O
THOU
IMPROPER,
THOU
UNCOMMON
NOUN

Although this volume will
never grace the shelves of your
library, I hope it will find
a home within reach of
the crapper. (see page 109)
Merry Christmas
"1980"
Tom Ferguson

OTHER BOOKS BY WILLARD R. ESPY

The Game of Words
An Almanac of Words at Play
Oysterville

THOU IMPROPER, THOU UNCOMMON NOUN ✖ A BOBTAILED, GENERALLY CHRONOLOGICAL LISTING OF PROPER NAMES THAT HAVE BECOME IMPROPER AND UNCOMMONLY COMMON; TOGETHER WITH A SMATTERING OF PROPER NAMES COMMONLY USED... AND CERTAIN OTHER DIVERSIONS ✖

WILLARD R. ESPY

CLARKSON N. POTTER, INC. *Publishers New York*
Distributed by Crown Publishers, Inc.

Library of Congress Cataloging in Publication Data

Espy, Willard R
    O thou improper, thou uncommon noun.

    Includes index.
    1. English language—Etymology. 2. English
language—Noun. 3. Names, Personal. 4. Names,
Geographical. I. Title.
PE1582.A3E8   422   78-15519
ISBN 0-517-53511-4

Published simultaneously in Canada by General Publishing Company Limited.
Second Printing, December, 1978
Printed in the United States of America.

Designed by Betty Binns

TO LOUISE

who worked as hard as I did

Learn the right
Of coining words in the quick mint of joy.

—*LEIGH HUNT*

CERTIFICATE OF AUTHENTICITY

I bring my bona fides forth
*   That all the world may marvel;*
For I researched my facts in North,
*   Who borrowed his from Carvel,*

Who owes his evidence to Morse,
*   Who filched from Connolly,*
Whose source was Bevan, who of course
*   Stole his research from me.*

ACKNOWLEDGMENTS

I STARTED this collection as a hobby, dropping into a file folder such uncommon, improper nouns as caught my eye in casual reading. The process went on for ten years before it occurred to me that I might have the makings of a book. And it was not until the first draft of my manuscript was actually complete that it entered my head to look for other books on the same theme. There might be, I thought, one or two suitable entries that I had overlooked. One or two? There were thousands. I proceeded to gorge myself on eponymous words like a starving cannibal bolting down a missionary. Unfortunately, I had room in my book for only the equivalent, say, of an arm and the lower half of a leg. If you want the whole missionary—and I promise you, missionaries taste mighty good—read the books listed in my reference key.

The discerning reader will discover in these pages a style, or several styles, more elegant than my usual hobbledehoy prose. This is because my own phrases connect those of better writers. Why should I cobble together a definition of canfield or sapphic when Webster has a staff that have spent their lives perfecting such definitions? By the nature of research, I owe all my facts and most of my speculations to others; am I not doing them honor if I also appropriate their language? Hoi polloi may accuse me of plagiarism; I apologize rather for the handful of instances where, by reconstructing an account in my own words, I have lowered the rhetorical standards of the original passage. At one moment I shandy, at another I namby-pamby; I am by turns Brown, Holt, Brewer, Benét, or Partridge.

I extend my thanks and admiration to all the historians and philosophers of language, living and dead, whom I have cannibalized. They are listed in the reference key. I have perhaps drawn most heavily on Benét, Brewer, Britannica, Brown, Evans, Funk, Holt, Partridge, Skeat, Webster, and Weekley. Partridge has supplied the plurality of entries; had I not already been well into my final draft before coming across his incomparable *Name into Word*, I would have abandoned this project.

Special gratitude is due to Timothy Dickinson, contributing editor of *Harper's* magazine, from whose cornucopic mind arcana rush like a spring freshet; any erudition in the following pages is his. Roger Angell made helpful comments on sports, as did Richard de Rochemont on food and Harry Randall on dance and musical instruments.

Louise read the manuscript with her artisan's eye for the plumb of a phrase, and vetoed a number of my infelicities. She did not, however, lay an impious hand on Benét, Brewer, Britannica, Brown, Evans, Funk, Holt, Partridge, Skeat, Webster, or Weekley.

My book would never have reached the publisher if Mignon Franco had not taken time from her overcrowded schedule to do the typing, often working until two or three o'clock in the morning. Now that my mother is gone, Mignon is the only person who can read my handwriting.

IN THE COURSE of a memorial service shortly after the death of
King George VI, Laurence Olivier reminded the mourners that
the oddly personal closeness they all had felt for their monarch
might be symbolically explained by a chain of linguistic deriva-
tions.

"The *Oxford Dictionary* tells us," he said, "that the Old English
word for king was *cyning,* which in turn came from *cyn,* meaning
kin. In short—one of us."

So, he went on to say, the people of the close-knit island realm
had always two families, their own and their royal family.

I bring up the example because it seems to me that Olivier was doing what Espy does in this book. He was illuminating the language. In the imaginative world where Espy roams, there are many such examples, but here he has limited himself to the rich fields of the proper noun.

Of course you will laugh as you read *O Thou Improper, Thou Uncommon Noun,* but I suspect you will also say again and again, "Aha!" or "Now I understand!" or "That explains something that's always puzzled me," or any other expression of enlightenment which will be appropriate to the many revelations which Espy has gathered into what at first appears a gallimaufry but is in fact a vade mecum for everyone who uses words above the level of who-where-how-much communication.

It is the organization of Espy's book which makes it not only more useful than the merely alphabetical compendia of oddities where *boycott* comes right after Bora Bora—although he had never been there—but also gives it a special shape. Instead of merely looking up words, one can go on various voyages of discovery through strange though chartable worlds.

Captain Espy of your verbal vessel, the S.S. *Cognomina,* makes a fine appearance on the bridge, but it is a deceptively casual one. Espy likes to be taken for a *boulevardier,* and with his waxed white moustache and boutonniere he appears ready to go on stage as the Ruritanian ambassador in some lighthearted operetta. One gets the feeling that he has an attention span measurable at somewhere between one and two martinis, and that his work, whatever it is, is something frivolous which begins at 10:30 A.M. and ends in the signing of a few letters before he goes to his club at noon.

He is the last man you would expect to be keeping vast notebooks full of cross-referenced arcana on the subject of word origins.

Every writer keeps what used to be called a commonplace book in which he jots thoughts or quotations or useful bits that he may someday stick into his own work. There is among some writers the wistful hope that if one becomes famous the commonplace book can simply be handed to a publisher and sold as the gleanings of a great mind, but for most of us it is just a ragbag in which the thing we need has either simply not been written into the book in the first place, or has been stuck into the pages in clipping form and fallen out somewhere, or is identified with what once seemed like an adequate hint. Such a clue as "See Trollope on l.d.h., page 348" is at least under *T* in my notebook, but there organization ceases. If I knew which of the great man's many novels discussed l.d.h. on page 348 I might then discover what l.d.h. means.

For all the time Espy spends twiddling his moustache into points and getting his cuffs to that length where the jeweled links peep out but don't parade themselves, he always knows what l.d.h. means because it is in the Blue File and the Red File and on the Master List. If you start figuring out the footpounds of work which went into this book you realize it was enough to take the Woolworth Building to the top of the Rockies (I get my statistical imagery from the *Book of Knowledge*).

In his Man of Fashion disguise Espy makes light of his own dedication and you would think from his account that assembling this volume was as pleasant as pressing ferns in an album or alphabetizing a collection of cigarette cards.

Samuel Johnson once gloomily remarked that a maker of dictionaries was "doomed only to remove rubbish from the paths of Learning and Genius, who press forward to conquest and glory without bestowing a smile on the humble drudge who facilitates their progress."

Unlike Espy, Johnson was a melancholy man whose linkless cuffs were stained with equal parts of ink and soup, but there is justice in his plaint about the position assigned to lexicographers. *O Thou Improper, Thou Uncommon Noun,* is not, of course, a dictionary but it is a work of lexicographic sophistication, and as you, dropping nuggets from it at parties, are taken for a person of Learning and Genius on the way to conquest and glory, I want you to make a small obeisance.

I don't ask you to admit that your Learning and Genius are secondhand, but when everyone around you cries out at your amazing knowledge, raise your glass in a silent toast to Willard Espy and bestow a smile on the man next to you.

If it's a really smart party there's a good chance the man will be Espy.

HEYWOOD HALE BROUN

BLOOMERS

CONTENTS

Earthly Words

BOX & COX

O
THOU
IMPROPER,
THOU
UNCOMMON
NOUN

HAVE NOT myself heard an Irishman say "Ah, wirra, wirra," or "Wirrasthru"; yet they often moan so, at least in books, shaking their heads and wringing their hands. To me wirra, sighing from Irish lips when something is badly wrong, smelled of "worry"; until I learned better, the two words ran together in my mind.

But the source of wirra is not worry. It is a proper name, indeed one of the dearest Proper Names of all, that of the gentle Mother Mary herself. Says Webster:

> **wirra,** *interj*. [Ir. O + *Muire*, Mary.] An exclamation expressing lament, grief, etc. Usually repeated, *wirra, wirra*.

As for wirrasthru, it cradles Mary and *truagh*, "pity," as well: "Mary, have pity."

Many words that seem as common as cabbages conceal provocative proper names. I call these name-words improper, uncommon nouns (though they may be in fact verbs, adjectives, or adverbs): improper, because they have ceased to be proper names; uncommon, because it is uncommon for proper names to become common.

"Words," says Barfield,

> may be made to disgorge the past that is bottled up inside of them, as coal and wine when we kindle or drink them yield up their bottled sunshine. It has only just begun to dawn on us that in our own language alone, not to speak of its many companions, the past history of humanity is spread out in an imperishable map, just as the history of the mineral earth lies embedded in the layers of its outer crust. But there is this difference between the record of the rocks and the secrets which are hidden in the language: whereas the former can only give us knowledge of outward, dead things—such as forgotten seas and the bodily shapes of prehistoric animals and primitive man—language has preserved for us the inner, living history of man's soul.

When Linnaeus, the 18th-century Swedish botanist, named a wild mint "collinsonia" after the English naturalist Peter Collinson, Collinson exclaimed that he had been given "a species of eternity." This book consists of names that have been given a species of eternity.

Words with unexpected backgrounds are as innumerable as the stars, but less orderly. One way to impose an appearance of order on the seething verbal universe is to select a handful of stars arbitrarily—eenie, meenie, minie, mo—and describe them in alphabetical sequence. Another way, adopted here, is to choose a single constellation—in this case, common words born of proper names—in which at least the principal stars can be listed.

In my telescope, an old whoremonger named Pamphilus turns into pamphlet. Gaya, an Italian woman's name, becomes *gazza,* magpie (for the same reason, I suppose, that our own magpie was named from some chattering Maggie); a *gazza* collects small bright objects, including coins; a certain Venetian coin becomes known as *gazetta,* "little magpie"; the coin happens to be the price of the first newspaper printed in Venice (not to mention that newspapers themselves have magpie characteristics). Gazette and gazetteer enter English. Presto! Gaya = newspaper; atlas.

Who would think that galley-west, as in "to knock galley-west," comes from Collyweston, a village in Northamptonshire? What was galley-west about Collyweston?

A recently published dictionary of eponymous words has twenty thousand entries. I have not dared to venture aboard that great ocean liner of verbal reference; nor shall I, until my own cockboat has found its way seaward through the surf. Else, from the discouragement of contrast, I might not launch at all.

Specialized lexicons list thousands of rocks, named for their discoverers. Others confine themselves to eponymous plants, or psychological, medical, or scientific terminology. I have thrown in a few of these to show how the game works. A greater number, I suspect, would bore both you and me.

I have included many commonplace words for comprehensiveness. But many words of uncommon, and occasionally improper, interest are missing, simply because they have not come to my attention. As James Sutherland says in *The Oxford Book of Literary Anecdotes*, "The only honest excuse for such omissions must be the one that Dr. Johnson gave to the lady who taxed him with a wrong definition in his Dictionary: 'Ignorance, madam, pure ignorance.' "

Sometimes I was planning to use a word, but I . . . well, I . . . just forgot. I am a great forgetter:

> *Illogic I abhor;*
> *   And yet I have to own*
> *That I've forgotten more*
> *   Than I have ever known.*

Even luminous delights vanish from my memory:

> *Such a lovely love affair!*
> *   One of those!*
> *But who, or why, or when, or where . . .*
> *   God knows.*

I might still be happily collecting improper, uncommon nouns if my wife, my editor, my publisher, and my creditors had not formed a united front against me. As one, they insisted that the time had come to stop collecting and start writing. They compared me scornfully to the small boy quoted by my friend Janice Block: "Oh, yes," he said, "I can spell bananas. It's just that I don't know when to stop."

When does a proper name become vernacular? One answer is, when dictionaries stop capitalizing it. Yet a word may be capitalized in one dictionary and lowercased in another; or it may retain its capitalization even when it has clearly assumed a generic meaning. I classify the latter sort as a Patient Griselda. Patient Griseldas are scattered throughout this book.

I include also words in transition, not common, but certainly no longer entirely proper. Examples are Charles Dickens's Pecksniff and, more recently, George Orwell's Newspeak.

Every name was once common. The will in will-o'-the-wisp harks back to Will, short for William; but William comes from will, meaning "determination; purpose," plus -helm: a William is helmeted in determination. Gods are named for the qualities they represent: *boreas* is Greek for "north wind"; Boreas is the Greek god of the north wind.

A word may plod along commonly for thousands of years, minding its own business; find itself through happenstance a capitalized celebrity; and return enriched to the vulgate. You would never have heard of apocalyptic, rooted in a routine Greek word meaning "to disclose," were it not for the blood-curdling Apocalypse that concludes the New Testament.

Man is a naming animal. Savages of certain tribes have secret names which they cannot reveal without yielding their souls to possessors of the secret.

The sun draws water skyward and releases it as rain. So with words. When the Greeks said *marnasthai*, meaning "to fight," the warrior-god Mars was born. When they used *aphrodisakos* for "sexual love," the goddess Aphrodite sprang from ocean foam. A Greek tree was a *drŷs*. The nymphs of trees were *dryádes*. In Latin they become *dryades,* and in English, dryads. All from the Greek for "tree."

Even the Pole Star drifts imperceptibly across the sky. Sometimes overnight, sometimes over the ages, proper names drift back into common ownership. A little of that drifting is traced in this book.

—W.E.

6

REFERENCES

AH: *American Heritage Dictionary* (American Heritage Publishing Company and Houghton Mifflin Company, 1969).

ANTHON: Charles Anthon: *A Classical Dictionary* (Harper & Brothers, 1892).

ASIMOV: Isaac Asimov.

BARFIELD: Owen Barfield: *History in English Words* (Faber and Faber, Ltd., 1964).

BENÉT: William Rose Benét: *Reader's Encyclopedia* (Thomas Y. Crowell, 1948).

BOMBAUGH: C. C. Bombaugh: *Gleanings for the Curious from the Harvest Fields of Literature* (1880s; reissued by Dover Publications, 1961; Martin Gardner, editor).

BREWER: E. Cobham Brewer: *Brewer's Dictionary of Phrase and Fable* (Centenary Edition, revised by Ivor H. Evans, Harper & Row, 1959).

BRITANNICA: *Encyclopaedia Britannica*, 1959.

BROWN: Ivor Brown: *I Give You My Word* (Jonathan Cape, 1945); *Say the Word* (Jonathan Cape, 1947); *A Word in Your Ear* (E. P. Dutton, 1969).

DE ROCHEMONT: Richard de Rochemont and Waverly Root: *Eating in America: A History* (William Morrow, 1976).

DOBSON: William Dobson: *Literary Frivolities and Poetical Ingenuities* (1880s).

EDWARDS: Gillian Edwards: *Uncumber and Pantaloon* (E. P. Dutton, 1969).

EVANS: Bergen Evans: *Comfortable Words* (Random House, 1962).

FARB: Peter Farb: *Word Play* (Alfred A. Knopf, 1974).

FUNK: Wilfred Fund: *Word Origins* (Grosset & Dunlap, 1950); Peter Funk: *It Pays to Increase Your Word Power* (Funk & Wagnalls, 1968).

GROSE: F. Grose (edited by Partridge): *A Classical Dictionary of the Vulgar Tongue* (Routledge and Kegan Paul, 1963).

HENDRICKSON: Robert Hendrickson: *Human Words* (Chilton Book Company, 1972).

HOLT: Alfred H. Holt: *Phrase and Word Origins* (Dover Publications, 1961).

HOUSMAN: A. E. Housman, *A Shropshire Lad* (1896).

JACOBS: Noah Jonathan Jacobs: *Naming Day in Eden* (Macmillan, 1969).

JENNINGS: Gary Jennings: *Personalities of Language* (Thomas Y. Crowell, 1965).

LAVER: James Laver: *The Concise History of Costume and Fashion* (Harry N. Abrams, Inc., 1969).

MOORE: John Moore: *You English Words* (Dell, 1961).

THE MORRISES: William and Mary Morris: *Dictionary of Word and Phrase Origins* (Harper & Row, 1977).

MURRAY: Alexander S. Murray: *Manual of Mythology* (David McKay, 1895).

OED: *Oxford English Dictionary*.

OXFORD: *The Oxford Companion to English Literature* (Oxford University Press, 1967); *The Oxford Companion to American Literature* (Oxford University Press, 1965).

PARTRIDGE: Eric Partridge.

ROSTEN: Leo Rosten: *The Joys of Yiddish* (McGraw-Hill, 1968).

SKEAT: Walter W. Skeat: *A Concise Etymological Dictionary* (Capricorn Books, 1963).

TIMOTHY: Timothy Dickinson.

WEBSTER: *Webster's New International Dictionary*, second edition (Merriam Webster, 1961).

WEDEK: Harry E. Wedek: *Classical Word Origins* (Philosophical Library, 1957).

WEEKLEY: Ernest Weekley: *The Romance of Words* (Dover Publications, 1961); *Words and Names* (E. P. Dutton, 1933).

WINDAS: Cedric W. Windas, *Traditions of the Navy* (Our Navy, 1942).

WARNING FROM THE AUTHOR:
Taken massively, Improper, Uncommon Nouns are dangerous to the health.
Try one here, one there. If there are no
disagreeable side effects, such as breaking out in a rash, taste again, but spar-
ingly and at intervals. Otherwise you may
become seriously ill.

EAVENLY
WORDS

ONE

THE GREEKS HAD A NAME FOR IT
WORDS FROM GODS, HEROES, AND MEN

Chaos to Olympus

DREAMED I was intermingled with nothingness that seemed deliberately to sort me out of itself, separating me as if I were needed for witness. Invisible about me there went on a laborious shifting and gathering, one that I neither saw nor sensed, yet knew and recognized; I was present at Creation. Chaos took form. For millions of years I watched the becoming of heaven and earth and seas, of gods and monsters and men.

This was Creation according to the Greeks. Because they

anthropomorphized all they touched or conceived, chaos itself, the vast and primal darkness, became Chaos himself, able to engender from nonexistent loins a son, Erebus, who went to dwell in Hades, and a daughter, whose name was Nox, or Night.

Nox was mother of the three Fates, or Moerae. These were Clotho, who spun the web of life; Lachesis, who measured the length of life and the element of luck that a person had the right to expect; and Atropos, inescapable fate, who finally cut the thread. The root of the Fates is the Latin *fari,* "to speak." Words connected with the three sisters include fame, fairy, nefarious, and preface.

ATROPINE

Atropine is named for Atropos, one of the three Greek Fates. They were conceived as occupied in spinning a thread of gold, silver, or wool; now tightening, now slackening, and at last cutting it off. Clotho put it round the spindle; Lachesis spun; and Atropos, the eldest, cut it off when someone's time had come to die. Atropine is a poisonous alkaloid obtained from belladonna.

FATA MORGANA

In Arthurian legend Morgan-le-fey (Fata Morgana), "the sea-borne fairy," is the sister of Arthur and wife of Urien, king of North Wales—possibly also god of the underworld. She treacherously tries to procure the death of her brother, and to slay her sleeping husband. In the end, she is one of the three queens who conduct Arthur to Avalon. In *Orlando Innamorato,* by the Italian poet Matteo Maria Boiardo (1434–1494), she appears as a personification of fortune, living at the bottom of a lake. A fata morgana is a mirage, especially one seen at the Strait of Messina, between Calabria and Sicily.

NOCTURNAL
NOCTURNE

The name of Nox (Nux, Nyx) lingers in nocturnal, "having to do with the night." It lingers too in nocturne: in music, a night piece; in painting, a night scene.

TERRESTRIAL

EARTH

Coeval with Chaos was Gaea, "deep-breasted earth." Her name lies at the heart of geography. *Gauleiter,* German for "district leader," adds a cousin word, Gaea (for land, hence district) to *Leiter,* "leader." Changing Gaea's name to Terra, the Latins broke ground for terrestrial, "of or pertaining to the earth or its inhabitants." The more down-to-earth word earth is a legacy from the Norse goddess Erda, or Jörd, wife of Odin and daughter of Nott. Etymologically, the Nordic Nott and the Greek Nox are twins.

PONTOON

Gaea, seemingly by parthenogenesis, gave birth to Pontus, the sea, and Uranus, the sky. Pontus left his name in pontoon, the floating understructure of certain bridges, seaplanes, boats, and such. The romance languages abound in *pont-* words referring to bridges, the Greeks having regarded the sea itself as a bridge from land to land.

URANIUM

Though Gaea took both her sons for husband as soon as they were up to the job, young Uranus was clearly her favorite. She made him the personification of the star-studded sky— "her equal," says Hesiod in *Theogony* (about 800 B.C.), "in grandeur, so that he entirely covered her." Uranium, a radioactive element found in pitchblende, is an extant reminder of the god. His majesty as an embodiment of the heavens has shrunk, however, until only a remote planet, nearly two billion miles from the sun, bears his name.

TITAN
TITANIC

The first progeny of Uranus and Gaea, indeed perhaps the first beings produced through standard generative processes, were the twelve Titans, six male and six female. A titan is one titanic in size or power, as "a titan of the automobile industry."

BRIAR

BRIAREUS

The primordial couple's next offspring were the Cyclopes—giants with but one eye apiece. Uranus grumbled at these malformations. His grumble turned to a roar when the next three babes turned out to be the abominable Hecatoncheires ("hundred-handed"): Cottus, Gyges, and Briareus. (Some contend that Briareus was the son of Pontus, not Uranus.) The briar, a kind of crosscut saw, may be so named for its multiple teeth, reminiscent of Briareus's hundred arms and fifty heads; and a person who seems to be in touch with everything is referred to in the literary set as a briareus. The briar bush would be an elegant derivation, but I fear has an Anglo-Saxon root. Uranus was appalled at these monstrosities; he threw them out, neck and crop, and confined them in the depths of the earth. This high-handed action, taken without concern for Gaea's maternal instincts, produced a rupture between the first married couple—the sort of rupture that, in our more permissive day, might lead to a divorce. Gaea, however, bided her time until she could persuade one of her sons, Cronus, to avenge her and his brothers. Provided by Gaea with a sickle, Cronus waited until Uranus was sleeping and then slashed off the god's genitals, which he cast into the sea. The blood dripping from this terrible wound gave birth to, among others, the Giants and three dreadful winged creatures with snakes for hair, the Erinyes, called in Latin the Furiae. It was their destiny to relentlessly pursue and punish doers of unavenged crimes. We have absorbed their

FUROR

FURIOUS
FURY

name in furor, "a general commotion"; in furious, "raging"; and in fury, "violent anger."

The debris of that hideous molestation, floating on the surface of the waves, became a white foam from which emerged the most enticing of all creatures, the goddess Aphrodite. As Aphrodite Urania, she was to become the patron of ideal, spiritual love; as Aphrodite Genetrix, the patron of marriage; as Aphrodite Porne, the patron of lust and prostitution. From this

PORNOGRAPHY

last aspect of the goddess comes pornography, "licentious and lust-provoking writing, painting, and the like." Moore believes that April reflects Aphrodite's name, as does of course aph-

APHRODISIAC

rodisiac, something which stimulates or intensifies sexual desire.

The children of Chaos—Erebus and his sister Nox—became husband and wife (after all, there was no one else around), and built themselves a palace in the lower world. Nox gave birth to two daughters. One was Hemera, or Day. There was a mother-and-daughter problem here; Night and Day were never home at the same time. When Day entered the palace, Night rode off in a chariot drawn by two black steeds, traversing the heavens till daybreak. On Night's return, Day left.

HEMERA

A hemera is the period of geological time in which any particular species "had its day"—i.e., was most abundant, as

HEMERALOPIA

indicated by remains in sedimentary rock. Hemeralopia is day blindness.

ETHER

Nox's other daughter was Ether. Ether is the name of the soul, or essential being, of the universe. It is also a flammable liquid obtained by distilling alcohol with sulfuric acid, widely

ETHEREAL

used in industry and as an anesthetic. Anything ethereal is intangible; delicate and exquisite; heavenly.

Besides Cronus, king of the gods, Hesiod lists the twelve Titans as Oceanus, Coeus, Creus, Hyperion, Iapetus, Theia, Rhea, Themis, Mnemosyne, Phoebe, and Tethys. Of these,

OCEAN

Oceanus was given charge of the oceans and all pertaining thereto. Iapetus remains a puzzlement. He has been equated with Japhet, son of Noah, and accordingly with the first human beings after the flood. In referring to the Caucasian language

JAPHETIC

family as japhetic, philologists give the appearance of lumping in one the Greek Titan and the survivor of the Flood.

The legend of the Flood comes down in many cultures. In the Greek version, the king of Athens at the time of the Flood

OGYGIAN

was one Ogygian; ogygian means "incomparably ancient; an-

FURY

tediluvian." Another word for terribly old—though younger than ogygian—is silurian, after the Silurians, a tribe of southern Wales who gave the Romans a great deal of trouble. Geologically, Silurian is part of the Paleozoic period, when land plants and reptiles first appeared. Mark Twain used the word to express doddering old age.

The satellites of the planet Saturn include Hyperion, Rhea, Iapetus, Phoebe, and possibly Themis. I say "possibly" because astronomers are not quite sure whether Themis, which would be the farthest satellite from its primary, is there or not. No vernacular words deriving from Hyperion, Theia, or Themis occur to me; theme is tempting, but has the wrong root.

Hyperion and Theia mated and produced a daughter, Aurora, the rising light of morning. Her job must have been to roust out Day when Day overslept. Aurora is the dawn. It is also a yellowish-red color, and half of aurora borealis.

When struck with a young man's beauty, Aurora would obtain immortal life for him. In the case of her own husband, Tithonus, however, she omitted to ask Zeus to provide not just immortality but also eternal youth. When white hairs appeared on Tithonus's head, his attraction for her waned. Says Murray, "He became quite helpless at last, and, to avoid the sight of his decrepitude, she shut him up in a chamber, where only his voice was heard like the chirp of a grasshopper, into which creature, it was said, he became transformed." There is no Tithonus order of grasshoppers; the order is Orthoptera. But a flower called the

tithonus turns its face toward the sun each dawn.

Tethys has taken to low company; she is a genus of large, often conspicuously colored, sluglike marine mollusks, which emit a purple liquid when disturbed.

Cronus, king of the gods, had a peccadillo: he swallowed each of his children as it was born. This propensity began to concern his sister-wife, Rhea. When she was about to give birth to Zeus she turned for counsel to her parents, Uranus and Gaea, who were together again, having decided to let bygones be bygones. At their suggestion, she hid herself in a Cretan cavern to bring forth her son. She then wrapped a great stone in swaddling clothes and presented it to Cronus, who swallowed it all unsuspecting. She later used the same trick to save Zeus's brothers Poseidon and Hades.

Zeus was reared in secrecy by his gentle old grandmother,

Gaea. So that Cronus should not hear the infant's cries, Gaea persuaded certain earth-spirits, the Curetes, to dance and sing around the cradle, beating clangorously on their bronze shields with their swords.

CYNOSURE

One of Zeus's nurses was Cynosura, a nymph of Mount Ida. On her death he changed her into the constellation Cynosure. Cynosure contains the North Star, to which the eyes of mariners and travelers were often directed. It thus came to mean a center of attraction: "The cynosure of all eyes."

Zeus eventually deposed his father by administering an emetic that forced the poor old Titan to vomit up not only the stones he had swallowed but also Zeus's brothers and sisters, who had been flourishing in Cronus's entrails as Jonah (and later Pinocchio) flourished in a great fish.

SATURNALIA
SATURNINE

MOLOCH

There is some debate about what happened to Cronus after that. Homer says he was enchained in the deeps of the earth. Others claim he was exiled to Italy, where the crusty old god seems to have turned over a new leaf, civilizing his people and ushering in a golden age as Saturn, god of sowing. Saturday bears his name. The annual festival in Saturn's honor, celebrated on December 17, was apt to wax so lively that we still call an outbreak of general license a saturnalia. Yet some of Cronus's dour characteristics persisted; we think of a saturnine person as one whose temper is heavy, gloomy, and dull. The metal connected with Saturn, astrologically, is lead. Saturn has been connected with the grim Tyrian deity Moloch, to whom children were regularly sacrificed. A moloch is any merciless all-devouring force.

JANUS-FACED
JANITOR

JANICEPS

Saturn ruled in Italy jointly with Janus, god of beginnings. Janus was depicted with two faces, one looking forward and one back, whence our expression janus-faced for a two-faced or deceitful person. January is named for him, as is janitor, Janus being also god of doors. In the temple of Janus, the doors were supposed to stand open during war and closed during peace. It is said that they were closed but four times in five hundred years. A janiceps (Janus plus Latin *caput,* "head") is a monster with two fused heads, the faces turned in opposite directions.

Under the Roman republic, there was a person styled king who had but two functions. One was to attend the temple of Janus. The other was to run away from a mob on the first of every year, indicating that the populace, not he, was boss.

The early gods embodied a number of different and sometimes incompatible characteristics, taking a different name for each. In one of his personifications, Jupiter was identified with Amen, the Libyan god of gods, and was worshiped as the ram-headed Jupiter Ammon. Suppliants who entered his temple left their camels grazing outside. A colorless, pungent gas, NH_3, now important as a base for fertilizers, was first observed in the dung of these camels. It is called ammonia after Jupiter Ammon.

AMMONIA

The Egyptians raised a splendid temple for the worship of cat-headed Baste, or Bubastis, goddess of love and fashion. Cats were worshiped as her surrogates. Whenever a cat died it was laid in a crypt in Baste's temple. The coffin was made from slabs of a local fine-grained, translucent gypsum, which might be white, pale yellowish pink, or yellowish gray. In honor of the goddess, this gypsum was called *a-la-Baste*, "vessel of Baste;" and alabaster it remains to this day.

ALABASTER

Hera, queen of the gods, Zeus's sister and principal wife, kept her name out of the vulgate until she removed to Rome and became Juno. A junoesque woman is one of stately bearing and imposing beauty. As Juno Moneta (Juno the Monitress), she presided over a Roman temple where gold was coined. Moneta became the eponym of money, and Moneta's temple a mint.

JUNOESQUE

MONEY
MINT

Zeus had other legitimate, though lesser, wives. Among these was Mnemosyne, aunt to him and Hera. Mnemosyne was the goddess of memory—whence mnemonics, the art of improving one's remembering. Zeus sired on her the nine Muses: Calliope, patron of eloquence; Terpsichore, goddess of dance; Clio, presiding over history; Erato, over lyric and amatory poetry; Euterpe, over music; Melpomene, over tragedy; Polymnia, over the sacred lyric; Thalia, over comic and bucolic poetry; and Urania, over astronomy. Muse refers either to a poet or his inspiration.

MNEMONICS

MUSE

Parnassus was the Greek mountain sacred to Apollo and the Muses. To climb Parnassus is thus to create poetry. A collection of poems is a parnassus.

PARNASSUS
TO CLIMB PAR-
NASSUS

Mosaic—a surface decoration made by inlaying small pieces of variously colored glass, stone, or other material—is traceable in name to the Muses—not, as one might think, to Moses and the Mosaic law.

MOSAIC

Calliope, chief of the nine, was mother of Orpheus and patron of eloquence and heroic poetry. She survives as the

CALLIOPE calliope, a musical instrument emitting a series of steam whistles, at one time a feature of every circus. Stephen Vincent Benét evokes her (mispronouncing her name for the rhyme):

> *Oh, pull on the rope of the calliope!*
> *Bang on the big bass drum!*

She also survives as the lovely calliope hummingbird.

TERPSICHOREAN
EUTERPEAN
EUTERPE Terpsichore was goddess of dance and choral song. Anything having to do with the dance is terpsichorean. Anything pertaining to music is euterpean, for Euterpe. A euterpe is in addition a graceful American palm.

IRENIC
PACIFIC Zeus dallied occasionally with his sister Themis, who conceived by him Irene, goddess of peace. Conciliation is irenic. The Romans referred to Irene as *Pax,* leading to our pacific, "peaceful."

HEBE Before the accession of Ganymede, the cupbearer of the gods was the virginal Hebe, goddess of youth and spring, daughter of Zeus and Hera. An innocently alluring young waitress is a hebe, pronounced with two syllables; pronounced with one, the word shortens Hebrew, and is a disparaging term for a Jew.

When Zeus took power, his grandmother, Gaea, though she had saved his life in infancy, incited two revolts against him. The first was by the Titans, brothers and sisters of deposed Cronus. Zeus won this war by releasing and commandeering the imprisoned Hecatoncheires and Cyclopes. "The Cyclopes," said Hesiod, "gave him the thunderbolt, and the Hecatoncheires put their invincible arms at his service." No sooner were the Titans put down than Gaea encouraged a new revolt, this time by the Giants. These had legs like serpents; their feet were reptiles' heads. In their war with the gods the Giants heaped Mount Pelion on Mount Ossa to scale the heights of heaven. But they

PELION ON
   OSSA failed to make it. To pile Pelion on Ossa is to perform prodigies in an almost hopeless cause. To defeat the Giants, Zeus required the aid of a mortal: Hercules. Having to call on a mortal for help was a portent of doom for the gods—a cloud no bigger than a

EX PEDE HER-
   CULEM man's hand. (Perhaps I should say a man's foot. *Ex pede Herculem,* "by the foot [one may judge] Hercules," is an expression indicating that the part is an index to the whole.)

Still unable to resign herself to the defeat of her children, Grandma Gaea raised up against Zeus a final monster, Typhoeus, her son by Tartarus, lord of the infernal regions. (After all, Uranus was sexually incapacitated, and a woman must live.) Typhoeus, says Larousse, "was a terrifying creature. From his shoulders sprang a hundred horrible dragons' heads, each with a darting black tongue and eyes which spurted searing flame. From his thighs emerged innumerable vipers; his body was covered with feathers; thick bristles sprouted from his head and cheeks. He was taller than the tallest mountain."

TYPHOON

Nonetheless, the thunderbolts of Zeus destroyed this final rival. Typhoeus is remembered now only as the source name of typhoon, a tremendous cyclone occurring at intervals in the region of the Philippines and the China Sea. Even that etymology is perhaps incorrect; "great wind" in Cantonese is *tai fung,* in Mandarin *tafeng*—close enough to typhoon as makes no difference.

The wars of the accession were over. The Olympians had triumphed.

Before the Heroes Came

OLYMPIAN

Zeus and his court lived on Mount Olympus. It follows that one majestic in manner, or superior to mundane affairs, is said to have an olympian way about him. As a child, being rather a mother's pet, I sometimes felt olympian myself; I lived with the fantasy that I had much in common with the dozen or so gods and goddesses at the center of things on Olympus. These were Zeus; his sons Apollo, Ares, Hermes, Hephaestus, and Dionysus; his daughters Artemis and Athena; his brother Poseidon; his queen-sister Hera; his other sisters, Demeter and Hestia; and, of course, the foam-born Aphrodite.

JOVIALITY

Zeus had two Latin names: Jupiter and Jove. The *Ju* of Jupiter and the *Ze* of Zeus are the same ancient root, meaning "shining sky"; Zeus *was* the shining sky. From the same root, *diu,* "bright," have sprouted such familiar words as Tuesday, deity, adieu, joss, diva (prima donna, from "divine"), Diana, adjourn, journey, sojourn, and July. In Rome he replaced the saturninity of Saturn with the joviality of Jove; persons born under the sign of the planet Jupiter are supposed to be jovial types. As Jupiter Pluvius he was dispenser of rain; *pluvius* means "rainy," and a jupiter pluvius is a rainstorm.

APOLLO

ADONIS

ADONIZE

APOLLONIAN

PYTHON

DELPHIC

SIBYL
SIBYLLINE

ORPHIC

ARTEMISIA

SELENEAN
SELENIUM
DIANA

Apollo, son of Zeus by Leto, the daughter of two Titans, was as handsome a god as one was likely to run across. An apollo nowadays is a handsome, masculine fellow. Nonetheless, a mortal, Adonis, rivaled him in masculine beauty. Though Adonis was beloved of Aphrodite herself, his consuming passion was the hunt. He challenged wild beasts day after day, until at last he lost his life at the tusk of a wild boar. His name survives in the adonia, a red or yellow flower of the buttercup family. An adonis is a preeminently beautiful young man; pejoratively, a dandy. To adonize is to dress up. Keats said, "When my spirits are low, I adonize myself."

Apollonian means rational and well ordered; harmonious. An ethereal alpine butterfly, white with eyelike markings on the wings, is called an apollo as a reminder of the god's beauty.

Apollo's earliest adventure was the single-handed slaying of Python, a flame-breathing dragon who blocked his way to Pytho (now Delphi), the site he had chosen for an oracle. From the name of this monster derives python, "any large snake."

The oracles of Delphi were susceptible to varying interpretations. One oracle told a Greek going to war, "Thou shalt go thou shalt return never by war shalt thou perish." She failed to explain where to place the commas. The Greek went, and was killed. Delphic is thus ambiguous; obscure in meaning. The Sibyls, women regarded as prophetesses by the ancients, were similarly vague in their predictions; a sibyl is a prophetess, and sibylline is prophetic in a mysterious fashion.

Apollo and the Muse Calliope were parents of Orpheus, whose lyre could charm beasts and make trees and rocks move. Orphic matters are mystic, esoteric, or entrancing, like the lyrist's music.

Apollo's twin sister, Artemis, presided over darkness and the moon, as he over sunlight, prophecy, music, and poetry. She is perhaps best remembered for lulling the reluctant Greek shepherd Endymion into a deep sleep to overcome his resistance to her caresses. The name Artemis is lowercased today for a genus of shrubs, artemisia, which includes wormwood and the western sagebrush; I wish I knew the association of ideas that went through the head of the person who gave sagebrush that name.

Artemis was also called Selene, triggering the words selenean (for matters having to do with the moon, and selenium), a nonmetallic element. The Romans worshiped her as Diana, a word poets lowercase for moon matters. Diana is a shade of blue; a monkey; and a handsome Appalachian butterfly.

LUNAR
LUNACY

Luna was an alter ego of Selene. The Latin name of the goddess and the moon comes from the former Etruscan city of Funa, on what is now the Gulf of Spazzio. The name survives in lunar, "pertaining to the moon," and lunacy, originally that insanity supposedly affected by the phases of the moon.

CEREMONY

An Etruscan city that may or may not have given its name to a common word is Caere. "Ceremony" in Latin was *caeremonia*; etymologists argue over whether the *caere* stands for the city or for *cura,* "cure."

MARTIAL

Ares, son of Zeus and Hera, better known by his Latin name, Mars, is protagonist of the martial arts. The month of March and the planet Mars bear his name.

HERM

Hermes, messenger of the gods, was son of Zeus; his mother was Maia, daughter of Atlas. Among Hermes's duties was the protection of boundary lines. The Greeks scattered about the countryside images consisting of a block of stone surmounted by a head of Hermes. Such a boundary marker is called a herm, and some still exist.

HERMETIC

There was a darker side to Hermes. As Hermes Trismegistus he was identified with the Egyptian god Thoth, author of the fabled Hermetic books on magic and alchemy. Presumably because alchemists employed in their researches the first well-sealed bottles, the word hermetic has come to mean "tightly sealed, so that nothing can enter or escape."

MERCURY
MERCURIAL
COMMERCE
MERCHANT
MERCER
MERCHANDISE

Hermes was known to the Romans as Mercury. He flickered in and out of sight so fast as he went about conducting souls to Hades, hiding thieves from justice, and carrying messages, that quicksilver, for its volatility, came to be called mercury. Mercurial is "volatile." Mercury was also a god of business, whence commerce, merchant, mercer, merchandise, and Mercator of the mercator projection, whose name Latinizes German *Kremer,* merchant. (See page 118.) Astronomically, Mercury is the nearest planet to the sun.

Zeus had by Hera, besides Ares and Hebe, a son named Hephaestus. Hephaestus was a master worker in metals. By one report, he was born lame and was thrown by his mother into the sea. There he set up his workshop, creating such marvels as Achilles's armor and, in a different mood, the first mortal

VOLCANOES

VULCANIZATION

VULCANIST

VESUVIATE

VESUVIAN

woman, Pandora. His Roman name was Vulcan. Volcanoes, the sites of his steaming forges, commemorate him, as does vulcanization, a process of treating rubber chemically to increase its useful qualities. A vulcanist is one who believes the world was created by fire. A principal forge of Vulcan was situated under Mount Etna, a volcano in eastern Sicily. To vesuviate, from Mount Vesuvius, is to erupt, and a match for lighting cigars was once called a vesuvian.

Hephaestus was given Aphrodite as wife—a symbolic union of craftsmanship and beauty. But Aphrodite did not long remain faithful to the ugliest and least graceful of the gods. At one time or another she dallied with all three of his brothers—Ares, Hermes, and Dionysus—and, according to some, even with Zeus himself. (Her romances with humans are not part of this chronicle.)

HARMONY

Hephaestus surprised her abed with Ares, but too late to prevent her from conceiving. The child of the union was Harmonia, goddess of harmony, demonstrating, say the philosophers, that from Love and Strife, attraction and repulsion, arises the order of the universe.

Hermes, slyer than his bluff brother, was never caught *in flagrante delicto* with Aphrodite. But their child Hermaphroditus came to a sad end, as we shall see later.

BACCHANTS

BACCHANAL

DITHYRAMB

Dionysus, Aphrodite's third immortal lover, was the son of Zeus and Semele. (Since Semele herself was the daughter of Cadmus and Harmonia, and since Harmonia was Aphrodite's own daughter by Ares, the degrees of relationship here are not easy to follow.) Dionysus, or Bacchus to the Romans, god and giver of the grape and wine—not to be confused with the mortal Dionysus of Syracuse—was worshiped with orgiastic rites. He was leader of a wild rout of bacchants (that is, worshipers of Bacchus), satyrs, and sileni (minor woodland deities, like the satyrs). The routs were called bacchanals. Another of his names was Dithyramb, which came to refer to songs or poems created in his honor and written in a wild, irregular strain. A poem, song, or speech delivered in an impassioned manner is a dithyramb.

DIONYSIAN

An event of ecstatic, orgiastic, or irrational character is dionysian, as opposed to apollonian. Dionysian is also applied to the philosophy of Nietzsche, which emphasizes creative imagination at the expense of the critical-rational power.

HYMEN

Aphrodite and Bacchus produced two children. One was Hymen, the god of marriage. Uncapitalized, hymen is marriage,

VOLCANO

or a wedding song. The virginal membrane is a hymen, and a wedding is a hymeneal rite.

Their other son was Priapus, the male generative power personified. He is described more fully in another chapter.

But one child of Aphrodite's so outshone all the rest that the Greeks argued whether his father might have been not Ares, Hermes, or Dionysus, but Zeus himself. Hephaestus, her husband, was not even considered.

The boy was Eros, the god of passionate love. He was the youngest of the gods, a winged, mischievous youngster armed with a bow and a quiver of arrows whose lightest prick was sufficient to ignite a firestorm of amorous passion. Often he shot his darts randomly or on impulse, and indeed he appears to do so still. Once he was burned by his own fire. Aphrodite, looking down from Olympus, saw a young girl so beautiful as to rival the love-goddess herself. She instructed Eros to rid her of this competition. But even Eros could not resist the gentle radiance shed by Psyche. Instead of arranging to have a monster eat her, as his mother had instructed, he wafted her to a magnificent palace, where each night he joined her in darkness, refusing to let her see his face. Unable to control her curiosity, she one night lit an oil lamp and found herself gazing upon the most adorable of countenances, that of the love-god himself. Unfortunately, a drop of scalding oil fell on Eros's bare shoulder and awakened him. God and palace instantly vanished. Seemingly endless tribulations followed for Psyche. Finally, however, Zeus consented to her marrying Eros.

EROTIC
PSYCHE
PSYCHIC
PSYCHOLOGY
PSYCHIATRY

From Eros comes erotic, "of or pertaining to sexual love." Psyche, quite the other way, is Greek for "soul." The get of the word includes psyche, one's rational and spiritual being; psychic, "sensitive to nonphysical forces"; psychology, the science which treats the mind; and psychiatry, dealing with mental illness.

CUPIDITY

KEWPIE

The Romans' name for Eros was Cupid. His embodiment of sexual desire grew in their minds to include excessive desire of any sort. Cupidity is generally avarice, an inordinate desire for wealth. In the early twentieth century Rose O'Neill trivialized Cupid delightfully, creating a cherubic doll, the kewpie, supposed to evoke his innocent aspects; it took the country by storm.

NEPTUNE
NEPTUNIST

Poseidon, brother of Zeus, was god of the sea and trainer of horses. The Romans called him Neptune, a word often used figuratively for the ocean. A neptune was once a copper or brass plate or pan used in trade with the natives of Africa. A neptunist

NEPTUNIAN
LUTIN
is one who believes the world emerged from water. A neptunian thing is one formed by the agency of water. Lutin, the name of a goblin in the folklore of Normandy, is corrupted from Neptune, and the goblin appears to have been a degenerate form of the god.

HELIUM

PHAETON

Apollo was the god of light, but Helios—perhaps another aspect of Apollo—was specifically god of the sun. His name is preserved in helium. Phaeton, his son, got in trouble by borrowing the chariot of the sun which his father drove daily across the heavens. Phaeton steered up, then he steered down; his want of skill had all but set the earth on fire when Zeus struck him down in the nick of time with a thunderbolt. The phaeton, a rickety contrivance, is named after the unfortunate youth because it is considered a risky sort of carriage. The moral for parents is to think twice when their son asks to borrow the car.

Persephone, daughter of Demeter, goddess of agriculture, was abducted by Hades (Pluto to the Romans), lord of the underworld. In despair and revenge, Demeter rendered the whole earth barren. She agreed to raise her proscription on sprouting, budding, blooming, and bearing fruit only when Hades consented to allow Persephone to return to the upper world for nine months of the year. Our three winter months, when plants are dormant, are those Persephone spends with Hades.

IAMB
IAMBIC

Demeter, mourning the loss of her daughter, was at last moved to smile by the jests of Iambe, a serving maid, and in gratitude immortalized the girl's name in the iamb of iambic verse. This rhythm, da *da* da *da*, is the most common in English prosody:

> *I thought that Carol caroled free;*
> *But Carol caroled C.O.D.*

The name Demeter, by the way, is philologically parallel to Jupiter: *Da* plus *pater*, "father," on the one hand; *Da* plus *mater*, "mother," on the other hand.

PLUTOCRACY

Hades, though a brother of Zeus, did not join the Olympian council; he went underground, emerging only to kidnap Persephone. He was prodigiously rich, a veritable Getty of a god, the subterranean world being the source of gold and precious stones. Government by the wealthy is a plutocracy, from his Latin name, Pluto.

Hades had few visitors, or at least few who ever returned to the upper world. No wonder; the traveler first had to pass the

STYGIAN inhospitable River Styx, over which Charon ferried the souls of the dead. From Styx comes stygian, meaning "gloomy; dark; infernal; hellish." On the farther shore waited Cerberus, a dog having at least three heads (Hesiod said fifty) and the tail of a serpent. Cerberus carefully inspected anyone coming in, and only once (in the case of Orpheus, whose music could move stones and trees—a dog didn't stand a chance) was known to let **CERBERUS** anyone out. Any vigilant, surly custodian is a cerberus. (So, by **SOP TO CERBERUS** the way, is an aquatic serpent of East India.) A sop to Cerberus is a bribe; it was a good idea to toss the monster a piece of meat to keep him occupied until one was safely past.

LETHARGY Lethe, a river running through Hades, caused those who drank from it to forget all that had gone before. Hence lethargy, "sluggish indifference; unconsciousness resembling deep sleep." Lethal, meaning "deadly," has a different source: Latin *lethum*, "death."

ACHERONTIC Also in Hades ran Acheron, the River of Woe. Whatever is infernal or dismal is acherontic.

PAEAN A paean, a song of joy or praise, recalls Paean, the physician of the gods. The paean was used especially as an invocation to Apollo, god of healing, of whom Paean may have been a man-**PEONY** ifestation. His name remains also in the peony, which he discov-**AESCULAPIUS** ered. The Romans worshiped him as Aesculapius, also the name of a harmless European snake once sacred to him.

PANACEA Aesculapius had a daughter Panacea, meaning "all-heal"; a panacea is a universal medicine or remedy. Another of his daughters was Hygeia, goddess of health, from whom we have **HYGIENE** borrowed hygiene. The Hippocratic oath for physicians (after Hippocrates, a celebrated Greek physician born about 400 B.C.) says in its preamble: "I swear by Apollo the healer, the Asklepios, and Hygeia and Panacea and all the gods and goddesses . . ."

Aeolian, meaning "carried by the wind," perpetuates Aeolus, Greek god of the winds, who dwelt on the island of Aeolia, or Strongyle, now Stromboli. Reports Anthon:

> Ulysses came in the course of his wanderings to the island, and was hospitably entertained there for an entire month. On his departure, he received from Aeolus all the winds but Zephyrus, tied up in a bag of ox-hide. Zephyrus was favorable for his passage homeward. During nine days and nights the ships ran merrily before the wind; on the tenth day they were within sight of Ithaca; when Ulysses, who had hitherto held the helm himself, fell asleep, his comrades, who fancied that

Aeolus had given him treasure in the bag, opened it; the winds rushed out, and hurried them back to Aeolia. Judging from what had befallen them that they were hated by the gods, the ruler of the winds drove them with reproaches from his isle.

AEOLIAN HARP

AEOLIAN TERRITORIES

AEOLIPILE

An aeolian harp is a stringed instrument adapted to produce musical sounds on exposure to a current of air. (A theremin, mentioned elsewhere, operates on the same principle.) Aeolian territories are areas whose soil has been deposited by the wind. In about the 3rd century A.D., Hero invented the aeolipile, or ball of Aeolus, consisting of a closed vessel with one or more projecting bent tubes. Steam is made to pass from the vessel through these jets, causing the vessel to revolve. This device has been called the first steam engine.

ZEPHYR

BOREAL

Zephyrus was the west wind. A zephyr is any soft, gentle breeze. The north wind was Boreus; boreal refers to anything northern.

HALCYON

A daughter of Aeolus, Alcyone, was deeply in love with her husband, Ceyx, a king in Thessaly. When Ceyx was drowned in a storm, her grief was so great that the gods permitted her husband to live again as a bird, the kingfisher, into which form she too was metamorphosed. The gods provided, moreover, that every year there should be from seven to fourteen successive days when the sea lies still and calm, so that Alcyone might brood over her floating nest. These are the halcyon days, the days of tranquillity and peace.

DEMON

To the ancient Greeks, a demon was an inferior divinity, such as a deified hero. The word was never a proper name; I throw it in because of the curious etymological parallel between *daimon*, "divinity," and demon, an unclean spirit. The same seed spawns both god and devil; the gods of the old dispensation become the devils of the new. Anatole France treated this symmetry in 1914 in his book *The Revolt of the Angels*.

SOMNOLENT

HYPNOSIS

HYPNOTISM

FANTASY

MORPHINE

Somnus was the god of sleep; somnolent means "sleepy." He was also called Hypnos, whence hypnosis and hypnotism. Phantasus, his assistant, tricked sleepers with hallucinations, or fantasies; but fantasy is also related to *phaethon*, meaning "to shine." The son of Somnus, Morpheus, was the god of dreams; from him derives morphine, an addictive narcotic.

NIKE

The nike—a rocket in the system established for the defense of the United States from nuclear attack—recalls Nike, goddess of victory, whose Hellenistic statue, *Winged Victory*, stands in the Louvre. Nikea in Greek was "a conquered place." Hence Nice, the city in southern France, and Nice biscuits from Nicaea, Turkey. Other gods drafted into our atomic arsenal are Poseidon and Zeus and that Titan who holds the world on his shoulders.

MOMUS

COMIC
COMICAL
COMA

If you are called a momus, be advised that you are considered a carping critic. Such was Momus, god of blame and ridicule. Comic and comical come from Comus, god of festive mirth. The god was occasionally found in a drunken stupor, giving us coma for any state of profound insensibility.

LAMP

The lamp, a vessel containing oil or alcohol burned through a wick for illumination, descends in etymology from Lampetia. She was daughter of the sun-god Helios, and sister of Phaethon.

PANIC

Sudden and groundless fear, such as the Persians were said to have suffered at Marathon, is panic, being caused by Pan in his capacity as god of the wilderness and its mysterious terrors. He was god also of pastures, with which his name is connected, and of animals. His name was interpreted as meaning "everywhere" and to be everywhere is perhaps the most alarming aspect of a god. Pan is shown often with the legs, ears, and horns of a goat. He is an occasional visitor to Wall Street.

TRAGEDY

The word tragedy in Greek means "goat song." The goat was none other than the great Pan himself. Singers in the first choral tragedies were clothed in goatskins, and represented satyrs. Perhaps the great Pan and the lowly satyr were in this case interchangeable.

Satyr, a sylvan deity, was often represented with the tails and ears of a horse. Sometimes he had the feet and legs of a goat, short horns on his head, and thick hair covering his body. Like Faunus, Satyr was multiple; there were as many satyrs in Greece as there were fauns in Rome. The deity's sexual attitudes are described elsewhere in this book.

CENTAUR

In present-day terminology, a centaur is a rider who seems almost part of his horse. When the Incas first saw Spanish horsemen, they thought that man and horse were one; when a rider dismounted, they reasoned that he had broken in two. The Centaurs (probably an ancient and primitive Thessalian tribe) were supposed to have the head, arms, and trunk of a man, but the body and legs of a horse. In Greek mythology they were descended from Ixion. Ixion is recalled as the first man ever to murder a relative, the victim being his father-in-law. He was once passionately attracted to Hera, queen of the gods, who, says one account, "deceived him with a cloud shaped like herself." The deception was so realistic that the cloud conceived; from this union sprang the Centaurs. But another legend says Zeus, in the form of a horse, seduced Ixion's wife, and so produced the Centaurs. The forms Zeus assumed to satisfy his carnal appetites include a cloud, a bull, a lion, a swan, a shower of gold, and a pigeon.

CHIMERA
CHIMERIC

The Chimera was a she-monster represented as vomiting flames and usually as having a lion's head, goat's body, and dragon's or serpent's tail. Sometimes, however, she had a lion's body and head, together with a goat's head rising from the back. A chimera is a fantastic creature of the imagination, or any frightful, vain, or foolish fancy. Chimeric is fanciful, unreal, fantastic.

Chimera's doom stemmed from the fury of a woman scorned. Antea, wife of Proetus, king of Argos, made certain improper suggestions which were righteously rejected by their handsome young house guest Bellerophon, grandson of the Sisyphus who to this day is trying to roll a stone up a hill in hell. Seeking vengeance, the queen accused Bellerophon of an attempt on her honor. Though Proteus believed her, he would not commit the impropriety of slaying a guest; instead he sent Bellerophon with a sealed letter to Iobates, the king of Lycia, and Proetus's father-in-law. This letter praised Bellerophon highly, but concluded with a request that he be put to death. (Hence

BELLEROPH-
ONTIC
LETTER

"bellerophontic letter," one containing material prejudicial to the person who delivers it.)

Iobates, wishing neither to violate the laws of hospitality nor to disoblige his son-in-law, compromised by setting Bellerophon the hopeless task of slaying Chimera. With Minerva's aid, however, Bellerophon managed to catch and tame the winged steed Pegasus, enabling him to surprise Chimera from the air and put an end to her.

PEGASUS
HIPPOCRENE

Pegasus, the steed of the Muses, stands loosely for poetic inspiration, as does Hippocrene, the fount that Pegasus called from the earth with a blow of his hoof.

SIREN

A siren is either an enticing, dangerous woman or an instrument producing a loud, penetrating signal or warning. Either way, the word was hatched by the ancient Sirens, who are generally shown with the breasts and arms of women, but otherwise with the form of birds. The most celebrated were those who lured mariners to destruction by their singing. Odysseus escaped them by filling his sailors' ears with wax and having himself lashed to the mast of his ship, so that he could listen without the power to yield.

PROMETHEAN

Prometheus, a son of Uranus, disobeyed the gods by taking clay and forming man. Worse, he stole fire from Olympus for man's use, making man an ultimate rival of the gods. Anything life-giving—daringly original or creative—is promethean.

IGNITE

Prometheus had his counterpart in Agni, the fire-god of the Hindus, born from the rubbing of sticks. When excited, Agni rushes among the trees like a bull. *Agni*, "fire" in Sanskrit, is a cousin word to Latin *ignis* and English ignite, "to cause to burn; kindle."

PANDORA'S BOX

PANDORA

To punish mankind for adopting fire, Zeus ordered Hephaestus to create the first woman—Pandora, "universal giver." From his own experience, he calculated that where a woman is, trouble follows. He was right. Pandora out of curiosity opened a forbidden box, letting loose all the ills to which flesh is heir. A Pandora's box is a present which seems valuable, but which in reality yields only trouble. Less cosmically, a pandora is a stringed instrument like the mandolin. It is also a type of marine bivalve. (What compels scientists to name ugly sea creatures after beautiful goddesses and legendary maidens?)

As for Prometheus, Zeus chained him to a rock and sent an eagle to eat his liver, which grew at night as fast as the eagle could devour it by day. But Zeus had locked the stable door after the horse was stolen: man possessed fire, and the gods were doomed.

The Great God Pan Is Dead

Plutarch relates that a ship was passing the Isles of Paxos when a loud voice was heard from shore calling Thamus, the pilot. On his responding, the voice said to him, "When you are arrived at Palodes, take care to make it known that the great god Pan is dead."

Or at least dying. The dim twilight of myth was receding before the clearer, less romantic daylight of history. But daylight was not quite arrived. Greece had still to pass through the era of heroes.

When not engaged in amorous episodes among themselves, the Olympian gods found themselves frequently and passionately drawn to mortals. What a god wanted, a god generally got. The objects of desire for the male gods were generally nymphs and princesses; for the females, kings and shepherds. Though some heroes were of human origin, more sprang from a fleeting union between a god and a mortal. Heroes died like the rest of us (though as a rule more violently), except when Zeus intervened. In that event they might be lifted to Olympus and immortality. Hercules was one who made it.

Hercules was so strong that on the day of his birth he was able to strangle two huge serpents, one in each hand. He also had wit enough to profit passably from the wisdom and virtue of his tutor, Rhadamanthus, son of Zeus and Europa, who for his exemplary justice on earth was made a judge of the souls of the dead. A dispenser of rigorous justice is rhadamanthine.

RHADA-
MANTHINE

Hercules committed a deadly crime, the crazed murder of his children. In expiation, twelve labors were imposed upon him. Some of these gave us words commonly used.

First, he was commanded to slay the Hydra, an enormous serpent with nine heads. Whenever one head was struck off, two grew in its place. Hercules resolved the problem by cauterizing each stump with red-hot brands as the head went tumbling. Anything having many heads, or many phases or aspects, is hydra-headed.

HYDRA-HEADED

AUGEAN STA-
BLES

He was also ordered to clean the foul Augean stables, where twelve magnificent bulls were confined amid heaps of dung. Hercules diverted two rivers so that they rushed through the cowsheds, sweeping all litter before them. Twentieth-century politicians running for office customarily promise to clean the Augean stables of the party in power.

ANTAEAN

Shortly after killing the earth-giant Antaeus (an antaean is one who draws force from earth and nature) by holding him away from the ground and throttling him, Hercules awoke in the desert to find himself under attack by the Pygmies, a race of tiny humans chronically at war with the cranes that ravaged their cornfields. The little fellows were seeking to avenge slain Antaeus, considering themselves his brethren because they too were earthborn. They assaulted the head, hands, and feet of

Hercules simultaneously. Arrows were discharged at him, his hair was ignited, spades were thrust into his eyes. The Pygmies removed doors from their hinges to cover his mouth and nostrils, hoping to suffocate him. But Hercules (unlike Gulliver under similar attack by the Lilliputians) was neither frightened nor annoyed; instead, the courage of his wee foes so pleased him that he gathered them all into his lionskin and brought them home as a present to Eurystheus, his master. A Pygmy, capitalized, is one of a dwarf people, generally under five feet, in central Africa. A pygmy, lower-cased, is a short, insignificant person; a dwarf. In Greek, *pygmé* was "fist." It was also a measure of length—the distance from the elbow to the knuckle.

PYGMY

HERCULEAN

A task requiring great strength is herculean. So is great strength itself.

PROCRUSTEAN

Procrustes was a robber who amused himself by tying wayfarers to an iron bed, then stretching or cutting off their legs to fit. Theseus, son of the king of Athens, killed Procrustes by using Procrustes's own methods. Arbitrary imposition of conformity is procrustean. ("Procrustean discipline is no longer to be found in our school," huffed the principal.)

Chiron the Centaur (not to be confused with Charon the ferryman) guided the education of the hero Jason, whose adventures left us the word argonaut. How that happened needs explaining.

A Greek king named Athamas traded in his wife, the mother of his two children, Phrixus and Helle, on a later model, the princess Ino. Ino, in order that her own son might inherit the kingdom, arranged to have the boy Phrixus, and his sister as well, offered up as a sacrifice. But a wondrous ram, with a fleece of pure gold, snatched them from the altar and bore them away through the air. As the ram was crossing the strait between Europe and Asia, Helle fell off and was drowned; the Hellespont is named after her. Phrixus arrived safely at Colchis, on the Black Sea. Since it was customary to sacrifice one's most valued possession in gratitude for such great services, he sacrificed the ram to Zeus—scarcely a grateful act from the point of view of the ram. He gave the Golden Fleece to the Colchian king.

Some years later, Jason was assured that his claim to be the rightful king of Iolcos would be honored if he brought home the Golden Fleece. He set out for Colchis with a crew of the greatest heroes of Greece, including Hercules, Castor, Pollux, and Orpheus, in a vessel called the *Argo*. It was piloted in the first stages by Tiphys, a pilot so skilled that the word has become lower-cased for an expert seaman. One of the crew, Linkeus, had eyes so sharp that he could see the precious minerals buried deep in the earth. Lynx-eyed refers not to the lynx, which happens to have rather poor vision, but to Linkeus, and Greek *leussein*, "to see."

At Colchis, the king's daughter, the enchantress Medea, helped Jason to obtain the Fleece, and then fled with him in the *Argo* back to Greece. The medeola, or wake-robin, a genus of North American trilliums, is the only common noun I know commemorating Medea. Even that is more than she deserves; she was a bloody sort, who liked to see old men slaughtered and boiled in caldrons.

The heroes who traveled in the *Argo* were called argonauts after their vessel. An argonaut is anyone who sets out on a fabulous and risky mission; the term was applied to the men who made their way to California in 1849 in search of gold, and later to gold seekers in the Klondike. A mollusk, the paper nautilus, is of the genus Argonaut.

Argos was also the name of Odysseus's faithful dog, which refused death until its master had returned home from his wanderings.

Argosy, "a fleet of vessels; a vessel of the largest size," does not derive from the *Argo*, but from a city, Ragusa, formerly spelled Arguze—perhaps the Sicilian city of that name, but more likely the one in Yugoslavia, now called Dubrovnik.

Here a genealogical twig:

Lacedaemon, son of Zeus, married the princess Sparta. When he conquered a section of Greece, he called the country Lacedaemon after himself, and its capital Sparta after his wife. Their daughter Eurydice, wife of the king of Argos, bore a daughter named Danaë.

Zeus seduced Danaë by means of a golden shower, a device much favored to this day. The result was the hero Perseus. The best-known accomplishment of Perseus was to slay Medusa, the only mortal among the three dreadful female creatures called Gorgons. The Gorgons' hair was entwined with serpents; they had wings of gold; their hands were of brass; their bodies were covered with impenetrable scales; their teeth were as long as the tusks of a wild boar; and they turned to stone all those on whom they fixed their eyes. A gorgon is any person, especially a

GORGONESQUE woman, who is very ugly or terrifying. To be gorgonesque is to be repulsive.

Daedalus, a very clever and unscrupulous Athenian artificer, having murdered his nephew, had to take refuge in Crete. There he built the famed Labyrinth, "double-headed axe," a maze in which the man-bull Minotaur was confined—the LABYRINTH prototype of all the labyrinths since then. This includes the LABYRINTHITIS labyrinth of the ear. An inflammation of that area is labyrinthitis.

A perhaps groundless legend says the first of these mazes was built not by Daedalus but by a king named Labarus, of whom nothing else is known, and that the original meaning of the term was "the abode of Labarus."

Daedalus incurred the displeasure of the king of Crete, and with his son Icarus was pent in the labyrinth he had built. They escaped on wings of Daedalus's devising. Icarus, however, flew so close to the sun that the wax binding the feathers of his wings ICARIAN melted, and he fell into the Aegean Sea. Icarian wings are perilously inadequate. An Icarian flight is one that soars too high for safety. Daedalus, more prudent than his son, flew at a reasonable altitude, and arrived safely in Sicily. Because he was so clever with his hands, any intricate, cunningly formed object is termed DAEDAL daedal. Air pioneers are called daedalists.

The word tantalize derives from Tantalus, a wealthy king, son of Zeus by the nymph Pluto (not to be confused with the god of the underworld). Tantalus committed an atrocious sin, gen- TANTALIZE erally believed to be that of serving up his son Pelops as a meal for the gods. His punishment in Hades was to be placed in the midst of a lake whose waters reached his chin but receded whenever he wished to drink, while above his head hung choice TANTALUS fruits just out of reach. To tantalize is to tease, torment. A tantalus is an article of glass furniture holding decanters for wine—visible, but out of reach.

Lycaon, a king of Arcadia, also served human flesh to the gods. As punishment, he was turned into a wolf. Hence the word LYCANTHROPY lycanthropy, insanity causing one to imagine himself to be a predatory animal.

SISYPHEAN Sisyphus, king of Corinth and a son of Aeolus, the god of the winds, was punished, according to some, because of his craft and avarice, or, according to others, because he gave away the fact that Zeus, in the form of a mighty eagle, had carried off the daughter of the river-god Asopus. Sisyphus was doomed in

37   THE GREEKS HAD A NAME FOR IT

Hades to try forever to roll a rock uphill which forever rolled back. Sisyphean labors require continual redoing.

With the help of Homer, the Trojan War turned scores of men, beasts, gods, and monsters into improper, uncommon nouns. The proximate cause of the war was the elopement of Helen, wife of Menelaus, king of Sparta, with Paris, son of Priam, king of Troy. Helen was supposed to have been the most beautiful woman who ever lived. She was apostrophized in a lovely ode by Edgar Allen Poe (1809–1849):

> *Helen, thy beauty is to me*
> * Like those Nicean barks of yore,*
> *That gently, o'er a perfumed sea,*
> * The weary, wayworn wanderer bore*
> * To his own native shore.*

HELEN
MILLIHELEN

Writers, seeking to measure the immeasurable, have used a helen as a unit of beauty; they speak of millihelens, kilohelens, and the like. But since Helen was the absolute, there clearly can be no kilohelens. Of millihelens there are many.

Some proper names that Homer turned into common nouns:

NESTOR
NESTORIAN

Nestor, king of Pylos, at an advanced age joined the besieging Greeks at Troy. He was revered as a wise counselor. A nestor is thus an old man especially noted for his wisdom. Nestorian means wise and aged. (There is a kind of parrot in New Zealand called the Nestor.)

STENTORIAN

STENTOR

Stentorian, meaning "extremely loud," comes from Stentor, a Greek herald during the war whose voice was "as loud as that of fifty other men together." A stentor has a loud mouth. Stentors, aquatic microorganisms, have mouths like trumpets.

THERSITES

In Homer's account of the Trojan War, a low-born Greek named Thersites took great pleasure in abusing Agamemnon and other heroes. Shakespeare referred to him in *Troilus and Cressida*. A thersites is anyone who scolds those who deem themselves his betters.

ACHILLES' HEEL

A mighty hero is an achilles. When Achilles was new-born, his mother rendered him invulnerable to injury by dipping him in the River Styx. But she had to hold him by the heel, which therefore was not protected. He was fatally wounded there by an arrow shot by Paris, the husband of Helen. Your vulnerable point (and you have one) is your achilles's heel. The achilles tendon, named from the same legend, is the hamstring at the back of the heel.

MYRMIDON

The Myrmidons, a Thessalian troop, accompanied Achilles to the war. Myrmidon is similar in spelling to the Greek word for "ant," which led to a report that the Myrmidons were ants before they were men. A myrmidon, once thought of as simply a loyal retainer or attendant, today is any subordinate officer who executes even the vilest orders without protest.

AMAZON

Among those who fell before the might of Achilles was Penthesilea, queen of the Amazons, who had brought her army to the aid of the besieged Trojans. The Amazons were a nation of female warriors, said to hack off the right breast lest it interfere with archery and swordplay. A tall, strong, masculine-appearing woman is described as an amazon. The Amazon River received its name because the Spanish explorer Francisco de Orellana, attacked there in 1541, believed he saw women fighting alongside the men.

HECTOR

To hector—that is, to bully—debases the name of Hector, perhaps the bravest of the Trojan warriors. He slew Patroclus, friend of Achilles, who in a fury then slew Hector. The word degenerated into its present pejorative meaning when a London street gang of the early 17th century styled themselves "hectors"—"heroes."

PANDER

To pander—"procure for; minister to; cater"—traces to Pandarus, who broke a truce between the Greeks and Trojans by shooting at and wounding Menelaus, the husband from whom Paris had stolen Helen. Chaucer, Boccaccio, and Shakespeare make Pandarus the procurer of Cressida, daughter of a Trojan high priest, for Troilus, son of the king of Troy. The match did not last, Cressida deserting her lover for a Greek. But if it is any comfort to Troilus, he has a beautiful memorial in the troilus butterfly, which is black, with yellow marginal spots on the front wings, and blue on the back. Cressida has no memorial at all.

TROILUS
BUTTERFLY

PALLADIUM

Troy was supposed to be safe from the Greeks as long as the statue of Pallas Athene remained undisturbed in the city. Odysseus and Diomedes managed to steal the statue, and Troy fell soon thereafter. A palladium is a safeguard: trial by jury has been called "the palladium of civil rights." The name endures in the asteroid Pallas and the element palladium.

The Greeks finally effected an entrance into Troy by pretending to lift their siege, leaving behind a huge wooden horse as a peace offering. The Trojans hauled the horse into their city, unaware that it was full of armed warriors. The priest Laocoön, according to Vergil, gave warning: *Timeo Danaos et dona ferentes*—"I fear Greeks even if they bring gifts." He was not only shouted down, but the gods sent two great serpents over the sea to kill him and his two sons. The *Laocoön*, a sculptural representation of the event, stands in the Vatican. A subversive group or device insinuated within enemy ranks is a trojan horse; a greek gift is one that is suspect.

TROJAN HORSE
GREEK GIFT

CASSANDRA

Cassandra, a daughter of Priam, also distrusted the Greeks, but her warnings went unheeded. Apollo had once wooed her, and given her the power of prophecy. When she rejected him, he could not take back his gift, but decreed that no one was to believe her prophecies. A cassandra is a true prophet of evil, never believed.

When Odysseus, king of Ithaca, left to join the Greek besiegers of Troy, he entrusted the care of his son Telemachus to his old friend Mentor, who trained the boy so carefully that

MENTOR

TELEMACHUS

ODYSSEY

CIRCEAN

mentor has come to mean "wise and faithful counselor." Telemachus grew up a prudent, dependable young man—too prudent and dependable for some tastes. A telemachus is still such.

An odyssey—"a long wandering or series of travels"—stems from the ten years it took Odysseus to reach home after the razing of Troy. For seven of those years he was detained on an island by the nymph Calypso, and for another year on another island, by the enchantress Circe, who transformed his crew into swine to prevent voyeurism. Circean devices lure by charm to degradation.

SCYLLA
AND
CHARYBDIS

One time, filled with rage that the sea-god Glaucus had scorned her love for that of a beautiful maiden named Scylla, Circe changed the maiden into a snaky monster with twelve feet, six terrible heads, and a voice like that of a young whelp. Scylla dwelt in a cave by the sea, whence she would thrust forth her long necks, seizing in each mouth a sailor from a passing vessel. On the opposite side of a narrow strait from her cave was the whirlpool Charybdis; a vessel seeking to avoid the snaky monster was drawn into the whirlpool. Hence the expression "between Scylla and Charybdis" for a choice between two equally great dangers. Odysseus lost six of his men as he sailed past Scylla, and was himself sucked in by Charybdis, but held to a mast till thrown out again.

PROTEAN

Menelaus had almost as much trouble getting home from Troy as Odysseus did. Menelaus was king of Sparta, brother of Agamemnon, and husband of that Helen whose elopement with Paris of Troy led to the Trojan War. His wanderings on the way back to Sparta lasted eight years. Once, detained for twenty days by want of wind on the island of Pharos, and running short of provisions, he was advised by a nymph that the sea-god Proteus, if forced, could tell him how to reach home. Menelaus found the god asleep, seized him, and held on despite Proteus's successive transformations into a lion, a serpent, a leopard, a boar, water, and a tree. (I would like to know how he managed to hold on to the water.) Proteus eventually provided the necessary instructions. Anything exceedingly variable or readily assuming many shapes—an amoeba, for instance, or, in a different sense, an actor—is protean.

PHAROS

In the 3rd century B.C., Ptolemy II made Pharos, just off Alexandria, the site of a huge lighthouse, one of the seven wonders of the ancient world. Pharos became generic for any lighthouse. It is an ecclesiastical chandelier as well.

UCALEGON

Just before Aeneas fled from blazing Troy, he saw the flames reach the house of Ucalegon, next to that of his friend Achates. A ucalegon is a neighbor whose house is on fire.

ACHATES

An achates is a faithful friend. Achates was a loyal companion of Aeneas after the Trojan War.

AENEAS

Aeneas—son, by the way, of Aphrodite herself—carried his aged father Anchises piggyback from the blazing city; hence the common noun aeneas as a model of filial devotion. Vergil calls him pious Aeneas. Enea Silvio de' Piccolomini, the last name meaning "little man," took the name Pius II when he became Pope in 1458, in respect for pious Aeneas.

The wanderings of Aeneas before he settled in Italy rival those of Odysseus. At one point he so aroused the amorous passions of Dido, queen of Carthage, that she immolated herself in a tremendous bonfire when he deserted her; sailing away at night, he could see the fire lighting the sky behind him. The 18th-century poet Richard Porson wrote:

When Dido found Aeneas would not come,
She mourned in silence, and was Di-Do-Dumb.

DIDO

A dido is an antic or caper, as in "to cut didoes." This definition may stem from the legend that when Dido, a refugee from Tyre, first arrived in her future kingdom, she was offered by the natives as much land as she could enclose by a bull's hide. She cut the hide into a single hairline thread, long enough to surround an immense tract, later the site of Carthage. Quite a dido.

TROJAN

The pluck and endurance of the defenders of Troy survive in such phrases as "to work like a Trojan." In old English slang, however, a trojan was less admirable. He was "a gay and perhaps somewhat dissolute companion."

JAKES

Ajax killed himself out of vexation because the armor of the slain Achilles was awarded not to him but to Odysseus. The name is punned on in the venerable English word jakes, for privy; in 1596 Sir John Harington (1561–1612) was banned from court for his Rabelaisian *Metamorphosis of Ajax*, largely devoted to this sort of schoolboy wordplay.

Besides transplanting Greek divinities, the Romans had innumerable gods and spirits of their own. Sir Frank Adcock remarked that "if the Romans had invented the automobile, they would have had a goddess Punctura."

Sors was the god of chance. From his name evolved *sortarius*, "a teller of fortune by throwing lots," which got around among the Celts. *Sortarius* emerged in Old French as *sorcier*, and in English as sorcerer, "a magician or wizard." Sort, as in "She's of the better sort," has the same origin.

Portus is Latin for "harbor." Portunus was the god who protected these havens. When *ob*, "before," was prefixed to the god's name, the result was opportune, "seasonable, timely": the ship waits for an opportune moment to enter the harbor. Opportunity, "a time or place favorable for executing a purpose," is a gift of the same god.

The Lares and Penates were household gods or ghosts, the Lares being beneficent ancestral spirits, and the Penates gods of the storeroom. Lares and penates, lowercased, are the sum of one's personal or household effects. The larva of an insect—the wingless and often wormlike form in which it hatches from the egg—takes its name from the larvae, "masked ones," the sinister and dimly seen cousins of the Lares and Penates.

A goddess or mountain nymph named Egeria was adviser to Numa Pompilius, second king of Rome. Her name came to represent the patroness of a public man, or indeed any woman who acts as an adviser. In 1624 Burton referred in *Anatomy of Melancholy* to "My Mistris Melancholy, my Aegeria, or my *malus Genius*." Three hundred and ten years later, in *Eleven New Cantos*, Ezra Pound found her still alive and well: "His wife now acts as his model and the Egeria / Has, let us say, married a realtor."

Vesta was the Roman goddess of the hearth, worshiped in a temple containing a sacred fire tended by virgins who were called vestal in her honor. A vestal is a virgin, or a nun.

A jovial old deity of rural stripe, living mostly in the woods, was Silvanus. To him we owe the word sylvan, as in a sylvan glen or landscape.

The Romans worshiped so many gods that they had to erect a special temple, the Pantheon ("all the gods"), to accommodate them all. A pantheon is any public building commemorating the great of a nation or profession.

Long after Zeus and Jupiter were only memories in Greece and Rome, Scandinavian Odin was attended by his Valkyries in Valhalla. The Valkyries were awful and beautiful maidens who conducted the souls of slain warriors to Valhalla, there to battle all day and carouse all night. Valkyrie persists today to describe a fierce woman, perhaps even more redoubtable than an amazon.

SAGA

Among those who drank from golden beakers with Odin was the goddess Saga, who has lent her name to "a poetic narrative having the real or fancied characteristics of an Icelandic saga." Outmoded gods often shrank into the equivalent of goblins; today a saga is a seeress or witch.

NIGHTMARE

The Scandinavian demon Mara, a kind of incubus, survives in nightmare—"a dream arousing feelings of inescapable fear, horror, and distress, or a situation that evokes such feelings."

OLD NICK

Not the devil but Nicor, a Scandinavian sea monster, is evoked when we call on Old Nick.

The Midas Touch

MIDAS TOUCH

King Midas, as a reward for a service to Dionysus, was granted one wish. He wished that everything he touched might turn into gold. The disconcerting results of that miscalculation are familiar to every schoolchild; even the king's own dear daughter became lifeless metal. The midas touch is the ability to turn everything into gold, whatever the consequences.

CROESUS

Croesus, a 6th-century B.C. Lydian king, was so rich that his name has become a synonym for an unimaginably wealthy person. Huck Finn said, "Rich as creosote." Tom Sawyer replied, "Rich as Croesus, you mean."

One might assume from the experience of Midas that gold is not synonymous with happiness; but few of us seem to have learned the lesson. We seek to lay our hands on every gold coin or its equivalent that we can find. Here are some of them, called after proper names, that would be worth collecting:

BEZANT

The bezant, a gold coin issued by the emperors at Byzantium (Constantinople), was circulated in Europe from the 6th to the 15th or 16th century.

BOB

A bob is a shilling, named speculatively for some Bob. But bob has other backgrounds, such as French *bober*, "to trick."

GUINEA

The guinea, a former British gold coin worth one pound and one shilling, was originally made of gold from the Guinea coast of Africa.

JOEY   A joey was London slang for a four-penny bit, commemorating some unknown Joey. (Joey, American slang name for a clown, is taken from Joseph Grimaldi [1779–1837], a famous clown of the period.)

JULY   The july is a coin whose only use is to pay the new Pope for his first Mass at St. Peter's. The name comes from its coinage under Julius II.

NAPOLEON   The napoleon is a former French gold coin of twenty francs named after Napoleon Bonaparte.

Other coins with names once proper:

Afghani (Afghanistan)
Albertin (Austrian Netherlands), from Archduke Albert
Alfonso (Spain), from King Alfonso
Argentino (Argentina)
Azteca (Mexico), from the Aztecs
Balboa (Panama), from Balboa, the explorer
Belga (Belgium)
Colon (Costa Rica and El Salvador), from Columbus
Florin (Austria, Great Britain, Montenegro, Netherlands, South Africa), from the city of Florence
Franc (Albania, Belgium, France, Switzerland, Virgin Islands), from France, Frank
Heller (Germany, Austria, Switzerland), from Hall, in Swabia, where it was first coined
Mahmudi, from the Mahmud, once the Muslim rulers in Persia and India
Mungo (Mongolia), from Mongol
Pahlavi (Persia), from Riza Khan Pahlavi, shah of Persia (Pahlavi was the chief Persian language from the 3rd to the 9th century)
Rand (South Africa), from the great South African goldfields of that name

A Meander Through the Attic

The traditional date of the Trojan War is about 1200 B.C. Some four hundred years later documented accounts of historic

45   THE GREEKS HAD A NAME FOR IT

events began to pile up in the attic of history. A meander through the Greek attic:

OLYMPIC GAMES

OLYMPIAD

The Olympic games, held at Olympia every fourth year, were first formally recorded in 776 B.C., but apparently had gone on long before that. The four-year interval between the games was called an olympiad. The word is now used for the quadrennial celebration of the modern Olympic games and, erroneously, for the games themselves.

DRACONIC
DRACONIAN
DRACONISM

The laws of Athens were first codified around 621 B.C. by the statesman Draco. Though fixed laws represented a major advance in civilization, the penalties Draco laid down for offenses were so severe that they were said to be "written in blood." Draconic or draconian is "barbarously harsh; cruel." Plato described draconism as "severe but honorable conservatism."

SAPPHIC

About 612 B.C., on the Aegean island of Lesbos, was born Sappho, a poetess of whose works few fragments remain. (Her presumed sexual predilections are mentioned in another chapter.) We know little more of her than that on Lesbos "burning Sappho loved and sung," and that she left behind a form of meter called sapphic. This is a logaoedic pentapody with a dactyl in the third place. I hope you know what that means. Sappho catches the reader unawares by dropping a choriambus (-˘˘-, as in "*chew*ing a *bone*") or perhaps a dactyl (-˘˘, as in "*Jef*ferson") into a series of feet of other lengths, especially trochees (-˘, as in "*go*ing, *go*ing, *go*ing"). Here is an imitation of the Sapphic stanza by Swinburne:

Heard the flying feet of the loves behind her
Make a sudden thunder upon the waters,
As the thunder flung from the strong unclosing
Wings of a great wind.

SAPPHO

A sappho is a learned and poetic woman. It is also a genus of hummingbird with a beautiful forked tail.

SOLON

In the 6th century B.C., Solon, a poet and statesman, instituted legal reforms in Athens, increasing the rights of all citizens to share in the government. A solon is "a legislator; wise lawgiver; sage." Members of the United States Senate are called solons, sometimes ironically.

THESPIAN

The first actor to appear separately from the chorus, speaking a prologue and set speeches, was Thespis, who won a prize for a tragedy in about 534 B.C. Thespian and actor are synonymous.

In 490 B.C., the town of Caryae, in Laconia, sided with the

Persians against the Greeks at Thermopylae. The victorious Greeks destroyed the city, slew the men, and made the women slaves. To immortalize the shame of Caryae, Praxitiles is said to have sculpted the draped figures of women from that city—perhaps representing the order of priestesses of Artemis—to serve as supporting columns for his temples. Such columns are caryatids.

CARYATID

The first great historian, Herodotus, who lived in the 5th century B.C., left a systematic account of the Greco-Persian wars from 500 to 479 B.C. Among the men he described was a stammerer named Battos. Battology is needless or excessive repetition in speech or writing.

BATTOLOGY

Timon of Athens, celebrated by Shakespeare in the drama of that name, lived during the Peloponnesian War (431–404 B.C.) He was noted for his misanthropy. Hence timon for a misanthrope or bitterly cynical person..

TIMON

Two tragedies of Sophocles (496–406 B.C.) featured Oedipus, king of Thebes, who was abandoned at birth and later was persecuted by Nemesis for unwittingly killing his father and marrying his mother. In psychoanalysis, the oedipus complex consists of libidinal feelings in a boy child for his mother, first manifested between the ages of three and five. The electra complex, the same feeling for a father on the part of his daughter, is named for Electra, a daughter of Clytemnestra and Agamemnon, king of Mycenae, who led the Greeks against Troy. Electra avenged Clytemnestra's murder of her father by killing her mother and her mother's lover. She was the subject of tragedies by Sophocles, Aeschylus, and Euripides, and the modern tragedy by Eugene O'Neill, *Mourning Becomes Electra*.

OEDIPUS COMPLEX

ELECTRA COMPLEX

Oedipus was first to answer correctly the riddle of the Sphinx of Thebes, a monster having a lion's body, birdlike wings, and the head and breasts of a woman. All who had previously guessed wrong had been destroyed. The riddle: What creature walks in the morning on four feet, at noon on two, and in the evening on three? The answer: Man—as a baby on hands and knees, later on his feet, and finally needing a staff. A sphinx is an enigmatic person, one who keeps secrets. The word is preserved in the sphincter muscle, which also keeps secrets. The spinnaker, a large triangular sail set opposite the mainsail on fore-and-aft-rigged yachts, may have been so named because yachtsmen find it refractory and mysterious, like the Sphinx. (But perhaps it derives from a nineteenth-century yacht named Sphinx, first to use the sail.)

SPHINX

SPHINCTER MUSCLE

SPINNAKER

47   THE GREEKS HAD A NAME FOR IT

SWORD OF DAMOCLES

Dionysius the Elder was a celebrated tyrant of Syracuse, where he was born in 430 B.C. He is famed for putting down one Damocles, a flatterer who extolled the tyrant's wealth, power, virtue, and felicity. Dionysius suggested that Damocles try the delights of absolute power for himself, and the flatterer eagerly assented. He lay on a purple couch, surrounded by vessels of gold and silver. Lovely slaves served him exquisite foods and obeyed his every whim. He thought himself at the summit of human happiness until, happening to cast his eyes upward to the richly carved ceiling, he perceived a sword, suspended by a single horsehair, directly over his throat. All delight instantly left him; he begged the tyrant to allow him to depart, since he no longer wished to enjoy this kind of felicity. The sword of Damocles symbolizes the precariousness of fortune.

DAMON AND PYTHIAS

Dionysius figures also in the famous tale of Damon and Pythias (or Phintia), shorthand for two inseparable friends. Pythias, having been condemned to death for conspiring against the tyrant, obtained leave to go home to arrange his affairs, on condition that Damon take his place and be executed should he not return. Pythias was delayed; Damon was led to execution; but his friend arrived just in time to save him. Dionysius was so struck with this instance of true attachment that he pardoned Pythias, and entreated the two to allow him to share their friendship.

ZOILISM

Zoilus, a bitter, envious, unjust critic of the 4th century B.C., has given his name to zoilism: "carping criticism."

DEIPNOSO-PHISTAI

It was around the 4th century B.C.—I have been unable to find the exact date—that Deipnosophistai of Athens won fame for promoting stimulating dinner conversations. If you are a skillful conversationalist, you are a deipnosophist.

PHILIPPICS

In 351 B.C., Demosthenes, the orator, launched a series of tirades denouncing King Philip of Macedonia for allegedly planning to take over Greece by force of arms. (Demosthenes was right.) Three hundred years later, the Roman Cicero's vitriolic attacks on Mark Antony were called philippics by analogy. Fierce and eloquent speeches loaded with ad hominem attacks, and made in critical times, still bear the name. Such speeches were not taken lightly. Demosthenes was ultimately forced to commit suicide, and Cicero was hunted down and put to death.

CICERONE

Cicero's name is perpetuated in cicerone, a guide to points of interest, presumably because he acted as Dante's guide to hell in the *Inferno*.

MAUSOLEUM

While Demosthenes was raging against King Philip, the Carians were building the monumental tomb of King Mausolus at Halicarnassus. It was considered one of the seven wonders of the ancient world. A mausoleum is any magnificent tomb.

GORDIAN KNOT

Alexander, son of the Philip against whom Demosthenes inveighed, was born in Pella in 356 B.C. and in his thirty-three years of life conquered most of the known world. At one point in his career he was confronted by the intricate Gordian knot, tied by Gordius, mythical founder of the kingdom of Phrygia. An oracle having declared that whoever untied the knot would be master of Asia, Alexander solved the problem by cutting it with his sword. A Gordian knot is an extreme or inextricable difficulty. To cut the Gordian knot is to dispose of the difficulty by summary measures. At one time the story was that Alexander actually unraveled the knot. The present version is a more cynical interpretation.

BUCEPHALUS

Alexander owned a high-spirited horse, Bucephalus, which only he could ride. Bucephalus carried his master throughout the conquests of Greece, the Persian Empire, and Egypt. A bucephalus is a riding horse, especially one that is full of life.

HYPERBOLE

Also in the 4th century B.C. there flourished in Athens one Hyperbolus ("far-throwing"), a demagogue who customarily used exaggerated statements as figures of speech. The word doubtless antedated the man. "I could eat a horse" is hyperbole.

COLOSSUS
COLOSSAL

COLISEUM

The Greeks had a word, *kolossioîos*, meaning "large"; we might never have heard of it had not Chares, about 280 B.C., built at Rhodes another of the seven wonders of the world: a statue of Apollo 120 feet high and called Colossus for its size. Thus reinforced, the word has stridden colossally down the generations. The huge amphitheater built in Rome by Vespasian and Titus in A.D. 75–80 was called the Colosseum. A coliseum, its spelling altered, is any building designed to hold large crowds. Thomas Telford, an English transportation expert of the 19th century, was called the "Colossus of roads."

Other ancient names that became common nouns:
The Greeks called non-Greeks *hoi barbaroi*, "the unintelligibles; the stammerers." The word was applied particularly to inhabitants of the Saracen lands of North Africa. These came to be known as Barbary, and the population as Berbers. Hence

BARBARIAN
BARBAROUS

barbarian, barbarous, a member of a primitive civilization or a person considered brutal or uncultured. In view of this source, I have often wondered why Barbara is so popular a name.

BARB

Barb is the name of a strain of horses from Barbary. From

three of these—the Godolphin barb, owned by the great Godolphin family of Cornwall; the Darley Arabian; and the Byerley Turk—are descended all thoroughbred horses. A barb, as in barbed wire, and barber, your haircutter, have their origin in an entirely different word—Latin *barba*, "beard."

SPARTAN

The Spartans were drilled in fortitude. Many a schoolchild has marveled at the Spartan boy who, rather than admit that he was concealing a stolen fox beneath his cloak, stood silent while the fox gnawed out his vitals. We refer to a person able to bear great discomfort or pain stoically as a spartan. The epithet is also applied to anyone who is especially frugal and austere.

HELOT

When first taking over Laconia, the Spartans overran the city of Helos and enslaved its inhabitants. A helot is a serf or bondsman.

LACONIC

Sparta was also known as Laconia, and Spartans as Laconians. Because the Laconians were sparing in speech and emotion, laconic means "terse; pithy; sententious." A foreign conqueror sent a message: "If I come to Laconia, not one brick will stand on another." The laconic reply was "If."

SYBARITES

Sybaris, an ancient Greek city of southern Italy, was the seat of folk addicted to luxury and pleasure, making them bywords. Sybarites are known for their hedonistic approach to life.

SOLECISM

The Athenian colonists at Soloi, near present-day Syria, spoke what the Greeks considered a corrupt dialect of Greek. Any ungrammatical combination of words is a solecism.

ARCADIAN

Arcadia, a mountainous district of Greece, was the abode of a simple people reputed to dwell in pastoral happiness. An existence ideally rural is arcadian.

MEANDER

The river Meander, now Menderes, twists and turns before joining the Aegean Sea on the west coast of Asia Minor. We meander when, in speech or action, we twist and turn.

ATTIC
ATTIC STYLE

ATTIC SALT
ATTIC FAITH
PUNIC FAITH

In classical architecture, the word "order" refers to the proportions of columns and the forms of their crowning members. The Attic order (from Attica) originally consisted of a small order placed above another of much greater height; hence attic for the top story of a building, especially a home. Attic style is simple, pure, and of refined elegance, as was that of the Greeks in Attica. Attic salt is elegant and delicate wit. Attic faith is inviolable faith. Its opposite is punic faith, not to be trusted. Punic, from Phoenician, was applied by the Romans to Carthage because Carthage was originally a Phoenician colony. The Carthaginians were proverbial among the Romans for perfidy, as no doubt the Romans were among the Carthaginians.

ATTIC STORY
BATS IN
THE ATTIC

In slang, the attic or attic story is the head, that being the highest part of the body; whence such epithets as bats (or rats) in the attic and queer in the attic story.

ARELY A line or two of this book remained undone, I thought, when I found myself chatting at a cocktail party with Timothy Dickinson, contributing editor of *Harper's* magazine. (Though I am not sure of Timothy's exact function there, I suspect they use him instead of a library.) He indicated a willingness to check the facts in my manuscript, and I leaped at the chance to exploit him. I might have been less eager had I realized I was opening my entire thesis to a revision and amplification that would result in a hopeless blurring between my uncommon, improper nouns and my Patient Griseldas. At Timothy's puckish touch, what had been a series of restrained, even costive definitions burst into exuberant chaos. A book virtually ready for typesetting was locked into manuscript form for an extra two months. And years will pass before my head stops whirling.

For a description of Timothy, I defer to George Plimpton in *Shadow Box* (published by G. P. Putnam's Sons in 1977):

> One can drop in at his office and ask him what he knows about Holstein's great work on the army ant, and it will be an hour before one is able to escape. . . . He speaks in quick explosions of verbiage, often shifting from one language to another, lacing himself on with "Think, Dickinson, *think!*" as he takes one back with him into fine labyrinthine areas of arcane knowledge. He looks like an overgrown schoolboy from the English public-school system—which indeed produced him—with his black morning coat and trousers (I have never seen him in anything else), a white boutonniere to brighten the ensemble, along with a watch-chain running across his vestcoat. He carries a silver-knobbed cane with him everywhere, even indoors, and when he stands and talks, he keeps it tucked away under one arm like a swagger stick. People behind him at cocktail parties get poked.

TITCH

In the land of improper, uncommon nouns, Timothy is not a titch, but a lambert. A titch, though it first meant something huge, now means something tiny. The evolution of the word proceeded in this fashion:

In March 1853 the heir to the Tichborne baronetcy was lost at sea, en route to Jamaica. Twenty years later an immensely fat man named Orton, a butcher by trade, came knocking at the Tichborne gates, claiming to be the missing heir. His account of himself was plausible enough to win him a lengthy legal hearing; and by the time he was declared an impostor, his name had become a byword throughout England. An infant named Harry Ralph, born at the height of the Tichborne affair, was nicknamed Titch for his fatness. Though he grew up to be phenomenally small, he kept the nickname; and since he was perhaps the most popular music hall entertainer of his time, titch became and remained synonymous with "little." This story illustrates my favorite moral, which is that you never can tell.

LAMBERT

Lambert too started out meaning someone or something extremely large, but retained that significance; metaphorically, a lambert is the ultimate of anything. The specialty of Daniel Lambert, who lived from 1770 to 1809, was putting on weight;

he hit a peak of 738 pounds. George Meredith referred to London as the Daniel Lambert of cities.

Timothy is a lambert of the forgotten or overlooked fact. He does not weigh 738 pounds, but he wears his budding embonpoint with pride. He marches incessantly about a room, his shoulders well back to balance the weight in front. One afflicted with such restlessness, he tells me, is known as a "wandering Jew"; but I have never heard anyone but Timothy use the expression in that sense.

Timothy talks faster than I can catch his sense; I am constantly saying, "Spell that word, Timothy," and "Spell that word again, Timothy," to give me time to catch up. The faster his speech, the higher his pitch. Sometimes, between the Oxonian accent and the linked-firecrackers delivery, I fail to understand him. I take the opportunity to clarify my notes when he pauses to gulp tea, spooning in sugar as he goes, so that the fullness of the cup scarcely diminishes. He also fancies apples, cheese, and a kind of chocolate cookie which Louise keeps around as bait.

"Something to nibble on?" I asked one night.

"Oh, I think not, thank you. Though if you happen to have one or two of those delicious chocolate tidbits . . ."

Louise had the tidbits. Timothy's hand found them out of habit, his eyes being engaged with the first of several crumpled sheets of once white paper. It was covered with sprawling notations, each some sort of trigger word. They were scribbled both horizontally and vertically, one intersecting another; this must be what is meant when handwriting is called chicken tracks.

"You have hanswurst and jack sausage, of course?" he began.

"I'm afraid not."

HANSWURST "Hanswurst was a 17th-century character in German low comedy. *Wurst*—slang for 'nonsense.' One of the great events in German theatrical history was the dramatic banishment of Hanswurst from the stage in 1723 by *die Nauberin*—the great actress whom Goethe evokes as Madame Kitty in *Wilhelm Meister*. JACK SAUSAGE Jack sausage is the English translation. They are generic now for the foods.

"Oh, did you know that Shakespeare's original name for Falstaff was Oldcastle? After Sir John Oldcastle—once close to Henry V, but then hanged as a Lollard rebel. A kinsman, Lord Cobham, objected to use of the name in the play, and Shakespeare changed it in 1598."

By the time I had finished writing "Oldcastle," Timothy was far down the road:

CESAREWICH "*Mmmm.* Pop-pop. Cesarewich. A son of the Russian czar."

"Why should I have cesarewich?"

"In 1839, when the future Alexander II visited England, a handicap race was named after him."

"So any handicap race in England is called a cesarewich?"

"Almost. Do you know why each floor of a house is called a story? Because in the 14th century the tapestries lining the walls told picture stories.

GALLERY
MARIANNE

"Marianne. The symbol of Republican France. She carries a flag, and wears a blue blouse with a bodice, and a red-and-white-striped shirt. Wooden shoes, I believe. And of course a Phrygian cap. A close-fitting affair, sometimes called a liberty cap or mob cap—a symbol of liberty as far back as the time of Caesar. The coins minted by Caesar's assassins showed two daggers flanking a liberty cap."

"Did Marianne become a common noun?"

"Indeed. The Société de Marianne was the Republican organization that operated against Napoleon III. They carried effigies of Marianne in their parades. The royalists would shout 'Marianne!' meaning whore. You can still find mariannes on Paris street corners."

I jotted down "Marianne."

BALACLAVA
HELMET

"Balaclava hemlet?" said Timothy. "In 1854, when the English, French, and Turks fought the Russians at Balaclava, both sides wore woolen masks because of the extreme cold. Skiers still wear them."

"May I fill your cup?"

"You are most kind. And if there happen to be more of those delicious chocolate tidbits about ... Do you have *facies Hippocratica*—the Hippocratic countenance? It is the look of those dying or wasted from long illness, as described by Hippocrates. A little like the Austerlitz look—the look on Prime Minister Pitt's face after the news of the French victory over the Austrians and Russians at Austerlitz in 1805: complete discouragement and exhaustion. 'Roll up that map of Europe,' he said. 'It won't be needed for ten years.' Within weeks he was dead."

HIPPOCRATIC
COUNTENANCE
AUSTERLITZ
LOOK

At about this stage in my recurrent engagements with Timothy, my mind is apt to flash back to the Plimpton analogy:

> He was great company [wrote Plimpton], though I always came away from him keenly aware of the empty stretches in my brain, knowing that if his was a cluttered *bibliothèque*-like vaulted chamber with balconies, great banks of volumes rising up, mine suffered badly in comparison—a broom closet off a corridor, a can of paint up on a shelf.

Timothy spooned more sugar into his tea. "Waterloo teeth?" he asked. "In Wellington's time, dentures had to be carved, like George Washington's, or else ripped from jaws. Dentists and their agents combed the battlefield at Waterloo, removing teeth from the mouths of the corpses. The day after Wellington's victory, he was inspecting the site with an aide, and saw a dentist blow out the brains of a dying French soldier to get at his teeth. 'Shoot that man!' ordered Wellington, and the dentist's brains joined his victim's. Summary justice."

Timothy paused, testing his own excellent incisors between thumb and forefinger, apparently to be sure they were not loosening. "Healthy young people," he said, "had the teeth bought out of their mouths. The prices were good. Long before that, the Romans used artificial teeth for show, and removed them for dining."

Timothy has a stick-tic. By this I mean that where others may suffer an uncontrollable twitch of the cheek or eyelid, Timothy when preoccupied unconsciously and endlessly somersaults his cane. He holds it by one end, flipping it so that it reverses direction in midair and returns to his palm aft end to. Now the stick was bouncing and turning like an acrobat on a trampoline. Timothy was unaware; his mind was on the wad of crumpled paper in his other hand. For a moment he was silent save for a murmured "Pop-pop-pop, yes yes." I seized my opportunity.

"I am pretty sure I have 'merry as a grig' right," I said. "Would you just check me? Latin *graecare* means to fool around like a Greek—high jinks, frequently sexual in nature. A person who specialized in such enjoyments was said to be 'merry as a Greek.'"

"Precisely. The English simply hobson-jobsoned Greek to grig, a kind of cricket, because the two words sound alike."

"Hobson-jobson?"

"From 'YāHasan! yāHusayn!'" said Timothy, twirling his cane faster. "It is a ritual cry at the Mohammedan New Year festival, mourning the assassination of Muhammed's two grandsons. The English changed two unfamiliar foreign words to two familiar English words, Hobson and Jobson. We are constantly doing that. Oh, by the way. You do know how Dahomey, the country in West Africa, got its name before it was changed to

Benin a few years ago? Dahomey—Dan-homey—meant 'stomach of Dan.' Tacondou, a king's son, went into the country of Dan, king of the Fons, demanding tribute and the right of passage for his armies. Dan was outraged. 'What!' he said. 'Do you propose to set yourself up on my stomach?' Tacondou then attacked and defeated the armies of Dan, beheaded him, and interred his body under the foundations of a new palace. *Danhomey*. Stomach of Dan."

There has to be a reason for Timothy's leap from one word derivation to another, but I have never been able to understand the principle. From Dan he vaulted to Hercules:

MONACO

"Monaco was first named Heracles Monoekos, 'Hercules dwelling alone.' Hercules exiled himself on the headland of what is now Monaco after going mad and killing his children. The Phoenicians and later the Greeks erected temples to him there. There is a pre-Indo-European word *mon*, meaning 'rock' or 'promontory'; so part of the name may be very ancient."

He continued: "Perhaps not germane, but worth remembering: *Hic Rhodus hic salta*. The people of Rhodes were great braggarts about their country—the Texans of the ancient world. One visiting Athens was telling how prodigiously the people of Rhodes could jump. *Hic Rhodus hic salta*, said his host (in Greek, not Latin, naturally): 'Very well; you are in Rhodes. Now jump.' "

I liked that, which led him to a further excess:

"*Et in Arcadia ega*? 'I too have dwelt in Arcadia?' Meaning I too have experienced the joys of unspoiled innocence—or, quite the other way, 'I, Death, dwell even in Arcadia'?"

There followed a partial recess, in which Timothy matched tea to my whiskey while he delivered himself of trivia. He mentioned that Podunk, generic for "small town," comes from the name of an Algonquin tribe once living on the Podunk River in Connecticut; that Woop Woop to the Australians means the ultimately rural, the ultimate tiny town; that Australians say speewah, perhaps the corruption of an aboriginal word, for biggest and best, as Texans say Texas; that sheila, from the name, is Australian for "girl"—"Smashing sheila, that!"; that the English still refer to emily-colored hands, though what color this is nobody knows, the word having appeared through a typographical error in a poem by Edith Sitwell.

PODUNK

WOOP WOOP

SHEILA

EMILY-COLORED
HANDS

"Perhaps," I said, "she was really playing a joke on A. A. Milne. You remember his verse about Emiline. She ran away from home when her mother scolded her for dirty hands, and returned saying something like 'I've been to London to see the Queen. / And she says my hands are *pufficly* clean.' "

"Quite possible," said Timothy. "By the way, you must make a note of divan. It first meant a register—"

"Timothy," I said loudly, " 'register' is *not* a proper name.

You know my book is limited to words from proper names—"

"... hence a government office; hence sitting around; hence, by extension, a comfortable place to sit. That is, a divan. I have said before that I don't expect you to use all my stories."

"But damn it," I protested, "they are too good to leave out even when they don't fit."

LAMBETH
QUADRANGLE

"Exactly. Lambeth quadrangle," Timothy resumed serenely, "certainly derives from a proper name. It was the four points proposed by the Anglican bishops in 1888 for the reunion of Christendom. They met at Lambeth, the Archbishop's seat."

CHICAGO
QUADRANGLE

"In America," I said, "we call it the Chicago quadrangle. Our bishops approved the four points before yours did."

"Very true," said Timothy. "By the way, the Archbishop of Canterbury has the right to confer honorary degrees called Lambeth degrees. The recipient must wear the gown of the university from which the serving Archbishop was graduated. The current Archbishop is Donald Coggan, from Cambridge, whose own doctorate was a Lambeth degree."

LAMBETH
DEGREE

"Is he the Archbishop who was so cross when Edward VIII abdicated to marry 'the woman I love'?" I asked.

"Ah, life is so short. That was back in 1936. The Archbishop was Cosmo Gordon Lang. Winston Churchill, by the way, wrote the abdication speech. Edward was a popular king, and many people were annoyed when Lang referred to the unfortunate episode in chilly terms over the wireless. One of Lang's ill-wishers sent him an angry anonymous verse, which his secretaries kept from him, but preserved. It goes this way:

My Lord of Canterbury, what a scold you are!
And when your man is down, how bold you are!
Of Christian charity, how scant you are!
And, auld lang swine, how full of cant you are!

"The whole verse builds to the last line—a pun on 'cantuar,' which is the name that the Archbishop of Canterbury signs instead of a surname. Surely *that* fits the guidelines of your book? Oh, have you heard this?

Lord K and Lord C
Will never agree.
So Lord C and Lord K
Must call it a day."

"No," I said, giving up. It was too late to get Timothy back on the track now, and besides, the train had disappeared over the horizon. "Who were Lord C and Lord K?"

"Lord Curzon and Lord Kitchener. They quarreled in 1905, when Curzon was Viceroy of India and Kitchener commander of the armed forces there. Curzon resigned to make his point, and was humiliated when the resignation was accepted. Do you remember that Ed Costikyan gave Ed Koch his margin of victory in the 1977 New York City mayoral primary? He was then abandoned by Koch. Very similar. Lord K and Lord C.

BRISTOL FASHION

"Shipshape and Bristol fashion, meaning done very professionally, are a tribute to the days when the superb ships and brilliant merchant class dominated the sugar—and, alas, the slave trade."

Then:

MASONIC

"Strictly Masonic?"

"Meaning?"

"Utterly confidential—a tribute to the rigor with which a Masonic oath is taken."

TYLER GRIPPE

Timothy riffled through his notes, murmuring "Bop-bop-bop-bop-bop. Uh . . . let . . . us . . . see. Tyler grippe?"

As usual, I was beyond my depth, and swallowing water. I said, "Suitcase, flu, or handshake?"

"Not suitcase. Tyler grippe was a severe chill said to be contracted by those who shook hands with President Tyler, due to his cold demeanor. There was an influenza epidemic at the time."

"Grip . . . grippe," I said sagely.

"Exactly. The Parliament of Dunces in 1404? It was called that because all lawyers were excluded.

MUNICH

"Oh . . . yes yes yes. Good. Munich, of course, for appeasement, from the meeting there between Prime Minister Chamberlain and Hitler. Chamberlain had to give Hitler all he wanted in order to buy time for Britain to arm. *Mmm-mmm-mm.* Punch

PUNCH AND JUDY

and Judy?"

"I do have that," I said rather crossly.

"You mistake me. Punch and Judy is the warning supposedly offered by bishops to young priests: 'Watch out for punch—strong waters—and judy—seductive women.' "

In quick succession I was then informed that:

CORK LIMB

A cork limb is a contraption designed by one Dr. Cork, and contains no cork at all.

APIKOROS

Apikoros, a rare name for atheist, is a Hebrew corruption of the name of Epicurus, the Greek philosopher.

SCANDAROON

The scandaroon, a homing pigeon, is called after an ancient seaport of that name in Syria, which in turn was named in honor of Alexander the Great after he defeated Cyrus there in 331 B.C. Alexander (Iskander) became Skander by aphesis, the gradual loss, as a result of a phonetic process, of a short unaccented vowel at the beginning of a word. Squire for esquire, said Timothy, is another example.

GRECIAN BENDS

The Grecian bends are caused by air blocking the bloodstream of divers rising too fast from the depths. The posture is similar to that forced on a woman wearing a bustle: curved spine, shoulders forced forward.

"Why are the bends called Grecian?" I asked.

"Some Greek statues were said to look that way. It became fashionable around 1868 to walk with the lower body slightly forward. The Alexandra limp was much practiced then too, in imitation of Princess Alexandra, who limped after pulling a muscle in some fashion.

ALEXANDRA
LIMP

"There is an Irish song about the Grecian bends."

Timothy struck an attitude, and recited at full voice:

She was just the sort of crayture, boys,
  that Nature did intend
To walk throughout the world, me boys,
  without the Grecian bend.
Nor did she wear a chignon, I'll have you
  all to know;
And I met her in the garden where the
  praties grow.

MORTON'S FORK

Morton's fork, continued Timothy, is a quandary devised by Cardinal Morton, Chancellor of Henry VII—a 16th-century Catch-22 of tax collection: if one is living poorly, one must be hiding a great deal of wealth; if one is living well, one obviously has a great deal; either way, one is heavily taxed.

VICAR OF BRAY

Something must have distracted me here, for when Timothy's voice next registered, he had got on to the Vicar of Bray. "Not an improper, uncommon noun," I protested, but Timothy flipped his stick and continued:

"He lived in the 16th century, and managed to retain his office during the religious upheavals of the reigns of Henry VIII, Edward VI, Mary, and Elizabeth; there is a song about him:

And this is the law I will maintain
Until my dying day, Sir,
That whatsoever king shall reign,
I'll still be the Vicar of Bray, Sir."

Timothy sang *con brio*, brandishing his stick, which barely missed a pitcher of daffodils. There was a pause while he tucked the stick under his arm and pulled down his vestcoat to reconnect with his trousers. He went on:

"A freeman of Bucks. You are familiar with the term?"

"I know Bucks is short for Buckinghamshire—"

"A freeman of Bucks is a cuckold: bucks have horns. A pun. The bride who throws away her bouquet is making a visual pun. She is abandoning her virginity: deflowered. By the way, Charles Michelson, P. R. man for the Democratic National Committee under Franklin Roosevelt, brought off some excellent puns. Brisbanalities, for instance, for the platitudes of Brisbane, the Hearst columnist. It was Brisbane who said a man could beat a gorilla in a wrestling match. But that was not a platitude, was it? Michelson also coined dupontification, from the Duponts, for
unenlightened business practices: the Duponts financed the Liberty League. And Californication for . . . no, that was not Michelson.

"*Mmm-mmm.* Bother. I wish the moho, the discontinuity between the earth's crust and the inner mantle, had been named after Moholy-Nagy, the artist, an admirable man; but it is named after A. Mohorovičić, the Yugoslav seismologist. So is the mohole, that hole scientists keep trying to drill down to the mantle; the word has probably caught on because it reminds people of a mole burrowing.

" 'In Oliver's days'—meaning the good old days, good times? The English used the expression when they looked back on the rule of Oliver Cromwell. Oh, and 'queer as Dick's hat-
band.' Nothing to do with homosexuality. It refers to the fact that the hatband, or crown, of Richard Cromwell, son of Oliver, was illegitimate. 'Dick's hatband is made of sand' was another way of putting it. The crown disintegrated; he was overthrown after only a year. 'Bonaparte's crown,' after Napoleon Bonaparte, is a briefly flowering plant. Richard lived another fifty-three years, most of the time under an alias. About 1692 he was insulted by a brash young lawyer in court proceedings. Mr. Justice Holt—some say Mr. Justice Hale—said, 'You shall not speak thus to one who sat sovereign in England.'

"You have the origin of mayonnaise: Port Mahon, capital of the Spanish island of Minorca. Yes. Named after Mago, the brother of Hannibal. Admiral Byng was sent there in 1756 to raise the French siege. He failed, and was executed. Voltaire said, 'The British shoot an admiral every so often—*pour encourager les autres.*' Voltaire had written in Byng's defense."

My head was drooping. Timothy is alert to such signals. He said, "I am wanted at home. I must be going. Three minutes more. Let me see, let me see. *Coup de Jarnac.* A foul blow. Guy Chabot, Sieur de Jarnac, in the presence of Henri II, dueled with M. de La Chataignerie—hamstrung the man with his sword, then slew him. Not sporting."

I missed something. The next thing I heard was "Ganser's syndrome is a compulsive inability to answer a question exactly. If a victim is asked, 'What is two and two?' he answers, 'About thirty-nine.'

"Thank you, Louise. Yes. Just one more of those delightful tidbits, and I am off. By the way, you no doubt have the Saut Lairds o' Dunscore. Petty squireens, so poor that the seven of them had to pool their resources to buy a block of salt. Saut Lairds o'Dunscore means an ancient name but no money. Like Lady Bareacres. *Mmm.* Dragon of Wantley? A very fierce dow-ager. Boniface's cup? Heavy drinking. Some Pope Boniface was supposed to have given an indulgence to anyone who would drink his health . . ."

The pencil dropped from my hand.

THREE

THE WORD WAS GOD

Old Testament Words

UTSIDE OF oaths, there are surprisingly few words that conceal the name of God. One is giddy,

GIDDY   from Anglo-Saxon *gyddig*, "God-possessed." Giddy means dizzy, or frivolous and flighty. One may doubt, however, whether our Jehovah was the god the heathen Anglo-Saxons had in mind.

It would simplify matters for the devout if God could be
GOOD   identified etymologically with good. But he cannot. Good arrives

from Old Norse sources unconnected with the deity. It once meant "bring together, unite" and also "fitting." The Gospel itself is not "God's tidings," as one might suppose, but "good tidings."

GOOD-BYE
GOSSIP

GOSSIP'S BOWL

The good in "good-bye" does distort God ("God be with you"); and gossip has descended—quite a distance—from God-sib, a "God-relation," usually a godfather or godmother. Brown says the gossip's bowl, mentioned by Capulet and Puck, was a christening gift. I try to imagine God gossiping, but the image will not come.

AGNOSTIC

Early Greek sects calling themselves Gnostics, from Greek *gnôsis*, "knowledge," claimed to know the reality of God through intuition rather than faith. The opposite side of the coin is an agnostic, from Greek *agnostós*, "one who disclaims any knowledge (of God)." An atheist, with a certain intellectual arrogance, knows there is no God.

MOLOCH

A blockbuster of a word, tetragrammaton, once capitalized, means the four consonants forming the Hebrew "incommunicable name" of the Supreme Being. In later Jewish tradition the name is not pronounced save with the vowels of Adonai or Elohim, so that the true pronunciation is lost. Webster says the four consonants are variously written IHVH, JHVH, JHWH, YHVH, and YHWH. Yahweh, variously spelled, is used by some for the tribal god of the ancient Hebrews, as contrasted with Jehovah, God of the Christian Bible. My copy editor says this explanation is not clear. In any event, the Hebrews had a way of changing consonants and vowels to alter the sense of a word. Melekh, for instance, meant "king," but when applied to the god of the Ammonites and Persians it became Moloch, the changed vowels turning a word of respect into an insult. An evil doctrine for which humanity is sacrificed is a moloch; so is a harmless but very spiny and ugly Australian lizard.

Yahweh proclaimed himself a "jealous god," and did not hesitate to destroy those who ignored his commandments. But he was no Moloch; nor did his lust for blood compare with that of his Hindu counterpart, Vishnu. In the 12th century, the worshipers of Vishnu built him a pyramidal temple at Puri, in Orissa, India. In an annual festival, his idol, Juggernaut ("Lord of the World"—a praise name for Vishnu) is dragged in his car (thirty-five feet square and forty-five feet high) over the sand to another temple. The car, says Brewer, has sixteen wheels, each seven feet in diameter. He adds that the belief that fanatical pilgrims cast themselves under the wheels to be crushed to death on the last day of the festival is probably without foundation. Nonetheless, juggernaut has come to mean an object of belief calling for blind devotion or senseless sacrifice. Humorously, it is applied to any large-wheeled car.

JOSS
JOSS HOUSE
JOSS STICK
JOSS PAPER

JOSS FLOWER

God in Portuguese is *Dios.* In the 15th century, Portuguese explorers and traders were among the earliest Western visitors to China. *Dios,* in the pidgin used for communications between whites and Orientals, became joss, referring to anything connected with religion: joss house (a Chinese temple); joss stick (made of the paste of odoriferous woods, and burned as incense before Chinese cult images); joss paper (gold and silver paper, burned in worship and at funerals in the form of coins and ingots); joss flower (the Chinese sacred lily).

In my childhood, the Bible was read more faithfully than it is now. A number of its principal characters lived in our village. We called our oldest inhabitant a methusaleh, our wisest a solomon, our strongest a samson. Our most fervid hunter was a nimrod, and our roughnecks were philistines. Such expressions seem to be retreating today from the vulgate.

BIBLE
BIBLICAL

Bible is traceable to Byblos, the city, down the coast from Tyre, which was the source of the papyrus on which Bibles were first written. A bible, lowercased, is "any authoritative work"; biblical is "authoritative."

ADAM'S APPLE

ADAM'S ALE
ADAM
   FURNITURE

Whatever bones you may pick with the Almighty, you must admit that he crowded his stage with lively characters. Whomever or whatever your mind may conceive, God conceived him, her, or it before you. Adam was not smart enough to dream up Eve; God did that. Adam, indeed, apparently dreamed up very little, and his own name grew few generic stalks. We sometimes equate him with humankind as a whole; when an unregenerate impulse overcomes someone, we are likely to say it is "the old adam coming out." An adam's apple is supposed to be a bit of the apple from the forbidden tree; it stuck in Adam's throat. Adam's ale is water. For most of us, "not to know from Adam" is not to know at all. Adam furniture relates not to the first Adam, but to brothers Robert and James Adam, architects who flourished under George III. Adam architecture is characterized by a delicate adaptation of Roman classical design and decorations. (Jesus Christ has been called the Second Adam; but that is another matter.)

One word Adam did leave the language was adamite, "one descended from Adam," sometimes denoting one who, like Adam before the apple, goes naked. With Eve's help, Adam also raised Cain—a troublemaking activity not uncommon among his descendants. The expression came into use in this country about 1840 as a euphemism for "raise the devil."

Pre-adamites may be either a sect that believes in the existence of men on earth before Adam, or those men themselves. In his novel *Vathek* (1786), William Beckford (1759–1844) depicted them as kings lying on great cedar beds, with their hearts globes of fire seen through their translucent bodies. Isaac Le Peyrère (1594–1676) promulgated a doctrine in 1655 that only the Jews are descendants of Adam, gentiles being descended from earlier man. Lilith, in medieval popular belief the first wife of Adam, would have been of this earlier race. She may have lived in the land of Nod, east of Eden (Genesis 4:16),
where Cain went after he killed Abel. A lilith, occasionally lower-cased, is an evil spirit who attacks children; but the word carries overtones of the irresistible sensual female.

Traditionally, Jews and Christians believe that Adam was the first man. The word man has its own likely origin in a proper name: a legendary teacher of the Hindus was one Manu, believed by certain classes to have originated their culture and religion. The male connotation of the word reflects the Aryan patriarchal system, which, though embattled, has not yet been overthrown.

Cain, son of Adam and Eve, killed his brother. A cain is a murderer. Cain-colored is reddish yellow, presumably the color of the blood shed by Cain.

God had his counterpart in Satan, or the Devil, chief of the rebellious angels. (See Beelzebub a little later.) Anything satanic is "infernal; extremely malicious or wicked." Present-day scientists call a speculative laboratory-developed bacterium or virus that might run amok a satan bug. The expression was coined by the novelist Alistair MacLean. Satan's chief lieutenant was Lucifer, the fallen archangel of the morning star who wound up as a kitchen match. Satan continues to reign in Tophet, the Old Testament name for a place where human sacrifices were made
by fire. Tophet is hell, and like hell has lost its upper case. Indeed, it has minced down from tophet to tunket; elderly New Englanders still say "as sure as tunket" for "as sure as hell."
Gehenna was a valley near Jerusalem where some Israelites

sacrificed their children to Moloch. Gehenna consequently became a place of abomination.

METHUSALEH

A methusaleh, anyone of extreme age, harks back to the five-times-great-grandson of Adam. Methusaleh lived 969 years. He begot Noah's grandfather Lamech at the age of 187, and numerous other sons and daughters thereafter.

NOAH'S ARK

Noah, familiar as he is to us all, has entered the vernacular only in the noah's ark, a children's toy representing the ark and some of the creatures it contained.

The three sons of Noah were Shem, Ham, and Japheth; Ham is considered in some traditions the ancestor of the Egyptians, in others of the blacks. One far-fetched linguistic theory holds that, of Japheth's sons, Gomer was the forebear of the Germans, Madai of the Medes, and Javan of the Ionians. Javan's sons included Elishah, ancestor of the Hellenes; Tarshish, of the Cyprians; Kittim, of the Cretans; and Dodanim, of the Dodecanesians.

NIMROD

Hunters are termed nimrods because Nimrod, son of Cush (Genesis 11:8-10), was "a mighty hunter before the Lord."

BABBLE

To babble—"to talk incoherently; to utter meaningless words"—is anteceded in a Middle English word descended from Greek *babbelin*, "prattle"; but for those who honor the insights of folk etymology, the word is inseparably linked with that cataclysmic day when mankind, being all "of one language, and one speech," started to build a city and tower at Babel, in the land of Shinar, "whose top may reach unto heaven." Mused the Lord (Genesis 9:6), "They have all one language . . . and now nothing will be restrained from them, which they have imagined to do." He therefore confounded their syllables, so that they could no longer understand one another. The Tower of Babel died a-borning, and people have been misunderstanding one another

BABEL

ever since. A babel is a place or scene of noisy confusion. To connect babel and babble etymologically is only a venial sin.

BETHEL

Genesis 12:8 recounts that Abraham settled on "a mountain on the east of Bethel . . . and there he builded an altar." Bethel in Palestine, a different place, was the scene of Jacob's vision of a ladder with angels ascending and descending. Webster traces the common noun bethel, "a house of worship, and specifically, in England, a chapel for Nonconformists," to the second Bethel; but it seems to me that the first would do just as well.

Jacob and his descendants dwelt happily in the land of Goshen (Genesis 14:10); land of goshen has become synonymous with a "good land," a place of peace and plenty. Canaan, which God promised to give to Abraham for his obedience, carries an even stronger connotation of serenity and abundance: "a good land and a large," says Exodus 3:8, ". . . a land flowing with milk and honey." Canaan stands figuratively for the land of promise, or heaven.

BAAL

Baal was any of various fertility and nature gods of the ancient Semitic peoples. The golden calf that awaited Moses when he returned with the tablets of the Ten Commandments was a baal (no connection with the *baa* of a calf). Jezebel, a Phoenician princess of the 9th century B.C., wife of Ahab, king of Israel, infuriated her subjects by attempting to raise Baal over Jehovah in the hierarchy of the gods. The rebel general Jehu finally put her and her cohort of heretics to death (dogs ate her body) and became himself king of Israel. A painted, flaunting woman is a jezebel.

JEZEBEL

JEHU

In 19th-century England, the name Jehu shrank to a mild joke. Because the Bible reported that he "rode in a chariot" when he went to war and that "he driveth furiously," a Victorian coachman who drove at a rattling pace was referred to as a jehu.

BAIN-MARIE

Moses's legendary sister Miriam (Marie) was an alchemist. She is said to be responsible for the bain-marie, a device consisting of a large pan containing hot water in which smaller pans may be set to cook food slowly or keep it warm. *Bainmarie* in French means "bath (or furnace) of Mary." Some prefer the Virgin Mary as a source of the word.

EXODUS

Exodus, as a book of the Bible or the flight from Egypt over which Moses presided, is capitalized and specific; when referring to the hasty departure of any number of people, it is lowercased and generic.

MOSES

A flat-bottomed boat is sometimes called a moses, perhaps in reference either to the ark of bulrushes in which the infant Moses was laid on the riverbank by his mother, or to the fact that a man poles a moses standing, and so may appear from a distance to be walking on the water—doubtfully a reference to the parting of the Red Sea to permit the passage of the Israelites fleeing from the Egyptians.

BEELZEBUB

Baal (a hostile play on Baalzebul, "Lord of the house") pops up occasionally as Beelzebub, lord of the flies and filth. In certain

JEZEBEL

medieval literature he is the chief associate of Satan. Milton in *Paradise Lost* made him next to Satan in power and crime. His role in real life, however, is modest; he is but a beelzebub, a South American monkey.

SABBATH
SABBATICAL

SABBAT

On the seventh day of creation, the Lord rested; it has been suggested that he quit a little too soon. However that may be, Exodus, the second book of the Bible, gives the name Sabbath to the seventh day of the week, set aside for rest and worship. Uncapitalized, sabbath is the sabbatical year, "a leave of absence with pay, usually granted every seven years, as to a college professor." In medieval terminology, a sabbat was a midnight assembly in which witches, demons, and sorcerers celebrated their orgies.

BALAAM

Balaam is the prophet who was supposed to curse Israel (Numbers 24) but blessed it instead. A balaam is thus a disappointing prophet or ally. The ass he rode is better remembered than he. It fell beneath Balaam when it saw the Angel of the Lord barring the way with a drawn sword; it uttered human speech when Balaam, to whom the angel was invisible, smote it with his staff. Cried the ass (Numbers 22:28-30):

> What have I done unto thee, that thou hast smitten me these three times? . . . Am not I thine ass, upon which thou hast ridden ever since I was thine until this day?

BALAAM'S ASS

At this point the Lord opened Balaam's eyes, so that he saw the angel standing in the way, and turned back. As far as the record shows, he made no apology to the ass, nor did that animal ever speak again; but Balaam's ass has become proverbial for a brute that knows more than its master.

GIBEONITE

In the days of Joshua, the Gibeonites attempted to trick the Israelite leader. Says Joshua 9:4-6: "They did work wilily . . . and took old sacks upon their asses, and wine bottles, old, and rent, and bound up. And old shoes and clouted upon their feet, and old garments upon them; and all the bread of their provision was dry and mouldy." So accoutered and provisioned, they persuaded Joshua that they were not in fact his near neighbors, but representatives of a far country, and he compacted to let them live. When he learned that they had deceived him, he maintained the compact, but decreed that they should be "hewers of bread and drawers of water" to the Israelites. A gibeonite is a slave's slave, a jack-of-all-work.

JOB

Humanity remains confused and troubled by the story of Job, a good man afflicted through no fault of his own. In the days when the Lord and Satan were still on speaking terms (per Job 1:7-11),

> The Lord said unto Satan, Whence comest thou? Then Satan answered the Lord, and said, From going to and fro in the earth, and from walking up and down in it.
> And the Lord said unto Satan, Hast thou considered my servant Job, that there is none like him in the earth, a perfect and an upright man, one that feareth God, and escheweth evil?
> Then Satan answered the Lord, and said, Doth Job fear God for nought?
> Hast thou not made an hedge about him, and about his house, and about all that he hath on every side? thou hast blessed the work of his hands, and his substance is increased in the land.
> But put forth thine hand now, and touch all that he hath, and he will curse thee to thy face.

JOBATION

The Lord acceded to this devilish urging, and the fortitude and faith of Job under tribulation has become a byword. A Job is anyone who entertains patiently a life of affliction; a jobation is a long, tedious scolding.

JOB'S COMFORTER

Job's comforters were Eliphaz, Bildad, and Zophar. A Job's comforter is anyone who tries to make you feel worse while purporting to make you feel better. (Boils, one of the early afflictions with which Job was smitten, are referred to as Job's comforters. This may be unfair to boils. They certainly make you feel worse, but they do not pretend to be making you feel better.)

BEULAH LAND

Beulah Land entered the language in Isaiah 62:4: "Thou shalt no more be termed Forsaken; neither shall thy land any more be termed Desolate: but thou shalt be called Hephzibah, and thy land Beulah; for the Lord delighteth in thee, and thy land shall be married." In Bunyan's *Pilgrim's Progress* (1678–1684), Beulah land is a place of heavenly joy where the pilgrims tarry till they are summoned to enter the Celestial City.

JEREMIAD

A jeremiad—"a dolorous complaint"—evokes the despair of Jeremiah the prophet, who lived in the 7th and 6th centuries B.C. In Lamentations 1:1-2, he mourns:

> How doth the city sit solitary, that was full of people! how is she become as a widow! she that was great among the nations, and princess among the provinces, how is she become tributary!
> She weepeth sore in the night, and her tears are on her cheeks; among all her lovers she hath none to comfort her; all

her friends have dealt treacherously with her, they have become her enemies. . . .

The harvest is past, the summer is ended, and we àre not
saved. . . . Is there no balm in Gilead? Is there no physician
there? . . . Her sun is gone down while it is yet day.

PHILISTINE

When he was not bewailing the moral decay of his own
people, Jeremiah was worrying about the Philistines, proverbial
enemies of the Jews. They were a martial people who in the 12th
century B.C. irrupted onto the southern shore of Palestine from
Crete or Asia Minor. A philistine, as an outsider, was by definition a boorish, militantly uncultivated person. (They were finally
assimilated by the native Semites. Once an outsider becomes an
insider, he ceases to be a philistine.)

SCHLEMIEL

A schlemiel is a luckless fool of fortune; the kind of man
who, were it raining soup, would have only a fork. The name
comes from one Shelumiel (Numbers 2:12), leader of the tribe of
Simeon. Of all the Hebrew captains of his day, he was the only
one regularly unsuccessful in battle. The tradition of the feckless
schlemiel was revived in 1814 by Adelbert von Chamisso
(1781–1838), part-French, part-German, who wrote *Peter
Schlemihls wundersame Geschichte*, the story of a man who gives up
his shadow to a gray stranger in return for Fortunatus's purse.
The word became a synonym for a person who agreed to a silly
bargain. Sholem Aleichim's stories made schlemiel an everyday
Yiddish word, and now it has a secure place in English.

SAMSON
DELILAH

Mighty Samson was born to deliver Israel out of the hands
of the Philistines. With the jawbone of an ass he slew a thousand
men. But as Achilles was vulnerable through his heel, so was
Samson through his hair. The Lord had ordered that "no razor
shall come onto his head." A Philistine harlot named Delilah
uncovered this secret, and caused his head to be shaved, render-
ing him powerless until it grew back. A samson is a man of great
physical strength; a delilah is a temptress.

GOLIATH

DAVID

DAVID AND
JONATHAN

When David slew the Philistine giant Goliath with a
slingshot, he established the David and Goliath legend: the little
man overcoming insuperable odds. A goliath is an especially
large giant, and a david a giant-killer. In the Civil War, Confederates called their submarines davids because they attacked the
goliaths of the Union navy. The love between young David and
Jonathan, son of King Saul, is prototypical of deep and abiding
friendship between one man and another. Jonathan loved David
"as he loved his own soul" (1 Samuel 20:17). Saul, considering
David a rival for his throne, constantly sought the youth's de-

struction; yet the two young friends managed to maintain not only their devotion to each other but their loyalty to the king. The pact between them (1 Samuel 20:42) became a benchmark of loyalty: "The Lord be between me and thee, and between my seed and thy seed forever."

The image evoked by the words David and Jonathan is one of manly love; that evoked by David and Absalom is one of parental grief. During David's rule over Israel, his son Absalom, though much loved of his father, rose against him, and was killed in defiance of David's orders (2 Samuel 18:33):

> And the king was much moved, and went up to the chamber over the gate, and wept: and as he went, thus he said, O my son Absalom, my son, my son Absalom! would God I had died for thee, O Absalom, my son, my son!

King Solomon, son of David, was known for his acuity. Solomonic is wise; a solomon "is any person of great wisdom." The act of wisdom usually associated with him was to order a baby cut in two, half for each of the two women who claimed to be its mother. The real mother withdrew her claim and was awarded the baby. I admire more Solomon's handling of the queen of Sheba, who came visiting to "prove him with hard questions." He answered so well that she gave him, for starters, "a hundred and twenty talents of gold, and of spices a great store, and precious stones." In return she received from him "all her desire, whatsoever she asked, besides that which Solomon gave her of his royal bounty." Not the least virtue of the Bible is that sometimes it leaves vice to the imagination.

More than one ambitious man or woman has spent a lifetime seeking to carve out a place in history, only to be remembered for a trifle. Two such were kings Jeroboam and Rehoboam. Jeroboam was the mighty man of valor who (says 2 Kings 3:3) "made Israel to sin" by separating her from Judah. Drunkenness

may have been one of the sins he encouraged; at least he popularized a container, called jeroboam in his honor, that contains two or more gallons of presumably intoxicating liquid.

Jerry, from jeroboam, is vulgar slang for a chamber pot; the jerrycan is a gasoline can in common use by the military. The Gypsies also have a word jerry, meaning excrement, but there is no proven link between the ordure and the king. Nor can he be

linked confidently to jerry-built, meaning built cheaply or insubstantially. The word may have come from Jerry Brothers, an erstwhile construction company of Liverpool. On the other hand, Partridge connects it with the walls of Jericho, presumably jerry-built, since they came tumbling down at the blast from Joshua's trumpeters.

REHOBOAM

When Jeroboam established the kingdom of Israel, in the 10th century B.C., Rehoboam, son of Solomon, remained king of Judah. He memorialized himself in the rehoboam, twice the size of a jeroboam, its capacity being sixteen quarts. Perhaps Rehoboam considered himself twice the man his rival was. The name is reasonable; *rehoboam* in Hebrew means "the clan is enlarged."

JONAH

The Book of Jonah, which consists of only four chapters and less than two pages, tells how Jonah, disobeying an order from the Lord that he cry out against Nineveh, in the customary manner of the old prophets, took ship for Tarshish. The Lord sent a great wind, and the mariners cast lots to see "for whose cause this evil is upon us." The lot falling upon Jonah, he was cast into the sea, which promptly "ceased from her raging." A great fish swallowed the unfortunate prophet, kept him for three days, and then vomited him out upon dry land. It follows that a person believed to bring ill luck or disaster is a jonah.

DAVY JONES'S LOCKER

In Welsh, by the way, Jonah evolved to Jones. Welsh sailors contributed the given name Davy, after the patron saint of their country; and "Davy Jones's locker" became the sea as a burial place for a sailor.

MACABRE

The word macabre has a macabre history, suggesting the horror of death and decay. It appears to have been inspired by the old French *danse macabre*, the dance of death. This in turn may have been corrupted from *danse macabe*, or "Maccabean dance," a traditional feature of morality plays. The dance probably represents the slaughter of Simon Maccabeus and two of his sons by Ptolemy, his son-in-law, in 135 B.C., after the Maccabees (an honorific meaning "hammerer"; the family name was Hasmon) had led a successful Jewish revolt against Syria.

Christly Words

JESUS FREAK
ANTI-CHRIST

It is as hard to find common words descending from Jesus Christ as it is from God. Jesus freaks, whatever else they are, are not common nouns. Anti-christs are enemies of Christ;

MACABRE

capitalized, with the hyphen dropped, the word refers to the Great Antagonist whom Christ at his second coming will conquer forever. The Jesuits, members of the Society of Jesus, founded by Ignatius Loyola in 1534 (and formally organized in 1539), are by repute dazzlingly casuistic in their arguments—whence jesuitic, "designing; crafty." "Accuse the Jesuits of killing three men and a dog," went the saying, "and they will triumphantly produce the dog alive." My acquaintances in the order, however, seem as straightforward as the run of devoted men. Christ, the honorific, is from Greek *christos*, "anointed; the anointed one"; Greek *chriein* is "to anoint." From *chrîsma* comes "chrism; consecrated oil; cream." Christ is the cream of the crop.

JESUITIC

To christen is "to give a name to," as in "christen a child," "christen a ship." Crisscross, "to mark with crossing lines," is a variant of christcross, the mark made for a signature by someone who cannot write.

CHRISTEN
CRISSCROSS

A word to bring a lump to the throat is cretin—a congenital idiot. Moore recalls that a special kind of mental deficiency was endemic in the Alpine valleys of Valoi and Savoy:

> It was associated with goitre, and the idiot-children were particularly horrific, having immense heads and swollen necks, protruding tongues and furrowed foreheads; their intelligence was much lower than that of the brutes. Nevertheless, being human, they must possess immortal souls, which set them utterly apart from the brutes. So the good peasants reasoned. And in pity and tenderness, they gave to the veriest monster the name which was an affirmation of immortality; for having been baptised the creature was at least *un chrétien*, and in due course would inherit the Kingdom of Heaven.

CRETIN

As *Dominus*, Latin for "Lord," Jesus worked his way into the vulgate in an odd fashion. *"Hoc est corpus Domini!"* was chanted at communion Mass. In Tudor times (from the reign of Henry VII through that of Elizabeth I), every fairground featured at least one conjuror who performed his sleight of hand while muttering the nonsense phrase "hocus-pocus," a takeoff on the religious chant. Hocus-pocus remains a nonsense phrase designed to cloak deception. A common playground rhyme is the equally nonsensical "hocus pocus dominocus." And we have the hokey-pokey, a combined song and dance:

HOCUS-POCUS

HOKEY-POKEY

> *Put your right foot in, put your right foot out,*
> *Put your right foot in, and shake it all about,*
> *And that's how you do the hokey-pokey.*

	In England, a hokey-pokey is an itinerant ice cream vendor, the name perhaps reflecting uncertainty as to what goes into cheap

In England, a hokey-pokey is an itinerant ice cream vendor, the name perhaps reflecting uncertainty as to what goes into cheap ice cream. From these derive hoax (a practical joke) and hokum (nonsense; fakery).

HOAX
HOKUM

BROUHAHA

Brouhaha, meaning uproar, disorder, is very likely from the Hebrew Barauk Habbah, "blessed is he who comes."

ANNO DOMINI
HALLELUJAH

In these secular days, Anno Domini, "the year of our Lord," is frequently, though improperly, lowercased by those to whom it is just another date. Anno domini is medical slang for old age: "Anno domini has got him." Hallelujah, "praise the Lord," is an improper, uncommon noun, since the Lord is part of it. It is often used as a simple expression of delight, with no religious overtone. Hosanna may communicate praise of anyone or anything; but it includes no proper name, and so is ineligible for consideration here.

LACHRYMA
CHRISTI
LIEBFRAUMILCH

Christ barely misses the vernacular in a smooth Campanian wine, *lachryma Christi*, "tears of Christ," which Weekley compares etymologically with the Rhenish wine *Liebfraumilch*, "milk of the Dear Lady." David Pilgrim's description of the drink in *The Grand Design* (1944) is quoted by Partridge:

> The wine was dark golden, very strong and very good. "This is an excellent wine," he said. "The tears of Christ, my boy, the tears of Christ," said Brother Thomas. " 'Tis a strange name for a wine grown on the slopes of Vesuvius, which is as near to hell as anyone can get in this world."

MARIGOLD
MARY LILY
ROSEMARY

The Virgin Mary is honored in the names of such flowers as the marigold and Mary lily.

MARIONETTE

LADY'S
BEDSTRAW
LADY'S GARTER
LADY'S SLIPPER
LADY BUG
LADY BIRD

The marionette traces back to the Virgin Mary. She becomes an expletive in "marry!" As Our Lady her name lingers in such plants as lady's bedstraw, lady's garter, lady's slipper. The lady bug, or lady bird, commemorates her in English and in German (*Marienkafer*, "Mary's beetle"). In French, the winsome little beetle is called after God: *bête à bon Dieu*.

GOSSAMER

There is a legend that gossamer is the raveling of the Virgin heaven, and so was God's seam, or God's thread. Other sugges-heaven, and so it was God's seam, or God's thread. Other suggestions are God's summer, and *gaze à Marie* ("Mary's gauze"). The most likely source is Middle English *gossomer*, "goose summer" (Saint Martin's summer; early November, when geese and their down are plentiful.)

When Jesus was born at Bethlehem, a multitude of the heavenly host, says Luke (2:14), sang, "Glory to God in the highest, and on earth peace, good will toward men." Ever since, on the anniversary of Christ's birth, carolers have gone about singing in church, street, and home of the transcendent event. **BETHLEHEMITES** Such carolers are bethlehemites.

MAGDALEN A magdalen is a reformed prostitute. This does an injustice to a great lady. Mary Magdalene, faithful follower of Jesus, accompanied him on the last journey to Jerusalem. She witnessed the crucifixion, found the tomb empty on the third day, and was first to speak with the risen Lord. Her only departure from virtue was involuntary; she was briefly possessed of seven devils (Luke 8:2), which Jesus drove from her. Yet for nearly two thousand years the poor woman has been confused with the unnamed harlot who in Simon's house anointed Christ's feet (Luke 7:37).

MAUDLIN Mary Magdalene is conventionally painted with eyes swollen and red from weeping for her lost Lord. Maudlin, a corruption of Magdalene, has come to stand for "tearfully or weakly emotional; effusively sentimental." It also means "drunk enough to be silly; fuddled," though no one contends that Magdalene ever touched a drop.

The 17th-century English poet Richard Crashaw wrote a curious poem about Jesus and Magdalene. It contains the following lines:

> And now where'er he goes
>   Among the Galilean mountains
> Or more unwelcome ways,
>   He's followed by two faithful fountains;
>   Two walking baths;
>   Two weeping motions;
> Portable and compendious oceans.

GADARENE Gadarene, meaning "swinelike; brutish," refers to Gadara, where Jesus cast the devils out of two demoniacs and into a herd of swine. "And behold," says Matthew 8:32, "the whole herd of swine ran violently down a steep place into the sea, and perished in the waters."

"Thou art Peter," said Christ (Matthew 16:18); "and upon this rock I will build my church." A triple-language pun: *cephas*, rock in Aramaic, becomes *pétros*, rock in Greek and Latin. It has **PETER OUT** been speculated that to peter out, "to come to nothing," may refer to the three times Peter denied Christ before his crucifixion. Despite his earlier protestations of loyalty, he petered out in the pinch.

Thomas, one of the twelve apostles, refused to believe in the resurrection of the Lord, "Except I shall see in his hands the prints of the nails, and put my finger into the print of the nails, and thrust my hand into his side" (John 20:25). A doubting Thomas is one who will not believe until he sees.

DOUBTING THOMAS

A Judas, capitalized, is "one who betrays under the appearance of friendship." Lowercased, it is a one-way peephole in a door, perhaps because only Jesus had any idea of what the renegade apostle was plotting. A treacherous kiss is a Judas kiss, because Judas kissed Jesus to identify him to his enemies. (Says George Eliot in *Mill on the Floss*: "A woman who was loving and thoughtful for other women, not giving them Judas-kisses with eyes askance. . . .") The judas goat is an animal used to lead others to destruction. The remorseful traitor is supposed to have hanged himself on the judas tree (*Cercis siliquastrum*) (though Acts 1:18 says instead that he became so swollen that he burst asunder). The judas tree stood in a field called Aceldama; lowercased, the word describes a scene of bloodshed.

JUDAS KISS

JUDAS GOAT

JUDAS TREE

ACELDAMA

When Judas died, his blood money for betraying Jesus was employed by the priests to buy "the potter's field," apparently a worked-out clay pit. Hence, "potter's field" as a burial yard for strangers and the destitute.

POTTER'S FIELD

Gethsemane, a garden outside Jerusalem, was the scene of the agony and arrest of Jesus. Uncapitalized, it means any place of great mental or spiritual suffering. Golgotha (from the Aramaic word for "skull"), the hill of Calvary where Christ was crucified, is lowercased for a place of torment or martyrdom.

GETHSEMANE

GOLGOTHA

The Cross is capitalized by Christians as a symbol of Christ's crucifixion, but began as a common name. From French and Spanish words meaning "marking with a cross" came Crusades, the name of the great efforts of the 11th, 12th, and 13th centuries to reclaim the holy places of the Christians from the Muslims. In the vernacular, a crusade is any vigorous, concerted movement for a cause or against an abuse.

CRUSADE

Few refer to a lungis, "lanky lout," these days, but it is a good word, distorted from Longinus, the supposed name of the tall centurion who thrust his spear into Jesus' side.

LUNGIS

The feast of Epiphany, from Greek *epiphaínein*, "to manifest," celebrates the coming of the Magi to Christ's manger as the first manifestation of Christ to the gentiles. An epiphany, lowercased, is a manifestation or apparition of God or Christ in his divine splendor. In literature, it means inspired intuition or insight. Epiphany was distorted into tiffany, a silky gauze, perhaps because of the transparency of the material.

Peter severely rebuked Simon Magus—a sorcerer converted by Philip (Acts 8:9-24)—for offering money to purchase the power of giving the Holy Ghost. Hence simony, the crime of buying or selling ecclesiastical preferment. The slang expression simoleon for a dollar may trace back to the same story.

A lazarus (from Aramaic *Eleazar*) is a diseased, especially a leprous, beggar, after the unfortunate described in Luke 16:19-25:

> There was a certain rich man, which was clothed in purple and fine linen, and fared sumptuously every day: And there was a certain beggar named Lazarus, which was laid at his gate, full of sores,
> And desiring to be fed with the crumbs which fell from the rich man's table: moreover the dogs came and licked his sores.

When the beggar and the rich man died, the first proceeded to Abraham's bosom and the second to hell, where he cried out:

> Father Abraham, have mercy on me, and send Lazarus, that he may dip the tip of his finger in water, and cool my tongue; for I am tormented in this flame.
> But Abraham said, Son, remember that thou in thy lifetime receivedst thy good things, and likewise Lazarus evil things; but now he is comforted, and thou art tormented.

There is no connection between this Lazarus and the one whom Jesus raised from the dead after he had lain four days in the grave.

A lazaretto is a pesthouse, once used especially for lepers. The word was originally nazarette, such a hospital having been founded at the former Church of St. Mary of Nazareth in Venice. Later the word became entwined with *lazaro*, "beggar." Lazaretto means also a building or vessel used for detention in quarantine, and in some merchant vessels is a space between decks for storage.

LIZARD   Some derive lizard from Lazarus, but this is a false etymology. Lizard, like alligator, stems from Latin *lacerta*, referring to either of these reptiles.

Of the various Jewish sects at the time of Jesus, the Pharisees were particularly noted for strict observance of rites and ceremonies of the written law. They gained as well a reputation for hypocrisy and self-righteousness. Perhaps particularly to Christians, the term pharisee, or pharisaical, means hypocritical and self-righteous.

PHARISEE

The Samaritans, named for the town of Samaria, are evoked in Jesus' parable (Luke 10:30-34) of a certain man who

> . . . fell among thieves, which stripped him of his raiment, and wounded him, and departed, leaving him half dead.
> And by chance there came down a certain priest that way: and when he saw him, he passed by on the other side.
> And likewise a Levite, when he was at the place, came and looked on him, and passed by on the other side.
> But a certain Samaritan, as he journeyed, came where he was: and when he saw him, he had compassion on him,
> And went to him, and bound up his wounds, pouring in oil and wine, and set him on his own beast, and brought him to an inn, and took care of him.

GOOD   The good samaritan became proverbial.
SAMARITAN

It is easy for me to accept Galilee, in Palestine, as the source of Galilean skull, since I know that a special sort of Neanderthal skull was found there in 1925; but I have never quite understood why Galilee became gallery—an enclosed narrow passageway, a verandah, a collection of paintings, cheap seats in a theater, and so on. Yet it so happened; Middle Latin *galilea*, later Italian *galeria*, was a vestibule, the inner perch of a church, and all else ensued therefrom.

GALLERY

In the 3rd century, Saint Jerome, with a little help from his friends, wrote the Vulgate Bible. (Jerome must have had a lovely grasshopper mind. It was he who referred to the Romans' "rabble of gods." It was he also who dreamed that God reproached him, saying, *"Ciceronus es, non Christianus"*—that is, "You are more interested in classical learning (like Cicero's) than in the simple pieties of Christianity." The Vulgate, designed for reading by those who did not know Greek, comes from Latin *vulgus*, the multitude. Use of the term as a title fixed it in the public mind; Vulgate entered the vulgate.

VULGATE

Jerome's Bible was based on the Septuagint. There is a tradition that between 278 and 270 B.C., at the request of

Ptolemy II, seventy-two emissaries from Jerusalem began translating the first five books of the Old Testament—the Pentateuch—into Greek. The Christian fathers later made the number of translators a round seventy—corrupted from the Latin, septuagint. Fourteen of the books came to be called the Apocrypha, Greek for "hidden" or "doubtful," by Protestants. These books were eliminated from the Protestant Bible on the ground that they are not an essential part of the Hebrew Scriptures. Eleven of the fourteen are accepted in the Roman Catholic canon. Any writing of questionable authorship or authenticity is termed apocryphal. Apocrypha is one more common noun that was saved from extinction by becoming proper, and then common again.

APOCRYPHA

ARMAGEDDON

Armageddon—any decisive conflict—derives from Har Megiddon, the mountain region of Megiddo, the site of several Old Testament and some modern battles. The Jewish national home was made possible by a British victory over the Turks there in 1918. Revelation 16:16 refers to Armageddon, the scene of a final battle between the forces of good and evil at the end of the world.

APOCALYPSE

No definition I have seen does justice to the word apocalypse. Apocalypse is not simply a prophetic disclosure or revelation; it is a revelation of transcendental and ominous portent. I prefer Apocalypse to Revelation as a title for the last book of the New Testament, which ends grimly:

> If any man shall add unto these things, God shall add unto him the plagues that are written in this book:
>   And if any man shall take away from the words of the book of this prophecy, God shall take away his part out of the book of life.

I was sitting forty thousand feet in the air in one of those airplanes that appear to be fifteen or twenty seats wide. From six or seven seats to my left, I heard, as clearly as if the speaker had been sitting next to me, these slurred words:

"Jezhus wazhn't no Jew. Hizh *fazher* maybe wazh a Jew; but his *muzher* was Eyetalian."

That was the end of it. The speaker lapsed into silence, and I could not even determine which of the passengers he was.

Thinking of all those Italian Madonnas by da Vinci, Michelangelo, Raphael, Bellini, Correggio, Giorgioni, and their kith, I could see the drunk's point about Mary. But he had to be wrong about the father of Jesus, since it is posited that the Saviour was sired by God himself.

For the next seven stanzas you are in recess from uncommon, improper nouns. I shall then return you—refreshed, I hope—to the theme of the book.

GENERATIONS SIXTY-ONE /
TIE THE FATHER TO THE SON

1.

*The
sower
soweth
the
word*

*No mortal mother bore the
    Man God emparadised;
No mortal man could store the
    Incarnate seed of Christ.
So, checking antecedents,
    I find it rather odd
(Indeed, exceeding credence)
    That Jē'sus, Son of God,
Should trace his generations
    (Some sixty-one by count)
Through temporal relations
    To Ăd'ăm, primal fount,
From Jō'seph, mate of Mā'ry,
    Who virgin bore our Lord,
When Jō'seph's seed was nary
    Involved in the accord.
By such a calculation,
    The Saviour was God's son
Through one sole conjugation
    And also . . . sixty-one.
His sire direct was fifty-
    Nine times his grandsire-great.
Men saintly and men shifty
    The chain concatenate:*

2.

*The
generations
from
Ad'am
to
Āb-rǎ-hǎm*

*Thus: After Cāin and Ā'bel,
    Came Ăd'ăm's third son, Sĕth.
First offspring at Sĕth's table
    Was Ē'nŏs, from whose breath
Ca-i nan sprang, and added
    Ma-hā'la'leel, whose zest
Sparked Jā'red. Jā'red dadded
    Mē-thūs'elah. Oppressed
By weight of years titanic,
    The ancient still contrived
A final act galvanic,*

And Lā'mech next arrived.
By custom forced to throw a

Superior sort of get,
This Lā'mech authored Nō'ah,
  Whose ark survived the wet.
Then, sotted, Nō'ah waxèd;
  Shĕm was the consequence,
Whose loins produced Är-phăx'ed;
  And Sā'lah issued thence.
Next Ē'bĕr, Pē'lĕg, Rē'u;
  Then Sē'rug, Nā'hôr too;
Then Tē'rah—ah, I see you
  Have hopes I'm nearly through;
For Tē'rah was the father
  Of Āb-ră'hăm, the root
Of the Hē-brā'ic pother
  And Jē'sus Christ, to boot.

3.

You're wrong: these procreations
  (Son's son to son's son's son)
From nineteen generations
  Must grow to sixty-one
Ere we see holy faces,
  And with the Godhead sup.
Sit down, then; take your places;
  The curtain's going up.

4.

*The
generations
from
Āb-ră-hăm
to
Dā'vid*

A reproductive dry sack
  Throughout a hundred years,
Abe finally sparks Ī'saac,
  Who Jā'cob gets and rears;
He, Jū'das. Out of Jū'das
  Stemmed Phā'res, he whose wee
Was Ēs'rom. There ensued, as
  Water from the sea,
Then Ā'ram. Using science,
  With bedroom as a lab,
And feminine compliance,
  He sired Ā-min'a-dab,
Who later got Na-as'son;
  He Sal'mon; Bō'ŏz next,
Who, duty-bound to pass on
  His bloodline, was perplexed

Till told if he disrobèd
    And called on God to bless, he
'd get a boy named Ō'bĕd,
    And Ō'bĕd would get Jĕs'se.
Now Jĕs'se's son was Dā'vid,
    Much storied for the fact
That he Go-li'ath bravèd.
    So ends my second act.

                    5.

The
generations
from
Dā'vid
to
the
Captivity

On mate of slain U-ri'ah
    Was Sol'o-mon begat;
Ro-bō'am got A-bī'a;
    And Ā'sa, Jōs'a-phat;
Whose Jōr'am got Ō-zī'as;
    Jō-a'tham Ā'chăz had;
From him sprang Ĕz-e-kī'as,
    Who was Ma-năs'sēs' dad.
Next Ā'mon; then Jō-sī'as;
    Then into Băb'y-lon
Was carried Jĕch-o-nī'as,
    Jō-sī'as' ill-starred son,
The fourteenth in transition
    From Dā'vid and his crown.
(Just one more intermission:
    We'll drop the curtain down.)

                    6.

The
generations
from
the
Captivity
to
Jō'seph

Undaunted, Jĕch-o-nī'as
    Begat Sa-lā'thĭ-ĕl;
Who in tradition pious
    Devised Zo-rŏb'a-bĕl;
And he Ā-bī'ud, who then
    Begat E-lī'a-kĭm;
Who reached adulthood too; then
    Ā'zôr sprang from him.
From Ā'zôr, Sā'dŏc; Ā'chim therefrom;
    E-lī'ud took a bow;
Then Ĕ-le-ā'zar, wherefrom
    Came Măt'thăn. You can now
Prepare the final curtain;
    For Jā'cob, Măt'thăn's son,
Got Jō'seph, who for certain
    Espoused the Virgin One.

7.

So down the years like thunder
  Pe-nā'tēs rolled, and lā'rēs.
And yet I sometimes wonder,
  Why Jō'seph's? Why not Mā'ry's?

The foregoing wordplay diverges at least four times from the Bible:

(1) It is not true that Methusaleh waited until his final years to beget Lamech;

(2) Judas is alternately spelled Judah;

(3) I doubt whether Bo'oz needed anyone's advice to disrobe in order to beget Obed;

(4) Joatham is properly accented on the second instead of the first syllable.

Oaths with a religious basis—"By God!" "Jesus Christ!" "Hell!"—are generally used either to give vent to strong feelings, or to shock, or, among semiliterates, simply to intercalate—that is, to stretch out a sentence without adding to its meaning. In the latter case they are a kind of vocal tic, no different from "er . . . ah" or "you know" or "like, wow, man."

VENTRE-SAINT-GRIS
VENTRE DE DIEU

PAR SAINCT GRIS

GOD'S NAILS
GOD'S TEETH

The favorite oath of Henry IV of France was *Ventre-Saint-Gris!*—"stomach of Christ!" (Having a Navarese accent, he pronounced Christ Gris.) *Par le ventre de Dieu* was also common in Renaissance France. Rabelais created the mighty pun *par sainct Gris*, alluding to Francis of Assisi, who was *ceint* (girdled) and clad in *gris* (gray). In England, "God's nails!" and "God's teeth!" were once common expletives.

PONTIUS
  PILATE'S EAR

The devout, for whom the First Commandment was a weighty sanction, preferred to mince their oaths by substituting innocuous, often meaningless words for those forbidden. Sometimes the reference was to an actual person, as in "By Pontius Pilate's ear!"

BY JOVE

"By Jove!" is a minced oath, Jove being a substitution of the Roman for the Christian god. Jove turned to Basque *Jinco* and English jingo. Jingo in the sense of "chauvinist" goes back to 1878, when Disraeli sent a fleet to Turkish waters to oppose the Russian advance. The chorus of a popular music-hall ditty of the time ran:

We don't want to fight, but by jingo if we do,
We've got the ships, we've got the men, we've got the money too.

Many of the following once-common minced oaths are borrowed from Mencken:

FOR GOD

dear (Irish for "dear Lord," as in "The dear only knows")

godfrey

golly

good grief

for goodness' sake

goramighty

gosh

for gosh' sake

gosh wallader

goshamighty

goshdal

by gravy

great guns

great horn spoon (my favorite record of the expression is from James Russell Lowell's *Biglow Papers*: "Sez Mister Foote, / 'I should like to shoot / The hull gang, by the gret horn spoon!' sez he."

great snakes

gum godfrey

swounds or zounds (God's wounds)

FOR GODDAMN

blimey (short for gorblimey, "God blame me")

coo blimey

consarn

coo lummy ("God love me")

dad-blame

dad-blast

dad-burn

dad-durn

dad-fetch

dad-gast

dad-gum

dad-rat

dad-rot

dad-shame

dad-sizzle

dad-swamp

ding-bust

gosh-darn

odd-rot

odd's bodikins ("God's little bodies," from communion bread, the Host)

FOR THE LORD

land

law

lawdy

lawks

lawsy

FOR CHRIST

crackey

crickey

cripes

for cripes' sake

Christmas

for crying out loud

FOR JESUS

gee

gee whillikin(s)

gee whittaker(s)

jeepers, jeepers creepers

jeez

jehosophat (king of Judah)

jemima

jeminy or jiminy (perhaps corrupting *Jesu Domini*)

jerusalem

jiminy crack—and I don't care

jiminy crickets

jiminy whiz

judas priest

FOR THE DEVIL	the dickens
Mr. Bogey	Hob
devilation (this was my father's strongest oath; I have often been told how he once said "devilation!" and the church fell down)	Old Boy
	Old Harry
	Old Nick

FOR HELL

blazes

Sam Hill

tophet

tunket

GREAT SCOTT

"Great Scott!" sounds like a minced oath, but perhaps refers to Old Fuss and Feathers, General Winfield Scott (1786–1866), who, when Whig candidate for President in 1852, was jeeringly called Great Scott by his political enemies.

BEJESUS

The Irish expression "bejasus," as in "I'll beat the bejasus out of you," seems to be no euphemism at all, but a full-fledged cussword.

HOLY MIKE

One can substitute inoffensive names for God or the Devil according to taste. Says John Buchan (1875–1940) in *Greenmantle*: "I could hear him invoking some unknown deity called Holy Mike. . . ."

GODDAM

LES SOMMON-BICHES

LA SONANA-GOGNA

Mencken reports that just as foreigners used to call the English goddams from one of the more frequent English oaths, so the French for a generation after World War I referred to Americans, and especially American doughboys, as *les sommon-biches*. The Italians, who apparently met troops of a more euphemistic turn of phrase, called them *gli sonanagogni*. The epithets are delightful, though they are not improper, uncommon nouns.

Saintly Words

There are many saints, but few have become generic. Of those that have, not all are authentic.

PUDENCY
PUDENT

Take Saint Pudentiana. Her name appears in pudency, meaning "morbid modesty"; pudent, meaning "bashful;

prudish"; and pudenda, the female genitals. Yet no one knows whether she ever existed. Father Pierre Jounel, a French liturgical scholar who drew up a revised calendar of saints in 1969, says she "may simply be an adjective who became a saint." Or she may have been a Christian echo of a heathen goddess. According to the Roman historian Livy, Pudicitia, personification of the chastity or modesty of women, was worshiped in a small shrine in the Forum Bovarium until at least 296 B.C.; but the cult degenerated along with the simple Roman virtues, and spiders wove their webs in her altars. It is a doubtful loss; goddess or saint, she could not have been much fun to know.

So, in the matter of saints, bear this caution in mind: before you ask one to intercede for you up there, you should make fairly sure that he or she is really up there. It would be embarrassing to discover too late that you have been praying to an adjective.

Another example is Saint Expeditus, advocate of urgent causes. Insist that Saint Expeditus present his bona fides before you commit any undertaking to his patronage. The story goes that he was a soldier in the Roman army, martyred at Meliteene, Armenia, in the 4th century, and that expedite—from Latin *expedire*, "to free from difficulties; to dispatch, send off"—is simply his name in the vulgate. His followers were few until, one day in the 19th century, a convent in Paris received a packing case containing relics from the catacombs of Rome. Edwards, tongue in cheek, recalls the event: "On the label was written Spedito, i.e., 'sent off,' and the date of dispatch. But the nuns mistook this for the name of the martyr and set to work with great energy to propagate his cult." Thereafter, Saint Expeditus thrived. There are earlier references to him, and he may indeed have lived; but it seems doubtful.

My question about another saint is not whether he existed, for he certainly did, but whether he really deserves credit for the adjective attributed to him. The saint is Bartholomew; you probably have seen him in Michelangelo's paintings, flayed alive and holding his own skin in his hands. He is patron of the feebleminded, wherefore it is claimed, most reasonably, that barmy (generally rendered "balmy" in the United States) is a corruption of Bartholomew. But the true source, one suspects, is "barm," an old word for the froth on beer. Too bad.

The almond-based confection called marzipan, frequently molded into the shapes of fruits and figurines, receives its name from the Latin *Marci Panis,* "Mark's bread." The bread was once used in the feast of St. Mark the Apostle.

VALENTINE

When those of us on the sunset side of the generation gap were still young, lovers on Saint Valentine's Day were accustomed to slip under the doors of their sweethearts anonymous cards decorated with broken hearts and arrows, bearing some such legend as "Would I were yours and you were mine! Won't you be my valentine?" The tradition grows from Saint Valentine's legendary practice of making secret gifts to the poor. But of the three Saint Valentines on record—two of whom were martyred in Rome on the same day in A.D. 276, the third following their example several centuries later—none left a record of anonymous good deeds, not even of that serendipitous sort, so agreeable to Charles Lamb, which are done by stealth, and found out by accident. Indeed, says Britannica, "The association of the lover's festival with St. Valentine seems to arise from the fact that the feast of the saint falls in the early spring, and is completely accidental."

FILBERT

There is no doubt that a French abbot named Philibert died in 684, that he was canonized, and that his feast day, August 22, coincides with the ripening season of a tasty, rounded, smooth-shelled nut, called in his honor a filbert; or at least did coincide until the calendar was put forward ten days in the 16th century.

TANTONY

Nor do I question for a moment the reality of good Saint Anthony, intercessor for swineherds. Since he is generally pictured with a piglet trotting after him, swineherds came to call the runt of each litter the "Saint Anthony pig," an expression still standard among English farmers in its shortened form, tantony. ("It is odd," remarks Brown, "that tantony never became a synonym for darling, for it is a darrlin' word, as Sean O'Casey's Joxer Daly would have said. If men could turn a moppet [little fish] into a term of affection, why not tantony, for little pigs are easy conquerors of the human heart?")

CATHERINE WHEEL

Also real was Saint Catherine of Alexandria. On the Fourth of July, a catherine wheel is a firework similar to a pinwheel; in a cathedral, it is a circular rose window filled with tracery. In A.D. 310 Catherine enraged Roman emperor Marcus Aurelius Maximinus by calling on him to abandon the worship of false gods. Though scourged and imprisoned for her pains, she managed from her cell to convert the empress and all her retinue, whom Maximinus thereupon put to the sword. He also ordered that Catherine be broken on the wheel; but it shattered at her touch. The executioner's axe proving more successful, angels bore her body to Mount Sinai, where Justinian I later built a monastery in her honor.

The name of a seabird derives from Saint Peter's bootless try at walking on water (Matthew 14:29–31). His faith deserting him, he began to sink, and would have drowned if Jesus had not given him a lift. Hence, says Evans, "The little birds often seen in mid-ocean are called *petrels* (or stormy petrels since they were thought to foretell and were sometimes seen in storms) because petrel (formerly peterel) is a diminutive of Peter. And the birds are called after St. Peter because, like him, they seem to walk on the sea."

PETRELS

Evans adds to his discussion of the petrel: "They are also called Mother Carey's chickens and this is an even more curious corruption because Mother Carey is a sailors' corruption of Mater cara ("dear mother," or the Virgin Mary). The French call them 'birds of our Lady' or 'birds of St. Mary.'"

MOTHER CAREY'S CHICKENS

PEDRO
PARROT
PARAKEET
PERUKE
PERIWIG
WIG

Peter is commemorated also in pedro, a card game, and, more controversially, in parrot, parakeet, and *perruque* (false hair presumably resembling a parrot's ruffled feathers). French *perruque* in English became peruke, then periwig—whence wig.

AUGUSTINISM

Augustinism—the theological system of Saint Augustinus (A.D. 354–430), bishop of Hippo, involving a dogma of grace—probably deserves a place in the vernacular. But such a place has more surely been achieved by one Pelagius, a saintly heretic of Augustinus's time, who insisted on the basic goodness of nature, including human nature. Saint Augustinus, while regarding Pelagius highly as a man, denounced pelagianism, since it conflicted with the concept of original sin. Rebecca West described the novelist Graham Greene as one "chasing pelagianism around the landscape with an axe."

PELAGIANISM

BEDLAM
TOM O' BEDLAM
BETH O' BEDLAM

As early as 1402, the name of the Virgin was used for the hospital of St. Mary of Bethlehem in Lambeth, London, a lockup for lunatics. Cockneys corrupted Bethlehem to Bedlam, which was quickly lowercased to mean any madhouse or any scene of utter confusion. A tom o' bedlam and a bess o'bedlam are wandering lunatics.

The English not only twisted the names of foreign-born saints; they were equally ruthless with their own. As Ethelreda, the virtuous if perhaps demented daughter of a 6th-century king of East Anglia, lay dying of a tumor of the throat, she reasoned that God must have sent her affliction to punish the follies of her girlhood, which consisted principally of liking to wear pretty necklaces. Hundreds of years later, when Ethelreda, her name shrunken to Audrey, had become patron saint of Ely, Cambridgeshire, the townfolk sold "necklaces of fine silk" to celebrate her feast day. Says Moore: "These 'Saint Audrey's laces' gave their name to the poor-quality stuff which was soon

TAWDRY   manufactured all over England; until by 1700 *tawdry* [a contraction of "Saint Audrey"] was a name for any cheap finery or trumpery thing."

VERONICA   There is a legend that Saint Veronica wiped the face of Christ as he carried the cross and that the handkerchief retained an imprint of his face. The veronica, a shrub, herb, or tree bearing blue, purple, white, or pink flowers, bears the saint's name.

JANSENIST   There were devout and holy men and women who never achieved sainthood. When the Jesuits and the Jansenists were at loggerheads in the 17th and 18th centuries, many on both sides were holy, but few were awarded halos. Cornelis Jansen (1585–1638) and his followers maintained the jansenist doctrine of total depravity and irresistible grace; the Jesuits maintained a more casuistic approach. I leave my saints with a prohibition posted at the entrance to a Jansenist cemetery in France in the 17th century:

> *Défense à Dieu*
> *De faire miracles*
> *Dans ce lieu.*

An English equivalent would be:

> *God must not*
> *Pass miracles*
> *Inside this plot.*

Saint Timothy

FRANCISCAN   "Franciscan from St. Francis," said Timothy. "Universally loving. He even spoke to the birds. His name was not Francis at all, you know; it was Giovanni. He was called Francisco because he spoke French so well. In the 1760s a rather nasty organization in Buckinghamshire, the Hellfire Club, called themselves Franciscans, but not from the saint. One of their patrons was a monstrous rake, Sir Francis Dashwood."

"Spell that last name, Timothy," I said. This was my last-ditch device for stopping him long enough to catch up in my note-taking.

"D-a-s-h-w-o-o-d. By the way—"

"Spell it again, Timothy."

SAINT MONDAY

"By the way," he repeated. "To keep Saint Monday? Meaning to take the day off?"

"Accepted with reservations," I said.

"Monday morning quarterback?"

"Now you are off the subject entirely."

GROBIAN

"Quite right. *Omm . . . ommm . . . omm.* Grobian? A grobian is a lout. Saint Grobianus is the patron saint of coarse people and you give short shrift to Saint Martin. As a soldier in Gaul, he gave half his cloak to a beggar. The remaining half was later carried around in the entourage of the Frankish kings, in a case, the capella, diminutive of *cappa,* 'cloak.' Hence chapel, a place of religious worship, and *cappelanus,* custodian of the cloak of Saint Martin. Hence 'chaplain.' And hence the name Kaplan, a substitute for Cohen, 'priest.' The Capelanos are literally custodians of the cape of Saint Martin. The Roman feast of Bacchus, carried over into the Christian era, became the feast of Saint Martin (November 11), but maintained its pagan traditions; everyone became horribly drunk. Martin drunk."

CHAPEL

CHAPLAIN

MARTIN DRUNK

"Spell it, Timothy," I said.

"Spell what?"

"Spell anything," I said, scribbling.

CUDDY

Timothy bit into a chocolate-covered tidbit. "Excellent!" he said. "Let . . . me . . . see. One more for the road. Cuddy. Common for 'donkey.' From Cuthbert. Probably, though not certainly, for the 7th-century English saint. Before his bones were finally interred, they were carried on donkeyback through northern England and southern Scotland."

He took a final sip of his tea and stood up. "I am waited for," he said. "God bless, Wede."

"*Pax vobiscum,* Saint Timothy."

PALEONTOLOGIST MAY reconstruct from a fragment of a thighbone not only some long-extinct beast but the sort of world in which it lived. So from the smattering of chronologically ordered words that follow, the reader may re-create the rise and fall of empires. "Words," says Barfield, "may be made to disgorge the past that is bottled up inside them, as coal and wine, when we kindle or drink them, yield up their bottled sunshine."

PARIAH

For three thousand years, one of the lower castes in India has been called Pariah, from Tamil *paraiyan*, "drummer." Though not lowest in caste ranks, the name in English has come to mean one despised by society. A pariah dog is a half-wild dog which scavenges in North Africa or southern Asia.

PYRRHIC VICTORY

The remorseless, clanking stride of Roman legions marching toward domination of the world is caught in the expression "pyrrhic victory," referring to a remark of King Pyrrhus after the battle of Asculum (279 B.C.). "One more such victory over the Romans," he said, "and we are utterly undone."

PELORUS

The first practical navigational aid, similar to the compass but lacking magnetic needles, was used about 203 B.C. by Pelorus in piloting Hannibal home from Rome. It is called the pelorus after him.

ARCHIPELAGO

Explorers and merchants sowed the seas with names. To the Romans the waters east of Greece, called by the Greeks the Aegean, were the Archipelago, or "chief sea." Since these waters are studded with small islands, archipelago has come to stand for either a large group of islands or a sea containing such a group.

CAESAREAN

CAESAR
KAISER
TSAR

The first delivery of an infant by cutting through the abdominal wall of the mother is traditionally the birth of Julius Caesar (100–44 B.C.). The procedure is named after him the caesarean section, often shortened to caesarean. It is possible that not he but one of his forebears was actually the person so born. The usage was reinforced by Latin *caedere*, "to cut out." In any event, Caesar immortalized caesarean. His own name became generic for emperor or autocrat. In Arabic it was *quysar*, in German *Kaiser*, and in Russian *tsar'*.

PALACE

Man's preoccupation with luxury and architectural beauty is summed up in the word palace, "a large and stately house." It traces from the Palatine Hill in Rome, named after Pales, goddess of fields. In the time of Nero (A.D. 37–68) the Palatine Hill was the turf of the beautiful people. Cicero and Cataline had lived there. Funk relates that Nero decided to preempt the location. He evicted the population, razed the fine homes, and replaced them with a single elaborate dwelling, the *palatium*. The word moved into Italian as *palazzo* and into French as *palais*. Therefore, palace. An officer of the imperial palace, or chamberlain, was a palatine; in the Middle Ages the name was applied to great feudatories exercising royal privileges, such as German rulers.

PALATINE

ZEAL
ZEALOUSNESS
ZEALOTRY

ZEALOT

SICARIUS

Zeal, ardor in the pursuit of anything, equates with zealousness. Zealotry is different—an excess of zeal. A zealot is a fanatically committed person. The root is from a Greek word meaning "zeal" (or jealousy) which became a proper name applied to the Zealots, after a fanatical Jewish sect that rebelled against the Romans in the 1st century A.D. They did not hesitate at murder, even of their own people, to gain their ends. The word sicarius for a murderer is borrowed from Sicarius, one of the most notorious of the Zealots.

LOMBARD

LUMBER

As persistent as zealotry among humankind is the need for money. This turned the name of a tribe into that of a length of wood. The Lombards ("long beards"), who seem to have been migrants from the lower basin of the Elbe, battled the Romans off and on from the days of Christ until the 6th century, when they established themselves in the Po Valley of Italy. This remained their seat until their overthrow by Charlemagne in 774. Thereafter, they won a name throughout Europe as moneylenders and pawnbrokers. Lombard Street in London was lined with pawnshops, where any miscellany could be sold or bought; the pawnbrokers, whatever their national origin, were called lombards. Because pawnshops were frequently repositories of useless articles, junk came to be called lumber, and the room where it was stored the lumber room. A passage in Alexander Pope's *Essay on Criticism* illustrates the usage:

The bookful blockhead, ignorantly read,
With loads of learnèd lumber in his head.

While lumber retains this meaning in Britain, in America it refers only to sawed wood. What Americans call lumber, Britons call timber.

MECCA

The doctrine called Islam by its adherents and Mohammedanism by its enemies swept the Arab lands in the 7th century, with Mohammed as its prophet. Mecca, his birthplace, is the holy city where all Muslims hope to worship before they die. In English the word has been extended to mean "a goal to which adherents of a faith fervently aspire," or, less nobly, "a place visited by many people."

ARABESQUE

STREET ARAB

The Arabs, forbidden by their religion to represent the face of God in their mosques, substituted the elaborate abstract traceries we know as arabesques. The word is applied also to a ballet position in which the dancer stands on one leg, the other leg extended backward with a straight knee. A street arab, "a wandering child of the street," reflects the nomadic habits of the Arabs and the prevalence of Arab vendors in Eastern Mediterranean ports.

HEGIRA

As the ancient Jews had their Exodus, the Arabs had their Hijrah, "flight," capitalized for the flight of Mohammed from Mecca in 622, Christian reckoning. The English is hegira, lower-cased for "any flight or exodus."

LAMA
LAMASERY

About a century after the advent of Mohammedanism, a form of Buddhism called Lamaism (*lama* or *bla-ma* was the title of the higher monks) was introduced into Tibet and Mongolia. The religion has an element of animism, and stresses celibacy. A lama is a priest of the sect, and a lamasery (*lama* plus Persian *serai*, "inn") a Lamaist monastery.

TATTER-
DEMALION

"Tatterdemalion" means "a ragged fellow; a ragamuffin. The "tatter" is probably from Icelandic *tötur*, a rag. But what about the rest? Webster is nonplussed. But correspondent A. Hefford owns an unidentified dictionary ("handled so much I had to recover it and cannot get the covering off without the printing too") that links the last two syllables to Old French *desmailler*, "to unlink." Darlene R. Ketten speculates that the whole word may corrupt French *tatin de Malines*—"tatting from Malines," the French spelling of a Belgian town noted for its tatting.

FRANK
FRANKNESS
FRANKLY

It is odd that the pleasant words frank, frankness, and frankly originate in javelin, but so it appears. The Franks were named after their national weapon, *frankon*, "spear," just as Saxons were named from theirs, *sahson*, "knife." The Francs, or Franks, were a Germanic people early on the Rhine. According to Partridge, "The Frankish conquerors in early France (*Frankreich*) were the only 'free' men, or nobles; hence Old French *franc* means of noble birth." In any event, frankness is candor, a happier association than those left by such other barbarian invaders as the Tatars, Vandals, and Huns.

Or Mongols. These tribes overwhelmed eastern Europe in the 12th and 13th centuries. The occupation of Hungary in 1241 was their high-water mark; when their king died that year, they retired to the east to argue over his succession. Their pigmentation was yellowish brown, their hair coarse, black, and straight, their cheekbones prominent, and their eyes dark with pronounced epicanthic folds. Since many of these features are pres-

FRANK

MONGOLOID
MONGOLISM

ent in children born with congenital idiocy, such unfortunates are known as mongoloids. The word was coined by a physician named J. L. H. Down, after whom mongolism is also called Down's syndrome.

"There are Asian nomads of all types," says Britannica, "the chief being the Mongols.". . . The Bedouins or Arabs of the desert are among the most familiar of all pastoral nomads, and their nomadism has no beginning. In popular usage, a bedouin is any nomad or wanderer.

BEDOUIN

Mogul, a corruption of Mongol, has also become part of common English. The Great Mogul was the emperor of Delhi; the highest-ranking playing cards were once called moguls because they had the emperor's picture on them. A mogul is any very rich or powerful person, except when it is a kind of heavy steam locomotive.

MOGUL

Lambert Le Bègue ("the stammerer") formed lay sister-hoods and brotherhoods at Liège in the 12th century. These

BEG
BEGGAR

mendicant orders were called *béguins* or *bégards*. Thus, beg; a *bégard* was a beggar. (But watch this one: middle English *beggen* also meant to beg.) The sisterhood of the Beguines came to be called Bigotes, by association with Bigot, a term applied in the 12th century to certain tribes of southern Gaul and to the Normans. Bigot was soon synonymous with "religious hypocrite." The word now means "one obstinately and intolerantly holding particular opinions, especially religious."

BIGOT

OTTOMAN

Around 1300 the Osmanli, "people of Osman," succeeded to the sultanate of Turkey. All that remains of them is their name, corrupted to ottoman, an upholstered seat or couch without a back.

TURKISH BATH

Speaking of matters Turkish, one sometimes hears "turkish bath" used for an intense experience, alluding to the intense heat of such baths: "They emerged depleted from a turkish bath of emotion."

BEYOND THE
PALE

The Norman conquerors of England sought in the 12th century to extend their conquest to Ireland. They managed to seize the region around Dublin and a few other coastal cities, but for five centuries the rest of Ireland remained more or less free. For protection from Irish attacks, the Normans, now become the English, fenced off their possessions with pales (Latin *palus*), or stakes. Pale became a proper noun meaning the territory or district under a particular jurisdiction. An untamed Irishman was "beyond the Pale." The word returned to the vernacular in this figurative sense; one within the pale is accepted; one beyond the pale is anathema to polite society. Said Shakespeare in *Richard II*:

> The wild O'Neal, with swarms of Irish kerns,
> Lives unmolested in the English pale.

HALLMARK

The development of an orderly society requires reliable benchmarks of quality and measurement. One such is the hallmark, the official mark stamped on articles of gold or silver to denote that they conform to agreed-upon standards. This assaying has been done since 1300 at Goldsmiths' Hall in London (and now at other places). Hallmark, literally, is a mark applied at Goldsmiths' Hall. Figuratively, it is any symbol of quality.

Though villainy is as ancient as man, one particular form of it was named only in the 14th century, when the sharp trading of men from Cerreto, a village about ninety miles north of Rome, made them notorious and their motives suspect. Under the

CHARLATAN

influence of Italian *ciarlare*, "to chatter," a Cerretano became a *ciarlatano*, and, in English, a charlatan, "one who pretends to unheld knowledge or ability."

PUCK

Impishness was personalized at about the same time in Puck, also called Robin Goodfellow. Shakespeare immortalized him as a household fairy in the service of King Oberon in *A Midsummer Night's Dream*. A puck is a hobgoblin, or, by extension,

PUCKISH

a person given to mischief-making: a puckish fellow.

Toward the end of the 14th century, the noble families of Percy and Douglas took turns raiding each other's territory in the neighborhood of the Cheviot Hills, along the English-Scottish border. Cheviot turned to Chevy in a popular 16th-century ballad, "Chevy Chase." One fine day in 1388, according to the song, Percy of Northumberland vowed he would hunt in the territory of Earl Douglas for three days, without leave. The Earl retorted, "Tell this vaunter he shall find one day more than sufficient." I have not read the poem; only one or two scraps have come to my attention, such as the haunting lines

> *O I ha' dreamed a dreary dream*
> *Beyond the Isle of Skye.*
> *For I dreamt that ae dead man wan a fecht*
> *For I dreamt that man was I.*

and

> *Fight on, my merry men all;*
> *For why, my life is at an end.*

CHIVVY

Historians say the ballad confuses the struggle between the two noblemen with the quite different Battle of Otterbourne, which occurred in the same year. In any event, Chevy endures as chivvy, "to chase or harass."

JACKANAPES

"Jack [here meaning monkey] of Naples," shortened to Jackanapes, is said to have been the nickname of William de la Pole, 15th-century Duke of Suffolk, whose badge was a figure of an ape with ball and chain. Suffolk was banished on a charge of aiming at the throne, and on his way to exile was beheaded off Dover in 1450. He was an unpopular man, and jackanapes became colloquial for "a silly, conceited fellow."

GYPSY

The Gypsies received their name from their supposed origin in Egypt, but actually came from India. In the vernacular, a gypsy is any wanderer. To gypsy is to live or roam like a Gypsy, either as a lifestyle or for amusement, as in camping or picnick-

GYP

ing. The Gypsies were considered great rascals by home-staying folk, not without reason. By the end of the Middle Ages gyp had assumed its present meaning of "to swindle; cheat; steal."

GHETTO

A symbol of restriction and oppression by reason of racial origin came into being in 1516 when the city of Venice expelled its Jews to the nearby Island of Ghetto, which was the site of a foundry, *ghetto* in Italian. A ghetto is a quarter in a city, especially a thickly populated slum area, inhabited by a minority group or groups, usually as a result of economic or social pressure. (But though Partridge gives this explanation in his *Origins*, in *Name into Word* he switches gears, deriving the word, like gypsy, from Latin Aegyptus, Egypt, "probably because the Jews dwelt so long in Egypt, perhaps also because so many Eastern Jews are swarthy—like the gypsies." While the island and the country may both have influenced the present usage, I make the Island of Ghetto the more dominant force of the two.)

PASQUINADE

A Roman tailor or barber of the 15th century, one Pasquino, was noted for his caustic wit. "After his death," says Brewer, "a mutilated statue was dug up and placed near the Piazza Navona. As it was not clear whom the statue represented, and as it stood opposite Pasquino's house, it came to be called 'Pasquino.' The people of Rome affixed their political, religious, and personal satires to it." Hence pasquinade, "a lampoon or political squib, having ridicule for its object."

FESCENNINE
FESCENNINITY

The city of Fescennia, in Etruria, was noted for a style of low, scurrilous, obscene poetry called fescennine verse. Fescenninity is an example of such verse, or scurrility generally.

DOLLAR

Eighty miles west of Prague, in what was then Bohemia, lies the valley once called Saint Joachimsthal. A rich mine of silver, highly regarded for its consistency, was discovered there in 1519. A coin minted from it was called a *Joachimsthaler*, a lubberly word that shrank to *Thaler*, rendered in English as "dollar." So dollar means "from the valley"; with prices continuing to climb, the valley grows ever deeper.

BAROQUE

The baroque style in art, typified by elaborate scrolls, curves, and other symmetrical ornamentation, became popular in Europe in the middle of the 16th century. The name may pay tribute to Federigo Barocci (1528–1612), an Italian artist who was a master of tender sentiment, with "a nervous, fluttering style and gay and juicy color." Baroque is applied also to a style of musical composition that flourished concurrently, marked by chromaticism, strict forms, and elaborate ornamentations. A large, irregularly shaped pearl, *barrueco* in Spanish; *verruca*, Latin for "want"; and Arabic *barak*, "pebble," are all allusory to baroque, and perhaps share credit for the word.

RIALTO

In 1590 the Venetians flung a great marble arch over the Grand Canal. It had a double row of shops, with a broad footway between. The bridge was called Pons Rialto, "bridge over the deep river," Rialto being short for *rivus altus*. The shortened form entered the vulgate for any arched bridge. Because of the commerce conducted on the original Rialto, the word was extended to mean a market or exchange. It was applied to the New York theatre district—first, I believe, by O. Henry—and now refers to any district frequented by players and playgoers.

LIDO

Lido, the name of a spit of land famous as a resort near Venice, is used generically for such a spit enclosing a lagoon, for a bathing beach or resort, or for a public open-air swimming pool.

GASCONADE

We have reached the 17th century now, and uncommon, improper nouns are dropping faster and faster from the tree of proper names. I start the modern era, incongruously, with the Gascons, natives of Gascony in southwestern France. D'Artagnan, in Alexandre Dumas's *Three Musketeers* (1844), was a Gascon. Their reputation for braggadocio was so well deserved that any appearance of exaggerated swashbuckling took on the name gasconade. Said Tobias Smollett, shortly before his death in 1771:

A peacock in pride, in grimace a baboon;
In courage a hind, in conceit a Gascoon.

PALLADIAN
ARCHITECTURE

PALLADIAN

Palladian architecture, developed in Italy by Andrea Palladio (1508–1580), was brought to England in the early 1600s by the great architect Inigo Jones. It is a revived classical style emphasizing Roman symmetrical planning and harmonic proportions. It underwent a major revival in Italy and England in the early 18th century. The name is reinforced by Pallas Athene, symbol of grace and intellect. Palladian in this sense refers to wisdom or learning.

On November 5, 1605, Guy Fawkes was arrested for trying to blow up King James I and the British Parliament as a protest against anti–Roman Catholic laws. He was horribly tortured and then hanged. The anniversary of the Gunpowder Plot is celebrated in England each November 5 with parades and the burning of Guy Fawkes in effigy. The stigma attached to his name made guy vulgar for "a fellow; a nobody." The verb first meant "to make or carry an effigy," and later "to make fun of; chaff." But though the Guy Fawkes affair undoubtedly sharpened the usage, guy was probably used earlier in a derogatory way. As far as I know, guy is always used in the third person; if addressing a guy, you will probably say "Hey, Mac!" Mac is the vocative of guy.

GUY

MAC

In 1631, Pierre Vernier (1580–1637), commandant of the castle in his native town of Ornans, in Burgundy, published a mathematical treatise in which he showed how a small auxiliary scale could be connected to a main scale to obtain a finer division, or adjustment, than had been considered possible previously. The vernier lived up to his billing, opening the way to revolutionary scientific and industrial advances.

VERNIER

Returning vessels brought home new words even when they had found no spices or gold. Sometimes the words evolved strangely. The French called the fugitive slaves of the Guianas and the West Indies *marrons*, "of chestnut color; wild and woolly." Refractory pirates, set ashore among these savages to shift for themselves, were said to be marooned, that is, "left in helpless isolation." The expression appears in print as early as 1738 (OED): "We were told that on the South Shore, not far from the Inlet, dwelt a Marooner that Modestly call'd himself a Hermit."

MAROONED

To shanghai means "to drug, intoxicate, or render insensible and ship as a sailor, usually to secure money or a premium." The victim woke in a bunk on a pitching vessel, as likely as not headed for Shanghai. There is a similar-sounding word in Gaelic meaning "forked stick," associated with the motion of stays in a ship, and thus perhaps facilitating the spread of the usage.

SHANGHAI

Where explorers, merchants, and settlers found the natives sufficiently complaisant, these were employed as unskilled laborers, particularly in the Orient. They came to be called coolies, perhaps from Kuli or Koli, an aboriginal tribe of Gujarat, India.

COOLIE

Isaac D'Israeli, father of the 19th-century British prime minister, found in a 17th-century pamphlet a curious origin of the word fudge, meaning "Nonsense! Humbug!" He quotes: "There was in our time one Captain Fudge, commander of a

FUDGE

merchantman [the *Black Eagle*], who upon his return from a voyage, how ill fraught soever his ship was, always brought home to his owners a good crop of lies; so much that now, aboard ship, the sailors when they hear a great lie told, cry out, 'You fudge it.' "

The 17th century also witnessed a change in the notes of the musical scale. For the preceding five hundred years, they had been *ut, re, mi, fa, sol,* and *la,* with *ti* added somewhere along the line. These were the initial syllables of a hymn (rising through a hexachord) to Saint John:

> <u>Ut</u> queant laxis <u>R</u>esonare fibris,
> <u>Mi</u>ra gestorum <u>F</u>amuli tuorum,
> <u>Sol</u>ve polluti <u>Lab</u>ii reatum,
>   Sancte Joannes.

DO

But in the 17th century *ut* somehow turned into *dō*. The new syllable has been associated by some etymologists with *Do*minus, "Lord." Others say the source is unknown. Still others point at an Italian musicologist of the time named Doni, who, they say, simply dropped the *ut* in favor of the first syllable of his own name.

TONTINE

In 1653 a Neapolitan banker named Lorenzo Tonti introduced into France a form of annuity shared by several stockholders, in which the shares of those who die are added to the holdings of the survivors until the last of them inherits all. The lucky winner would necessarily be of advanced years, with little time left in which to enjoy his riches, but tontines were very popular for a while, leading to lovely melodramatic chicaneries and, a few years back, a funny motion picture.

BRUMMAGEM

Brummagem distorts Birmingham, England. Because the town was noted for its output of cheap trinkets, toys, and imitation jewelry, brummagem became a pejorative term for any article of cheap or flimsy manufacture, not excluding counterfeit coins. In the 1680s high Tory friends of the Duke of York, later King James II, disparaged supporters of the Exclusion Bill (which forbade Catholics to hold public office) as Brummagens, short for "Birmingham counterfeit Protestants."

Such opponents of royal prerogative also were damned as Whigs, identifying them with the authors of the 1648 Whiggamore Raid in which a rabble of Scottish Covenanters marched on Edinburgh. (Whiggamore, apparently from Gaelic *whig*, "to drive," plus mare, was a term applied to horse thieves.) The term

Tory itself started as disreputably as Whig. It derived from Irish *toraidhe*, "pursued man; robber," after the Irish who, rising against the English in Ulster in 1641, killed thousands of colonists and were reviled as despicable savages. It was the most offensive name the Whigs could dredge up; but the Tories soon adopted it with pride, as their opponents did the name Whig. A tory is one whose leanings are conservative, and a whig one who leans to the liberal side.

TORY
WHIG

MUGWUMP

The term Mugwump, originally an Algonquin term for "great man," was used respectfully by colonists in America for a tycoon. Its meaning deteriorated to "one who backs down or withdraws." Brown says, "An American writer recently explained a mug-wump as one who sits on the fence with his mug on one side and his wump on the other."

Two cities named Niagara Falls are situated in New York and Ontario, at opposite ends of the celebrated waterfall. Niagara, of Iroquois origin, has become vernacular for any overwhelming torrent: "a niagara of abuse." To firemen, a niagara is a large revolving nozzle, mounted on an elevated platform. ("Would it not be more impressive," asked Oscar Wilde, on seeing Niagara, "if it flowed the other way?")

NIAGARA

MONADNOCK

A mountain or rocky mass that has resisted erosion and stands isolated in a plain is a monadnock. Though there are many monadnocks, the usage derives from Mount Monadnock in New Hampshire. Other uncommon, improper nouns from geological terminology are champaign ("level and open country; a plain"), from the flat Middle Italian province of Campagna; munro (for any mountain more than three thousand feet high in Scotland), from Sir H. T. Munro, who in 1891 made a list of all such mountains; and guyot, a submarine mountain or plateau, from the Swiss-American geographer and geologist Arnold Henry Guyot (1807–1884).

CHAMPAIGN

MUNRO

GUYOT

18th Century

PETTIFOGGER

Pettifogger now means "a petty, quibbling, unscrupulous lawyer," but at the turn of the 18th century was applied to hucksters generally. The etymology is questionable. "If it be true that fogger is derived from the great Bavarian merchant house of Fugger," says Brown, "then he is a huckster on the grand scale, reduced by prefixing the word petty." *If*.

KIT-CAT

A portrait of less than half-length, measuring twenty-eight by thirty-six inches, is called a kit-cat, after a club formed in London in 1703 by the leading Whigs of the day. The name is from Christopher Catt, a cook in whose house the club first met. There were at least forty-two members, including Steele, Addison, Congreve, Vanbrugh, Walpole, Lord Stanhope, and the Earl of Essex. Sir Godfrey Keller painted portraits of the forty-two, adopting the odd size required to accommodate the paintings to the height of the clubroom. This was not the Catt house, but a later meeting place, in the villa of the secretary, Jacob Tonson, who commissioned the paintings. Catt's mutton pies, a favorite at the club, were also known as kit-cats, as were certain short biographical essays.

PINCHBECK

Two years before his death in 1732, Christopher Pinchbeck, a London watchmaker who took his name from Pinchbeck, Lincolnshire, invented an alloy of copper and zinc which he used to imitate gold in cheap jewelry. Pinchbeck is "sham; spurious; counterfeit"; sometimes "an affected, unsuccessful imitation." In a misogynistic moment, novelist William Makepeace Thackeray called women's tresses pinchbeck.

ARTESIAN WELL

In 1750, at Artois, France, a clever fellow drove a well through rock strata to reach water capable of rising to the surface by internal hydrostatic pressure. Artois gives artesian. Artesian wells provide significant yields; a set of eight wells at Camberwell, London, produced 1.5 million gallons of water per day.

MACARONI

A macaroni is a coxcomb. The term originated with the Macaroni Club, founded about 1760 by young men described by Brewer as "exquisite fops; vicious, indolent, fond of gambling, drinking, and duelling. Having travelled in Italy, they prided themselves on the consumption of macaroni, whence the club name." Said a periodical in 1770: "There is indeed a kind of animal, neither male nor female, a thing of the neuter gender, lately started up amongst us. It is called a Macaroni. It talks without meaning, it smiles without pleasantry, it eats without appetite, it rides without exercise, it wenches without pleasure."

"Yankee Doodle," written in the Revolution to deride the

colonists but adopted by them, refers to the usage in the lines:

Yankee Doodle came to town,
A-riding on a pony;
Stuck a feather in his hat,
And called it Macaroni.

JACOBIN

During the French Revolution of 1789 a society of radical democrats accepted from its enemies the name Jacobin, after its meeting place in an old Jacobin convent in Paris. A jacobin is a violent radical or turbulent demagogue—except, of course, when the name is borne by a breed of fancy hooded pigeons, or a tropical American hummingbird.

MESMERISM
MESMERIST

Mesmerism is hypnosis, and a mesmerist is a hypnotist. Franz Anton Mesmer (1734–1815), an Austrian physician, became convinced that his hands held a healing power, which he called "animal magnetism." He made striking cures, especially of hysterical patients, but was driven from Vienna at the instance of orthodox physicians, and in Paris was investigated for charlatanism by a government commission including Benjamin Franklin, then U.S. Commissioner to France. The investigators concluded that the cures were genuine but the cause unknown.

LUDDITE

While Dr. Mesmer was sending shivers through the medical establishment, a halfwit from Leicestershire named Ned Ludd was giving sleepless nights to burgeoning industrialists and manufacturers. About 1779 he broke up textile machinery (for making stockings) to save his job, setting an example later followed by organized bands of workmen. A luddite is a person who tries to prevent the use of labor-saving machinery by breaking it, burning factories, and the like; or, these days, anyone who simply opposes scientific advances on principle.

19th Century

DAVENPORT

I hesitate to trivialize the accomplishments of the 19th century by starting out with the davenport, which is only a large upholstered sofa, often convertible into a bed (or, in England, a small kind of writing desk). But Webster concedes that this word comes "from the name of some maker." Surely a stingy way to confer immortality.

With the industrial revolution in full swing, it was inevitable that a number of uncommon, improper nouns of the 19th century should deal with labor-saving devices. A stillson wrench, once trademarked after some Stillson, is a pipe wrench having an adjustable L-shaped jaw sliding in a sleeve that is pivoted to and loosely embraces the handle. Pressure on the handle increases the grip. A monkey wrench is a wrench with a fixed jaw and an adjustable jaw set at right angles to the handle. Tradition says it was first devised by a London blacksmith named Charles Moncke, Moncke changing to monkey by folk derivation. A difficulty with this theory, as Mencken has pointed out, is that the British monkey wrench is a spanner, which is not adjustable. In 1932–33, the *Boston Transcript* traced the invention to 1856, crediting it to a Yankee named Monk, employed by the firm of Bemis and Call in Springfield, Massachusetts.

STILLSON
WRENCH

MONKEY
WRENCH

The plimsoll line might best be described as a lifesaving rather than a labor-saving device. Samuel Plimsoll (1824–1898) was a British reformer who directed his first efforts against "coffin ships"—unseaworthy and overloaded vessels, often heavily insured, in which unscrupulous owners risked the lives of their crews. Plimsoll induced Parliament to pass an act prohibiting overloading. The plimsoll line conspicuously painted on the sides of all British (and now American) merchant vessels indicates the limit of submergence allowed by law. The plimsoll, a sneaker still worn in England, was named after the resemblance of its mudguard to the plimsoll line of a ship.

PLIMSOLL LINE

PLIMSOLL

The peavey is a wooden lever with a metal point and a hinged hook near the end, used by lumbermen to handle logs. It was invented around 1870 by Joseph Peavey, a New England blacksmith who later served on the faculty of Oregon State Agricultural College.

PEAVEY

For one's name to be mud dates from at least 1820; the mind instantly analogizes between the slimy, sticky stuff and the contumely of society. Lincoln's assassination, however, simultaneously tied the expression to a proper name and locked it into the vernacular. John Wilkes Booth, the actor-assassin, broke his leg while jumping from Lincoln's box to the stage after firing the fatal shot. During the twelve days before his capture, he was

YOUR NAME IS
MUD

treated by Dr. Samuel Mudd, a prominent physician of the area. It was not proved that Dr. Mudd knew the identity of his patient, but he was nonetheless tried for conspiracy, convicted, and sent to the fever-infested Dry Tortugas in Key West to serve his term. His selfless treatment of the hundreds of yellow fever victims among his fellow prisoners won him sympathy, and when the post-assassination hysteria died down he received executive clemency. His descendants wear their name as a badge of honor. One of them greeted Christopher LaFarge, the poet, at a cocktail party: "My name is Mudd," she said casually, and turned away.

CRAPPER

CRAP

The crapper has saved millions the grief of making their way to outdoor privies in inclement weather. It is a hopper for defecation, fitted with a device for flushing the bowl with water. To crap is to defecate. The float, metal arm, and siphonic action by means of which toilets can flush without flowing ceaselessly were developed in the 1870s by Thomas Crapper, a London sanitary engineer. Yet an earlier account indicates that somebody beat Mr. Crapper to the crapper, if not the name; "When in 1596 Sir John Harrington, one of Queen Elizabeth's courtiers, invented the modern indoor toilet, with its flushing arrangements, he announced it in a work with the punning title of The Metamorphosis of Ajax (A-jakes)." (The privy in England was a jakes.) Middle English had *crappe*, "residual rubbish"; and there may also be an etymological connection with crop, agricultural produce. But though "to crap" may have antedated Mr. Crapper, he undoubtedly nailed the word to the mast.

NEANDER

In 1856, in the Neanderthal Valley of the Rhine province, paleontologists discovered what appeared at first to be parts of a normal human skeleton, but turned out to be the remains of a hitherto unknown variety of man, long extinct and only collateral to *Homo sapiens*. The creature was reconstructed as hulking, with a flat, sloping forehead and enormous ridges above the eyes. From the place where he was found, he was called neanderthal man. Actually, that should not have been his name at all. In the 16th century the Germans had undergone a rebirth of learning, in the course of which many of them changed their names into Greek. A certain Herr Neuman became Neander; the valley (*Thal* in German) was named after his great-great-grandson, J. C. Neander (1650–1680), a poet and hymn writer. So the neanderthal man is really "the man from the valley of the new men." He is the "new man"—the wave of the future. Perhaps those UFOs are piloted by neanders.

RAMAPITHECUS
Ramapithecus, a highly developed ape whose remains were found in India, is named for Rama, hero of the Hindu epic *Ramayana*.

SPOONERISM
The Reverend William A. Spooner (1844–1930), beloved warden of New College, Oxford, was noted (some say unfairly so) for helplessly twisting his words. A spoonerism is an accidental transposition of sounds, usually the initial sounds, of two or more words. Some familiar spoonerisms, yours to disentangle:

A well boiled icicle

A blushing crow

Our shoving leopard

Our queer old dean

Please sew me to another sheet; someone is occupewing my pie.

Kinkering congs

When the boys come home from France, we'll have hags flung out.

My boy, it's kisstomary to cuss the bride.

JUMBO
An ancestral spirit in Senegal was portrayed on appropriate occasions by someone wearing a particular costume and going through particular rites. Since pompons, or balls of feathers, were an important part of the costume, the spirit was prayed to as *mama dyambo*; that is, "ancestor-pompon." The English hobson-jobsoned this expression to mumbo-jumbo. In 1882 the American showman Phineas Taylor Barnum (1810–1891) brought to the States an elephant that stood ten feet nine inches at the shoulder. The brute was named Jumbo, probably with reference to its African origin. By the time it was killed by a railway engine three years later, Jumbo had become a household word for anything of large size, as a "jumbo-size" package. The Boeing 747 and the DC 10 are jumbo jets.

JESSE
England had an early zoo elephant called Jesse. The word for a time was used generically for any pachyderm, and later became a synonym for thick-skinned or resistant: "Thick as jesse."

BARNUM
BARNUMISM
BARNUMIZE
A sucker is born every minute, said Barnum. He applied this concept so assiduously that barnum has become a synonym for humbug, and barnumism for humbuggery. If you permit me to barnumize you, you are among those suckers who are born every minute.

GRIMTHORPE   Toward the end of the century, Lord Grimthorpe undertook the restoration of the west front of St. Albans' Abbey (Hertfordshire, England) and its window. The good lord's name entered the language deplorably: to grimthorpe means "to do a rotten job of restoration."

20th Century

MAFFICK   On May 17, 1900, the British finally raised the siege of Mafeking, in South Africa, beset by the Boers since October 12, 1899. The deliverance was wildly celebrated in England, and maffick came to mean "to celebrate with boisterous rejoicings or hilarious behavior." The English author Saki wrote, "Mother, may I go and maffick, / Tear around and hinder traffic?" Maffick is not much used nowadays, perhaps because we seem to have little to maffick about.

RITZY   In 1906 the Swiss hotelier Cesar Ritz built the Ritz Hotel in Piccadilly. With the later Ritz in Paris and Ritz-Carlton in New York, he set a new standard for fashion and luxury. Ritzy is "ostentatiously or vulgarly smart in appearance or manner."

ROBOT   In 1923 the play *R.U.R.*, by the Czech writer Karel Capek, took Broadway theatergoers by storm. The initials in the title stand for "Rossum's Universal Robots," the name of a firm which manufactures mechanical beings, enslaved to work for men. In the play, the robots revolt. The notion that man might eventually be destroyed by his own creations was disturbing in 1923, and is even more disturbing today. A robot is an externally manlike mechanical device capable of performing human tasks, or any device that works automatically or by remote control. The name is applied also to a person who works mechanically, without original thought. Robot in various Slavic languages is cognate to our "orphan." It means hard, usually forced labor, especially that of peasants, for a manorial lord.

REUBEN
RUBE GOLDBERG   Rube Goldberg (1883–1970), one of the dearest men who ever lived, prospered for more than half a century by developing cartoon equivalents of the mountain that labored to give birth to a mouse. The reuben, a prize for cartoonists, is named for him. A rube goldberg is an intricate contraption designed to effect relatively simple results.

TO TAKE A
GALLUP

The Gallup poll was the first renowned scientific sampling of public opinion; to conduct such a poll is increasingly referred to as "to take a gallup."

PLIMP

Time magazine foresees a verb, to plimp, for "the participatory journalism . . . in which the amateur ventures lamb-like among the wolves of professional sport—and then writes about how to be a lamb chop." The eponym is George A. Plimpton, a writer who has vied with the professionals, usually unsuccessfully, in such risky sporting events as playing football for the Detroit Lions and boxing with former light-heavyweight champion Archie Moore.

PAP TEST

The pap test for uterine cancer, which has saved the lives of thousands of women, uses the first syllable of the surname of Dr. George Papanicolau (1883–1962), who originated it.

GESTAPO

WASP

Two vernacular acronyms of the 20th century are gestapo, for *Ge*heime *Sta*ats *Po*lizei, Hitler's secret state police; and wasp, for White Anglo-Saxon Protestant. The wasp is currently the punching bag of scores of ethnics who are happily repaying him in kind for the slights and injuries they feel they have taken from him in the past.

MACH

The next time you fly in a Concorde, you may notice on the cabin speed dials that you are traveling at, say, mach 1.5. Mach is the ratio of the speed of an object through a medium to the speed of sound in the medium; mach 1 is its speed at sea level (1088 feet per second at 32°F.). The word pays its respects to Ernst Mach (1838–1916), Austrian physicist, a philosopher of sensations and student of sound.

There is no end in sight to the creating of uncommon, improper nouns. As long, that is, as there is anybody around to create them.

FIVE

THE GROVES OF ACADEME
DEEP, DEEP WORDS

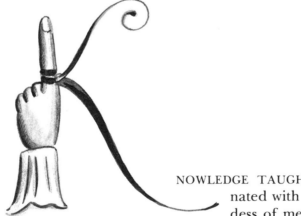

MNEMONICS

KNOWLEDGE TAUGHT by rote originated with Mnemosyne, goddess of memory and mother of the nine Muses. She was the daughter of Uranus, the most ancient of the gods, and Gaea, the goddess of earth. Mnemonics is any system designed to improve or develop the memory. I tried several such systems, until I decided I was better off forgetting.

A long time ago there lived in Attica a man named Academos ("on the side of the people"). Academos disclosed to

Castor and Pollux the place where Theseus had secreted their irresistibly beautiful young sister Helen, whom he had kidnaped with lustful intent. (This is the same Helen who was later to desert her husband for Paris—an event which led to the Trojan War, the *Iliad,* the *Odyssey,* and a poem by Edgar Allan Poe.)

The people of Athens made much of Academos for his tittle-tattling, though it is hard to see why they should have cared, since Helen was a Spartan. A lovely and spacious garden, the Academe, was named in his honor.

ACADEME
ACADEMY

In the 4th century B.C., the philosopher Plato opened a school for his followers in the grove of Academe. Ever since, the word has been inseparately connected with learning. An academy may be an association of scholars, or of artists (as in London's Royal Academy of Fine Arts); or a school for special instruction; or a secondary or college-preparatory school.

PLATONISM

Platonism, from Plato ("broad-shouldered"), is a philosophy holding that perfect, eternal realities are the objects of true knowledge; that the things of the senses are but distorted shadows of reality; that the soul, in its highest, rational form, is immortal; and that pleasures of the body, while they may be harmless and even virtuous, are to be subordinated to the plea-

PLATONIC LOVE

sures of the mind. Platonic love has come to be associated with love having no element of sexual desire.

Plato was a pupil of Socrates, who developed the inductive method and the conception of knowledge or insight as the foun-

SOCRATIC
IRONY

dation of virtue. Socratic irony is pretended ignorance, or a willingness to learn from others assumed for the sake of making

SOCRATIC
METHOD

their errors conspicuous. The Socratic method consists of a series of questions, the object of which is to elicit a clear and consistent expression of something supposed to be implicitly known by all rational beings.

Socrates' love for outdoor discussion, away from home, appears to have been augmented by domestic difficulties, his wife Xanthippe ("roan horse") outdoing Mrs. Caudle in her

XANTHIPPE

scolding. A xanthippe is a shrewish, peevish, quarrelsome wife.

At the opposite pole from platonic idealism is aristotelianism, after Aristotle (384–322 B.C.), who is said to have exercised greater influence upon Western attitudes than any other one man. Aristotle ("best objective") espoused the empiri-

ARISTO-
TELIANISM

cal or scientific in methods and thought. Aristotelian logic is built around the syllogism, a form of deductive reasoning consisting of a major premise, a minor premise, and a conclusion.

LYCEUM

The gymnasium at Athens where Aristotle taught was named the Lukeion, after the neighboring temple of Apollo Lukeios ("wolf-killer"). The word has come down to us as lyceum. (The lyceum movement, an association for debate and educational and literary improvement, flourished in the United States before the Civil War, having three thousand branches in 1834.)

ATHENEUM

Philosophy was taught also at the Athenaion, the temple of Athena. Rome adopted the word for a school of art, and today atheneum, like academy, has become common for any institution, such as a library or reading room, that disseminates learning.

CYNIC

Antisthenes (born about 444 B.C.), like Plato a student of Socrates, founded the school of the Cynics (named improbably for a dog), who believed that virtue is the only good, and that its essence lies in self-control and independence. It is curious that this noble doctrine entered the vernacular with a nearly opposite meaning: today's cynic believes all men are motivated by vulgar selfishness.

EPICUREANISM
EPICURE

The turnabout in the meaning of cynicism is matched by that of epicureanism. Epicurus, born seven years after the death of Plato, was so chaste a man that one of his enemies sought to deny him merit by saying he was without passion. He did not marry, in order that he might devote himself to philosophy. His conviction that it was human duty to maximize pleasure and minimize pain, however, led to an impression that epicureanism stood for a life of indulgence. Today an epicure is considered one given to luxury or sensual gratification, modified by delicacy and refinement.

SOPHIST
SOPHOMORE
SOPHISTICATED

The Sophists (5th century B.C.) received their name from the Greek word for "skilled" or "clever." They were not personified in any one leader, but the best of them were undoubtedly among the most learned men of the period. They were the first to offer systematic education beyond the rudiments, antedating even Socrates. But they later came to be disparaged for oversubtle, self-serving reasoning, and that is the way a sophist is thought of today. Sophomore ("wise fool"), sophisticated, and the like, have the same origin. Your Aunt Sophie is a wise old woman.

About 308 B.C., Zeno taught that men should be free from passion and calmly accept all occurrences as the unavoidable

STOIC

result of divine will. He taught in a porch *(Stoa)* in Athens, which led to the appellation stoic for persons apparently or professedly indifferent to pleasure or pain.

EUCLIDEAN

Euclid, father of geometry, was born about 300 B.C. It was he who warned Ptolemy I that "there is no royal road to geometry." Euclidean means "lucid and orderly in the exposition of evidence," even if geometry is not in question.

PYRRHONISM

Between 365 and 275 B.C. there lived in Greece a man named Pyrrho, who believed that all perceptions are of doubtful value, so that the supreme good is to preserve tranquillity of mind. Such a belief is pyrrhonism. It has nothing to do with pyrrhotism, from Greek *pyrrhotes*, "redness," the quality of having red hair.

EUHEMERISM

Euhemerism is the doctrine that gods were great humans who grew in the telling, that myths are embellished accounts of historical personages and events. The Sicilian philosopher Euhemeros (meaning "good day") lived around 300 B.C. His interpretation relies upon an account of early history which he said he had discovered on a golden pillar in a temple on the island of Panchaia when on a voyage around the coast of India. The voyage and the island appear to have been a figment.

CYRENAIC

When Jesus was walking toward his crucifixion, the Roman soldiers, says Matthew 27:32, "found a man of Cyrene, Simon by name: him they compelled to bear his cross." A Cyrenaic is a disciple of the hedonistic school of philosophy founded in Cyrene by Aristippus ("best horse"), who believed that pleasure is the only good in life. There's no reason to think the biblical Simon was of that school.

DUNCE
DUN

One generation's genius may be the next generation's half-wit. Johannes Duns Scotus (c. 1265–1308), born in Duns, Scotland, was the greatest of British medieval philosophers. Called the "subtle doctor" for his intricate reasoning, he won a large following for his objections to many of the changes brought about by the Reformation. After his death these "Dunsmen" persisted blindly in their opposition to the revival of classical learning, and eventually came to be considered a stupid lot. Hence the present-day significance of dunce: "one backward in book learning; a dull-witted person." Dun, for an old, broken-down horse, may have the same point of departure.

Atlas was either a divinity having charge of the pillars which upheld the heavens, or a Titan forced, for warring against Zeus,

EUCLIDEAN

to bear the heavens on his head and hands. A picture of Atlas, supporting not the heavens but the ball of earth, was commonly prefixed to map collections at the beginning of the Renaissance. This led Gerhard Mercator (1512–1594), the Flemish geographer, to call the collections atlases. Mercator created the mercator projection, a map in which the meridians and parallels of latitude appear as lines crossing at right angles. The scale along the meridians increases away from the equator; any oblique line maintains a consistent compass direction.

ATLAS
MERCATOR
PROJECTION

DARWINISM

The theory that species of plants and animals develop through natural selection of viable variations is called darwinism, after Charles Robert Darwin (1809–1882), the British naturalist who propounded it in 1858. A social darwinist is said to use this subtle doctrine as justification of individual callousness—every man for himself.

SOCIAL
DARWINIST

FREUDIAN

A freudian is one who practices the theories of Sigmund Freud (1856–1939), the pioneer psychoanalyst, in psychotherapy; or who applies those theories to other disciplines such as history or literary criticism; or who simply approves and preaches them. *Freude* in German means "joy; gladness," emotions not generally associated with the father of psychiatry. A "Freudian slip" could be called a *Felix culpa*.

NEWTONIAN
NEWTON
EINSTEINIAN

Newtonian derives from the work of Sir Isaac Newton (1642–1727) in mechanics and gravitation (the newton, a unit of force, is named after him), and einsteinian from the theories of Albert Einstein (1879–1955) on general and special relativity.

CHAUTAUQUA

After the Civil War, Americans became fascinated by the chautauqua, a traveling show, often performing under canvas, and including vaudeville acts as well as lectures. Chautauquas were reinforced by a system of home study. The name derives from the county and lake in southwestern New York where the first chautauqua was held in 1874. Chautauqua was a word of the Seneca Indians, who attributed several meanings to it, one being "the place of easy death." In view of the uneasy state of present institutions of learning, one wonders whether we should not give the chautauqua another chance.

BRAILLE

Louis Braille (1809–1852), a Frenchman who lost his sight through an accident at the age of three, developed a dot system of printing (first suggested by Captain Charles Barbier) which can be read by touch, and easily written with a simple instrument. Braille defines any similar system.

Summa Cum Laude, Timothy

BERKELEIANISM "Oh," said Timothy, turning the last page of the chapter face down, "berkeleianism. Subjective idealism. The doctrine that so-called material things exist only in being perceived. After Bishop George Berkeley, the Irish philosopher. His dates are 1685–1753. He inspired this anonymous witticism:

There was a young man who said: God
Must think it exceedingly odd
  That the juniper tree
  Just ceases to be
When there's no-one about in the quad.

Monsignor Ronald Knox replied:

Dear Sir, Your astonishment's odd;
I am always about in the quad;
  And that's why the tree
  Will continue to be,
Since observed by
                Yours faithfully,
                God.

BERKELIUM "You might wish to include berkelium, the appropriately transient element with a half-life of four and a half hours. Named for Berkeley, California, which in turn is named for Bishop Berkeley."

He also insisted on my including "Priscian's head." Priscian, a Latin grammarian who flourished at Constantinople around A.D. 500, was so highly regarded during the Middle Ages that the phrase "to break Priscian's head" became a byword for the violation of rules of grammar.

TO BREAK PRISCIAN'S HEAD

OCKHAM'S RAZOR Ockham's razor, too, noted Timothy, has become generic: "William of Ockham. A Franciscan. His dates were about 1300 to about 1349. A pupil and later a rival of Duns Scotus. His famous doctrine was 'Entities are not to be multiplied'—that is, one must slice away all nonessential constituents in the subject being analyzed. Hence Ockham's razor."

ALGORISMUS

I suddenly remembered something. "Algorismus!" I exclaimed. "Wasn't it invented by someone named Algor?"

"Ah," said Timothy. "A name applied in the Middle Ages to arithmetic employing the Indo-Arabic numerals. Ah . . . yes. Bop-bop-bop."

I was much set up to have thought of a word he had missed. He went on: "Early European writers indeed thought it came from Algor, a king of India. A manuscript written around 1300 said, 'Ther was a kyng of Inde the quich heyth Algor, he made this craft. And aft his name he called hit algory.' I will write that out for you. But the origin is *Liber Algorismus*, 'the Book of al-Khowarizmi,' by Mohammed ibn Musa al-Khowarizmi."

"But it is an uncommon, improper noun," I said. "Khowarizmi—algorismus."

"Exactly. Ah, Vitruvian man?"

VITRUVIAN
MAN

Vitruvius was a Roman architect of the 1st century B.C. To show the normal proportions of the members to the body, he sketched the Vitruvian man in the two classic positions with arms and legs outthrust: one around which could be drawn a perfect circle; the other around which could be drawn a perfect square. Leonardo da Vinci created a similar figure. It would have done your heart good to see Timothy demonstrate the two positions, arms and legs stiffly spread, his stick aloft in one hand. His agility was admirable.

His final contribution was the Greek cynic philosopher Diogenes, supposed to have lived in a tub and to have gone about with a lantern in daylight, looking for an honest man.

"Alexander the Great admired him extravagantly," said Timothy. " 'If I were not Alexander,' he said, 'I would be Diogenes.' The admiration appears not to have been returned. When the ruler of the world inquired, 'Is there any way I can serve you?' Diogenes replied, 'You can step out of my light.' "

I protested: "Diogenes has left us no improper, uncommon nouns. Nor Patient Griseldas either, as far as I know, unless you consider Diogenes's lantern in that category."

DIOGENES CRAB
DIOGENES' CUP

"You forget the terrestrial hermit crab that destroys crops in the West Indies," said Timothy. "The Diogenes crab. And the cuplike hollow formed by the hand and the fingers: Diogenes's cup."

Magna cum laude, Timothy. Summa cum laude.

SIX

ALWAYS SCRIBBLE, SCRIBBLE, SCRIBBLE, EH, MR. GIBBON?
LITERARY WORDS

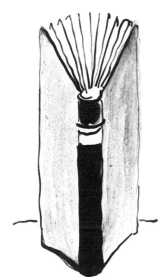

N 1788, Edmund Gibbon presented the sixth volume of his monadnock of scholarship, *The Decline and Fall of the Roman Empire*, to the Duke of Gloucester. "What—another damn thick square book! Always scribble scribble scribble, eh, Mr. Gibbon?" said the duke tolerantly.

But if it were not for the scribblers, who would remember the dukes? Homer, whose scribbling was done with a lyre—and of whom nothing more is known; he may have been one person or many; he may have lived in any century between the 11th and the 8th B.C.—made common nouns of hosts of gods, monsters, heroes, and nymphs. Even his own name became common in such expressions as homeric combat and homeric laughter—combat and laughter as hearty and unreserved as that of the gods themselves.

The origins of many fairy tales are lost in antiquity. Cinderella, for instance, appears to stem from remote Oriental folklore. Her fairy godmother raised her from a fireplace drudge to a prince's bride, and she lived happily ever after. (Hollywood, TV, and the like, furnish us with many cinderella stories, but the girl seldom lives happily ever after.) A cinderella is a despised, neglected person who eventually achieves recognition or affluence.

As far as I know, the first specifically fictional character to become vernacular was Amaryllis, the "beloved shepherdess" hymned by Theocritus in the 3rd century B.C. Her name was to become an endearment; Milton, before he fell sightless and stern, could conceive of no more blissful pastime than "to sport with Amaryllis in the shade." A great historian, Sir Stephen Runciman, reflected on the transformation of the garden of the Greeks into the wilderness of the Mafia:

While Corydon sported with Amaryllis in the shade their goats devoured the bark from off the trees.

Our current crop of poets has abandoned Amaryllis for less beautiful subjects; the beloved shepherdess survives only as a lily. Still, the amaryllis, with its bell-shaped white or rose-colored blossoms, is a sweetheart of a flower.

Theocritus remains unmatched for the love and faithfulness with which he depicted peasants, animals, and the countryside. We remember him in the word theocritan, meaning idyllic or pastoral.

A century later, the Roman comic poet Terence (Publius Terentius Afer, c. 190–159 B.C.) created for his comedy *The Eunuch* a Captain Thraso, so boastful that a braggart today is still marked down as a thrasonical fellow. *Veni, vidi, vici,* Caesar's report of his fast victory over Pharnaces II, is a thrasonical boast.

Vergil opens the first Eclogue of the Aeneid with "Tityre, tu" ("O Tityrus, thou"), addressing one Tityrus, who spent all his

TITYRUS

time indoors. The word came to mean a lurker in doorways, and during the Restoration a tityre-tu was one of a gang of brawling bucks in London. If a mugger lunges at you, address him politely as "Mr. Tityrus."

HORATIAN

The odes of Horace (65–8 B.C.) were so remarkable for their urbanity, form, and fitness that horatian has become synonymous with "elegant."

MAECENAS

Maecenas (c. 70–8 B.C.) was so loyal a friend to the poets Horace and Vergil, and so generous in his support of them, that his name has become a term of praise for any liberal patron of literature or the arts, or indeed any patron at all.

ANECDOTE

In the 6th century A.D., Procopius wrote *Anekdota*, from a Greek word meaning "unpublished." The title returned to the vernacular meaning a short account of some interesting or humorous incident. An anecdote also means "hitherto undivulged particulars of history or biography."

GALAHAD

At about the time of Procopius, there lived in the British Isles a shadowy hero-king named Arthur. First mentioned in English literature by Geoffrey of Monmouth about 1148, his story was given permanent shape in Malory's *Morte d'Arthur*, about 1470. One of his Knights of the Round Table, Launcelot, might have become an everyday word signifying chivalry and bravery but for his adulterous affair with Guinevere, Arthur's queen. Launcelot, however, did sire a son, Galahad, a knight so pure and noble that his name is vernacular for any young man particularly pure in heart.

PAMPHLETS

A Latin poem of the 12th century, *Pamphilus, or Concerning Love*, drew so deft and devastating a picture of Pamphilus ("all-loving"), an old whoremonger, that the popularity of the poem continued unabated for hundreds of years. With the advent of printing, it was issued for greater convenience in booklet form. Such booklets are pamphlets.

ROMANCE

ROMAINE LETTUCE
ROAM
ROME

The word romance, "made in the Roman manner," is now applied to books about fictional love affairs, as well as to stories about love affairs that are not fictional. The first romances described in prose or verse the adventures of chivalric heroes. Romaine lettuce is named for Rome; so is rum. Old French *romier*, "pilgrim to Rome," may be the source of roam, "to wander." In Elizabethan slang, rome was anything particularly large or great.

123   ALWAYS SCRIBBLE, SCRIBBLE, SCRIBBLE

The Italian poet Dante Alighieri (1265–1321) is author of the *Divina Commedia*, consisting of the *Inferno*, the *Purgatorio*, and the *Paradiso*. It was written in terza rima, lines of eleven syllables arranged in groups of three and rhyming a-b-a, b-c-b, c-d-c. A present-day example of the form:

Behold my Editor, whose roweled pen
Tames my Bucephalus, my Gift of Gab!
Turns wheeling eagle into barnyard hen,
And Amaryllis into Biddy Drab!
But I forget—she'll edit this complaint.
No sweat—she'll know I do but write in jest.
She deals in miracles; the girl's a saint—
A paragon, a trump, a brick, the best!
(You may think I am foolish, but I ain't.)

DANTESQUE

Dante's work was so graphic, intense, and rich in allegorical significance that dantesque became the highest praise to be bestowed on poetry of exalted, visionary style. Since the *Inferno* is the best known of the three books, dantesque is also used as a synonym for "hellish."

BEATRICE
LAURA

Beatrice, Dante's unattainable beloved, is represented in the *Divine Comedy* as conducting him through Paradise. The guide and inspiration of a lovesick artist is often referred to as a beatrice—unless she is a laura, after the Laura who inspired the sonnet sequence in celebration of an unattainable mistress by Petrarch (Francesco Petrarca; 1304–1374). Strictly, Beatrice and Laura are Patient Griseldas rather than uncommon, improper nouns.

LIMBO

The limb of a planet, from Latin *limbus*, "border," is the very edge between visibility and invisibility. The same root yields Dante's Limbo, a specific place on the borders of hell, eternal home of the "praiseless and blameless dead," including Old Testament saints. Unbaptized babes were supposed to dwell eternally in Limbo. Today the word means any place or condition of neglect or oblivion.

ALEXANDRINE

The alexandrine, a verse form with lines of twelve syllables, became popular in 12th-century France to embroider the exploits of Alexander the Great. Pierre de Ronsard (1524–1585), "prince of poets," gave the form its vogue. It is little used in English, the problem being, says Britannica, "that in attempting to give dignity to his line, the poet may only produce heaviness, incurring the criticism of Pope:

A needless alexandrine ends the song,
That, like a wounded snake, drags its slow length along.

CURRY FAVOR

In a French satirical poem of the 14th century, the *Roman de Favel*, all classes of society soothed and lovingly tended a yellow or chestnut horse named Favel to gain the goodwill of his master, who happened to be king. To "curry Favel" was thus to seek advancement by ingratiating oneself with the powerful. Across the Channel, the English soon hobson-jobsoned curry Favel into curry favor.

CHAUCERIAN

Geoffrey Chaucer (c. 1343–1400) is noted for his humor, his realism, his psychological insight, the accuracy of his observation, and the technical excellence of his style. Abundant, worldly narratives of human social life are styled chaucerian.

TERMAGANT

HAM

Termagant was believed by Christians to be a Mohammedan deity. He was depicted in morality tales, farces, and puppet shows of the 14th and 15th centuries as vociferous and tumultuous; Hamlet says of a player visiting court, "I would have such a fellow whipped for o'erdoing Termagant." The deity managed eventually, goodness knows how, to change his sex; the termagant of the 1970s is "a boisterous, brawling, turbulent woman; a virago." Shakespeare's critic of overacting became a word for an overactor: from Hamlet comes ham.

SKIRMISH

Soon afterward came Scaramouche, a creature of Italy's commedia dell'arte. Brown describes him as a "boastful poltroon . . . a person always threatening to, or beginning to, fight but never going on with the job." The English applied the name to minor encounters in war between small bodies of troops, and by extension to preliminary conflicts or disputes of any sort. To skirmish is to scaramouche—which is as it should be, since *scaramuccia* was Italian for "skirmish" in the first place.

RODOMONTADE

Italy is also the source of that great drumrattle of a word, rodomontade. In Boiardo's *Orlando Innamorato* (1487) and Ariosto's sequel, *Orlando Furioso* (1532), Rodomont is a Saracen king who besieges Charlemagne in Paris. He is depicted as a braggart, but a brave and fierce warrior. The bravery has been forgotten; his name stands for "vain boasting; empty bluster."

An anti-hero in *Orlando* is Philander ("lover-man"), Dutch knight of the roving eye. He trifles scandalously with Gabrina, a married woman. Though a Philander had already been the lover of Phillis in an earlier ballad, and another was to flirt with Erota in John Fletcher's *Laws of Candy* (1647), it was Orlando who made philander a verb meaning "to trifle amorously." To turn the verb back into a noun, one adds -er: philanderer.

In 1516 a book appeared describing an imaginary island whose inhabitants enjoyed near-perfection in their customs, politics, and laws. Sir Thomas More called the island Utopia, a Greek combining form meaning "nowhere." (Dystopia, by contrast, is an imaginary place or condition in which everything is as bad as possible.) To say a person is a utopian is to imply that his idealism includes a preponderant admixture of the visionary. (The title of Samuel Butler's novel *Erewhon* [1872], a satire on utopian concepts, is "nowhere" all but spelled backward.)

UTOPIA
UTOPIAN

Early in the 16th century, a brilliant Italian physician, Girolamo Fracastoro, concluded that venereal disease was transmitted through the passage of minute bodies, capable of self-multiplication from the infector to the infected. In 1530 he published a widely read medical poem, *Syphilis sive morbus gallicus* — "Syphilis, or the French Disease." (It is an old habit of one nation, when it finds something offensive, to blame it on another; the British still refer to syphilis as "the French welcome.") Syphilis probably derives from Greek *suphilos*, "lover of pigs," and means swineherd. In the poem, says Hendrickson, Syphilis was a shepherd whose blasphemies prompted the sun-god, Apollo, to afflict him:

SYPHILIS

> *He first wore buboes dreadful to the sight,*
> *First felt strange pains and sleepless past the night;*
> *From him the malady received its name.*

In France, meanwhile, François Rabelais (1494?–1553) was swinging at accepted values with so indiscriminate a broadsword that rabelaisian assumed a permanent place in the language for anything "boisterously satirical; grotesque, extravagant, and licentious in language." One of his creations was Gargantua (from the Spanish for "gullet"), a giant famous for his great appetite; in his infancy, 17,913 cows were needed to supply him with milk. Gargantuan has come to mean enormous, inordinate, great beyond all limits.

RABELAISIAN

GARGANTUAN

Gargantua was tiny compared with his son Pantagruel — from a combined Greek and Arabic word meaning "thirsty," because he was born during a drought which lasted thirty-six months, three weeks, four days, thirteen hours, and a few minutes more. The year of his birth was noted for having three Thursdays in one week. Pantagruel, last of the giants, was so enormous that his tongue alone formed a shelter for a whole army:

> Then did they put themselves in close order, and stood as near to each other as they could, and Pantagruel put out his tongue half-way, and covered them all, as a hen doth her chickens.

PANTAGRUELISM Pantagruelism is coarse and boisterous buffoonery.

Voltaire (1694–1778) created the incurably innocent Candide, who bore every ill with philosophical indifference before finally discovering life's secret: *Il faut cultiver notre jardin*. His tutor, the philosophic Dr. Pangloss, insisted despite the most blatant evidence to the contrary that "all is for the best in the best PANGLOSSIAN of all possible worlds," so giving us panglossian for incurable optimism and ability to explain facts away. Candide's sweetheart, Cunegonde, stayed pure in heart while relishing rapes by entire regiments of soldiers. Though particularly common clay, to my knowledge she has never appeared as a common noun.

In 1555, one Nostradamus, a French physician and astrologer who had made several startlingly correct predictions at court, published a set of rhymed prophecies still awaiting their NOSTRADAMUS final proof. A nostradamus is a soothsayer.

RIBALD Ribald, "obscene or coarsely offensive," has been connected with Jean Ribaut (1520–1565), who laid claim to the territory of Florida for France and wrote an account of his expedition there. But his account was not ribald, and the etymology appears doubtful; Old High German *Hriba*, "prostitute," is probably the origin.

In John Lylie's *Euphues: The Anatomy of Wit* (1578), followed in 1580 by *Euphues and His England*, the title character's comments about the world around him are so highly exaggerated in form and substance and so overloaded with alliteration that we EUPHUISM now call any affectation of speech a euphuism. Gongorism, with GONGORISM a similar meaning, derives from the Spanish poet Luis de Gongora y Argote (1561–1627).

BRAGGADOCIO Braggadocio, who appears in Spenser's *Faerie Queene* (1590), is as great a boaster as Rodomont or Thraso, without their redeeming courage. The root of the word goes back to Middle English. In *Jack Brag* (1837), a novel by Theodore Hook, the eponymous hero is a vulgar pretender who seeks to creep into aristocratic society by lying about his antecedents and accomplishments.

The beaten-gold doors of the 17th century swung open. Cervantes and Shakespeare emerged.

In Spain, Cervantes's Don Quixote tilted at windmills to personify immortally the visionary and impracticable—the quixotic (*Quixote* in Spanish means "thighbone." The last name of Sancho Panza, the dolorous knight's shrewd yet credulous squire, means "paunch.") Rosinante, the rack of bones on which Quixote bounced and from which he frequently fell, nowadays represents any ancient nag. Dulcinea, Don Quixote's name for the mistress of his knightly dreams, has become generic for "sweetheart."

QUIXOTIC
SANCHO PANZA
ROSINANTE

DULCINEA

In England, Shakespeare thronged the boards with heroes and villains larger than life: Hamlet, the epitome of tragic indecision; Shylock, the merciless creditor who could still cry, "My daughter! O my ducats! O my daughter!"; Benedick, so reluctant a lover that bachelors roped kicking into marriage have been known as benedicks ever since; Falstaff, the embodiment of self-indulgence, bragging, good humor, fatness. And so on and on.

HAMLET
SHYLOCK
BENEDICK
FALSTAFF

Lesser authors, too, created characters who moved from printed pages into the hearts and onto the tongues of hoi polloi.

In 1610, Honoré D'Urfé created in his play *Astrée* a wan lover named Celadon. In despair at Astrée's jealousy, Celadon tries twice to commit suicide before being reconciled to his love. In a poem by James Thomson (1700–1748), a lover of the same name has even worse luck; his sweetheart, Amelia, is killed by lightning in his very arms. Not surprisingly, both Celadons grew wan, and celadon is literary for any wan lover. The French variety is courtly, and the English rustic. Celadon is also a muted greenish color, and a pale green or sea-green porcelain from China.

CELADON

In the Beaumont and Fletcher play *The Scornful Lady* (1613), one Abigail was so quintessential a lady's maid that ladies' maids have been abigails ever since. Beaumont and Fletcher perhaps borrowed the name from the Abigail in the Old Testament who was the wife of Nabal, a churlish fellow whom David had marked for destruction (1 Samuel 25). Abigail intercepted David, fell on her face before him, and offered him . . . well, it was a generous offer, hard to resist. David exclaimed, "Except thou hadst hasted and come to meet me, surely there had not been left unto Nabal by the morning light any that pisseth against the wall." Soon afterward Nabal conveniently died, and David lost no time marrying Abigail.

ABIGAIL

TARTUFFE

Tartuffe, the title and leading character of a play by the French dramatist Molière (1622–1673), is a hypocritically religious devotee who swindles his benefactor and seeks to seduce his benefactor's wife. A tartuffe is any hypocrite, but especially one who affects religious piety.

PANDEMONIUM

The capital of Hell and the site of Satan's palace in *Paradise Lost* (1667), by John Milton (1608–1674), was Pandemonium, coined from Greek *pan*, "all," and *daimon*, "demon": "Pandemonium, city and proud seat / Of Lucifer." Pandemonium is generic for "any wild uproar or infernal noise; a wildly lawless or riotous place."

LOTHARIO

In 1703, Nicholas Rowe (1674–1718) produced at Lincoln's Inn the tragedy *The Fair Penitent*, featuring a lover of women, Lothario. Lothario's name now typifies either a "heartless libertine" (per OED) or a "gay seducer" (per Webster). Apparently the jury is still out on whether seduction is a sin or a peccadillo.

BONIFACE

Pope Boniface VI, who reigned for fifteen days in 896, is alleged to have promised an unspecified indulgence for anyone who would drink his health. This may be why in his play *The Beaux' Stratagem* (1707), George Farquhar called an innkeeper Boniface, Latin for "do-good." The name took root; an innkeeper is now a boniface. Among the characters in *The Beaux' Stratagem*:

> Sullen's a sorehead, and Scrub does the hall;
> Aimwell and Archer throw darts at the wall;
> Gibbet's a highwayman; Bagshot's the same;
> Cherry's been plucked, and requires a new name.

LADY BOUNTIFUL

Another proverbial character from *The Beaux' Stratagem* is Lady Bountiful, who cures all her neighbors of their distempers and spends half her income in charity. A wealthy, generous, but perhaps overbearing woman is a lady bountiful.

MARPLOT

In *The Busy Body* (1709), Susannah Centlivre created a stupid and officious meddler, Marplot, whose interference compromised any undertaking. We still call meddlers marplots. In *A Bold Stroke for a Wife*, presented eight years later, she gave her audiences an indomitable Pennsylvania Quaker who beat back villainy to prove his right to his own name, Simon Pure.

SIMON-PURE
THE REAL M'COY

Ever since, anything simon-pure has been the real article, beyond dispute. (The McCoy of "the real McCoy," by the way, was a boxer named Norman Selby [1873–1940], whose fighting name was Kid McCoy.)

Jonathan Swift published *Gulliver's Travels* in 1726. Gulliver encountered, among others, the Lilliputians, six inches high, and the Brobdignagians, as tall as steeples. Hence lilliputian for "tiny" and brobdignagian for "gigantic." He also fell in with the Yahoos, a filthy race subject to the Houyhnhnms, horses endowed with reason. A lout or a bumpkin is a yahoo. The name may have been taken from the Yahoos, an Indian tribe at the border between Brazil and French Guiana. Swiftian literature (after Jonathan Swift) is savagely mocking.

Namby-pamby, applied to verse, means "insipid; weakly sentimental." It was a nickname bestowed on the poet Ambrose Philips (1674–1749) by Henry Carey, the dramatist. Alexander Pope agreed that the name fitted Philips's "eminence in infantile style."

Robinson Crusoe, by Daniel Defoe (1660?–1731), appeared in 1719. Stranded on a desolate island, Crusoe was lucky enough to be joined as a castaway by a black man whom he named Friday, that being the day they met. Friday turned out to be a cheerful,

hardworking helper, and such a companion is called a man Friday to this day. A girl Friday is a young female acting as a general helper, doing whatever has to be done.

Speaking of days of the week, Qwassi (from *Kwasi*, "Sunday," in the Ashanti and Fanti tongues of West Africa) was a term applied to Negro Christians by the tribes, on account of the day on which they worshiped. One Graman Quassi in 1730 discovered the usefulness of the root of a certain tree as a bitter tonic and as a remedy for threadworm. The tree was named quassia in his honor.

Casanova (1725–1798), an Italian adventurer and rake, wrote toward the end of his life memoirs describing his rogueries, adventures, and amours in most of the countries of Europe. A casanova is a promiscuous, irresistible man; a libertine. Casanova appears, however, to have been a likable sort, meaning no harm to anyone; he simply loved women. I considered him in a clerihew:

> *As Casanova*
> *Marveled over*
> *Each new breast,*
> *He cried, "You're the best!"*

Don Juan, supposed to have been the son of a leading family of Seville in the 14th century, killed the commandant of Ulloa after seducing his daughter. "To put an end to his debaucheries," says Benét, "the Franciscan monks enticed him to their monastery and killed him, telling the people that he had been carried off to hell by the statue of the Commandant, which was in the grounds." It is told similarly of Romulus that the Roman senate murdered him and sneaked his dismembered parts out under their togas, saying he had been carried up to heaven. In Mozart's opera *Don Giovanni* (1787), Don Juan's valet says his master has "in Italy 700 mistresses, in Germany 800, in Turkey and France 91, in Spain 1,003." A don juan is more twisted in his sexual drives than a casanova:

> At college, Don Juan
> Carried on
> Till they changed his major from Biology
> To Abnormal Psychology.

Music and morality are beguilingly intermingled in this *World Book Encyclopedia* synopsis of *Don Giovanni*:

> The handsome Giovanni (baritone) has broken the heart of countless girls. As the opera opens, he breaks the heart of Donna Anna (soprano) and then kills her father Don Pedro (bass) in a duel. Only Donna Elvira (soprano), whom he deserted during a previous elopement, remains true to him . . .

No contraltos . . .

The title of the provincial governors of Mogul India was from the Arabic nuwāb, "deputies," a plural applied to each governor to emphasize his importance. Asimov reminds us that these governors "used their power to grow rich indeed." As the British East India Company infiltrated India, its officials, enriching themselves in their turn, came to be styled "nabob" after their predecessors. The name became familiar to the British public with the success in 1772 of *The Nabob,* a play by Samuel Foote (1720–1777). (A later novel by Alphonse Daudet had the same title.) Foote's play satirized the corruption and stolen wealth of the East India Company so effectively, says Asimov, that "a common word in India became a proper name in England in order to become common again." A man of wealth and prominence is a nabob.

In 1742, Henry Fielding (1707–1754) published the novel *Joseph Andrews*, featuring one Parson Trulliber. Trulliber was a fat clergyman, ignorant, selfish, and slothful. He has become a byword for a coarse person who does not do his job.

DON JUAN

NABOB

PARSON TRUL-
LIBER

GRANDISON   If you are a grandison, you are a perfect gentleman, so full of virtues as to be supremely dull. You take your name from the title character of *Sir Charles Grandison* (1753), by Samuel Richardson (1689–1761).

BOSWELL
BOSWELLIZE   Boswell's biography of Samuel Johnson appeared in 1791. Ever since, a boswell has been an intimate, entertaining, undiscriminating biographer. To boswellize is to write a hero-worshiping biography.

SERENDIPITY   In 1754, Horace Walpole (1717–1797) wrote a friend that he had coined a new word, "serendipity," based on the title of the fairy tale *The Three Princes of Serendip* (as Mohammedan traders called Ceylon). The princes repeatedly discovered, by chance or sagacity, rewards they were not seeking. Serendipity is the gift of finding valuable or agreeable things not sought for.

SHANDY   To shandy is to digress, as did Laurence Sterne (1713–1768) in his novel *The Life and Opinions of Tristram Shandy, Gentleman*, which appeared in several installments in the 1760s. Sterne shandied so continuously that it took three volumes to get the hero born, after which the author found time to write his preface.

MALAPROPISM   Until 1775, *mal à propos* was simply a French expression meaning "unseasonable" or "inopportune." That year, in a play called *The Rivals*, Richard Brinsley Sheridan (1751–1816) introduced a personality named Mrs. Malaprop. She distinguished herself through such verbal blunders as "a progeny of learning" and "illiterate him quite from your mind." Any grotesque misuse of a word is a malapropism. "I was so hungry I gouged myself," remarked a young lady of my acquaintance. Said my handyman, "I don't like him and he don't like me, so it's neutral." He also commented, "You can't stop a dog from barking, it's only human nature."

STURM UND
DRANG   A German phrase commonly used in English is *Sturm und Drang,* literally "storm and stress." It comes from the title of a play by F. M. Klinger presented in 1776.

MÜNCHAUS-
ENISM
MÜNCHAUS-
ENIZE   A münchausenism is a lie so outrageous as to be comical. The improbable travels of Baron Münchausen were the subject of a book published by Rudolf Raspe in 1785. To münchausenize is to tell a whopping untruth.

MRS. GRUNDY   A character in Thomas Morton's comedy *Speed the Plough* (1798), Mrs. Grundy, has become proverbial for a narrow-minded bigot. When anyone in the play was contemplating some mildly unconventional action, the question would arise, "What will Mrs. Grundy say?"

DIDDLE

In 1803 the English dramatist James Kenney (1780–1849) presented a farce called *Raising the Wind*. The principal character, Jeremy Diddler, continually borrows small sums which he never repays. His sponging is memorialized in the verb diddle, "to cheat or victimize."

COLLINS

In England, a collins is a bread-and-butter letter written to one's hosts as a courtesy after a visit. The name is from Mr. Collins, in Jane Austen's *Pride and Prejudice* (1813). He was a self-important toadying clergyman whose thank-you letters were particularly effusive.

GANDERCLEUGH

In *Tales of My Landlord* (1817), by Sir Walter Scott (1771–1832), Gandercleugh was the home of the hypothetical editor of the book. A gandercleugh ("folly-cliff") is that mysterious place where a man makes a goose of himself.

FRANKENSTEIN

Mary Shelley (1797–1851), and her husband, the poet Percy Bysshe Shelley, spent the summer of 1817 with Lord Byron in Switzerland. It was unseasonably wet, and they passed much of their time indoors, amusing themselves by reading, writing, and telling ghost stories. Mary Shelley's contribution, developed into a long story at her husband's suggestion, was *Frankenstein*, published the following year. Frankenstein, a student of natural philosophy, learns the secrets of imparting life to inanimate matter. He constructs the semblance of a human being and gives it life, with dreadful results. A "frankenstein monster" is popular usage for something that destroys its creator. Frequently the phrase shrinks to "a frankenstein."

BYRONIC

In poetry, the early 19th century was known as the Byronic era, Byronic (often lowercased) meaning world-weary and contemptuous. Byronic rather than Keatsian, or Shelleyan, or Wordsworthian—perhaps because Byron was the most dramatic and colorful, if by no means the best, of the poets of the period.

TOM AND JERRY

Corinthian Tom, who takes his name from the reputation of Corinth in the ancient world as a pleasure city, and his friend Jerry Hawthorne were a pair of rakes and sporting men in Pierce Egan's 1821 novel *Tom and Jerry, or Life in London*. Their first names linger in a hot intoxicating drink, the tom and jerry. (In a once-popular animated cartoon, Tom and Jerry are a quarreling cat and mouse.)

ROORBACK   A roorback—a false or scandalous story used for political advantage—perpetuates Baron von Roorback, fictional author of *Roorback's Tour Through the Western and Southern States in 1836*. A passage from the book was quoted before the election of 1844 in an effort to disparage candidate James K. Polk.

BAEDEKER   The first baedeker, now synonymous for a tourist's guidebook, was developed in Germany by Karl Baedeker (1801–1859). Hitler is said to have ordered that all the officers of his invading armies be equipped with baedekers.

TAUCHNITZ   The tauchnitz, a paper-back reprint of books in English, was issued beginning in 1841 by the Tauchnitz publishing firm in Leipzig. In Paris, in 1931, I first read *Lady Chatterley's Lover*, banned in the United States, in a Tauchnitz edition. I lacked courage to try to smuggle it past the customs officer when I came home, though bowdlerized versions were available in the United States even then.

BOWDLERIZE   Word-mincing was developed to a high art by Dr. Thomas Bowdler (1754–1825), an English gentleman who undertook to exorcise from literature any reference that might "raise a blush on the cheek of modesty." The technique of bowdlerizing is well illustrated in his *Family Shakespeare* (1807), where he turns Lady Macbeth's haunted cry, "Out, damn'd spot!" to "Out, crimson spot!" Some say his sister did most of the bowdlerizing; many a reference must have raised a blush on her modest cheek. Chaucer and Mark Twain are two notable victims of bowdlerizing. One editor even dropped the reference to Queequeg's underwear in Melville's *Moby Dick*.

This quatrain by Matthew Prior (1664–1721) has been cited as impossible to bowdlerize:

> *No, no; for my Virginity,*
> *When I lose that, says Rose, I'll die;*
> *Behind the elms, last Night, cry'd Dick,*
> *Rose, were you not extremely sick?*

GRANGERIZE   A somewhat different offense against the muse was committed by the Reverend James Granger (1723–1776), who illustrated his *Biographical History of England* (1769) with engravings taken from other books. To cannibalize in such a manner is to grangerize.

COMSTOCKERY Comstockery, though the word was coined by George Bernard Shaw only in 1905, has found a permanent place in the language as a synonym for blue-nosed censorship. The reference is to Anthony Comstock (1844–1915), moving spirit of the New York Society for the Suppression of Vice, which advocated the banning of all literature deemed to be salacious or corrupting.

PAUL PRY An inquisitive busybody is considered a Paul Pry, from John Poole's 1825 farce of that name. The titular character was a prying journalist.

COUNT OF MONTE CRISTO A Count of Monte Cristo is someone enigmatic, and fabulously rich. The allusion is to Edmond Dantès, hero of *The Count of Monte Cristo* (1844), a romance by Alexandre Dumas (1802–1870). Imprisoned on a false charge, Dantès learns from a fellow prisoner where an immense treasure is hidden. He escapes, acquires the treasure, and uses it to exact a fearful revenge from those who have wronged him.

TADPOLE AND TAPER Tadpole and Taper were characters who sidled through two novels—*Coningsby* (1844) and *Sybil* (1845) by Benjamin Disraeli (1804–1881), later to become Prime Minister of England. Today, tadpole and taper are bywords for political hacks.

CAUDLE LECTURE A caudle lecture is a querulous, lengthy reproach of a husband by his wife after they have retired for the night. The expression was coined by Douglas W. Jerrold, who in 1845 and 1846 contributed to *Punch* a popular feature called *Mrs. Caudle's Curtain Lectures*. The lectures, addressed to Mr. Caudle as he tries to sleep, are reproofs for his mildly convivial habits, exhortations to take the family to the seaside, or disquisitions on similar domestic subjects.

BOX AND COX To play box and cox is to alternate privileges—as if, say, one were to entertain two lovers in turn, neither knowing of the other's existence. The usage arises from the one-act farce *Box and Cox* (1847), by John Maddison Morton (1811–1891). Mrs. Bouncer, a lodging-house keeper, lets her room to Box, a journeyman printer out all night, and Cox, a journeyman hatter out all day. The arrangement is upset when one arrives home out of turn.

Bohemia, like Egypt before it, was once mistakenly considered to be the starting point of the Gypsy tribes that roamed through western Europe as early as the 15th century. Bohemian

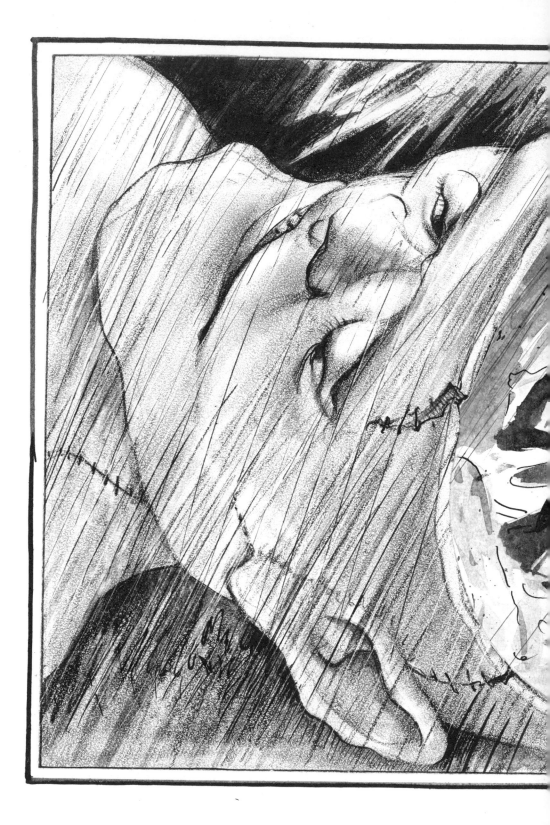

FRANKENSTEIN'S MONSTER

became synonymous with rootless. William Makepeace Thackeray (1811–1863) extended the word when he called Becky Sharp in *Vanity Fair* (1847–48) a "Bohemian by taste and circumstances . . . of a wild, roving nature." The next year Henry Murger (1822–1861) published a popular series of stories called *Scènes de la Vie Bohème,* describing the lives of impoverished artists and writers. Bohemian is now an established epithet for a poor artist or writer who lives in an unconventional manner.

BOHEMIAN

During this period Charles Dickens was injecting scores of characters into the veins of the vernacular. He gave us Mr. Pickwick and his club, in which pickwickian remarks were esoteric, not to be taken seriously. He gave us Mr. Micawber; a micawberish person "remains doggedly optimistic, despite constant adversity, about an inevitable change for the better." (Harold Wilson called Harold Macmillan, his predecessor as British Prime Minister, "an inverted Micawber waiting for something [the visibly overheating economy] to turn down.") He gave us Mr. Pecksniff; pecksniffian means "characterized by hypocrisy or unctuous insincerity." A wellerism, a saying or action of loyalty and cockney-like shrewdness, recalls Mr. Pickwick's man Sam Weller. A Bumble is a malignly pompous minor official, from Mr. Bumble, the overbearing beadle in *Oliver Twist.* A fagin, from the thief-trainer in the same novel, is a keeper of a thieves' kitchen and a receiver of stolen goods. Bill Sikes, who took more while Oliver only asked for more, has come to stand for any professional burglar. Scrooge was the curmudgeon in *A Christmas Carol*; despite Scrooge's reform, a scrooge remains a curmudgeon today. Uriah Heep, in *David Copperfield*, epitomizes a sanctimonious hypocrite, full of sharp practices. Dickens himself has entered the vernacular; dickensian is common usage for "grotesque, larger-than-life, as if caricatured by Dickens." Other Dickens bywords:

PICKWICKIAN

MICAWBERISH

PECKSNIFFIAN
WELLERISM

BUMBLE

FAGIN
BILL SIKES

SCROOGE
URIAH HEEP

DICKENSIAN

GRADGRIND

A gradgrind is a person who measures everything by rule and compass, allowing nothing for human nature. From Thomas Gradgrind, in *Hard Times.*

SPENLOW AND JORKINS

Spenlow and Jorkins are a pair, the invisible one carrying the blame for the other's decisions, after the partners in a *David Copperfield* law firm.

PODSNAPPERY

PRUDHOMMERIE

Podsnappery is self-satisfied philistinism, exemplified by Podsnap in *Our Mutual Friend.* He bears a resemblance to Joseph Prudhomme, of *Les Mémoires de Monsieur Joseph Prudhomme*

(1857), by Henri Monnier. Podsnappery in France is *prudhommerie*.

TWANKY

Twanky, or twankay, is a barely surviving Victorian term: first for China tea, often imported from Twankai, and later for tea in general. ("We'll have a pot of Twankay," says Thackeray.) British pantomime imports into the story of Aladdin a widow Twanky—"the pantomime English," says Brown, "for a tea-swilling old woman."

BOVARISM

Madame Bovary (1857), by Gustave Flaubert (1821–1880), tells in grim detail the inexorable degeneration of the title character. She has lover after lover, piles up enormous debts, and finally commits suicide. One of the first novels of the realistic school, and considered one of the masterpieces of 19th-century literature, it gave rise to the term bovarism for "the power granted to man to see himself as other than he is; that is, to establish an assumed persona, as did Madame Bovary." Aldous Huxley remarks that "people have bovarized themselves into the likeness of every kind of real or imaginary being."

UNCLE TOM

SIMON LEGREE

TOPSY

TO GROW
LIKE TOPSY

In 1852 bookstands began carrying a novel by Harriet Beecher Stowe (1811–1896) called *Uncle Tom's Cabin*. Uncle Tom was an idealized, elderly black, pious, faithful, brave toward his oppressors. The term is often lowercased today for a black held to be humiliatingly subservient to whites. Billie Holliday said of Satchmo Armstrong, the black trumpet player, "Satchmo toms, but he toms from the heart." A Simon Legree, from the name of the brutal slave dealer in the book, is a cruel taskmaster. A topsy, symbol of that which originates spontaneously and develops aimlessly, is from the young slave girl whose ignorance and unconscious humor provide comic relief to the book. Asked about her origin, Topsy says, "I spect I growed." "To grow like Topsy," unattended, has become a byword.

JOHN ALDEN

A John Alden is one who woos a maid for another, only to find himself the object of her affection. Longfellow made the theme popular in his *Courtship of Miles Standish* (1858); Alden relays Standish's proposal of marriage to Priscilla, who replies, "Why don't you speak for yourself, John?"

ENOCH ARDEN

In 1864 Alfred Tennyson wrote the narrative poem *Enoch Arden*, about a seaman who after being long shipwrecked on a desert island returns home, learns his wife is happily and prosperously remarried, departs without making himself known, and dies of a broken heart. An Enoch Arden is that rare creature who truly loves someone else better than himself.

HORATIO ALGER In the second half of the 19th century, Horatio Alger (1834–1899) wrote innumerable books for boys, built around the formula of a poor but worthy hero who inevitably, as Benét puts it, "surmounts impossible obstacles, and achieves the heights of success." A Horatio Alger hero moves from rags to riches through sheer grit and determination (though serendipity is involved; not every bootblack has the chance to stop a runaway horse, thus saving the life of the daughter of the richest man in town, thus winning the undying gratitude of the richest man in town, thus assuring that the bootblack ultimately will become the richest man in town).

POOHBAH A politician who holds many offices is a poohbah. The name is straight out of Gilbert and Sullivan's light opera *The Mikado* (1885), in which one Pooh-Bah is "Lord High Everything Else."

JEKYLL AND HYDE A Jekyll and Hyde is a person who is alternately completely good and completely evil. In Robert Louis Stevenson's *The Strange Case of Dr. Jekyll and Mr. Hyde* (1886), the gentle and proper Dr. Jekyll discovers a potion by means of which he can change himself into the monstrous Mr. Hyde and back again. He is ultimately trapped in the Hyde personality.

LITTLE LORD FAUNTLEROY A Little Lord Fauntleroy is a spoiled or effeminate small boy, too good to be true. The seven-year-old hero of the 1886 book of that name by Frances Hodgson Burnett (1849–1924) becomes heir to an earldom on the death of his father, disinherited for marrying an American. The boy, living in poverty with his mother in New York, is called back to England by his grandfather and wins the hearts of all his relatives there for both himself and her.

DORIAN GRAY In 1891 Oscar Wilde (1854–1900) wrote *The Picture of Dorian Gray*, an allegory about the title character, who remains youthful while his portrait, reflecting his evil life, grows old and hideous. A dorian gray is a person whose countenance remains fair and innocent despite his villainy. Journalist Henry Fairlie said of the English politican Hugh Gaitskell, leader of the Labor Party from 1955 to 1963, that he had a portrait upstairs that grew more youthful and wholesome as Gaitskell's face became more sinister and dishonest.

SVENGALI *Trilby*, a novel published in 1894 by George Du Maurier (1834–1896), features as villain a musical genius named Svengali, who hypnotizes the heroine into becoming a great singer. If you exercise a mysterious control over other people, you are a svengali.

WELLSIAN   H. G. Wells (1866–1946) spun early science fiction. Futuristic writing is frequently called wellsian.

ORWELLIAN   Orwellian refers to the style and pessimistic social views of George Orwell (1903–1950), author of *1984*. Orwell is a pen name taken from the peaceful River Orwell. The author's real name was Eric Blair; to me, blairian suits his skeptical spirit better than orwellian does.

Cartoons can be great art. Perhaps they are also a form of literature. "Literature for the illiterate," I once called them to Charles Addams, master of monster cartoons; but I was not serious. If I could evoke in a sentence what Charles Addams evokes in a cartoon, I would not fear mortality. When you refer

PALOOKA   to a slow-witted fellow, particularly a prizefighter, as a palooka, you are paying tribute to Joe Palooka, title character of a comic strip popularized by Jack Conway before World War II. I have referred elsewhere to the long-generic wimpy, and to a hawkshaw as a detective. Casper Milquetoast was the hero of H. T. Webster's cartoon series *The Timid Soul,* a favorite in the first half of this century. Milk toast is a bland dish of hot buttered toast in warm milk, often associated with frail persons. A

MILQUETOAST   milquetoast is a timid sort who habitually lets himself be pushed around.

By the opening of the 20th century, George Bernard Shaw (1856–1950) had become so widely known for his unorthodox

SHAVIAN   theories of social and political organization that the word shavian was invented to describe one espousing such heretical views.

It is too soon to predict which literary creations of the present century will continue to live as symbols of some human conceit. These, at least, have a chance:

In the first decade of the 20th century, George Barr McCutcheon wrote a series of hair-raising romances sited in Graustark, an imaginary petty kingdom of Europe. Something

GRAUSTARK   impossibly melodramatic is graustarkian.

POLLYANNA   A foolishly and sugarily optimistic person is forever a pollyanna, a sort of juvenile pangloss, after the title character of the 1913 novel by Eleanor Porter. Pollyanna saw the bright side of everything from a headache to a heart attack.

BABBITT   A babbitt is a member of the American middle class whose attachment to its less laudable ideals is such as to make of him a model of narrow-mindedness and self-satisfaction. The prototype is George F. Babbitt, main character in Sinclair Lewis's novel *Babbitt* (1922). His natural habitat is *Main Street*, title of another Lewis novel (1924), satirizing the middle class.

WALTER MITTY   Walter Mitty is the hero of a story by James Thurber (1894–1961). In his daydreams Walter Mitty might be anything from a war hero to a ladies' man, a racing car driver, or a martyr. Until we can all act out our fantasies, the Walter Mitty component in us will help to keep us sane.

HECHTASCAL-ANDER   I propose the word hechtascalander for a form of double-dactyl verse invented by poets Anthony Hecht, Paul Pascal, and John Hollander, all still living. The first line is a nonsensical double-dactyl. The second line names the subject; the sixth is a single double-dactyl word; and the fourth and eighth are the rhyme lines. This double-dactyl memorializes the inventors of the arrangement:

> *Tribble a scribble, a*
> *Hecht on you Hollander*
> *Pascal vobiscus you*
> *Lyrical three!*
>
> *Write me a poem in*
> *Proceleusmaticus;*
> *Then I'll concede you are*
> *Better than me.*

CLERIHEW   Edmund Clerihew Bentley (1875–1956), an English journalist, managed to implant his middle name firmly in the pantheon of word-makers by developing in the first half of the 20th century the clerihew—a humorous, unscanned quatrain about a person named in the first line. For example:

> *George the Third*
> *Ought never to have occurred.*
> *One can only wonder*
> *At so grotesque a blunder.*

And again:

> *The Art of Biography*
> *Is Different from Geography.*
> *Geography is about Maps,*
> *But Biography is about Chaps.*

It has been argued that the net effect of the invention of printing by Gutenberg half a millennium ago has been to hound literature to the borderline of illiteracy. This is a harsh charge, and I do not accept it. But it is undeniable that printing has resulted in a proliferation of typefaces named after persons or places, some lowercased, some not. I for one cannot tell most of them apart. A few of the type families:

Arabic	Corvinus	Hess
Baskerville	Custing	Janson
Bernhard	Eden	Lombardic
Bodoni	Egyptian	Scotch Roman
Bruce	Ethiopian	Spartan
Bulmer	German	Syriac
Caledonia	Grandon	Weiss
Caslon	Greek	
Coptic	Hebrew	

BEN DAY

Other printing processes, once capitalized, have become to all intents and purposes generic. One of these is ben day, a means of quick, mechanical production of stippling, shading, or tints on line engravings, eliminating the shading of a drawing by hand. It was developed about 1879 by Benjamin Day (1838–1916), a New York printer, grandfather of the writer Clarence Day.

Timothy and the Muse

Timothy thought I should have included Ultima Thule among my literary derivatives.

In the 4th century B.C. a Greek navigator named Pytheas visited an island in the northern seas—perhaps Shetland, coastal Norway, or even Iceland—which he called Thule. To the ancients, Thule, where the night and day were both six months ULTIMA THULE long, was the northernmost part of the inhabitable world. Ultima Thule, sometimes lowercased, stands for any mysterious distant region or remote goal.

"But it is *not* a literary derivative," I said.

"Polybius wrote an account of Pytheas's voyage," said Timothy. "Around 150 B.C."

"By that kind of reasoning," I said, "everything ever written would be eligible."

"Besides which," continued Timothy, unmoved, "Henry Handel Richardson wrote a book called *Ultima Thule*. In 1930. Last of a trilogy. You know Henry Handel Richardson?"

"Never heard of him."

"Her. An Australian. She was born Henrietta Richardson in 1880, her married name was Robinson, and she died in 1946."

I know when I am beaten. "All right," I said, making a note. "In goes Ultima Thule."

BAYARD "And where," he went on, "do you have bayard, for a person of singularly beautiful character? Seigneur de Bayard, 1475–1524. *Le chevalier sans peur et sans reproche*."

"Same objection," I said. "Not a literary figure."

"Sir Philip Sidney," Timothy continued as if I had not spoken, "was called the British bayard. Robert E. Lee was the bayard of the Confederate Army. *Mmm*. Pop-pop-pop. Did you know that the pronunciation and meter of Chaucer were distorted for three hundred years, until the 1760s? Thomas Tyrwhitt, the English classicist, pointed out that the final *e* in a Chaucerian word was meant to be sounded—a hangover from Norman French. Before Tyrwhitt, we pronounced 'When that Aprille with his shoures soote' as if it were written 'When that Aprill with his shoors soot.' Awful."

"Awful."

Timothy riffled through his notes. Then, bop-bopping, he began to pace the floor, his stick under his arm. I watched him with the kind of hypnotized attention a mouse must focus on the purposeful approach of a cat. "O-*kay*, Wede," he said at last. "Coming . . . *at* you."

There being no mousehole available, and Timothy being in fact a very gentle sort of cat, I readied my pencil and pad.

CYRANESQUE "Cyranesque for terribly romantic? After Cyrano de Bergerac. He did exist, you know—a 17th-century poet and atheist philosopher, contemporary with Molière. And he did have a very large nose, and fight duels. In Edmond Rostand's 1898 play about him, Cyrano wins Roxanne for his friend Christian by writing her eloquent letters in Christian's name, though Cyrano loves Roxanne himself.

"*Mmmm* . . . Yes yes yes. Good. *The Rivals*. You have Mrs.
BOB ACRES Malaprop; how about Bob Acres for a man who incites a confrontation but loses his nerve? Bob Acres found his courage

'oozing out of the palms of his hands' after he challenged his rival to a duel."

I said, "Yes yes yes. Good."

CALIBAN'S RAGE "Caliban's rage. Referred to by Oscar Wilde in *The Portrait of Dorian Gray*. Censuring our own faults in others. Shakespeare's monster Caliban fell into a rage on first seeing his own face in a glass."

"Excellent," I said.

DOGBERRY "Exactly. And you might mention dogberry for an officious, incompetent policeman. After Constable Dogberry in *Much Ado About Nothing*."

"I played Dogberry once at college. I shall test you, Timothy. I am Dogberry. You are the watch." I pointed an imperious finger:

" 'This is your charge: you shall comprehend all vagrom men; you are to bid any man stand, in the prince's name.' "

" 'How, if a' will not stand?' " replied Timothy.

" 'Why, then, take no note of him, but let him go; and presently call the rest of the watch together, and thank God you are rid of a knave.' "

" 'If he will not stand when he is bidden, he is none of the prince's subjects,' " said Timothy. He shook his head. "But it was not the watch who said that. It was Dogberry's partner, Verges."

"All right," I agreed, conceding defeat. "Next item, Timothy."

He refilled his teacup, mostly with sugar, and I poured myself another Scotch. He shuffled his notes.

TENNYSON BINDINGS "Oh, by the way. Tennyson bindings. For affectation of culture. A *nouveau-riche* matron was showing a friend of similar stripe her library, which had been stocked by interior decorators. 'And here,' she said, 'is my Tennyson.' 'No no, darling,' corrected her friend. 'Those are green. Tennyson is *blue*.'"

I smiled wanly.

OSSIANIC "Bop-bop-bop-bop," said Timothy. "Ossianic, meaning romantically epic? From Ossian, the legendary 3rd-century Gaelic bard. As in the Ossianic poems quasi-forged by James Macpherson in the 18th century. He was a learned Scot who enlarged fragments of ancient poems and stories into a romance of his own composition. At least so Samuel Johnson charged, adding, 'On whatever hypothesis, *Ossian* is the work of a Scotsman.' Malcolm Lain declared Macpherson had no ancient sources at all. In any event, he was a great romantic writer.

"Ah. Ibsenity? The magazine *Punch*'s notion of the doctrines of Ibsen, the Norwegian dramatist?"

I said, "You must watch those puns, Timothy."

"Dickensian villain. Richard Crossman, the British politician, said of his colleague Roy Hattersley, "Hattersley is a Dickensian villain, and like a Dickensian villain will be found out in the last chapter.""

Timothy paused, tapping his teeth with the butt of his pen. "Off our subject, I fear," he said, "but worth mentioning. Dead Sea fruit. Thomas Moore wrote in *Lalla Rookh*, 'Like Dead Sea fruits, that tempt the eye, / But turn to ashes on the lips.' Prime Minister Macmillan told Henry Fairlie, 'Power in politics is Dead Sea fruit, Fairlie! Dead Sea fruit!' "

"I'll find a place for it," I said.

SEVEN

THE GINGHAM DOG WENT BOW-WOW-WOW!

Disputed Words

AID EUGENE Field:

The gingham dog went bow-bow-wow!
And the calico cat replied, "Mee-ow!"
The air was littered, an hour or so,
With bits of linen and calico.

Eventually, as lovers of Eugene Field will recall, the dog and cat ate each other up.

Students of word origins, though less lethal in their disputes than the gingham dog and calico cat, do sometimes fill the air with bits of linen and calico.

BRONZE   Webster and AH say bronze derives from Italian *bronzo*, "perhaps of Persian origin." Weekley, however, credits Brindisi, formerly Brundisium, a seaport of southeastern Italy on the Adriatic Sea.

BUCKRAM   Britannica traces buckram to old French *boucaran*, a coarse cloth common in book binding, without mentioning, as do other authorities, that the cloth was originally from Bukhara, in the Uzbek S.S.R.

CORSAIR   I have heard Italians insist that Corsica, an island in the Mediterranean belonging to France, is responsible for the word corsair—meaning a privateer, formerly a Turk or Saracen of the Barbary Coast authorized by his government to harass the commerce of Christian nations. A more likely source is Medieval Latin *cursus*, "plunder," from Latin *currere*, "to run." (A scorpaenoid fish of the California coast and a reduviid predatory bug of the genus *Rasahus* are both called corsair. Mark this information down; it might come in handy.)

FRIEZE   A coarse, shaggy woolen cloth with an uncut nap is called a frieze. Weekley attributes the word to Friezland, a province of the Netherlands. Webster prefers French *friser*, "to curl." AH says frieze, the ornamental horizontal border, derives from Phrygia, an ancient country of Asia Minor noted for its embroidery.

GAGA   According to AH, gaga, a slang expression meaning "mentally unbalanced," mildly corrupts the same word in French, where it means a "foolish old man." Holt, however, connects the word with the French Impressionist painter Paul Gauguin (1848–1903). Some critics saw signs of mental unbalance in Gauguin's paintings, and the tongue slips easily from Gauguin to gaga. Webster avoids this argument by omitting gaga altogether.

GIBBERISH   Gibberish—"rapid, inarticulate, foolish talk"—probably corrupts the imitative "jabber." But Dr. Samuel Johnson, king of lexicographers (though occasionally he nodded on his throne: once he called an attic the highest room of a house, and the cockloft the room over the attic), attributed gibberish to Geber, the name of a legendary Arabian alchemist.

GRINGO   Gringo, the pejorative term applied by some Latin Americans to foreigners, is usually assumed to corrupt *griego*, Spanish for "Greek," as in "It's all Greek to me." But there are those who insist on locking the name into the Bobby Burns ballad "Green Grow the Rushes, O," reportedly sung by Yankee soldiers in the

Mexican War. Some say again that it refers to Major Samuel Ringgold, a gallant officer killed in that war. As it happens, the latter two attributions are impossible; the word is defined in its present sense in *Diccionario de Americanismos*, published in 1787.

POSH

Partridge gives short shrift to the superstition that posh is an acronym for "port out, starboard home," the preferred accommodations for British civil servants shuttling by steamer to and from British India. Rather, says Partridge, the word simply corrupts "polish." But it is not quite that simple. "Port out, starboard home" was a specific ticketing procedure for the passage to India in the days before air-conditioning. The passengers wished to be out of direct sunlight in both directions, and P.O.S.H. was stamped on their tickets. As so often happens, two etymological streams flowed together to make a linguistic river.

JOSH

The origin of josh, "to banter; to make fun of good-humoredly," bewilders etymologists. Suggestions range from joss, the plump Chinese divinity, to Joshua, who made the sun stand still. Holt remarks that out of local pride he would have attributed josh to the 19th-century American humorist Josh Billings (Henry W. Shaw), except that the word clearly predated the humorist. Color josh "origin unknown."

MASCOT

Holt appears to take pride in being odd man out in some of these etymological set-tos. As one example, most authorities attribute the word mascot (meaning a person, animal, or object believed to bring good luck) to French *mascotte*, "sorcery; talisman," perhaps with a bow to *masque* ("born with a caul and therefore lucky"). Holt, however, claims the word entered English by way of the opera *La Mascotte* in 1880.

MERINO

AH takes a minority position on the origin of merino, a hardy, gregarious breed of fine-wooled white sheep originating in Spain. While Skeat and Webster agree that the word is Spanish for "roving from pasture to pasture," and that a merino is likewise an inspector of sheep walks, AH credits the name to the Beni Merin, the tribe that developed the breed. This appears to be, if not a chicken-and-egg, in any event a sheep-and-shepherd argument.

MERRY-ANDREW

Most experts cite no origin for merry-andrew—"one who makes sport for others; a buffoon; a clown." But Thomas Hearne (1678–1735) declared that the first merry-andrew was one Andrew Boorde (c. 1490–1549), who to his vast learning added great whimsicality.

The name for a grayish-white metal, used principally in alloys, is nickel, from German *Kupfernickel (kupfer,* "copper," and *Nickel,* "demon.") Skeat says that the demon referred to by A. F. Cronstedt, the Swedish mineralogist who gave the metal its name in 1754, was not Old Nick, the devil, but Nix (or Nicorus), a mythological half-human, half-fish water sprite.

What is the origin of runcible spoon, "a three-pronged fork, as a pickle fork, curved like a spoon and having a cutting edge"? Perhaps Roncesvalles, a village in the Spanish Pyrenees which boasts less than two hundred inhabitants but is famous in history and legend for the defeat of Charlemagne and the death of Roland in a bloody battle there in A.D. 778. Webster says the spoon, having a cutting edge, may have received its name "in jocose allusion to the slaughter." AH prefers to believe the word was coined by British nonsense writer Edward Lear (1812–1888) in his *Nonsense Songs* (1871), wherein the Owl and the Pussycat

> *. . . dined on mince, and slices of quince,*
> *which they ate with a runcible spoon.*

In the preface to his book, Mr. Lear presents a self-portrait:

> *His body is perfectly spherical,*
> *He weareth a runcible hat.*

The runcible hat did not outlast Mr. Lear and evokes no vision in my mind; but the runcible spoon cuts on.

A three-legged stand of iron or other metal, used for supporting cooking vessels in a fireplace, is a trivet. The usual explanation of the word is that Latin merges *tri,* "three," and *pes,* "foot," to mean three-footed. But Holt, again odd man out, cites as other possible sources one Truefits, a wig manufacturer, and an Admiral Trivet, who escaped unscathed from an undescribed sea disaster.

The expression Grub Street, "allusive for the ill-fed corpus of literary hacks," comes, says Partridge, "not from an actual Grub Street but from that street in Moorfields, London, which has, since 1830, been known as Fore Street." Very well; yet Samuel Johnson named it as a specific street "much inhabited by writers of small histories, dictionaries, and temporary poems; whence any mean production is called grubstreet." Frank Muir, as English as Partridge, says Grub Street was renamed Milton Street in 1830, and by the end of the 19th century "had sunk to its lowest as the lodging-house centre for impoverished dictionary compilers, and writers of 'small histories' and 'temporary poems.' " In the 1970s, he adds, the street disappeared without a trace beneath the concrete of the Barbican building scheme.

CINCHONA   And what, by the way, is the origin of the word cinchona, the tree whose bark yields quinine? AH and Webster nominate as eponym Francisca Henriques de Ribera (1576–1631?), Countess of Chinchón, saying she recovered from a fever through the use of quinine and introduced it to Europe. Not so, says Britannica: "The oft repeated tale was completely disproved by A. W. Haggis in 1941, as the wife of the Viceroy of Peru never had malaria, died at Cartagena on her way to Spain, and hence could not have carried cinchona back to Europe."

Take it from there, AH and Webster.

Fraudulent Words

From time to time in this book I have mentioned examples of doubtful or false etymology. This chapter contains nothing else. I see no reason to leave out some of my favorite stories simply because they are not true.

Some apocryphal origins were jokes taken seriously. Thomas Costain, for instance, pretended in one of his novels that during the Middle Ages there lived a Britisher who wove fine wool covers. The name of this man was Blanket, an anglicization of Blanquette. As a result, the word blanket is now applied generally to bedcovers.

BLANKET

Mr. Costain's tongue-in-cheek invention has been gravely cited as authority for the provenance of blanket. But if there was indeed a Mr. Blanket who made blankets, his name came from French *blanc*, "white," hence white cloth.

WALLOP   Similarly, in Tom Stoppard's *Lord Malquist and Mr. Moon* (1966), Lord Malquist tells his friend: "In the 13th century Sir John Wallop so smote the French at sea that he gave a verb to the language. But there must be less energetic ways of doing that." Mr. Stoppard did not invent this tall story; he simply passed it on. In reality, wallop descends from Old French *waloper*, "to gallop."

Russell Baker, the humorist and satirist, attributed the word pragmatism (a philosophy holding that the truth is to be tested by the practical consequences of belief) to one Giovanni Pragma, described as a 19th-century Florentine councilman and bungler. When I wrote expressing skepticism, Mr. Baker replied that the provenance came to him direct from his friend Nino, who manages a trattoria on Wisconsin Avenue in Washington, D.C. Mr. Baker said Nino would be glad to confirm the story in person if I would first buy a bottle of Bollo to loosen his tongue.

So don't be surprised if in the Fourth or Fifth Edition of Webster's you find an attribution like this:

prag-ma-tism (prag′ma-tism), *n.* [from G. Pragma, It. statesman]

Some apocryphal origins have an element of truth. They give the word with which they are associated a richer meaning and perhaps a longer life. Take rickets, a disease of infancy or early childhood caused by defective nutrition, affecting the growing bones and frequently causing bow legs. The post-Elizabethan gossip John Aubrey (1626–1697), discussing monstrous births and other obstetrical wonders in *Brief Lives*, asserts:

I will while 'tis in my mind inset this Remarque, viz.: about 1620 one Ricketts of Newberye, a Practicioner in Physick, was excellent at the Curing of Children with swoln heads and small legges: and the Disease being new, and without a name, He being so famous for the cure of it, they called the Disease the Ricketts: as the King's Evill from the King's cureing of it with his Touch; and now 'tis good sport to see how they vex their Lexicons, and fetch it from the Greek Παχις, the back bone.

Those who vexed their lexicons had the right of it; the word does stem from Greek *rhachîtis,* "inflammation of the spine." But without John Aubrey's story, folk etymology might by now have changed it to cricket or crackers.

A Dr. Ricketts is indeed the eponym of the microorganism that causes typhus. It was discovered in 1906 by an American pathologist named Howard Taylor Ricketts, and is called rickettsia after him.

In the first half of the 19th century, Colonel E. G. (or E. S.) Booze purveyed whiskey in a bottle bearing his name and shaped like a log cabin. The whiskey and the name became popular in the presidential campaign of 1840, when General William Henry Harrison, the successful Whig candidate, boasted that he had been born in a log cabin. The old bottles are collectors' items now. Booze traces back to Middle English *bousen*, "to carouse"; but as a synonym for hard, cheap liquor, it could not have reeled on so persistently but for the redolent rotgut of Colonel Booze.

BOOZE

CANT

A similar intermarriage involves cant, "whining speech, as used by beggars; hypocritically pious language; thieves' argot." In 1711 the *Spectator* attributed the word to "one Andrew Cant, who, they say, was a Presbyterian Minister . . . who by exercise and use had obtained the Faculty, alias Gift, of talking in the pulpit in such a dialect that it's said he was understood by none but his own Congregation, and not by all of them." An Andrew Cant (1590–1663) was a minister in Aberdeen, all right, but he was a clear, not confusing, speaker. Edwards suggests that the only relationship between his name and the common noun is that both probably descend from Latin *cantare*, "to sing."

False etymology attributes the invention of the tram, or tramway, to Sir James Outram (1803–1883). Sir James was a well-known English general, a hero of the Indian Mutiny. To the best of my knowledge he did not use trams in the Indian fighting, or indeed anywhere else; nor did Benjamin Outram, a quarry owner in Derbyshire, who is sometimes given credit for the name. Tram originates in an Old Norse word meaning "beam."

TRAM

GINGERLY

In his book *Phrases and Names*, Trench Johnson attributes gingerly ("mincingly; often with an implication of distaste for what one has to do") to none other than Queen Guinevere, on the grounds, first, that the lady had red hair; second, that the nickname for a red-haired person is Carrots; and third, that both a carrot and a ginger plant have edible roots. Hence, Guinevere = gingerly. But gingerly is simply a comparative form of Old French *gent*, "nice." The ginger plant is of the genus *Zingiber*, from which its name was corrupted.

DIMITY

GINGHAM

The cotton fabric dimity is so called not from Damietta, Egypt, as is often said, but from Greek *dimitos*, "double thread." Nor does gingham, another cotton cloth, usually in stripes or checks, come, as once supposed, from Guingamp, a town in Brittany, but from Malay *ginggang*, "striped."

TOBACCO

Tobacco is named not from the island of Tobago, but from the native name of the tube through which the Caribs smoked it.

CABAL

Intriguing (using the adjective advisedly) is the persistent assertion that cabal, "a conspiratorial group of plotters or in-

BOOZE

triguers," is an acronym of Clifford-Ashley-Buckingham-Arlington-Lauderdale, a clique of intriguers in the ministry of Charles II. That the first letters of their names could be juggled into cabal was coincidence. The word comes from Hebrew *qab-balah*, meaning "tradition"—hence a particular body of esoteric, mystical doctrine.

GIN

Another pleasant fraud is the attribution of gin, the alcoholic beverage flavored with juniper berries, to Geneva. The word does indeed derive from geneva liquor, but the geneva has nothing to do with the city. It is a variant of the aforementioned juniper, which is no proper name at all.

PHONY

As an instance of how a phony derivation may strengthen a correct one, I give you phony. A phony is a counterfeit. Partridge says the word goes back to the British underworld "fawny," from Irish *fainne*, meaning finger ring, hence ring switching and gyp. No doubt he's right, though there are zealots who insist on blaming the word on the early telephone, because of the distorted squawks produced by that instrument. But phony would not be the colloquial standby that it is had not one Mr. Forney made a good thing of selling imitation jewelry to Americans in the 19th century. Mr. Forney was a grand phony.

BLOODY

In England, the vulgar slang usage bloody ("Bloody well right!") is commonly, but incorrectly, considered a degenerate form of either "God's blood" or "by 'er Lady," perhaps with some allusion to menstruation. Though etymologists agree that these are incorrect provenances, there is no generally accepted alternative. Bloody is still regarded as indecent by many Englishmen, though they don't know why. In 1913 all London trembled when George Bernard Shaw put bloody into the mouth of the elegant Mrs. Patrick Campbell in his play *Pygmalion*. "The interest in the first English performance," said *The New York Times*, "centered in the heroine's utterance of this banned word."

The Australians use bloody with less trepidation than their English cousins; Mencken calls the word "the great Australian adjective." Australian troops stationed in Newfoundland in 1942 sang:

No bloody sports, no bloody games;
No bloody fun with bloody dames;
Won't even tell their bloody names;
Oh, bloody, bloody, bloody!

A recent London *Times* letters-page tournament revolved about that trusty British breakfast companion, marmalade—a pulpy jam of quince, plum orange, or the like. Was it invented by the English, the Scots, a French chef, the Portuguese, or the Spanish? One correspondent said it took a canny Scot to see value in the peel that others threw away; another said Gervase Markham (1568–1637) created the recipe in his book *The English Housewife.* The most common suggestion was that marmalade corrupts Marie Malade ("sick Mary"), because the jam, once a rarity, was among the few things that Mary Queen of Scots was able to hold in her stomach during an illness.

The fact is that marmalade comes from Greek *melimēlon,* "sweet apple."

ROSEMARY

The rosemary, a fragrant shrub, is often traced to the Virgin: the "rose of Mary." Its true origin is Latin *ros marinus,* "sea dew."

WOG

During the British administration of the Suez Canal, the native workers wore shirts bearing the stenciled letters WOGS. Wog became a slighting reference to these workers, and eventually to any nonwhite of the lower classes. There is a tradition that the acronym stands for "wily (or Westernized) Oriental gentleman." Of course it does not; a correspondent named Patricia Lamb has reminded me that the word uses the first letters of Working on Government Services. Ms. Lamb also mentioned the acronym OHM. Ohm is not the electrical measurement (though another ohm, the practical unit of electrical resistance, is indeed an uncommon, improper noun, being named after the German electrician G. S. Ohm). No, Ms. Lamb's ohms are British civil servants, from the franking of government mail with the letters OHMS: On His (or Her) Majesty's Service.

OHM

TARIFF

It is commonly held that since payment of a fixed scale of duties was demanded by the Moorish occupants of a fortress on Tarifa promontory, which overlooked the entrance to the Mediterranean, all taxes on imports came to be called a tariff. The Moors of Tarifa may indeed have levied tariffs, but the association of the word with the fortress is simply a happy coincidence. Tariff, like French *tarif,* Spanish *tarifa,* and Italian *tariffa,* all meaning a list or schedule of prices, comes from Arabic *ta'rifa,* "inventory," out of *'arafa,* "to notify."

EIGHT

"I WAS NEVER SO BETHUMP'T WITH WORDS"

—SHAKESPEARE, *King John*

WORDS OF STATE

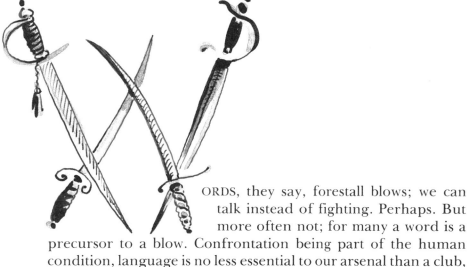

ORDS, they say, forestall blows; we can talk instead of fighting. Perhaps. But more often not; for many a word is a precursor to a blow. Confrontation being part of the human condition, language is no less essential to our arsenal than a club, bow and arrow, cannon, or atom bomb. We declaim, fighting. We fight, declaiming.

The subject of this chapter is the uncommon, improper nouns that have emerged from the ongoing confrontation between state and state, or between state and citizen.

DANEGELD

Take as a starter danegeld, meaning public blackmail. The danegeld was levied to pay off the Danes who invaded the British Isles regularly in the days before William the Conqueror. Warned Kipling:

> If once you have paid him the danegeld
> You never get rid of the Dane.

PEEPING TOM

In 1040 the Lord of Coventry, a town near Birmingham, England, agreed to his wife's plea that he reduce certain oppressive taxes, but only on the condition that she in turn agree to ride naked through the city. This she did, and the townspeople so revered her that all averted their eyes. The exception, a tailor named Tom, was struck blind for his impudence. A peeping tom is a voyeur.

COVENTRY
SENT TO
    COVENTRY

During the open war between Charles I and Parliament that began in 1642, Coventry was a Parliamentary stronghold, where the most difficult Royalist prisoners were sent for safekeeping. The citizens of Coventry shunned not only the Royalists, but even the soldiers of their own side. Any young woman seen talking with one of the military was shunned. Coventry is thus a state of ostracism; to be sent to coventry is to be cut off from normal pleasures as a form of social disapproval.

COVENTRY
    BLUE
TRUE BLUE

Coventry blue means something quite different—"extraordinarily loyal," resulting from the town's reputation for producing a fine blue dye that did not run. "True blue" has the same origin in dyeing. Prussian blue, in the 19th century, was a term of endearment: Sam Weller called his father My Prooshan.

BOURBON

Bourbon, signifying a rigid and anti-democratic approach to government, recalls the Bourbon dynasty, which reigned over France for three hundred years prior to the revolution of 1789. Bourbons were said never to forget and never to learn.

ROI D'YVETOT

In the days before the study of history became a misdemeanor, a person of mighty pretensions but little real power was referred to as a roi d'Yvetot, "king of Yvetot." The overlord of Yvetot, in Normandy, through some legal quirk bore the title of king from the 14th to the 16th century; but he was more or less subject to the king of France.

CISATLANTIC
TRANSATLANTIC

The Latin prefix cis- means "on this side of," as opposed to trans-, "on the other side of." The function of the two prefixes is illustrated in cisatlantic and transatlantic.

In the days when a number of northern churches were loosening their ties to the papacy, conservatives were called transalpines or ultramontanes because they looked across the Alps to Rome for guidance. Persons who formed their religious opinions without regard for the Pope's were, conversely, cisalpines. As far as I know, the two words have shrunk back to their original sense, one meaning the far side and the other the near side of the Alps.

VATICANISM
VATICANIZE
**VATICAN-
IZATION**

The Vatican contributed a full share of improper, uncommon nouns to the language. The doctrine of absolute papal supremacy is vaticanism; to bring under the authority of the Vatican is to vaticanize; and the neutralization of holy places is vaticanization.

**MACHIA-
VELLIAN**

Niccolò Machiavelli (1469–1527) was a Florentine diplomat, statesman, and writer who contended that a ruler is justified in using any means to establish and maintain a strong central government. Machiavellian is "characterized by political cunning, duplicity, or bad faith."

MARTINET

Jean Martinet, a French general, built the first modern army in Europe during the reign of Louis XIV. His introduction of a precise and persistent system of drill improved the fighting ability of his men, but did not add to his popularity. At the siege of Duisburg in 1672 he was accidentally killed by his own artillery. Says Britannica: "His death, and that of the Swiss captain Soury ("mouse") by the same charge, gave rise to a *bon mot*, typical of the polite ingratitude of the age, that Duisburg had cost the king only a martin and a mouse." A strict disciplinarian, one who demands rigid adherence to rules, is a martinet.

DEWITT

A public official killed by a mob is dewitted. The expression refers to the murder in 1672 of the brothers Jan and Cornelius DeWitt, Dutch patriots. Jan fought the British to a standstill at sea for William of Orange. He also, however, stoutly maintained republican principles against William at home. On both counts, he is considered one of the great patriots of his age. But that did not prevent a crowd of William's adherents from seizing the two brothers, tearing them to pieces, and hanging their mangled remains by the feet from a lamppost. To make the affair even more curious, William III of the Netherlands soon afterward was invited by the British to become William III of England.

BILLINGSGATE

Billingsgate was a gate in the Old Wall of London, on the Thames below the London Bridge. A fishmarket near there became notorious in the 17th century for foul and abusive language, and such language has been called billingsgate ever since. A similar expression, more at home in England than here, is

LIMEHOUSE

limehouse, "abuse of one's political opponents." The usage commemorates a 1909 speech delivered by Lloyd George in Limehouse, a district in the East End of London. The audience was delighted because the future Prime Minister "spoke their language" of harsh invective.

SILHOUETTE

Étienne de Silhouette (1709–1767), made Controller General of France through the influence of Mme. de Pompadour, slashed the budget of the regal household, tripled the tax on bachelors, discontinued the tax exemption of municipal officeholders, and succeeded in making himself so disliked that he had to resign. To ridicule his parsimony, men's clothing was designed without pockets—*à la silhouette.* His hobby, which later became that of other famous personages including Goethe, was to cut profile portraits out of black paper. These were taken as symbols of his stinginess and so were given his name: silhouette. (In the 20th century, the 12th Duke of Bedford had his suits made without pockets because "a duke should not need them.")

TAMMANY

A pre-Revolutionary Indian chief is resurrected in the word tammany—meaning any corrupt organization, but especially one engaged in politics. Tammany Hall dominated New York politics from about 1800 through the first half of this century. Its full name is Sons of St. Tammany, the aforementioned chief. The name was chosen at the time of the Revolution as a gibe at such Tory clubs as the Sons of St. George, Sons of St. Andrew, and Sons of St. David.

JEDBURGH
JUSTICE

In Britain, execution before trial is termed jedburgh (often shortened to jeddart) justice. Jedburgh is a small town in Roxburghshire, Scotland, where in the reign of James I a gang of rogues was eliminated cavalierly at the instance of Sir George Hume. The expression, says Britannica, "seems to have been a hasty generalization from a solitary fact . . . but nevertheless passed into a proverb."

LYDFORD LAW

At Lydford, where the courts governed Cornish tin mines, the rule of thumb was said to be "First hang, and then draw. Then try the case at Lydford law." Excessively harsh justice is frequently referred to as Lydford law.

LYNCH

Charles Lynch (1736–1796), a Virginia planter and justice of the peace, employed extra-legal methods in trying and punishing Tories during the Revolution, often hanging them out of hand. Hence lynch for "to execute without due process of law; to hang." Some etymologists prefer to trace the word to

James Lynch, a 15th-century mayor of Galway, Ireland. There is credit enough for both.

CHAUVINISM

Nicholas Chauvin, of Rochefort, France, a soldier of the First Republic and Empire, was famous among his companions for his demonstrative patriotism and adoration of Napoleon. During the disturbances of the 1830s he was used as a character in a popular play. His name became a byword; xenophobia is now named chauvinism.

GERRYMANDER

To gerrymander is "so to divide the voting districts of a state, county, or city as to give unfair advantage to one party in elections." Elbridge Gerry, soon to become Vice President of the United States, was governor of Massachusetts in 1812, when the state's districts were redivided for political purposes. The shapes of the towns forming one particular district in Essex County, when drawn on a map, had a somewhat dragonlike appearance. Such a map hung over the desk of Benjamin Russell, an anti-Gerry editor. The celebrated painter Gilbert Stuart, coming into the office one day, added with his pencil a head, wings, and claws, and exclaimed, "That will do for a salamander!" "Better say Gerrymander!" growled Russell. Though Governor Gerry had nothing to do with juggling the districts, the outlandish name caught on.

BUNCOMBE

BUNK

In the Sixteenth Congress (1819–21), the county of Buncombe, North Carolina, was represented by one Felix Walker. From time to time Congressman Walker made irrelevant speeches, explaining on the side that his constituency expected them, and that he was not speaking for the ears of his fellow Congressmen, but rather for Buncombe. Buncombe came to mean "anything said, written or done for mere show; nonsense." Nowadays the second syllable is dropped, leaving bunk.

MAVERICK

The literal meaning of maverick is "an unbranded animal, especially a motherless calf." By extension, the word means someone who refuses to abide by others' rules—that is, declines to be branded. In the 1930s Congressman Maury Maverick, a veteran of World War I who still carried unextracted bullets in his body, was the quintessence of the maverick; neither the House leaders nor the President could tell him how to vote. Congressman Maverick was descended from Samuel Maverick. In the last half of the 19th century, Maverick, a Texas banker, had to take a herd of cattle in settlement of a debt. Lacking land, he leased an island for his stock in the middle of the Nueces River. His agents, inexperienced, failed to confine the calves or to brand them. In the winter, when the river shrank to a trickle, the calves waded across into adjoining pastures. "Must be another one of Sam Maverick's calves," the neighboring cattlemen would say; or, later, "There's another Maverick." I find no evidence for the old canard that Maverick burned his brand into the hides of other ranchers' still-unbranded calves.

MARXISM

MARXIAN

Scientific socialism, as enunciated by Karl Marx (1818–1883) and Friedrich Engels (1820–1895), made Marxism a code word for certain social and economic doctrines, including dialectical materialism and the class struggle. Though the validity of these doctrines is hotly disputed, Marxism has played a major role in the shaping of modern thought. Marxian, lowercased, means "economically doctrinaire."

BOYCOTT

In 1880, Captain Charles Cunningham Boycott was land agent in County Mayo, Ireland, for an absentee owner, the Earl of Erne. Though the harvest had been disastrous, Captain Boycott refused to reduce rents and attempted to evict any tenants who could not pay in full. As a result, he became the object of the earliest known effort to force an alteration of policy by concerted nonintercourse. His servants departed en masse. No one would sell him food. Life became so miserable for him that at last he gave up and returned to England. To boycott is "to combine in abstaining from, or preventing dealings with, as a means of intimidation or coercion."

QUISLING

Quisling, meaning traitor, took quick root in the language during World War II. Vidkun Quisling (1887–1945) was a Norwegian whose willingness to serve the German conquerors of his country in 1942 made him despised throughout the world. After the war he was found guilty of treason and was shot.

McCARTHYISM

McCarthyism, shorthand for witch-hunt, was coined by opponents of Joseph R. McCarthy. He was charged with using such tactics during investigations into Communist activities held by the House Un-American Activities Committee between 1946 and 1957.

BEVINISM

To end on a lighter note, bevinism is the type of marvelous confusion of metaphor associated with Ernest Bevin, who served in the cabinets of both Clement Attlee and Winston Churchill after World War II. A typical bevinism: "If you open this Pandora's box, you will find it full of Trojan horses." Two of the best-known American counterparts of bevinism are the

GOLDWYNISM goldwynism, from motion-picture producer Samuel Goldwyn ("An oral contract isn't worth the paper it's written on") and the

STENGELISM stengelism, from baseball manager Casey Stengel ("He's so lucky he could fall in a hole and come up with a silver spoon").

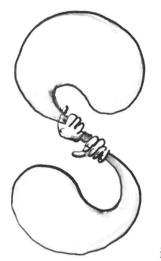
INCE VIOLENCE of all sorts has pretty much died out these tranquil days, it is as well that a few words remain to remind us of stormier times.

In 1829, William Burke, a navvy, was hanged in Edinburgh, Scotland, for a series of particularly odious murders. With the help of William Hare, it was his custom to suffocate his victims and sell their bodies to Dr. Robert Knox, an Edinburgh surgeon who paid a handsome price—£8 to £14 per corpse.

BURKE

Burke and Hare, with their wives, lured fifteen people to their deaths before being apprehended. Burke's name quickly lost its capitalization: to burke is "to murder by suffocation, so as to leave the body intact and suitable for dissection." The villains are memorialized in a popular quatrain of the day:

> *Up the close and down the stair*
> *But and ben with Burke and Hare.*
> *Burke's the butcher, Hare the thief*
> *And Knox the boy that buys the beef.*

"But and ben" in Scottish dialect means "into the outer and inner apartment of the house." Burke is now used more metaphysically than literally, as in "to burke an issue"; "the bill was burked."

BISHOP

Two years later, one Bishop, probably influenced by the example of Burke, drowned a boy in order to sell the body. In *The Ingoldsby Legends* (1840), Richard Barham says, "I burk'd the papa, now I'll bishop the son." To bishop is to murder by drowning.

BLUEBEARD

There is a move afoot to eliminate Bluebeard from fairy stories, on the ground that he might implant a predisposition in small boys to grow up and burke their wives. The story, a folk tale of punished curiosity, probably was extant long before 1697, when Charles Perrault put it into print along the following lines: Fatima, a pretty young thing, married the sinister Bluebeard against her brothers' wishes. Before leaving on a business trip, he gave his bride the keys to the castle, but warned her not to open a certain door. She, out of curiosity, disobeyed, and found the remains of six previous wives hung up like beef. Surprised by her husband, she was about to suffer the fate of her predecessors when her brothers arrived and saved her. A bluebeard is a man who murders the women he marries. The name has been connected with Gilles de Rais, a 15th-century grandee and friend of Joan of Arc, who passed long winter evenings torturing children, probably doing away with well over a hundred of them.

JACK THE RIPPER

In 1888 and 1889 in London, a madman killed and disemboweled young women, particularly prostitutes, almost faster than their corpses could be counted. His identity has never been established. Charges have been laid against individuals ranging from a prince of the blood royal to Prime Minister Gladstone. Whoever the perpetrator was, he is remembered as Jack the

Ripper, a name now prototypical of a mad killer who mutilates his victims. He named himself in a note found on one of the bodies:

I'm not a butcher, not a yid,
Nor yet a foreign skipper,
But just your old good-hearted friend,
Yours truly, JACK THE RIPPER.

In the 1890s an Irish family named Hooligan, or Houlihan, proliferated in Southwark, London. Patrick Hooligan, according to *Punch*, "walked to and fro among his fellow men, robbing them and occasionally bashing them." His name first appeared in print in January 1899, when the *Pall Mall Gazette* reported: "The proprietor of Lord Tennyson (in wax) says it was a certain young man who, with others, when called upon to desist, Hooliganed about and threw the late Laureate's head at him." Overnight the *H* shrank to *h*. Hooligan entered the vulgate for a "loafer, ruffian, or hoodlum." The Russians use it with particular frequency, though they have not yet claimed they invented it. They call it "gooliganism"—they cannot pronounce the letter *h*—and consider it a serious offense. In the 1978 border warfare between the Cambodians and the Vietnamese, the Cambodian government referred indignantly to the other side as hooligans.

HOODLUM

Weekley suggests that hoodlum, similar to hooligan in meaning, may be a perverted back-spelling of Muldoon. Back-spelling has been a specialty of cockney Londoners since the 1830s. Police becomes ecilop, corrupted to slop; Muldoon becomes noodlum, corrupted to hoodlum.

LARRIKIN

Hooligans and hoodlums are an English variety of Australia's larrikins. This term probably evokes the name Larry, though it could be simply a corruption of "larking." Larrikins act much like their English equivalents. Their style of dress, excessively neat and severe in color, is the antithesis of their conduct.

APACHE

An apache is a member of a class of criminals in Paris, once notorious for their violence, but now best known for the violent apache dance that fascinates tourists. They borrowed their name from the Apache Indians, a ferocious, wily, and stubborn tribe that was not finally subdued until 1886.

MOHOCK

In the early 18th century, London streets were vandalized by young aristocrats of antisocial bent called after the Mohocks, a subdivision of the Iroquois. There were also street ruffians

HAWKUBITES

called hawkubites, combining Mohawk with Jacobite, an adherent of James II and III, exiled Stuart kings.

THUG

While the French and English were borrowing apache and mohock from us, we were borrowing thug, for "ruffian; assassin," from northern India. The Thugs, members of a fraternity suppressed by the British in the 1830s, were worshipers of the goddess Kali, in whose name murder, usually by strangling, was considered a meritorious act.

BERSERK

Though not legal criminals, some savage tribes in ancient times did cut up. Their approach to society was epitomized in Berserk, a legendary Norse hero of the 8th century, so named for the *berserk* (bear skin) that he wore into battle. He was famous for the reckless fury with which he fought. Berserk's twelve sons were known with their father as Berserkers. The name was eventually applied to a class of wild warriors who in battle howled like wolves or growled like bears, bit their shields, foamed at the mouth, and were dreaded for their enormous strength and apparent invulnerability. To go berserk is to go into a frenzy of rage.

GOTHIC

GOTHIC
ARCHITECTURE

GOTHIC ARMOR
GOTHIC SCRIPT

GOTHIC TYPE

The Teutonic Goths overran the Roman Empire in the early Christian centuries. Like the Britons, they were considered by their victims to be, if not out-and-out criminals, at least rude types. As an adjective, gothic reflects roughness and fierceness. It also means romantic, as opposed to classical. It was a critically dismissive word when first applied to architecture. A gothic building is not simply an affair of pointed arches, but a stone skeleton of pillars, props, and ribs, upon which rests the shell of vaulting. Gothic armor is a 15th-century style of beautifully designed and well-constructed plate armor. Gothic script is a minuscule affair in which the curved parts are replaced by angles. Gothic type is black and square-cut, with no serifs.

HUN
HUNNISH

The Huns, perhaps native to the Caspian steppes, poured into Europe about A.D. 372. Under their inspired leader Attila (meaning "daddy" in Turkish) they eventually obtained control of a large part of eastern and central Europe, forcing Rome itself to pay tribute. Attila's death in 453 terminated their empire. The people were described as of squat muscular figure, flat of face, ugly, and low in culture. A hun is a wantonly destructive person; the word was applied to the Germans in World War I. Hunnish is the adjective. In 1898 the Germans sent an expeditionary force to avenge the murder of two German missionaries in China. The Kaiser told them: "Behave as the Huns of old."

VANDAL

In 455, just two years after the withdrawal of the Huns, the Vandals, a Germanic tribe dwelling south of the Baltic between the Vistula and the Oder, overwhelmed and sacked Rome, destroying many monuments of art and literature. Hun and vandal are now used interchangeably.

OGRE

An ogre is a monster or hideous giant of fairytales and folklore who devours human beings—by extension, any hideous or cruel man. The derivation is either from Byzantine *Ogor*, "Hungarian"—in the old days the Hungarians were doubtless tough customers—or from Orcus, Roman god of the underworld.

TARTAR
TO CATCH A
TARTAR

In the early 13th century the Tatars, a Turkish-Mongolian mix, swept into eastern Europe by way of Tatary, in Siberia. Genghis Khan, their leader, began his career as the chief of an unknown tribe. He died, in 1227, one of the greatest conquerors in history. The Romans are said to have found the Tatars so intractable that they changed the name to Tartar, after Tartarus, the ancient version of hell, "as far below Hades as Hades is below the earth." Generally, a tartar is a person often underestimated by his opponent. "To catch a tartar" is to take on more than one had bargained for.

CANNIBAL

Though cannibalism has erupted at various times and places, the name refers to Indians called Carib in Cuba and Caniba in Haiti. Their disagreeable habit of serving up their enemies for supper was described to Christopher Columbus during one of his explorations of the West Indies.

NAZI

The National Socialist German Workers' Party, generally shortened to Nazi, wrote a page of indelible shame in world history by its indiscriminate slaughter of millions of Jews and other minority groups in the 1930s and the 1940s. A nazi is a fascist of the most monstrous type.

MORGUE

By the nature of things, crime is often violent, resulting in death. Society has to find a place to keep the slain bodies during identification, processing, and arrangement for burial. For this purpose the Parisians used a building called Le Morgue. The origin of the word is obscure; it appears to have nothing to do with Latin *mors*, "death," or with such cognates as "mortuary." "As late as 1611," says Partridge, "the French term was defined as 'a place where prisoners were examined on entry into prison.'" In any event, other nations picked up morgue for any such building. By extension, a morgue is also a reference file in a newspaper or magazine office.

BOBBY
PEELER

Society requires armed guardians. Among these are the bobby of England and the peeler of Ireland. Both are named for Sir Robert Peel (1788– 1850). As Home Secretary he established London's Metropolitan Police in 1829. He had formed the Irish Constabulary when Chief Secretary of Ireland a decade earlier.

CHARLEY

Before Sir Robert's time, the night watch were called Charlies, perhaps after Charles I, in whose disorderly reign the police system was reorganized.

COSSACK

Perhaps because the Cossacks of the Russian Steppes have a warlike and brutal reputation, it is common in left-wing circles to describe police who break up demonstrations as cossacks.

NOSY PARKER

Matthew Parker (1504–1575), Archbishop of Canterbury early in the reign of Elizabeth I, sent questionnaires to all the parishes in England concerning the way in which priests and people conducted their church affairs. He won a reputation for nosiness which has made his name a byword in England. A nosy parker is one who pries into others' affairs.

DARBIES

To control refractory prisoners, the police sometimes employed darbies, or handcuffs. The expression is probably derived from a personal name; Brewer says the phrase "father Derbie's bands" for handcuffs is found in George Gascoigne's *The Steel Glass* (1576).

BILBO

Sometimes the feet of prisoners were shackled with bilbos, iron bars with sliding fetters. These originated in Bilbao, Spain, famous for its steel- and ironworks. The name also applies to a rapier.

BRODERICK

The police are not always gentle with suspects. John Joseph Broderick, a first-grade detective on New York City's police force, won headlines as "the world's toughest cop." From 1923 to 1947 he subdued gangsters with his fists, and left the force with eight medals for valor. The Morrises say the heavyweight champion Jack Dempsey, who occasionally used Broderick as a bodyguard, pronounced him the only man he would not care to fight outside the ring. To broderick someone is to clobber him.

TYBURN TREE
TO RIDE BACK-
WARD UP HOL-
BURN HILL
GREGORIAN
TREE
GREGORY

Executions by hanging were so common at Tyburn, London, that the gibbet came to be called the tyburn tree. "To ride backward up Holborn Hill" (Tyburn being at the top) was to go to be hanged. Three successive Tyburn hangmen of the 17th century bore the name Gregory, so that the tyburn tree is also called the gregorian tree. To gregory is to execute by gibbeting or hanging.

A particularly barbarous hangman of the period was Jack Ketch (c. 1662–1686); his brutality at the execution of political offenders such as the Duke of Monmouth became legendary. A jack ketch is any hangman. It has been speculated that he is memorialized in the ketch, a fore-and-aft rigged sailboat with a mainmast and mizzen, but I doubt it; more likely the sailboat is called a ketch because it ketches the wind.

Goodman Derrick, another Tyburn hangman, was as adept with the axe as with the noose; he cut off the head of the Earl of Essex in 1601. But it was his adeptness at gibbeting that won him vernacular immortality. Any hoisting apparatus employing a tackle rigged at the end of a spar is a derrick.

CLINK

BRIDEWELL
NEWGATE

NEWGATE
FRINGE
BASTILLE

A prison may be referred to as the clink, a bridewell, a newgate, or a bastille, according to taste. Says *London and Environs*, a 1761 guidebook: "Clink prison in Clink Street belongs to the liberty of the Bishop of Winchester, called Clink liberty. It is a very dismal hole where debtors are sometimes confined." (The bishop's liberty was the area over which he exercised jurisdiction.) There was another Clink prison somewhere in England; Partridge suggests too that the name may be associated with the clinking sounds of manacles and chains. Until 1864, Bridewell was a house of correction in the Bridewell section of London. Newgate was the main prison for the city of London from the 13th century until its razing in 1902; the hangman's noose is called a newgate fringe, and hair worn around the jawline, reminiscent of that noose, is also a newgate fringe. The Bastille, stormed and destroyed in the French Revolution, remains as a name for a notorious dungeon. Americans commonly refer to a prison or jail as a hoosegow, but this is not an uncommon, improper noun. It stems from Spanish *juzgado*, "a court or place of judgment."

In this country, under-age criminals are consigned to institutions once optimistically known as reform schools. The more common term now is "training schools"; presumably the children emerge well trained in criminal techniques. Dickens's Fagin conducted an illegal but not dissimilar school. He trained his boys and girls only to be pickpockets, however, neglecting such profitable fields as mugging, drug dealing, prostitution, check kiting, and the like.

English reform schools are called borstals, from Borstal, a village in Kent. The Borstal Association, established by an act of Parliament in 1909, runs them; it is supposed to subject offenders to highly organized supervision after dismissal. I have no idea whether the British system produces more expert criminals than ours.

Penknives, jackknives, and the like are only incidentally associated with crime; the rolling pin with which Maggie used to hit errant Jiggs in the comic strip could as reasonably be called a murderous instrument, to be banned by act of Congress. But one type of single-bladed jackknife, the barlow knife, deserves mention, first because it takes its name from some forgotten maker named Barlow, and second because it was held in awe ("a sure 'nuff Barlow") by Tom Sawyer and Huckleberry Finn.

BARLOW KNIFE

Every suspect is entitled to his day in court, with a lawyer to defend him. In the 1840s one of the most effective criminal lawyers was a man named Scheuster, who, says Webster, "was frequently rebuked for pettifoggery." The name shrank to shyster, "one who is professionally unscrupulous, particularly in law or politics." An echo from Shakespeare's Shylock may have helped make shyster a common noun. So may *scheissen*, a gross German word meaning "to defecate."

SHYSTER

It will come as no surprise to lexicographer Peter Funk, son of lexicographer Wilfred Funk, that a peter funk is a confidence man, or someone employed to build up prices at an auction. At the turn of the century a gang operated shadily at auctions, presumably under the leadership of one Peter Funk.

PETER FUNK

At about the same time Raffles, now lowercased as a classification, came to stand for a gentleman burglar; Ernest W. Hornung, an Australian writer, created him in a collection of stories published in 1899.

RAFFLES

Dr. J. I. Guillotin (1738–1814) considered gibbeting barbarous. He proposed beheading instead. "With my machine," he informed the awestruck French Assembly in 1789, "I can whisk off your head in a twinkling and you feel no pain." The instrument he promoted was for a while called the *louisette* or *petit louison*, after Dr. Antoine Louis, secretary of the Academy of Medicine, who designed the version Guillotin espoused, and fittingly died under its knife. Italy had used decapitators named *mannaia* to execute criminals of noble blood as early as the 13th century. The antiquarian museum of Edinburgh still displays the rude "maiden," a similar cutting device which did in the regent Morton in 1581. Holinshed's *Chronicles* reports that such a machine was used in the Yorkshire town of Halifax. Its blade dropped "with such violence that, if the neck of the transgressor

LOUISETTE
PETIT LOUISON
GUILLOTINE

were as big as that of a bull, it should be cut in sunder at a stroke and roll from the body by a huge distance."

Dr. Guillotin was the right man in the right place at the right time. So many Frenchmen died by his machine in the ensuing Reign of Terror (he barely escaped himself) that it now bears his name. To guillotine is to behead by the doctor's improved device. To guillotine a bill in Congress or Parliament, by the same token, is to behead it.

MULLER

The muller, remarks Hendrickson, is probably the only hat in history that was named for a murderer. He might have added that the hat was named after the first man to commit a murder on a railway train. Mr. Muller wore a low-crowned felt affair pulled down over his face for concealment, but was identified and hanged nonetheless. That was in the middle of the 19th century. From 1855 to 1885 a kind of deerstalker hat was known in England as a muller.

TOMMY GUN

The tommy gun was a submachine gun much favored by gangsters of the Capone era. The name abbreviates the Thompson submachine gun, invented by J. T. Thompson and John Blish. The gun is easily fired from either hip or shoulder; it is highly recommended if you propose to kill seven at one blow, like the little tailor in the fairy tale.

MAFIA

The Sicilian dialect contains the word *mafia*, "lawlessness"; by background, boldness. *Mafia* in turn derives from Arabic *mahyah*, "boasting." The Mafia is a secret terrorist organization that has operated in Sicily since the early 19th century. Internationally, it is a criminal organization allegedly dominant in the organized crime of Italy and the United States. In the vernacular, a mafia is any organization using terrorist methods to control an activity.

WABASH

Not all crime is violent. Fraudulent land speculation was so rife in early Indiana that the name of an Indiana river was given it; in slang, to wabash is to defraud.

PONZI

A ponzi, or confidence group, appropriates the name of Charles Ponzi, who in December 1919 advertised a scheme involving the supposed purchase of International Postal Reply coupons in countries where the exchange was low, their exchange for postal stamps at face value in a country where the rate was high, and sale of the stamps at a great profit. Within six months, 20,000 individuals invested nearly $10 million in the project. Ponzi bought no coupons whatever; he simply paid early investors with money received from later ones until the bubble burst.

Sometimes a crime leaves the authorities looking so ridiculous that the public is less outraged than amused. A caper of this sort occurred in 1906 at Köpenick, a suburb of Berlin, when a tailor obtained a captain's uniform from an old clothes shop, arrested the mayor, and took over the city treasury, trading on the Germans' instinctive respect for authority as embodied in uniforms. The incident became the basis of a play, *The Captain of Köpenick*, popular in the 1920s in London and on Broadway. To köpenick is to impersonate. In Saki's story "Ministers of Grace," the Duke of Scaw remarks:

KÖPENICK

> Do you understand what I mean by the verb to köpenick? That is to say, to replace an authority by a spurious imitation that would carry just as much weight for the moment as the displaced original; the advantage, of course, being that the köpenick replica would do what you wanted, whereas the original does what seems best in its own eyes.

Timothy the Detective

ROSCOE

"Roscoe," said Timothy. "The pistol of the professional criminal. This origin is speculation—but plausible: Roscoe Conkling was a powerful politician of the 1870s and 1880s; in 1873 he was offered the post of Chief Justice of the Supreme Court (now called Chief Justice of the United States), but turned it down. Conkling quarreled with President Garfield over patronage at a time when Vice President Arthur was among Conkling's lieges. On July 2, 1881, a Conkling zealot named Charles J. Guiteau pistoled down Garfield, shouting, "Arthur is now President!" Garfield died seventy-nine days later. My suspicion is that criminals began calling pistols roscoes after Roscoe Conkling. A Scots verdict, to be sure."

SCOTS VERDICT

"And what is a Scots verdict?"

"Scots juries were noted for returning verdicts of 'not proven.' By the way, after Garfield's assassination Conkling wrote a moving passage:

How can I wrestle with a shroud?
How can I shout into an open grave?
Silence is a duty and a doom.

Timothy added two heaping spoonfuls of sugar to his tea, took a slow, luxurious swallow, and carried on:

HOTTENTOT
ARKANSAS
   TOOTHPICK
PINK

"Okay . . . okay . . . okay. A hottentot for an uncouth person—from the South African crossbreeds? Arkansas toothpick, from a stabbing knife? Pink for a detective, from Pinkerton, the noted detective agency?"

"You are going too fast, Timothy."

G-MAN

"G-man? When the FBI trapped Machine Gun Kelly, he called, 'Don't shoot, G-men, don't shoot!' The expression outlasted Machine Gun Kelly. It is commonly considered a shortening of 'Goverment-man.' But Kelly was recently from Ireland. I believe his mind had leaped back to the secret arm of the British police in Ireland—Section G."

"Scots verdict?"

"Precisely. Bengal lancer? After the Bengali troops that fought for the British in India?"

"Why bengal lancer?"

BENGAL LANCER

BLACK HOLE OF
   CALCUTTA

"A bengal lancer," said Timothy patiently, as if everybody but me knew, "is a rough with a razor. *Mmm* . . . Bop-bop. The black hole of Calcutta? Any place of horrible confinement. In 1756 the nawab of Bengal is said to have confined 146 British prisoners, including at least one woman, in a prison measuring eighteen feet by fourteen feet ten inches. Only twenty-two men and the woman escaped suffocation."

I shut my mind to the black hole of Calcutta.

NEWGATE
   CALENDAR

PADDINGTON
   SPECTACLES

Timothy continued: "Newgate prison; add newgate calendar—a who's who of leading criminals. And Paddington—another London prison. The hood placed over the eyes of one about to be hanged is called paddington spectacles.

"*Mmmm* . . . Oh, by the way. You have mentioned the Huns. Do you recall the Russell versus Russell divorce case in London in 1925? The husband was accused of unspecified 'hunnish practices.' "

"I am much too young to have followed that trial, Timothy."

"Oh—quite. Exactly. I am sorry."

Recall 1925 indeed! Sometimes Timothy is positively hunnish.

A Discharge of Rifles

NTONED VERGIL in the first line of the *Aeneid*:
Arma virumque cano, "Of arms and the man I
sing." Though his line is more sonorous, I
consider this quatrain of mine more profound:

> *To abort little Willy*
> *Is silly.*
> *That's what war*
> *is for.*

PARTING SHOT

Wars raged even before there were any little Willies to abort. Jehovah defenestrated Satan. The pagan gods vied in cannonades of mountains and thunderbolts. Zeus flexed his lightning, and Thor his hammer. Dawn man killed with rocks and clubs as enthusiastically as twilight man juggles atom bombs.

GREEK FIRE

The Byzantine Greeks invented greek fire, an incendiary mixture that blazes up on wetting.

PARTING SHOT

Parting shot, "the last word, as in an argument," dates back to the ancient Parthians, a Turkomanic people living to the southeast of the Caspian Sea. After each discharge of their bows, they would turn their horses as if in flight; "whence," says Partridge, "Parthian shot; whence parting shot."

In the 5th century B.C., Xerxes boasted that he would "go to Attica and eat the figs"—i.e., conquer Greece. Try as he might, he never got there. Things much coveted but not attained are

ATTIC FIGS

attic figs.

CHAERONEIA

A chaeroneia is a defeat for liberty, called after the battlefield where Philip of Macedonia finally crushed democratic Athens in 338 B.C.

CAPUA

To capua is to weaken by luxury, an expression referring to the erroneous belief that after Hannibal's Carthaginian troops went into winter quarters in 216 B.C. at Capua, south of Rome, they were so weakened by the opulent life of the city that they lost their fighting spirit. To be capuaed is the equivalent of Mencken's phrase "to be wobbled." In reality, the decline of Hannibal's fortunes after Capua was due to the new strategy of Fabius—never to accept battle when the enemy offered it, never to offer it on equal terms, but to destroy the enemy force little by little according to time and opportunity. Hence the expression

FABIAN

fabian for "cautious; dilatory." The fabian socialists, organized in England in 1884, were so named because they proposed to spread socialism, but gradually.

CARTHAGINIAN
PEACE

A carthaginian peace is a treaty so severe as to cripple, if not destroy, the defeated nation. The expression stems from the Third Punic War in the 2nd century B.C., when the Roman orator Cato's daily cry was *Delenda est Carthago!*—"Carthage must be destroyed!" The Romans spread salt over the site of Carthage in order that not even plants might grow there.

When Claudius invaded Britain (A.D. 43) he found his armies confronting a kind of hastily thrown-up breastwork which

BRATTICE the Romans called *brattice*, approximating the name of the British defenders. Brattice is no longer a fighting word; it is a partition, particularly one used in a mine for ventilation.

CHEVAL-DE-FRISE

CHEVAUX-DE-FRISE
Another breastwork is the *cheval-de-frise*, or "horse of Friezland" (also the name of a region of the Netherlands). In the Middle Ages the Frisians had no horses of their own. To protect themselves against cavalry attacks, they erected timber or iron posts traversed with iron-pointed spikes or spears. Today a *cheval-de-frise* is a sawhorse used as an obstacle, or any protecting line of sharp points, as spikes or nails along the top of a fence or wall. The jagged edges of women's skirts and caps in the 18th century were called *chevaux-de-frise*.

BUNDEEK
A crossbow made in Venice was called by the Arabs a *bundeek*, from Banadik, which was as close as they could come to pronouncing the name of the Italian city; a later musket bore the same name.

ADMIRAL
A man in authority is saluted as 'Amir in Arabic. A man in yet higher authority is an 'Amir a' ali, which to Westerners easily becomes *admiral*. During the crusade of 1249, the French adopted *amiral* from the Genoese, who had taken it from the Arabs. It entered English as admiral soon afterward. There is a folk-etymological enhancement from Latin *admirari*, since an admiral is "to be wondered at" for his rank and accomplishments; but the direct source is Arabic. Brown, joining the two strains, comments, "Our chief naval commanders are, by origin, Praiseworthy Pashas."

GUN
Guns (not small arms, but cannon; the small arms came later) were introduced into warfare in the first quarter of the 14th century. Though Webster speculates that gun traces back to Latin *canna*, "pipe or reed" (which certainly is true for cannon), Britannica approves Skeat's suggestion that the word "conceals a female name, Gunnhilde or Gunhilda," of which Gunne is a diminutive. Both *gunne* and *hilda* mean "war" in Old Norwegian. An inventory of war material at Windsor Castle in 1330–31 lists *una magna balista de cornu quae vocatur Domina Guinilda*: loosely, "a large and powerful missile thrower named Lady Guinilda." The case for Gunnhilde as the mother of gun may not be watertight, but it does not leak much.

VERDUN
In the 16th century, a long rapier was called a verdun after its place of manufacture in Verdun, France—the same Verdun that was to be the scene of some of the bitterest fighting between the French and Germans in World War I.

TOLEDO BLADE

Concurrently, finely tempered swords were being made at Toledo, forty miles southwest of Madrid. The best were said to be those tempered by having passed through a human body. The high quality of the blade soon made toledo blade generic; the name of an Ohio steel-town newspaper, the *Toledo Blade*, puns on the sword.

BAYONET

The first bayonet emerged from the factories of Bayonne, France, about 1575.

PISTOL
BISTOURY

Pistol probably derives from Pistoia, Italy, origin also of the extremely sharp blade called bistoury, used in surgery for minor incisions.

DAMASCUS STEEL

An excellent steel, damascus, is named for the capital city of Syria; it makes as effective a plowshare as a sword.

CARBINE

A form of small firearm which came into use near the end of the 16th century, shorter than the musket and used chiefly by mounted men, was the carbine, now a shortened version of the ordinary rifle. Carbine has been traced to the scarab, or dung beetle; but Partridge considers it a corruption of Calabria, where the weapon was first manufactured.

In passing—it really has nothing to do with my thesis—the word offhand comes from rifle shooting. It is the vertical position used in competitive shooting; kneeling and prone are the other two. Offhand shooting is less reliable than the others.

ISABEL

A perhaps apocryphal story asserts that the color isabel, a shade of brownish-yellow, takes its name from the underwear of the Infanta Isabella of Spain, who, with her husband Albert, reigned over Belgium from 1598 to 1621. The Infanta had vowed never to change or wash her unmentionables until her husband took the city of Ostend by siege; this required three years.

ANDREA FERRAS

Elizabethan literature frequently mentions the Andrea Ferrara, a Scottish broadsword attributed by Scots to a drill sergeant named Andrea Ferras. The true maker was probably Andrea dei Ferrari ("Andrew of the Smiths"), a 16th-century Italian swordmaker; but one way or another, the Scots got the sword.

STEENKIRK

A kind of cravat or lace, negligently worn, is known as a steenkirk, because of a turn in the weather at the Battle of Steenkirk, Belgium, in 1692. The day was so hot that the officers of the opposing French and British forces removed their neckwear and in some instances turned their shirts backward.

HANNAH   The nickname hannah for a female marine, common for British Wrens in World War II, goes back to Hannah Snell of Worcester (1723–1792), who, passing herself off as a man, took part in the attack on Pondicherry, India, in either 1761 or 1778.

BLUNDERBUSS   The English jeered at the Dutch *donderbus* ("thunder gun") as a "blunderbuss" because, like all 17th-century muzzleloaders, it was clumsy, inaccurate, and unreliable. "Blunder" was folk etymology, while the remainder of the name seems to have been a reminder of Good Queen Bess. Her name is also incorporated

BROWN BESS   in the brown bess, an equally inefficient British smooth-bore musket of the same period.

CARRONADE   The carronade, named after its place of manufacture at Carron, Scotland, was a light cannon used on shipboard in the 18th century to sweep enemy decks, and sometimes on shore as a howitzer.

SHRAPNEL   In 1804, in Dutch Guiana, the British first fired in anger a hollow projectile containing a number of balls and a charge of powder to burst the shell. This was shrapnel, a foretaste of bigger and better wars. It was the explosive brainchild of Lieutenant General Henry Shrapnel (1761–1842). Anything hit by a shell fragment in warfare, whatever the source, is "shrapneled."

(Excuse me for another irrelevance, referring neither to an uncommon, improper noun nor to a proper name used commonly. Still, it is a good story: After the Battle of Vittoria in 1813, the 14th King's Hussars captured Joseph Bonaparte's carriage and retained a silver chamber pot as a trophy. They commemorated the event by styling themselves the Emperor's Chambermaids, a euphemistic title which they bear proudly to this day.)

COPENHAGEN   The British destroyed the Danish fleet in 1807 without declaration of war, giving rise to the phrase "to copenhagen" for such unsanctioned attacks.

STRAIGHT FROM THE HORSE'S MOUTH   It sticks in Drew Middleton's mind, and I take his word for it, that in the Peninsular Wars the Horse Guards—i.e., the offices of the secretary of war in the old Guards barracks in Whitehall—were frequently the source of information not otherwise available—much to the annoyance of the Duke of Wellington, who preferred to keep military matters under his own cocked hat. "Straight from the horse's mouth" came to mean any fact imparted on impeccable authority. (There are similar expressions that I cannot resist including, though they are not uncommon, improper nouns. "A pig in a poke," for instance, stems from the fact that pigs were once tied up in sacks for marketing, in order to prevent them from wriggling loose. As a result, the customer could not see what he was buying. It might turn out to be not a pig but a cat; whence "let the cat out of the bag.")

WATERLOO
On June 18, 1815, at Waterloo, Belgium, Napoleon was finally defeated by a combined British and German army operating under the supreme command of the Duke of Wellington. A waterloo is a decisive defeat or reverse. Timothy points out, however, that this definition is arbitrary, since if the battle represented the irremediable overthrow of one man, it also signaled the consummate triumph of another; it could logically be considered a synonym for victory. Language often disregards logic.

DUKES
The Duke of Wellington's nose compared in magnitude with those of Cyrano de Bergerac and Schnozzola Durante. His troops called him "Nosey." Cockneys began to call noses dukes in his honor. Fists, by extension, were duke-busters. Duke-buster shrank back to duke, but retained the meaning "fist." When you are ordered to put up your dukes, you are being challenged to fisticuffs.

CONGREVE

CONGREVE ROCKET
The first friction matches made in England (they were evil-smelling things) were called congreves by the inventor after Sir William Congreve (1772–1828), whose own inventions were numerous. His best known is the congreve rocket, a loud, smoky affair probably more suitable for a Fourth of July celebration than for war. Nonetheless, it was effective against the French, largely through the fearsome sound of its exploding shell. In the Burmese War of 1825, a congreve rocket had a lucky first shot: it landed in the midst of the Burmese high command and killed them all, including their chief, Mahul Bandula. The Burmese fled incontinently, awestruck and demoralized. The campaign, if not the war, was won by a firework.

PROMETHEAN

LUCIFER
The early friction match changed its name as the years passed—first to promethean, after the Titan who gave men fire, and then to lucifer, after the star of morning who rebelled against Jehovah.

BLIGHTY
For the 18th- and 19th-century fighting men in India, blighty meant "home; England." The word shows the mutation of Hindi *wilāyatī* ("foreign country"; ultimately the foreign country England) into *bilāytī*. A common noun in Hindi, to the British

it was first a proper name and then a common noun once more. In World War I a blighty became a wound which got one sent home.

Around 1812, a girl named Fanny Adams was murdered at Alton, in Hampshire, England. Her body, cut into pieces, was thrown into a river. The British troops, when tinned mutton became a staple of their rations, called the meat fanny adams. The equivalent in the merchant navy was a harriet lane, after another murder victim. A fanny (besides the vulgar meaning) was a naval mess kettle. It is erroneous, however, to assume a similar connection between Dixie, a collective designation for the Southern states, and the dixie, another mess tin used in camp; dixie hobson-jobsons Hindi *degeí*, "kettle."

The early 19th century was the heyday of Karl von Clausewitz (1780–1831), a Prussian army officer whose studies profoundly altered military theory. To refer to a man as a Clausewitz is to rank him a seminal genius on the tactics and strategy of war.

War, according to an account in an 1866 issue of the *Mexican Times,* is responsible for the word humbug. During the wars between the German states, says the story, so many false reports emanated from Hamburg that one expressed disbelief by saying "You had that from Hamburg," which became corrupted to humbug. The Century Dictionary says the word was first used about 1735.

Colonal James Bowie (1796?–1836), an American adventurer who was once an associate of the notorious pirate Jean Lafitte, probably never bothered his mind over abstruse military strategy. He did, however, spend considerable time sharpening his knife, an ugly, single-edged instrument curved at the tip and about fifteen inches long. The bowie knife was used indiscriminately to cut the throats of deer or of men. Whether the colonel or his brother Rezin designed it is in dispute, but the colonel wielded it with historic effectiveness until the Mexicans outknifed him at the Alamo.

A particularly nasty bullet of 19th-century provenance is the dumdum, which expands upon impact. It is named from its place of manufacture, Dum Dum, near Calcutta. Which reminds me (such references pop from nowhere into my delighted mind) that in the 18th and 19th centuries the heat of the Punjab in India was deemed to cause amnesia and confusion; to this day

PUNJAB HEAD the English say one suffering from such an ailment has the punjab head.

COLT In 1835, Samuel Colt (1814–1862) patented the first practical revolver, a single-barreled pistol with a rotating breech. The Colt was to become the universal handgun. In Wild West days it would have been a foolhardy cowboy indeed who ventured into a saloon without his Colt as an "equalizer." It remains the most ubiquitous of revolvers.

GARIBALDI RED Garibaldi red is named from the color of the shirts worn in battle by Giuseppe Garibaldi (1807–1882), liberator of Italy. Patriotic Italian women favored a shirtwaist of the same color.

INDIANA VOLUNTEER Among the troops serving under General Zachary Taylor in the Mexican War (1846–1848) were a number of Indiana volunteers. It was charged that these men headed homeward when the situation grew awkward at the Battle of Buena Vista. Someone who looks like a hero until the bullets begin to fly is an Indiana volunteer.

MAGENTA SOLFERINO In 1859, the French and Austrians had a bloody set-to at Magenta, Italy. A purplish dye discovered in the same year was named magenta because of the supposed resemblance of its color to blood. Another bluish-red is called solferino, for the other great battle of that campaign.

DERRINGER Before the Civil War, Henry Deringer (1786–1868), a Philadelphia gunsmith, invented and gave his name (with an added r) to a short-barreled pocket pistol with a grip shaped like the head of a bird. John Wilkes Booth used a derringer to assassinate Abraham Lincoln.

BILLY JOHNNY STONEWALL "There's Jackson's brigade standing like a stone wall," said the Confederate general B. E. Bee, perhaps somewhat ruefully (for he could have used a bit of help himself) at the first battle of Bull Run. Thomas Jonathan Jackson, then Colonel but soon to be General, was known thenceforth as Stonewall Jackson. Less than two years later this tactical genius was accidentally mortally wounded by his own men, perhaps destroying the johnnies' last chance of victory. (Union soldiers were billies, Confederates johnnies—short for billy yank and johnny reb[el].) Stonewall returned to common usage as an expression meaning not to yield an inch. During the Watergate scandals, the Nixon Administration stonewalled to the bitter end.

CUSTERISM

To engage in foredoomed confrontation with a superior enemy is custerism. The allusion is to the last stand of Major General G. A. Custer (1839–1876), who was ambushed and massacred with his entire command by Sioux Indians under Crazy Horse.

BOLD AS BEAUCHAMP

JACQUERIE

But history, or legend, recalls military triumphs against even greater odds than Custer faced. In 1346, Thomas Beauchamp, Earl of Warwick, is said to have overthrown at Hogges, in Normandy, with the help of one esquire and six archers, one hundred armed men, giving rise to the expression "bold as Beauchamp." In 1358, one Captal-de-Buch, with but forty followers, allegedly cleared the Jacquerie (French peasant insurrectionists) from the town of Meaux, killing seven thousand of them. A jacquerie is any peasant revolt, but especially a very bloody one. The name is from the contemptuous title Jacques Bonhomme, given by the nobles to the peasants.

GATLING GUN

R. J. Gatling (1818–1903), a North Carolinian whose inventions include a screw propeller, a grain-sowing machine, a hemp-breaking machine, and a steam plow, perfected in 1862 a gun that fired the then incredible total of 350 shots a minute. The gatling gun was eventually adopted, says Britannica, "by almost every civilized nation." "Civilized" is a bemusing word in the context. If you watch gangster melodramas on television, you will find that gat, short for gatling, has become established underworld usage for a pistol or revolver. Timothy says the gatling gun was not used against human beings until the New Orleans riots of 1866, at about which time someone wrote the imperialist couplet:

> *Whatever happens, we have got*
> *The gatling gun, and they have not.*

MAUSER

The mauser, a breechloading rifle used for a generation by the Germans, was invented in 1867 by the brothers Peter Paul and Wilhelm Mauser. Peter Paul invented the mauser magazine rifle in 1897. There is also a mauser pistol.

CHASSEPOT

The French lost the Franco-German War of 1870–1871 despite the advantage of an excellent breechloading rifle invented in 1866 by Antoine Chassepot. The chassepot, which had contributed to the rout of Garibaldi at Mentana in 1867, proved markedly superior to the Germans' highly touted "needle gun."

By the end of the century, inventors were rationalizing that their improved weapons, by making war more destructive, rendered it less likely. Alfred Nobel (1833–1896) asserted that his invention of nitroglycerin made further warfare "unthinkable." Nonetheless, he gave his name not to the dynamite but to the Nobel Peace Prize.

BALKANIZE

The Balkan wars of 1912–1913 split the states of Rumania, Serbia, Greece, Montenegro, and Bulgaria into hostile units. To balkanize a region is to divide it into inimical parts.

ARCHY

World War I gave us, among other name-related words, archy for German anti-aircraft guns. The expression is supposed to have stemmed from British flyers' habit of greeting each new burst of fire with a catch phrase from a current music hall hit: "Archibald, certainly not!" Archie was already generic for an upper-class young man.

FURPHY

Furphy, rather onomatopoeic Australian slang for "latrine rumor," referred to Furphy Brothers, who furnished field latrines to the Australian troops. The expression may have been reinforced by one John Furphy (1843–1913), an Australian, who wrote tall tales under the pen name of Tom Collins.

IMMELMANN
TURN

An immelmann turn, developed by the German pilot Max Immelmann (1890–1916), is a maneuver in which an airplane completes a half-loop and then makes a half-roll to resume a level position. This evasive action enables the craft to revert quickly to an offensive (or defensive) position. A German officer named Lufen perfected the lufen turn, a similar piece of acrobatics.

LUFEN TURN

BIG BERTHA

The big bertha, a heavy siege gun, alludes in its name to Berta Krupp von Bohlen und Halbach, head of the Krupp steel works, which made most of the large guns of the German army in both world wars. From this ugly eminence the expression declined into a genial slang term for a stout woman.

DEB

World War I also launched the term deb for one who commits his forces only after the battle is won or the enemy has been drawn off. General Marie Eugene Debeney, an associate of Marshal Foch, was charged with such shenanigans.

RUPERT

A barrage balloon—a small captive balloon from which wires or nets are suspended as protection against air attacks—is called a rupert, from Rupert of Bavaria (1869–1955), apparently a bulgy fellow. Through his mother he was a descendant of the Stuart kings of England and in the succession to the British crown. He was given chief command of the northern group of German armies on the western front in World War I.

ASDIC

SONAR

Asdic is an acronym for Anti-Submarine Detection Investigation Committee—forerunner of sonar, itself an acronym for SOund NAvigation Ranging. (In Hindi, a sonar is a gold- or silversmith.)

FLAK

Flak is surely one of the more felicitous acronyms to emerge from World War II. It first referred to anti-aircraft guns, or, more commonly, their exploding shells. Flak is now slang for excessive criticism or abuse: "Don't give me any more flak." The word unites the initial letters of German *Fl(ugzeug) A(bwehr) K(anone),* "aircraft defense gun."

BREN GUN

Another war-born acronym was the British bren gun, combining Br(no), Czechoslovakia, where it was first made, and En(field), England, where it was manufactured in large quantities.

FINLANDIZATION

In 1940 Russia failed to overwhelm Finland by force of arms, though she came closer a year or so later. Her power remains so near and overwhelming, however, that Finland dares not risk an independent foreign policy. Ascendancy without conquest is finlandization.

PEARL HARBOR

JAP

American military participation in World War II began on December 7, 1941, when a Japanese air attack, delivered while the two nations were still technically at peace, sank or severely damaged much of the U.S. Pacific Fleet. For a long time to come, any devastating military blow under cover of peace, once called a copenhagen, will be known as a pearl harbor. To jap, is to take by surprise; an unexpected test at school is a jap.

WIMPY

A gluttonous character in *Popeye*, a comic strip by E. C. Segar (1894–1938), was J. Wellington Wimpy, so addicted to hamburgers that he would commit any enormity to obtain them. Not only did hamburgers in England become wimpies (a name now applied also to the stands where hamburgers are sold), but British airmen in World War II referred to the Wellington bomber as a J. Wellington Wimpy, soon shortened to wimpy.

MOLOTOV
COCKTAIL

In the face of the Nazis' 1941 blitzkrieg, the poorly armed Russians supplemented their conventional weaponry with a makeshift incendiary bomb consisting of a breakable container filled with flammable liquid and provided with a rag wick. This device had been used against the Russians in the Finnish war of 1939–1940, but now became known as a molotov cocktail, after the Soviet Foreign Minister, V. M. Molotov. Molotov, a veteran of the Bolshevik revolution, was a tough old boy. He gave his

MOLOTOV BREADBASKET	name also to the molotov breadbasket, a cluster of small bombs dropped from an airplane.
JACK JOHNSON	A jack johnson, a heavy explosive emitting a column of dark smoke, salutes the boxer who in 1908 dethroned James Jeffries, becoming the first black to attain the heavyweight championship of the world. Efforts to find a white man who could defeat him gave rise to the phrase "great white hope."
MOANING MINNIE	The moaning minnie, a six-barreled German howitzer, was named from the rising shriek it uttered when fired. The personalization was limited to the Allied side; the Germans considered the weapon a simple *minenwerfer*, "mine thrower."
QUONSET HUT NISSEN HUT	A portable shelter frequently employed by the military was the quonset hut, a prefabricated edifice first built in Quonset, Rhode Island. Its semicylindrical roof of corrugated metal curves down to form walls. Similar in concept is the nissen hut, designed by Lieutenant Colonel Peter N. Nissen (1871–1930), a British mining engineer.
CHICAGO PIANO	The chicago piano, a pompom or 20-millimeter antiaircraft cannon, recalls the city where in Prohibition days the pianos of Al Capone and his henchmen played deadly music.
GONE FOR A BURTON	RAF slang for "dead; missing; absent" was "gone for a burton," probably shortened from "gone for a drink of Burton's ale." Burton's ale was, and still is, a popular thirst quencher, in England. The slang term was a reminder that many airmen lost their lives in the sea—the "drink"—particularly in the first years of the war.
STOKES GUN LEWIS GUN	The stokes and lewis guns were two elementary machine guns, perhaps remembered best because Lawrence of Arabia called two of his men Stokes and Lewis because they operated these guns.
G.I.	In World War I, American soldiers were called doughboys, perhaps because their large military buttons resembled dumplings of that name. Though a doughboy is not an uncommon, improper noun or a Patient Griselda, a G.I. is. The Yanks of World War II were first Government Issue Joes, then G.I. Joes, and then simply G.I.'s.
HERSHEY BAR	A hershey bar is a stripe for overseas service. The reference is to the candy, with an infusion from Lieutenant General L. B. Hershey (1893–1976), wartime director of the Selective Service System.

CATCH-22

Catch-22 designates the small print that makes any enterprise hopeless from the start. In Joseph Heller's novel so titled, the hero sought to leave the Army on grounds of insanity only to be informed that you could not be crazy if you wanted to get out of the Army.

Uncommon, improper nouns from Korea, Vietnam, the Middle East, and other recent or impending wars are yet to come in.

Timothy in Arms

Timothy sat tapping the barrel of his pen against his teeth and breathing *Omm-mmm-mm-mmm* until I thought he had become a Zen Buddhist.

"Is anything the matter?" I asked.

"Not really. But you did omit a bit."

I thought I had covered the waterfront.

"*Mmm-mmm* . . . yes. The wars in India, for instance. Where is pandy?"

"Where?" I echoed. "*What* is pandy?"

PANDY

"A pandy is a mutinous native soldier. From Pande, a common Bengali given name."

"How could I have missed it?"

POONA

Timothy ignored the sarcasm. "Poona," he continued inexorably. "Meaning terribly stuffy. Poona was a major British base in India. In Poona, the Indian Civil Service did not speak to the box-wallahs—"

BOX WALLAH

"What is a box-wallah?"

"Merchant out from England. The Army did not speak to the Civil Service. The infantry officers regarded themselves as superior to the Indian officers, and the cavalry officers spoke only to themselves."

"And perhaps to God," I said, "like the Lowells?"

"The Cabots," Timothy corrected gently. "Exactly. Oh, by the way—Beecher's Bible?"

BEECHER'S BIBLE

"Weren't rifles called Beecher's Bibles because Henry Ward Beecher agitated against new slave states, and his followers took that to mean armed resistance?"

"Exactly. Bleeding Kansas and all that. Now . . . let . . . us . . .

MATA HARI

see. World War I. Mata Hari? For a woman spy? She was really not so dreadful, you know. Nor so beautiful. But very stupid. Of Dutch origin—Netherlands Indies—pseudo-Malayan. Any secrets she gave the Germans were of little value. The French executed her to prove their resolution. At about the same time they shot a man named Bolo because he had said the French could never whip the Germans.

BLOOEY

"Blooey, meaning gone to pot? One suspects it originated at Blois, where a military hospital was located. The word is not recorded before 1920.

"It is hard to believe," he went on, "that as late as World War I, England remained a completely stratified society. Lord Curzon passed some Tommies bathing in the vats of a huge Belgian brewery that had been destroyed by shellfire. He said to his companion, 'Dear me, General, I had no idea the lower classes had such white skins.'"

"What was Palmerston's remark of the same sort to Victoria?" I asked.

"She was reviewing volunteers in Windsor Great Park with Palmerston, then Home Secretary. In 1853. The day was warm, and the odor from the ranks was rank. 'Esprit de corps, your Majesty,' explained Palmerston."

"A rank pun."

TO BE HULLED

"Precisely. *Omm.* Good good good. Oh, to be hulled. General William Hull invaded Canada in the War of 1812, expecting an easy victory, but was forced to capitulate ignominiously. The Americans court-martialed him and sentenced him to be shot, but let him live because of his service in the Revolution."

I mused, "If I started to count the number of times I have been hulled—"

BLACK-AND-TAN

"Exactly. Black and tans? They were the irregulars used by the English in the early 1920s to harass and torture the Irish. Named for a pack of hounds with extraordinary markings. The Irish used to say, 'Evil as a black-and-tan.'

BAEDEKER
RAIDS

"Bop . . . bop . . . bop. Baedeker raids, of course. After the famous guidebook—because in World War II the Germans launched obliteration raids against historic English cities. It has been asserted that Oxford was spared because so many of the German leaders had studied there."

He wadded his notes and stuffed them into a side pocket. I said, "Is that all, Timothy?"

LONGACRE

"Ah . . . one . . . thing . . . more. Longacre. One who talks of himself endlessly. At the Congress of Vienna, Sir Sidney Smith went into such detail about how he had compelled Napoleon to raise the siege of Acre in 1799 that the Prince de Ligne referred to Smith as Longacre."

"That reminds me," I said. "Do you remember the story of the little girl who received a gift book about penguins and had to write a thank-you note? She wrote, 'Thank you so much for the book. It taught me everything I had always wanted to know about penguins. Even more than I wanted to know.' Do you think we may be crowding this book with just a little more than anyone really wants to know?"

Timothy said, "Goodnight, Mr. Longacre."

EARTHLY WORDS

ELEVEN

THE WAY OF ALL IRISH
✕
A BROGUE OF WORDS

HE IRISH have enriched English with Gaelic words; in addition, they have uncovered a spangled heaven of new suns and constellations in their second tongue. English, Irishly spoken, must closely resemble the music of the heavenly spheres.

Breakers on the Irish coast may be simply breakers to you, but not to an Irishman. To him they are O'Donahue's white horses, because every seventh year O'Donahue, the monster hero, comes riding back to Ireland through the surf.

The image is pure Irish. It is not enough to say the Irish are born with a harp in the throat; their silliest sentences come out like the goose girl's in the fairy story, all emeralds and pearls. Sweet talk was the only ally available to the defenders of Blarney Castle, County Cork, when an overwhelming English force besieged it in 1602; but persuasion and promises served so well that the English, distracted, failed to overrun the castle before an Irish relief force arrived to raise the siege. Blarney, atrociously defined by Webster as "cajoling flattery," is confined to the Irish; it is not for export. Some etymologists see a parallel between blarney and baloney, "nonsense." Which is what the parallel is, nonsense; no Italian sausage can aspire to compete with so noble a product of the silver Irish tongue.

BALLYHOO

If blarney fails to bring an Irishman his heart's desire, he may escalate to ballyhoo, "clamorous advertising; noisy uproar." In the old days, a Patrick out for a lively time would walk the bogs to Ballyhooly, where he could expect the singing and roistering to continue into the dawn. I hold this origin of ballyhoo to be self-evident, notwithstanding the captious pedants who would derive it from bally (a euphemism for the expletive "bloody") and hooey.

TWISS

It is hard to have the last word with an Irishman. Richard Twiss (1747–1821) did his best to put them down in his travel book *Tour in Ireland.* The Irish responded by manufacturing a chamber pot called the twiss, with a portrait of Twiss at the bottom captioned:

Let everyone piss
On lying Dick Twiss.

Irish tongues can be as rough as their fists, and far more deft. You will have to go far to match the invective of the last two lines of the James Stephens poem "A Glass of Beer," in which an Irishman execrates the barmaid who denied him credit for a drink:

May she marry a ghost and bear him a kitten, and may
The High King of Glory permit her to get the mange.

The co-managers of the Gate Theatre in Dublin were of a minority persuasion in their sexual conduct. Who but the Irish would have called them "Sodom and Begorra"?

I am convinced, regardless of the evidence, that it was an Irishman who first referred to blue patches in a stormy sky as "Dutchman's breeches."

If Irish eloquence is traditional, so are such Irish bulls as this:

> A priest in a country parish asked his flock to raise money for a chandelier. One of the parishioners arose to say, "Yer Riverince, I am opposed, for three reasons. First, there's nobody within tin miles can spell chandelier. Second, there's nobody within tin miles could play one. And third, what we really need is more light."

LIMERICK

Limerick, little more than a wide place in an Irish road, gave its name to the most pervasive of all verse forms—an arrangement, often nonsensical, of five anapaestic lines. The form has existed since Roman times. It was popularized by Edward Lear in his *Book of Nonsense* (1846), and became a popular subject for improvisation at convivial parties. Between each new offering, the guests would sing, "We'll all come up, come up to Limerick," and the verse soon took the name of the village. Limericks gained their worldwide popularity with such thought-provoking observations as these:

> *There was an old man at the Cape*
> *Who made himself garments of crape;*
> *When asked, "Will they tear?"*
> *He replied, "Here and there,*
> *But they keep in such beautiful shape!"*

and

> *There was a young man who said "Damn!*
> *It is borne upon me that I am*
> *An engine which moves*
> *In predestinate grooves.*
> *I'm not even a bus; I'm a tram."*

Britannica says the best limericks are those with the largest amount of improbable incident or subtle innuendo (often sexual) that can be crowded into the available space:

> *There was a young maid from Madras,*
> *Who had a magnificent ass;*
> *Not rounded and pink,*
> *As you probably think—*
> *It was gray, had long ears, and ate grass.*

MICK

JARVEY

Mick, from Micky, from Michael, was once applied in this country to Irish immigrants, and indeed to all immigrant workers. A jarvey, from Jarvey, was the driver of an Irish stagecoach; but the name is not Irish in origin. It comes from Saint Gervaise,

BIDDY

depicted in paintings bearing a whip, as a coach driver did, because he was whipped to death. Biddy, a serving maid, shortens Irish Bridget. In America, biddy is applied also to a hen, and in Australia to a woman teacher.

MULLIGAN
STEW
MURPHY

Mulligan is a stew of various meats and vegetables. Murphy remains popular slang for the Irish potato. They are hearty dishes, though rough, the mainstay of many a Mulligan and Murphy; the taste of the Irish is less refined in food than in literature. Indeed, a recent survey shows that the Irish, followed closely by the Americans, are the heaviest eaters among North Atlantic peoples.

MURPHY BED

In my early childhood I slept with my brother and sister in a murphy bed, one that folds or swings into a closet for concealment. It was designed by an American inventor named William Lawrence Murphy (1876–1959), obviously Irish by heritage.

KELLY POOL

GET THE
IRISH UP
SHILLELAGH

SCOT

Precious as the blarney, ballyhoo, and limericks may be, they are not the most precious product of the Green Isle. Nor is kelly pool, named for some Kelly, an irresistible variety of pool in which each player draws a number and, while playing on the object balls in numerical order, aims to pocket the ball bearing his number. No, the pinnacle of Irish achievement is Irish whiskey—usquebaugh, "water of life." The whiskey goes down well with a spot of agreeable violence. A disgrace to the Irish is the lad who when offended fails to get his irish up and fight— not with gun or knife, mind you, but with his two fists, reinforced perhaps by a cudgel of oak or blackthorn, called a shillelagh after the town of the same name. The British sometimes speak of "getting the scot up"; but scot (for Scotsman) has nothing like the same flavor as irish, and will never catch on. (The scot in "scot-free," meaning tax-free or without penalty, is another word altogether. It is from the North Country, and comes from "shoot; a shooting.")

PADDY WAGON
PADDY
SHAMUS

When the sons of Erin boiled into the slums of the United States in the 19th century, their brawls were so frequent and vigorous that the police wagons which carted them off to the hoosegow (a word of Spanish, not Irish, antecedents) were called paddy wagons, after the nickname for Patrick. The paddies were the police, not the brawlers. A common term for a detective, shamus, is from Seamus, Irish for James.

BRANNIGAN

An Irish brawler, one Brannigan, was so renowned for his prowess that to this day his countrymen call any confused quarrel a brannigan.

DONNYBROOK

The annual fair at Donnybrook was for centuries the setting, according to Bergen Evans, of "cheerful violence, open-hearted pugnacity, and sociable clouting of skulls by shillelaghs." A donnybrook is "an uproarious or riotous occasion."

Mencken cites Irish as an element in many English compounds, chiefly of a derogatory or satirical significance:

Irish promotion, a demotion (often the loss of a job)
Irish evidence, perjury
Irish apricots, potatoes
Irish legs, thick ones
Irish beauty, a woman with two black eyes
Irish dividend, an assessment on stock
Irish spoon, a spade
Irish clubhouse, a police station
Irish bouquet, a brickbat
Irishman's dinner, a fast
Irish chariot or buggy, a wheelbarrow ("the greatest of human inventions, since it taught the Irish to walk on their hind legs")

IRISH KISS

Mencken omits one of my favorites—an Irish kiss for a slap.

This chapter is a paean to the Irish, but I will grant a closing paragraph or two to other nationalities. We have vernacular references, often uncomplimentary, for several.

TOMMY ATKINS
UNCLE SAM
BROTHER JONATHAN
JOHN BULL
MARIANNE
FRITZ
JERRY
IVAN
GEORDIE

Tommy Atkins personified a British soldier in World War I; Uncle Sam (after one Samuel Wilson, who helped finance the Revolution) stands for the United States; an American citizen was long called Brother Jonathan; an Englishman is still John Bull; Marianne stands for republican France; a German may be a Fritz or Jerry; an Ivan is a Russian; a Geordie comes from northeast England.

TO WELSH

Terms for strangers, and especially foreigners, tend to be pejorative. To welsh, for instance, means to default on an obligation. The usage may derive from a nursery rhyme:

Taffy was a Welshman, Taffy was a thief,
Taffy came to my house and stole a leg of beef . . .

The Welsh are not named after a place. Welsh means "foreigner," and was applied by the invading Saxons to the tribes they drove before them into what is now Wales. The Welsh refer to themselves as *cymru*, "comrades."

BOHUNK A bohunk (from *Bo*hemian and *Hung*arian) is in U.S. slang an unskilled laborer, especially from former Austro-Hungary.

DAGO Dago, a contemptuous reference to persons of Mediterranean origin, is from the common given name Diego, from San Diego de Compostela, patron saint of Spain.

MOSEY Mosey, slang for "to stroll," evokes the slouching manner of early Jewish vendors, burdened down by their wares, many of whom were named, or in any event styled, Moses.

YID
YIDDISH
JEW
JEWFISH
JEWISH LIGHT-
   NING
JEW DOWN
Yid, a disparaging term for Jews, derives from Yiddish, which is an anglicism for German *jüdisch*, from Jude-Deutsch (Jewish-German). Jew comes from Judah. A jewfish is a rough-scaled, voracious, sluggish variety frequenting deep water in warm seas. Jewish lightning is arson. To jew down is to bargain for a lower price.

BOOR

SLAVE
Boor is contemptuous for the Boers of South Africa, whom the British patronized until the Boers proved tartars in the Boer War of 1899–1902. Slave, even more pejorative, refers to the Slavs of eastern Europe, often overrun and forced into peonage.

TWELVE

OCH, JOHNNY, I HARDLY KNEW YE!
✕
WORDS FROM NICKNAMES

KATYDID

ROBIN

HY ONE given name rather than another is applied to such a concept as maleness or femaleness, or to certain plants, or animals, or tools, or toys, or attributes, or states of mind, is an etymological mystery beyond resolution. Sometimes the reason may have been simple onomatopoeia—an insect sound, for instance, suggesting a girl's name (*katydid* . . .). In many cases, an individual bearing the name in question was probably not involved at all. Robin is short for robin redbreast; Robin is a diminutive of Robert; but God alone can identify the Robert, if any, who gave his name to the bird. He may have been the same

ZANY

DOBBIN	Robert whose pet name, Dobbin, is now attached to a farm horse, so that we call any gentle, faithful old nag a dobbin. Or the Robert whose nickname Robbekin turned into rabbit. Or the Bob o' Lincoln recalled in bobolink. Or the Bob of bobwhite.
RABBIT	
BOBOLINK	
BOBWHITE	

JOHN and its nickname Jack are ubiquitous uncommon, improper nouns. A johnny-come-lately is a tardy adherent to a cause or fashion. A johnnycake is a corncake (though the johnny here is probably a folk shift from "journey," such cakes being taken along for sustenance on trips); a johnny-jump-up is a fast-growing plant, usually a violet or pansy; a john-a-dreams is a dreamy, idle fellow; a johnny-on-the-spot is someone ready and available to act when necessary; a stage-door johnny is one who waits at stage doors for actresses to emerge; a john chinaman is a Chinese; a john dory is a type of Atlantic fish (perhaps, however, named from John Dory, a 16th-century privateer who was the subject of a popular music hall ballad); a johnny darter, a small, quick fish of American streams; a john is a toilet, or the room containing one; and in a "dear john" letter a girl ends her relationship with her sweetheart, usually on the ground that she has found someone she loves better. A john is also the customer of a prostitute.

(Labels in left margin: JOHNNY-COME-LATELY, JOHNNYCAKE, JOHNNY-JUMP-UP, JOHN-A-DREAMS, JOHNNY-ON-THE-SPOT, STAGE-DOOR JOHNNY, JOHN CHINAMAN, JOHN DORY, JOHNNY DARTER, JOHN, DEAR JOHN LETTER)

APPLEJOHN An applejohn is small withered apple (James Madison was called Applejohn from his build and appearance).

ZANY Zany, meaning one who plays the foolish or simple fellow, sometimes on purpose, is a Venetian form of Giovanni—John in Italian—the name assigned to the "tom-fool" character in the commedia dell'arte. If you name your son John, don't nickname him Zany.

JOCK In Scotland, the diminutive of John is Jock. A jock in America is a macho sort, more interested in sports than studies. A jockey is a professional rider of horses in races, and sometimes a cheat.

JOCKEY

Why does jack denote the male in jackass? What does it mean in jack rabbit and jackdaw? Why is it so commonly employed for tools—bootjack, kitchen jack, tire jack? How does it manage to cover so wide a range—steeplejack, jackknife, jack-in-the-pulpit, flapjacks, manjack (a tree), man jack (an individual: "Every man jack was there"), jacks (a children's game played with specially shaped pieces of metal), jack-of-all-trades, jack off (to masturbate)?

(Labels in left margin: JACKASS, JACK RABBIT, JACKDAW, BOOTJACK, KITCHEN JACK, TIRE JACK, FLAPJACK, MANJACK, MAN JACK, STEEPLEJACK, JACKS, EVERY MAN JACK, JACK UP, JACKKNIFE, JACK-IN-THE-PULPIT, JACK-OF-ALL-TRADES, JACK OFF)

BLACKJACK	Why is a blackjack at once a small leather-covered bludgeon with a short flexible strap, a card game, a type of oak tree, and a tankard made of tarred or waxed leather? (General John Pershing was called Black Jack and Nigger Jack because he once commanded black cavalry.)
HIJACK	There is jack up as in jack up a wheel. There is hijack—to steal property in transport (presumably the miscreant would call to someone, "Hi, Jack!" and then hit him over the head).
CRACKERJACK	Crackerjack or crackajack means something especially fine or splendid. As a proprietary term, it is a sweetened compound
APPLEJACK	chiefly of popcorn and syrup. Applejack is brandy produced by freezing hard cider. To skyjack is to commandeer an aircraft.
SKYJACK	To skyjack is to commandeer an aircraft.
JACK-IN-THE-BOX	Jack-in-the-box may be a child's toy, a kind of firework, a hermit crab, or a cuckoopint (an herb of Europe and Asia); a
JACK-O'-LANTERN	jack-o'-lantern is a hollowed pumpkin with carved-out eyes,
JACKPOT	nose, and mouth, and lighted from the inside; a jackpot in poker is a pool which cannot be opened until some player has a hand with a pair of jacks or better. In the 1760s rioters against John Stuart, Lord Bute, punned their protest by burning a jackboot in
JACKBOOT	effigy.
TOMBOY	Take Thomas—or, rather, its diminutive, Tom. A tomboy is no boy at all, but a romping girl who wants to play the rough
TOM, DICK, AND HARRY	games her brothers play. Tom, Dick, and Harry is everybody. In England and Scotland, a tommy is a loaf of bread, or provisions
TOMMY	
TOMCAT	of all sorts. Tomcat is the other side of the coin from gib cat (from Gilbert), a castrated male; Gilbert is not a popular name among
TOMFOOL	cats. Tomfool, tommyrot, tomtit (a bird), long tom (a large,
TOMMYROT	
TOMTIT	long-range gun), tom noddy (an idiot), mad tom (a catfish with
LONG TOM	poisonous pectoral spines), tommy knocker (an unexplained
TOM NODDY	sound in a mine), tommy shop (a company store—christened in
MAD TOM	
TOMMY KNOCKER	one of Disraeli's novels), a soft tommy (a soft touch)—these are but a sampling. Webster lists at least forty vernacular words from
TOMMY SHOP	
SOFT TOMMY	that one given name.
GOOD-TIME CHARLEY	A good-time charley is someone whose principal interest is social pleasure.
MAGPIE	The magpie, a chattering bird, is called after some Mag, a
NANNY GOAT	pet form of Margaret. The nanny in nanny goat adopts the pet
NANNY	name for Ann. Since infants were frequently fed goat's milk, the

LAZY SUSAN

goat may also connect with nanny, a children's nurse, though some contend that this originated as baby talk for "nursie." French children call a nanny a *nounou*. Nelly, a large hyperborean bird, shortens Ellen, Helen, or Eleanor. A nice nelly is a milksop. A nervous nelly is one unduly concerned over the risks attending an undertaking.

NELLY
NICE NELLY
NERVOUS NELLY

LAZY SUSAN

The lazy susan, a revolving food tray, apparently dates from the beginning of the century, being named for some unknown servant.

BROWN BETTY

American brown betty is a baked pudding of chopped or sliced apples, bread crumbs, raisins, sugar, butter, and spices. It is also the coneflower. But who was Betty? The brown bess is not only a flintlock rifle, described in another place, but the prairie wake-robin. A charlotte russe is a cold dessert of Bavarian cream, set in a mold lined with ladyfingers. But who was Charlotte? A chuck wagon is a wagon equipped with food and cooking uten-

BROWN BESS

CHARLOTTE
RUSSE
CHUCK WAGON

CRÊPE SUZETTE — sils, as in a lumber camp. But who was Chuck? Suzette is a pet form of Suzanne in French, and a crêpe suzette is a thin dessert pancake, usually rolled with hot orange or tangerine sauce, and often served with a flaming brandy or curaçao sauce. But who was Suzette?

MARGARITA — On a spirituous level, a margarita is a cocktail made of tequila, lemon or lime juice, and Triple Sec, usually served with salt encrusted on the rim of the glass. In Latin it is a pearl; in the church it is the vessel in which the consecrated Host is preserved. Clearly, Margarita was quite a girl. I am sorry I never knew her.

HODGE

HOB
INNOCENT
NINNY
SIMPLE SIMON
RUBE
YOKEL

Language has not been fair to some given names. It is not the fault of Roger that his nickname, Hodge, became an epithet for bumpkin, nor of Robert or Robin (as in Robin Goodfellow) that the shrunken form Hob became a rustic, clown, or elf. The gentle word innocent, in the past often a given name, has sunk to ninny. A nursery rhyme turned the perfectly respectable name Simon into a simpleton, partly through association of sound. A rube, an unsophisticated country fellow, is a nickname for Reuben. Yokel derives from the biblical name Jacob; in Bohemia, it came to be spelled Jokel (read yokel), and a jokel was condemned as an ignorant peasant. Jokel along the upper Rhine, became Janke (pronounced Yankee). Webster considers the possibility that Yankee for an American may be an Indian corruption of English, but prefers the theory that it stems from Jan, pronounced Yan, for John, applied by the early Dutch of New York to the English of Connecticut.

SMART ALEC — We first began referring to cheaply clever, bumptious fellows as smart alecs in the 19th century. Why Alec? Why not Archie or Alfred? I can think of a possible explanation: there was a 16th-century scholar named Alexander Ross, to whom Samuel Butler referred in *Hudibras* (1663–78):

> *There was a very learn'd philosopher*
> *Who had read Alexander Ross over.*

HUDIBRASTIC — Which reminds me of another uncommon, improper noun that belongs elsewhere. It is hudibrastic, meaning "mock heroic," after the hero of Butler's satire against the Puritans. Hudibras was a sort of English Don Quixote who set out on a half-blind old horse to reform abuses and enforce repressive laws.

CHARLEY HORSE — Charley horse, a painful cramp in a limb resulting from muscular strain, was named, I must assume (for it is unlikely that anyone knows), for some crippled horse named Charley.

CRÊPE SUZETTE

BLUE PETER	The blue peter, a blue flag with a white square in the center, is flown to signal that a ship is ready to sail. The source in the name Peter may be erroneous; perhaps the word corrupts the message signifying "repeat."
DICKY DICKY BIRDS HICK GILES COLIN	Words deriving from the nickname for Richard include dicky, generally a false shirt front; dicky birds, most often hedge sparrows; and hick, a country bumpkin. Giles, also for country bumpkin, is vestigial from Old Norman French, as is Colin, Norman French for shepherd. (Norman French survived in restricted environments as late as the 1500s. At least two hundred years after the language had vanished elsewhere in England, the nuns of Lacock Abbey in the Midlands still spoke it.)
DICK PETER CLYDE	The dick in mystery stories has no connection with Richard, being a compression of "detective." But dick, vulgar slang for penis, is indeed the given name. Other given names applied to the male sex organ are peter and, more rarely, clyde. Clyde also means "fellow."
DAVIT	The davit, from David, is any of various types of small cranes, usually made of shaped steel tubing and used on ships to hoist boats, anchors, and cargo.
JIMMY BETTY	Jimmy (in England, Jemmy), pet form of James, is the name of a short crowbar with curved ends, regarded as a burglar's tool. Another short bar similarly used is the betty, a humorous derivation from the diminutive of Elizabeth.
EVEN-STEVEN	Even-steven is an intensive of even, or fifty-fifty. In Dean Swift's *Journal to Stella*, he remarks, " 'Now we are even,' quoth Stephen, when he gave his wife six blows for one."
BILLY BILLY GOAT WILL-O'-THE- WISP WILLY BOY LITTLE WILLY HILLBILLY	A billy, from the pet form of William, is a short wooden club. A billy goat too goes back to Billy; but a billy in Australia, meaning a metal pot or kettle used in camp cooking, comes from *billa*, a native word for "can." Will-o'-the-wisp (also called ignis fatuus, "a misleading or deluding object") may derive from William, as does Willy boy or little willy—that is, someone not quite a he-man. A hillbilly is a bumpkin. In German tradition, the willies were ghosts of maidens who had died under distressing circumstances. In English, to have the willies is to experience extreme uneasiness.
HUMPTY-DUMPTY	Weekley suggests that humpty-dumpty, meaning "dumpy," from the nursery rhyme hero, incorporates Humpty, from Humphrey.

FANCY DAN	In the military reorganization following World War II, General Omar Bradley referred to certain admirals as "fancy dans" who would not cooperate in the changes. A fancy dan is one vain, arrogant, and narcissistic.
SKIP TO M' LOU	In "Skip to m' lou," a country dance popular in 19th-century America, lou, shortened from Louise, was generic for "girl."
LULU	Lulu, also a pet form of Louise, is slang for any remarkable object, action, or idea. The name has nothing to do with the controversial lulu that means "a flat payment to members of a legislature in lieu of itemized payments." The trigger words here are "in lieu of."
JILT JENNY WREN JENNY HOWLET SPINNING JENNY JENNY SCAFFOLD JENNY WINCH FANNY DOLL JEMIMAH	To jilt comes from Jill, through Gillian. Jenny, nickname of Jane, indicates the female of certain animals: jenny wren, jenny howlet. It also specifies certain contrivances—the spinning jenny, jenny scaffold, jenny winch. Fanny, vulgar for the buttocks, shortens Frances; the British use this slang expression to denote the female's front as well as her rear. Doll, a familiar form of Dorothy, meant a mistress or sweetheart before it meant a toy. A jemimah was once common for a serving maid.
MAUDE MATILDA MERKIN GRIMALKIN	The names Maude and Matilda were formerly slurring references to servant women, and, by extension, to slatterns or drabs. The diminutives of the two names were Merkin and Malkin. A mop for cleaning cannon was at one time called a merkin; this is still the name of a wig for the female pubis. I do not know whether merkins are currently in vogue. The almost forgotten word grimalkin—a witch's familiar, her connection with Satan; generally, though not always, a black cat—comes from Malkin.
TIN LIZZIE	Tin lizzie is an endearment for the legendary Model-T Ford, the most successful automobile in history. The first to be mass-produced, it was cranky and bumpy; but it kept on going. It could be repaired by anyone handy with string or baling wire. The Morrises represent the name as short for "tin limousine." But AH (which William Morris edited) says the use came about by analogy with the common tin can "+ *Lizzie*, pet form of *Elizabeth*."

Pejorative terms from unknown women:

MOP MOPPET	Mop is from Mabel, once a common name among scullery maids. Moppet, meaning a young child or little girl, has the same origin. *Mappula*, a Medieval Latin word, means "towel or cloth"; perhaps Mabel was named for the tool she used.

MOLLY-CODDLE	In old British slang, Molly, a pet form of Mary, meant milksop. A molly-coddle is a person of weak character who seeks to be pampered and protected. A gunman's moll, semantically identical, is no molly-coddle. Literature and history are rife with such hardbitten molls as Moll Cutpurse, Moll Flanders, and Molly Mog, not to mention moll blood, Scottish slang for the gallows.
MOLL MOLL BLOOD	
JUG	Weekley says, "A 17th-century etymologist regards [the word *jug*] as identical with the female name *Jug,* for *Joan* or *Jane.*" Webster agrees (citing Joanna instead of Jane), and gives "a woman" as one meaning of the word, though the common definition is of course "a pitcher or ewer."
'ARRIET PHYLLIS	An 'arriet is a low-class cockney girl; a phyllis is a country girl. (The Greek prefix *phyll*, meaning green leaf, is incorporated in chlorophyll.)
REAL GEORGE	Real george is slang meaning "All wool and a yard wide." "All wool and a yard wide" means the very best.
ROUND ROBIN	Round robin is a discussion in which each participant speaks in turn; perhaps from "round Robin Hood's barn," meaning the long way around.
AUNT SALLY	An aunt sally is a target at a fair, and by extension, one who is fair game to be abused.
JAKE	Jake, from Jacob, means excellent, admirable, fine.
MARIE	Marie is a type of plain white cookie.

If one of the above names is yours, feel no responsibility for the uses to which it has been put. Nobody knows how the names slipped away from their owners in the first place.

THIRTEEN

FORTY L'OEUF
SPORTY WORDS

ODY SPORTS antedate history. They evolved
from hunting and war, or from training for
hunting and war, or from the inextinguish-
able competitiveness that peaks in hunting and war. Even cere-
bral games like chess euphemize warfare.

Wrestling was attributed by the ancient Greeks to the hero
Theseus, but probably was introduced from Egypt or Asia. It
entered the Olympic games in 704 B.C. Boxing, recorded in
Crete nearly a thousand years before, followed in 688 B.C. There

is a four-thousand-year-old rock carving of a skier, now in the ski museum in Oslo, Norway; snowshoeing and skiing were prehistoric responses to the challenge of snow. Men have hunted horseback (and fought horseback too) as long as they have had horses to ride. Modern lawn tennis dates from the invention of Major Walter Winfield in 1874; but a similar game was played by the Greeks and Romans. Golf may have been brought to Britain by the Roman invaders.

Hazard, or dice, was already an old game when the Roman soldiers cast lots for the seamless robe of Jesus. A variety of chess was played in India as long as five thousand years ago; by the 11th century, King Canute is said to have played it in England. Card games are far older than cardboard itself. Though there is no mention of poker in the United States before 1834, men from time immemorial have played some version of the game.

Sports are often called after their nature—baseball, football, and the like. Sometimes, however, the denominator is the place where the game originated or the name of the person who invented it.

MARATHON

A marathon is any kind of endurance contest—running, dancing, bicycling, flagpole-sitting. It is named for the narrow valley in Greece where in 490 B.C. the Athenians, under Miltiades, pinned down superior Persian forces so that they could not use their cavalry, and proceeded to slaughter them. The Persians lost 6,400 men in the battle; the Greeks, 192. Miltiades, fearing that Athens might surrender to a Persian attack by sea in ignorance of the victory at Marathon, dispatched Pheidippides, his fastest runner, to take home the good news. Though nearly exhausted, having already run to Sparta and back, Pheidippides raced twenty-some miles to Athens, gasped out "Rejoice—we conquer!" and fell dead.

The modern marathon road race is exactly 26 miles and 385 yards long. It was first staged at the revival of the Olympic Games at Athens in 1896. Boston's marathon is held every year on Patriot's Day (April 19) and commemorates such Bostonian matters as Paul Revere's ride. New York City too has an annual marathon run; apparently one of the conditions is that at least one contestant be in a wheelchair.

CHRISTIANIA
CHRISTY

The christiania, or christy, is a familiar ski turn in which the body is swung from a bent-knee position to change direction or make a stop. The source is Christiania, the former name of Oslo, Norway, early capital of skiing.

NELSON	Wrestling involves several holds called nelson. In the half
HALF NELSON	nelson, the applier thrusts one arm under the corresponding
	arm of the opponent, generally from behind, and applies pres-
FULL NELSON	sure with the palm upon the back of his neck. In the full nelson,

NELSON
HALF NELSON

FULL NELSON

Wrestling involves several holds called nelson. In the half nelson, the applier thrusts one arm under the corresponding arm of the opponent, generally from behind, and applies pressure with the palm upon the back of his neck. In the full nelson, both hands are so used. Some wrestler named Nelson may have been responsible for these holds, unless the word comes from the northern English town of Nelson, famous for wrestling. Or one may even speculate that the term traces back to Admiral Nelson, who had one arm out of commission.

COLONEL
BOGEY
BOGEY

MR. BOGEY

Golf, Middle English for "club," is connected with at least three proper names. The first is the legendary Colonel Bogey, a bit better than a dub, but no whiz. In America, a bogey is a stroke over par on any hole. In Britain, it is the number of strokes a good player may be reckoned to need for the course or a hole. The Devil is sometimes called Mr. Bogey, for reasons every golfer understands. The word originated with a song called "The Bogey Man," popular in 1890. One Major Wellman, playing for the first time against the newly introduced "ground score," now called par, exclaimed that his mysterious and well-nigh invincible opponent was a regular "bogey-man." The word filled a need, and has been around ever since.

MULLIGAN

The mulligan, apparently called after some Irishman, is a stroke not counted on the score card. It may twit the supposed Irish passion for giving blows.

NASSAU

The third common golf term originating in a common name is the nassau, from Nassau in the Bahamas. It is a golf match in which winning the first nine holes counts a point, winning the second nine counts a point, and winning the eighteen counts a point.

RHUBARB

Roger Angell mentioned to me that rhubarb, meaning an argument, was popularized by Red Barber when Barber was broadcasting the Brooklyn Dodgers baseball games. I do not know how rhubarb took on the meaning of "quarrel"; the usage may be a localism from the Deep South. In the early days of motion pictures, crowds making ominous noises were told by directors to keep repeating "Rhubarb, rhubarb!" In any event, the echo between "Red Barber" and "rhubarb" intrigued me; I wondered whether the coincidence of sound had played a part in fixing the word in the public's consciousness, and looked up the origin. Rhubarb comes from Greek Rha, the Volga River, plus *barbaros*, "foreign; rude; ignorant." So! Our common garden plant is a barbarian from the Volga! All is now clear; when barbarians confront one another, as in a baseball game, a rhubarb is inevitable.

It is surprising that few, if any, names of baseball heroes have entered the vulgate. Babe Ruth is the symbol of the home run, but nobody says "to ruth" or "hit a ruth" for hitting a homer; no one says "throw a johnson," after Walter P. Johnson, meaning to pitch a fast ball; no one says "do a speaker," after Tris Speaker, for making an astonishing centerfield catch.

TINKER TO
EVERS TO
CHANCE
Baseball expressions, however, permeate the language. "Tinker to Evers to Chance" signifies any flawlessly executed maneuver; it can be used in football, or on Wall Street. Tinker, Evers, and Chance made up the infield of the Chicago Cubs before World War I. Wrote F. P. A. in the *New York Evening Mail*:

These are the saddest of possible words:
"Tinker to Evers to Chance."
Trio of Bear Cubs, and fleeter than birds,
"Tinker to Evers to Chance."
Ruthlessly pricking our gonfalon bubble,
Making a Giant hit into a double—
Words that are heavy with nothing but trouble:
"Tinker to Evers to Chance."

Curiously, Tinker and Evers despised each other. They are said never to have exchanged a word off the field.

John O. Herbold II lists in *Verbatim*, the language quarterly, some baseball terms that are part of everyday conversation:

1. He was born with two strikes against him.
2. He couldn't get to first base with that girl.
3. He sure threw me a curve that time.
4. I'll take a rain check on it.
5. He went to bat for me.
6. I liked him right off the bat.
7. He was way out in left field on that one.
8. He's a foul ball.
9. I think you're way off base on that.
10. It was a smash hit.
11. Let's take a seventh-inning stretch.
12. I hope to touch all the bases on this report.
13. Could you pinch-hit for me?
14. He doesn't even know who's on first.
15. I just call 'em as I see 'em.
16. He's only a bush-leaguer.

17. Major League all the way.
18. We'll hit 'em where they ain't.
19. He was safe a mile.
20. He has a lot on the ball.
21. He really dropped the ball that time.
22. We'll rally in the ninth.
23. No game's ever over until the last man's out.

"And is there any term in our language," he adds, "more synonymous with failure than 'strike out'?"

TENNIS

Britannica says the word tennis corrupts French *Tenez*, "Hold!" But according to Webster the source is Tinnis, a town in Lower Egypt noted for the cloth long used in tennis balls. Either way, tennis is of ancient and honorable descent. Henry II (1519–1559) of France was described as the best tennis player in the country. Under Henry IV tennis was so popular that there were said to be "more tennis players in Paris than drunkards in England." Modern lawn tennis was first played on an hourglass-shaped court known as Sphairistiké, Greek for "spherical." The word, sometimes shortened to "sticky," was for a time used as the name of the game. The expressions "fifteen-love, thirty-love, forty-love," constantly chanted against me when I was still trying my racquet at the game, refer to nothing cuddlesome; "love" is simply our version of French *l' oeuf*, that is, "the egg; zero."

PELL-MELL

Pell-mell means "headlong; in reckless confusion." The word comes, says Brewer, from Pall Mall, in the 16th century the dignified London center of clubland. Earlier, it was an alley where pall-mall was played. The game is described as one "wherein a round box ball is struck with a mallet through a high arch of iron, which he that can do at the fewest blows, or at the number agreed upon, wins." It sounds like a pioneer sort of croquet. The players of pall-mall rushed heedlessly to strike the ball, and pell-mell for "headlong" survives long after the game that gave us the word has vanished.

HUNTING PINK

Fox hunting became fashionable in the 17th century. A hundred years later in London a tailor named Pink designed the jacket that is called hunting pink in his honor. It is not pink, but scarlet.

The 12th Earl of Derby in 1784 gave his name to an annual horse race for three-year-olds held at Epsom Downs in Surrey. He is supposed to have tossed a coin with Sir John Hawkewood to decide after which man the event should be called; Derby won the toss, but Hawkewood's horse beat his in the first race. Various such events, most notably the Kentucky Derby at Louisville, have adopted the name. A derby nowadays is any formal race with a more or less open field of contestants. The soapbox derby is a familiar example. The expression "hermit's derby," common among English racing fans for "an upset," refers to Hermit, a long shot that won the Derby of 1868. Timothy says the horse's name lodged in the mind of the public for two related reasons. First, the Marquis of Hastings lost his entire fortune betting on the favorite. Second, the upset victory provided revenge for Hermit's owner, Henry Chaplin, whose fiancée had run off with and married Lord Hastings.

There is a tradition that whenever the race is about to be run, some dog ventures onto the track and has to be chased off; a derby dog is thus a reference to some inevitable cause of delay.

The racing term "garrison finish," in which the jockey holds his horse back until the homestretch, when he whips it into a furious, winning rush, is a reference to one "Snapper" Garrison, who introduced this tactic successfully when riding Montana in the 1882 Suburbia, standing high in the stirrups and bending low over the horse's mane.

About 1800, when New Orleans was a French city, Bernard Marigny introduced dice playing from France. From the slighting reference to a Frenchman as a Johnny Crapaud ("toad"), dice playing became known as Johnny Crapaud's game, and was shortened to craps. At least that is what Brewer says. Webster and OED state less romantically that the origin was crabs, the lowest throw at hazard, plural of English slang "crab."

An Englishman named Richard W. Clarke (1845–1930) was a famous Indian fighter and express guard in the Black Hills of South Dakota. He became proverbial as Deadwood Dick (perhaps from Deadwood, South Dakota) through the dime novels written about his exploits by Edward L. Wheeler. In the minds of millions, however, he was Dead-*eye* Dick, in reference to his accurate shooting; I am one of these millions. Though, like Butler's Hudibras, I comply against my will, I am of the same opinion still. Not Deadwood Dick but Dead-eye Dick lives in my heart.

Another straight shooter was Annie Oakley (1860–1926), who for forty years starred in Buffalo Bill's Wild West Show, often tossing a playing card into the air and shooting holes through all its pips. The punctured cards reminded theater performers of their meal tickets. These tickets came to be called

ANNIE OAKLEY annie oakleys. The expression is now applied to a complimentary pass to a stage performance or other event.

There is a natural affinity between cards and shooting, or at least there was in the old West. The dead man's hand, aces over eights, is not properly an improper, uncommon noun, but at least it has a connection with a man's name: in a saloon at Deadwood, South Dakota, Wild Bill Hickok dropped those cards when he was shot in the back at a poker game.

Two popular American sports were invented in the 1890s. I find it impossible to mention one and omit the other, though the first is not connected with a proper name, and the connection of the second is apocryphal:

Basketball was invented in 1891 by James Naismith, then an instructor at the YMCA training school at Springfield, Massachusetts (later Springfield College). He hung up peach baskets at each end of the gym and told his students to try throwing a soccer ball into them. (At first he used square boxes. If he had not changed, the name might have been called box-ball.)

VOLLEYBALL Four years later, G. Morgan, physical director at the YMCA in Holyoke, Massachusetts, invented volleyball, played by men and women for whom basketball was too arduous. The name comes from the fact that a leather-covered rubber bladder is vollied back and forth across a net. I wish I could believe Arthur Kopit's more diverting account of the origin of the game. Mr. Kopit says that every evening in King Louis XV's prison compound a court official named Jacques de Vollet supervised eight nude chambermaids as they, four to a side, batted a loaf of sour bread hither and thither across a line draped with their underclothing. The bouncy play of the young ladies greatly agitated the manacled prisoners looking on. When the bread had been beaten into morsels too small to bat, the chambermaids tossed the remnants to the inmates for supper. Hence, logically, volleyball. If you doubt this story, ask Arthur Kopit. Or ask Jacques de Vollet.

BADMINTON Badminton, played with racquets and shuttlecocks, owes its name to Badminton, the Gloucestershire seat of the Duke of Beaufort, where the game, an import from India, was played from 1873 on. Claret cup, a drink of red wine, brandy, lemon, borage (an herb), sugar, ice, and carbonated water, is also called badminton. Human blood, especially that sprayed about in pugilistic matches, is sometimes called claret from the color, and sometimes badminton from the duke's claret cup.

RUGBY SOCCER	Rugby School, at Warwickshire, England, started rugby football; soccer, now tardily taking over the United States, corrupts Association, in turn shortened from the Football Association, started in England in 1863.
SPOOF	To spoof, "to deceive; hoax; swindle," derives from the name of a foolish card game, Spoof, invented in the 19th century by the English comedian Arthur Roberts (1852–1933). The name has outlasted the game.
ENGLISH BODY ENGLISH	To english a billiard ball—that is, to impart a spin to it by striking it off center—is said to have been taught Americans by an English player named English in the middle of the 19th century. Whether or not such a man existed, body english is body language; there is doubtless body French, body Russian, and as many more such as there are languages. The word English evolved from the Angles, whose homeland in Schleswig had the shape of a fishhook, *Angul* in early German.
QUEENSBERRY RULES	The queensberry rules, governing boxing matches in which gloves are worn, were formulated in 1865 by the 8th Marquess of Queensberry and John G. Chambers. The British Boxing Board of Control replaced them with the present rules in 1929.
DINNY-HAYSER	Ancient devotees of boxing still remember a dinny-hayser—a tremendous knockout blow. The word memorializes a 19th-century British pugilist named Dinny Hayes, who apparently packed quite a punch.
RUSSIAN ROULETTE	Roulette is a popular gambling game in which the banker spins an ivory marble counter to the movement of the inside of a bowl (roulette wheel); the players win or lose according to the compartment at the bottom in which the ball comes to rest. Russian roulette is a riskier game; the player places to his temple a revolver in which, say, one of five chambers contains a bullet, and pulls the trigger. If there is no bullet in the chamber, the player wins; if the trigger strikes a bullet, the player . . . loses.
MOXIE	A term employed frequently by sports fans is moxie, meaning courage of a high order, but also, according to the Morrises, nerve or gall. Its standing in the language was reinforced by the soft drink Moxie, popular in New England since 1884.
GENOA	I do not know why the large, tricky jib used on yachts when sailing close-hauled is called a genoa. The inhabitants of Genoa, Italy, are noted for their maritime achievements, but not for their trickiness.

LATEENER   The lateener is a vessel with a lateen (from "Latin") sail, a triangular arrangement extended by a long yard from a low mast.

BOSEY   What is a googly? It is a bosey. What is a bosey? It is a deceptive cricket delivery, "depending on hard action by the bowler in which an off-break is bowled to a right-handed batsman with what appears to be a leg-break action." B. J. T. Bosanquet, a British cricketer, introduced the throw during an Australian tour in 1903–1904.

PING-PONG   An indoor modification of lawn tennis, played with small round bats and a light, hollow celluloid ball on a large table divided in the middle by a net, was trademarked as Ping-Pong, but became so pervasive that it lost its capitalization. In official competition it is called table tennis.

FRISBEE   Frisbee is the proprietary name in the United States for a concave plastic disk which spins when thrown into the air and is used in a catching game. Anyone who lower-cases Frisbee (and many do) runs the risk of being sued by the maker, the Wham-O Manufacturing Company of San Gabriel, California. The idea for the disk came from the airworthy pie tins once used by the Frisbie bakery in Bridgeport, Connecticut; the spelling of the name was modified to avoid legal problems.

CHECKMATE   Checkmate in chess is an exclamation made by a player when he puts his opponent's king in a position from which there is no escape. It is a hobson-jobson of Arabic-Persian *Shah-mat*, "The shah [king] is dead."

HAZARD   Also Arabic is hazard, once a game of chance played with dice but now, to the best of my knowledge, existing only as a word meaning "risk; danger; peril." Evans says it "was a French corruption [*hasart*] of an Arabic name [*Ain Zarba*] of a castle in Palestine. The castle stood a long siege, and to while away the time the game was invented." In Webster the word sallies not from the castle but from *az-zahr*, the die that was cast in the game.

FARO   Faro, a card game in which the players lay wagers on the top card of the dealer's pack, is a variant spelling of Pharaoh, perhaps because the king of hearts was once supposed to represent the Egyptian monarch.

TAROT   Tarot is said by Britannica to be the oldest card game, from which others borrowed such features as competitive bidding; the scat or widow; the joker; and the effort to capture specific counting cards. A set of twenty-two tarot cards is used in fortune-telling, the various cards depicting vices, virtues, and elemental forces. The name salutes Tar, Egyptian god of the nether world, Tartarus to the Greeks.

NAPOLEON

Napoleon, or nap, named for the emperor, is a card game in which each player holds five cards and each in turn must bid. The highest bidder leads a trump, pays a chip for each trick he loses, and is paid a chip for each trick he wins. A player bidding

NAP

nap wins ten chips from each player if he succeeds, or pays five to each if he fails. In a variant called wellington (after the emperor's great adversary), a player can overcall a nap bid with

WELLINGTON
BLÜCHER

wellington, which doubles his penalties if he fails. This may be outbid again by a blücher, after the Prussian general who saved Wellington at Waterloo. A blücher redoubles the penalties, but does not increase the rewards for success.

PAM

A card game similar to napoleon is called pam, after *Pamphile*, French for the knave of clubs. Some trace Pamphile to the fictional Greek rogue Pamphilus.

BUNGAY

The English call a stupid play in whist, such as leading with the highest scoring card, a bungay, from the old town of Bungay in Suffolk, sometimes called "silly Suffolk." The expression may have lodged in the language because of the similarity of sound between Bungay and bungle. Robert Greene (1560?–1592) wrote a play entitled *The Honorable Historie of Friar Bacon and Friar Bungay*, in which Roger Bacon and Thomas Bungay make a head of brass and, conjuring up the Devil, learn how to give it speech. It is to utter its first sentence within a month; but "if they heard it not before it had done speaking, all their labour should be lost." After watching day and night for three weeks, the two men fall asleep, leaving Bacon's servant Miles to watch. The head says, "Time is." Miles, fearing to anger his master by waking him for so little, lets him sleep on. The head presently says, "Time was," and finally, "Time is past," when it falls down and breaks. I cannot understand why this story has been cited as an example of the stupidity of Bungay, when the fault clearly lies with the indolence of Bacon.

In *Britannia*, a guidebook of Britain published in 1586 by William Camden (1551–1623), Lord Bigod of Bungay presents a kindlier picture of the town:

> Were I in my castle of Bungay
> Upon the river of Waveney,
> I would ne care for the king of Cockney.

The man who "would rather own a castle in Bungay than be king" is one who prefers ease to glory.

WHITECHAPEL

Like bungay, whitechapel in whist denotes an unskillful play, such as leading from a one-card suit in order to trump, in short-sighted pursuit of immediate profit. The word comes from Whitechapel, long a Jewish quarter in the East End of London.

FAIRBANKS

In contract bridge, a hand full of kings and queens is sometimes referred to as a fairbanks, the allusion being to the particular pleasure Douglas Fairbanks Jr. is said to take in the company of royalty.

YARBOROUGH

A yarborough, quite the other way, is a hand of thirteen cards in which there is no card higher than a nine. Such discouraging hands occur seldom, but to their victims seem to come oftener. In the early 19th century a gentleman gambler named Lord Yarborough capitalized on this defeatist view by offering to bet a thousand to one that a particular player would not get such a hand (that is, a total bust) on the deal about to commence. Since the proper odds on being dealt a yarborough are 1,860 to 1, in the long run Lord Yarborough nearly doubled his money.

KLONDIKER

Miners in the Klondike used to while away long winter hours in their cabins playing a species of solitaire, similar to patience, the object being to see how many cards can be built up in sequence and suit on a row of aces. (In passing, the gold hunts in and around Alaska led to the use of the word klondiker for one who guts abandoned buildings for their metal fixtures.) The game migrated to the States, where it almost, but not quite, became a generic term for a card game which one person can play alone. That distinction was reserved for a refined form of Klondike developed toward the end of the 19th century by Richard C. Canfield (1855–1941), an American gambler who frequented the fashionable resort of Saratoga Springs, New York. When not at the gaming table, Mr. Canfield played a solitaire of his own devising. It became the most popular game of its kind in the world: canfield.

CANFIELD

BARANI ROLL

In gymnastics, a barani roll is a one-and-a-half-times twist in the air. Timothy suggests that the name may be a shortening from Robert Báráni (1876–1936), Austrian physician who won the 1914 Nobel Prize for his research into the human vestibular apparatus—that is, loosely, the sense of balance. But I have no proof.

The following evolution has been suggested for kitty, the pot to which poker players contribute:

Catherine turned to Kate, and Kate to Kitty. Some Kittys were no better than they should be, and Kitty became one of the many epithets applied to prostitutes. Spirited Johns—not yet lower-cased for a prostitute's customer—used to amuse themselves by tossing coins into the lap of Kittys, as poker players today throw their antes or bets into a kitty in the hope of getting a winning hand. The sequence cannot be proved—no one will talk—but it seems plausible.

EX goes back a long way; not even the
Russians claim to have invented it. Indeed, it goes back to the gods themselves. I
have described some of their amorous exploits; I must point out
now that these were not confined to members of the opposite
sex, to other divinities, or to humans made in the divine image.
Bestiality was an Olympian amusement; the gods not only con-
joined delightedly with beasts, but frequently wooed in bestial
form. The bulls, rams, serpents, horses, swans, and the like who

consorted carnally with humans would make a spectacular zoo. Nobody seemed to mind.

CATAMITE
GANYMEDE

Catamite, "a boy kept for unnatural purposes," distorts Ganymede, name of a beautiful Trojan youth who so took Zeus's fancy that the greatest of the gods, assuming the form of an eagle, carried him off to Olympus. There, when not cupbearing for the immortals, he performed functions impracticable for his predecessor, the fair Hebe. A young bartender or waiter is still referred to, with humorous intent, as a ganymede.

The Greek gods concentrated on the immediate carnality of love. Aphrodite was no remote, unattainable vision; she was the epitome of seductive, sexually exciting sensual beauty; and when she wanted a god, or a man, she got him. Her temple at Paphos was served by priestesses of such amiable wantonness that pa-

PAPHIAN

phian became synonymous with "strumpet."

ATHANASIAN
WENCH

The expression "athanasian wench" for a round-heeled woman alludes to the ecumenical Athanasian Creed (probably dating from the 4th century), which begins, "Whosoever desire . . . "

HARLOT

HOOKER

Arlette, attractive daughter of the tanner Falbert of Falaise, was surprised naked, washing her clothes, by Robert le Diable, Duke of Normandy. The result was William the Bastard, better known as William the Conqueror. But Arlette was not, as sometimes claimed, the source of the word harlot. That appears to descend from Old German *Hari*, "army," and *Lot*, "loiterer": "a camp follower." A later word for a prostitute is hooker, so called, says Windas, for a line of small vessels that used to trade between British ports and the Hook of Holland, where ladies of the night lay in wait (or more likely stood in wait, and lay afterward), eager to comfort a poor sailor far from home. There are other possible sources. The word appears in print in 1845 in a passage by E. N. Eliason that reads, "If he comes by Norfolk, he will find any number of pretty hookers in the Breck row not far from French's hotel." Hookers hook their man any way they can; in an 1857 print they are shown using the hooks of their parasols for the purpose.

Another story says Civil War General Joseph Hooker ruled the red-light districts of Washington, D.C., off-limits for his men, who retaliated by calling the objects of their passion after their commander. There was some logic to the name; the general was reputedly a dissolute man, whose headquarters were described as "half barroom, half brothel."

HOOKER

From *hoeker*, Dutch for "fishhook," derives hooker for a clumsy ship (or Irish fishing smack), doubtless reinforcing the allusion.

WARREN

Timothy tells me that prostitutes are often called warrens after Mrs. Warren, the title character in Shaw's *Mrs. Warren's Profession*. Corinth was notorious for them in the 3rd and 2nd centuries B.C. There was a saying, "Are you married or do you come from Corinth?" Another Timothy term for whores is Winchester geese. In the 16th and 17th centuries the Winchester countryside was dotted with white geese. There was also a thriving industry in prostitution, and the whores were called after the geese. The successive bishops of Winchester owned the land and houses where the whores operated, and owed a considerable part of their income to venereal activities. "One might call them meta-pimps," says Timothy, "or mega-pimps." Profits from the Winchester geese paid for the founding and upkeep of a number of Oxford's most prestigious foundations—including New College, Magdalen, and Corpus Christi.

WINCHESTER GEESE

APHRODISIAC

The effect of Aphrodite on the male of the species gave rise to the word aphrodisiac, "that which (as a drug, or certain foods) excites to venery."

EROTIC

Eros specialized in erotic—i.e., "amatory"—rather than spiritual attraction; but his appeal was passionate rather than pornographic.

PRIAPUS

Priapus, protector of herds, bees, and fish, personified the male generative power. He was born with an extraordinary deformity, a phallus so enormous that it struck even his mother with horror, so that she disowned him. A phallic symbol of stone was commonly placed as a protector in orchards and gardens. A priapus is thus a phallus or penis—by inference one of enormous proportions.

Hermaphroditus, begot on Aphrodite by Hermes, was a shy, savage youth, whose chief pleasure was hunting. One humid day, in Carya, he chanced to cool himself by bathing in the fountain of the nymph Salmacis, who at the sight of him was seized by ravening passion, and leaped into the water to embrace him. When he repulsed her advances, she cried out in anguish, "O ye gods! Grant that nothing may ever separate him from me, or me from him!" On the instant, their two bodies were merged into one, neither man nor woman, yet both; whence hermaphrodite, "an individual having both male and female sexual organs." A hermaphrodite brig is so called because it is square-rigged forward and schooner-rigged aft.

HERMAPH-
RODITE

HERMAPH-
RODITE BRIG

The demigods emulated the sexual activities of the gods. No mean contender in the field was Satyr, a sylvan deity referred to previously. A satyr is "a lecherous man; one having satyriasis"—insatiable venereal appetite in the male. The female equivalent, from the mythological nymphs, is a nymphomaniac.

SATYR
SATYRIASIS

I am not sure whether the nymphs in ancient Greece or Rome were ever upper-cased, but a word about the darlings will not come amiss. They were inferior divinities of nature, represented as beautiful maidens. Dryads were wood nymphs with a life span matching that of the tree that was their home; hamadryads were of the same ilk. Naiads inhabited lakes, rivers, springs, and fountains. Nereids were sea nymphs. The oceanids, three thousand in number, were daughters of the Titan Oceanus and his wife Tethys. Oreads were the nymphs of mountains and hills. Today a nymphet is an adolescent wanton, typified by Lolita, the title character of Vladimir Nabokov's 1955 novel; her name is on its way to becoming a vernacular term for such a person.

LOLITA

Pious Greeks felt it their duty to emulate their gods in sexual as in other activities. Among the most devout in this respect was Sappho. She was a Lesbian by birth, and reputedly a lesbian by inclination—that is, "a woman who is attracted sexually to other women rather than to men." As the island is eponym of the word lesbian, so is her own name of sapphic—"relating to the type of erotic indulgences practices by Sappho and her pupils." In *Don Juan*, Lord Byron evokes

LESBIAN

SAPPHIC

The isles of Greece, the isles of Greece!
Where burning Sappho loved and sung . . .

Two legendary demons deeply involved with sex were Incubus and Succubus. Incubus lay with women in their sleep. An incubus is any oppression, burden, or nightmare; to incubate is to brood, as on eggs, for hatching. Succubus was a female demon who lay with sleeping men. A succubus is a strumpet or whore. A concubine, "a woman lying down with a man," contains etymological elements of both incubus and succubus. Since the Evil One cannot engender, the semen of Incubus was obtained from that deposited by a man in Succubus.

INCUBUS
INCUBATE
SUCCUBUS
CONCUBINE

The Hebrews were as preoccupied with sex as the Greeks, though they seem to have been less able to relax and enjoy it. I think I have mentioned the curious parallel between the story of Iaphetus, the Greek Titan, and Japhet, the son of Noah. A similar parallel has been drawn between the castration of Uranus by his son Cronus and the treatment of Noah as described in Genesis 9:20-21:

> And Noah began to be an husbandman, and he planted a vineyard.
>
> And he drank of the wine, and was drunken; and he was uncovered within his tent.
>
> And Ham, the father of Canaan, saw the nakedness of his father, and told his two brethren without.
>
> And Shem and Japheth took a garment, and laid it upon both their shoulders, and went backward, and covered the nakedness of their father; and their faces were backward, and they saw not their father's nakedness.

More than one scholar contends that this is a bowdlerized version. The sons of Noah, they say, actually castrated their father in his drunkenness, as Cronus had unmanned Uranus in his sleep. The Greek and Semitic myths merge into one.

Two of the most familiar names in the roll call of sexual perversion date back to the first book of the Bible. "The men of Sodom," says Genesis, "were wicked and sinners before the Lord exceedingly." Equally wicked were the men—and, since it takes two to tango, the women—of neighboring Gomorrah. The Lord therefore (Genesis 19:24-25) "rained upon Sodom and upon Gomorrah brimstone and fire from out of heaven; and he overthrew those cities, and all the plain, and all the inhabitants of the cities, and that which grew upon the ground."

SODOMY
GOMORREAN

It is assumed that the definitive sin of the men of Sodom was copulation in any of certain unnatural ways, including bestiality. These perversions are lumped together as sodomy. An associated word, gomorrean—"an inhabitant of Gomorrah, or one of similar conduct"—has the same meaning, with a dash of lesbianism added for flavor. The similarity of sound with "gonorrhea" is fortuitous.

BUGGER

In England, a sodomist is a bugger; as a verb, the word means to sodomize. It traces back to the Volga River, from which the Bulgars took their name. In Middle Latin, *Bulgarus*, Bulgarian, meant "heretic" or "sodomite"; the transition from Bulgar to bugger was easy. This is a form of etymological river pollution.

NANCE

In Spanish, by the way, a male homosexual is a *marica*, from Maria, a woman's name. The epithet nance in English, presumably deriving from Nancy, is now rarely used.

ONANISM   Onancock, Md., is not named for Onan. In Genesis 38:7-10 Onan made onanism synonomous with masturbation:

> And Er, Judah's firstborn, was wicked in the sight of the Lord; and the Lord slew him.
> And Judah said unto Onan, Go in unto thy brother's wife, and marry her, and raise up seed to thy brother.
> And Onan knew that the seed should not be his; and it came to pass, when he went in unto his brother's wife, that he spilled it on the ground, lest that he should give seed to his brother.
> And the thing which he did displeased the Lord; wherefore he slew him also.

Which goes to show that there are some days when a man should have stayed in bed.

CONDOM   The condom is a thin rubber sheath (in the beginning, sheep linings) designed to prevent disease and impregnation from sexual intercourse. It is said to have been invented by one Contin, Condon, or Condum. By some accounts he was a French physician; by others a London doctor in the court of Charles II; and by still others a Colonel Condum of Britain's Household troops. The word first appeared in print in 1665. I am told that some American tourists find it amusing to send home postcards from the city of Condom, in southwestern France.

SADISM   Two terms, sadism and masochism, describe opposites in abnormal sexuality. Count Donatien Alphonse François de Sade (1740–1814) embraced the perversion that bears his name. His novels are filled with fantasies of the gratification to be obtained by torturing the object of one's desire. The French in 1772 condemned de Sade to death for "an unnatural offense, and for poisoning" (the latter presumably a natural offense). He escaped by fleeing to Italy. His life thereafter was an endless series of perversions, interspersed with arrests, imprisonments, escapes, and rearrests. His writing began in the Bastille, and continued when he was removed to the Charenton Lunatic Asylum. He was discharged from the asylum, but was recommitted as incorrigible in 1803 and remained incarcerated until his death in 1814.

MASOCHISM   De Sade's opposite number, Leopold von Sacher-Masoch (1836–1895), an Austrian novelist, was fascinated by the pleasure certain lovers appeared to find in being physically and emotionally abused as part of the sexual act. He dealt with this subject so relentlessly that his name was appropriated for the emotional sickness he described.

Sex, from the foregoing accounts, sounds more like a sickness than a sport. Let us end on a gentler and more positive note. A simple kiss, you will agree, is surely a harmless and agreeable exchange. Not long ago there lived among us a man whose very name became a synonym for kissing. He was handsome Richmond Pearson Hobson (1870–1937), a naval lieutenant who tried to block the harbor of Santiago de Cuba in the Spanish-American War by sinking the collier *Merrimac*. Hobson returned home a hero; kisses from worshipful women rained on him like April showers. (There is no evidence that May flowers resulted; he was a very upright man.) His name entered the dictionary briefly as a verb. If you are asked to hobsonize, a half-minute demonstration will fix the meaning of the word in your mind forever.

HOBSONIZE

SOUL KISS

In the days before sex became permissive, a soul kiss was considered a long, lovely step down the road to damnation. It consisted, if memory serves, of adding to the usual labial contacts titillations made possible by a sort of wordless conversation between male and female tongue. The origin of the expression is uncertain; but as likely an explanation as any is that it shortens and hobson-jobsons the name of the actress Olga Nethersole, whose passionate onstage kiss caused her to be prosecuted after she appeared in Daudet's *Sapho* in the 1880s.

Something not of the natural or proper color is off-color; hence dubious; hence in poor taste; whence "off-color joke." It is my impression that the British are better than the Americans at using off-color remarks to make important points. Thus when Sir Samuel Hoare made arrangements with Paris that the English government found disadvantageous, King George V was able to tell his Foreign Secretary, "No more coals to Newcastle; no more Hoares to Paris." "Coals to Newcastle" is self-explanatory; so, to anybody who walked Paris streets after midnight before World War II, is "Hoares to Paris." Again, during Lord Curzon's term as Foreign Secretary, he received word that the monks at Mount Athos were violating their vows. In the transcript, the word vows had turned into cows. Curzon scribbled in the margin of the message: "Send them a papal bull."

HOARES TO
PARIS

FIFTEEN

EAT, DRINK, AND BE MERRY

Gastronomic Words

WANTED to give an appearance of cohesiveness to this chapter, so I built it around a theoretical menu consisting of dishes with names drawn from persons or places but now considered generic. I further decided that the man selecting his meal from this menu would be Anthelme Brillat-Savarin (1755–1826), a Frenchman who wrote in 1825 a lively book on the arts of cookery and eating, *La Physiologie du*

BRILLAT-SAVARIN *goût.* His name sometimes is seen uncapitalized; a brillat-savarin is "an authority on cooking." A savarin is a kind of egg bread, and a brand name for coffee. Had M. Brillat-Savarin been Chinese, he would doubtless have lived in Chuanchow.

As one of the world's leading non-authorities on cooking, I suspected some of my facts might be skewed, so I sent a first draft of this chapter to Richard de Rochemont, a bit of a brillat-savarin himself. Some of his comments follow:

> The fundamental premise is right, a truly Lucullan meal could be organized using dishes and products named after people or places, or even events. But Brillat-Savarin would never have started his meal with fruit, though if it were lunch he might have ended with fruit and cheese. May I suggest his dessert (sweet) might have been *Savarin à la Chantilly*, thus honoring a man and a town at one swoop.
>
> I won't try to follow through with the defense of Brillat-Savarin against the curious mélange you impute to his specter, but leaving the planning of the menu to you, I just want to say that had Proust found meringue on his madeleine, *A la Recherche du temps perdu* might never have seen print.

The Proust passage in *Swann's Way* to which Mr. de Rochemont refers begins ". . . my mother, seeing that I was cold, offered me some tea . . . She sent out for one of those short,
plump little cakes called 'petites madeleines,' which looked as though they had been molded in the fluted scallop of a pilgrim's shell." The thought of that madeleine set off in later years the chain of reminiscences that constitute *A la Recherche du temps perdu*. Its name also bridges time, commemorating Madeleine Paulmier, a 19th-century pastry cook.

I decided that to fit my framework, Brillat-Savarin was going to have to start his meal with fruit, even if, as Mr. de Rochemont says, he would never have considered doing so. But I was forced to admit that meringue on a madeleine would be an odd combination; I eliminated that arrangement.

If he wished to start with a fruit, he would have a choice of the bartlett pear, named after Enoch Bartlett (1799–1860), who first distributed the variety in America (in France it is known as the *bon chrétien*); the baldwin, a yellowish-red, slightly acid apple, which honors in its name Loammi Baldwin (1740–1807), the American engineer and army officer who first grew the species; or the spitzenberg, a red or yellow apple first found on a hill at Esopus, New York, and named by the Dutch (*spits*, "pointed," plus *berg* "mountain").

RIBSTON PIPPIN   He might peel a ribston pippin, an apple which can trace its ancestry to a single pip. At Ribston, England, in 1707, only three seeds were left of a certain variety of apple. Sir Henry Goodriche planted all three, but only one survived. From it derive all existing ribston pippins. Hilaire Belloc commemorates the crisp tartness of this fine winter apple:

> I asked of heart, How goes it?
>   Heart replied,
> "Right as a ribston pippin!"
>   But it lied.

ROQUEFORT   If Brillat-Savarin wished to eat his fruit with cheese, he had a choice of dozens named from their place of origin. Roquefort, first made from ewe's milk in the Roquefort area of France and stored in rocky caves to ripen, is now produced by a Roquefort Association that insists the name be capitalized. For practical purposes, it's a losing battle; the cheese joined the vulgate long since. Yet Roquefort takes its legal ownership of the name seriously. When Frank O. Fredericks, president (and legal representative) of Roquefort, learned that a recipe in an impending book treated blue cheese as an alternate ingredient to Roquefort, he threatened legal action, arguing that "blue cheese is made from cows' milk and Roquefort cheese from sheeps' milk. The two milks, and therefore the two cheeses, are chemically substantially different despite the surface appearance of similarity." The reference to Roquefort was dropped from the book; the blue cheese remained. To an outsider, Roquefort would appear to have cut off its nose to spite its face. But apparently Roquefort would rather not be mentioned at all than to be coupled with blue cheese.

CAMEMBERT   Camembert is unpressed cheese from the Normandy town;
CHEDDAR   cheddar, a pressed cheese of acid flavor and smooth texture,
CHESHIRE   takes its name from a village in Somerset; cheshire (from the same area as Lewis Carroll's wonderful Cheshire cat, which fades gradually from view, its grin disappearing last) originated in the northwestern English county of that name. Other cheeses called
BRIE   for their places of origin include brie, from that French district, a
EDAM   soft cheese ripened by mold; edam, from Edam, Netherlands, a pressed yellow cheese made in balls weighing three or four
GORGONZOLA   pounds, and usually covered with a coat of red wax; gorgonzola, much like roquefort, from a village of that name near Milan,
GRUYÈRE   Italy; gruyère, a whole-milk cheese, usually without holes, from
SWISS   that district in Switzerland; swiss, white or pale yellow, with many

PARMESAN

STILTON
LIMBURGER
GERVAIS

large holes, from the same country; parmesan, a skim-milk product, hard, dry, and sweet, with an even distribution of gas holes, from Parma, Italy; stilton, rich, unpressed, waxed, and when ripe permeated with a green mold, from Stilton, England; limburger, a soft white cheese with a strong odor and flavor, from the region in Belgium and the Netherlands. Gervais, a soft creamy cheese, derives not from a locale, but from the French maker, Charles Gervais (1830–1892).

KRAFT

If none of these proved satisfactory to M. Brillat-Savarin, he might choose from trade-named varieties like Kraft, an Australian cheddar made by the Kraft-Walker Cheese Company of Melbourne.

MADRILÈNE

An excellent soup would be consommé madrilène, after Madrid. It is commonly flavored with tomato, and generally chilled.

YORKSHIRE
PUDDING

WELSH RABBIT

M. Brillat-Savarin might like to try yorkshire pudding, from Yorkshire, England, a popover batter made of eggs, flour, and milk, and baked in the drippings of roast beef. He might try a welsh rabbit, made of melted cheese, seasonings, and sometimes ale, served over hot toast or crackers. (Rabbit, not rarebit. When poor Welshmen had no meat, they made do with this cheese, and called it welsh rabbit.) Other dishes at his disposal, all named for their places of origin:

MELTON
MOWBRAY

For Melton, England, the melton mowbray, a high-quality meat pie.

FRANKFURTER

For Frankfurt, Germany, the frankfurter (called by Americans in World War I "victory steak").

HAMBURGER

For Hamburg, Germany, the hamburger.

WIENERWURST
WIENER
SCHNITZEL

For Wien (Vienna), Austria, the wienerwurst and the wiener schnitzel.

BEEF
BOURGUIGNON

For Burgundy, France, beef bourguignon.

BOLOGNA
SAUSAGE
BALONEY

For Bologna, Italy, the bologna sausage (the corruption "baloney" has come to mean "nonsense"; "all sausages," according to Partridge, "being gastronomic inferiors").

The menu would offer dishes named after people as well as places. A 19th-century Russian diplomat, Count Paul Stroganoff, so favored thinly sliced beef fillet sautéed and served with mushrooms and sour cream that the dish became perma-

BEEF
STROGANOFF
CHATEAUBRIAND

nently known as beef stroganoff. Chateaubriand, a double-thick tender cut of beef tenderloin, appears to have been invented by the chef of a conspicuous figure in French literature during the First Empire, François René, Vicomte de Châteaubriand (1768–1848). The servant created the dish; the master gave it his own name.

DUXELLES

A similar linguistic appropriation of a servant's product by his master is duxelles, a purée of mushrooms and onions named for the 17th-century Marquis d'Uxelles, but created by his chef, François Pierre de la Varenne. Hendrickson calls de la Varenne the "founder of French cuisine."

CHICKEN À LA
KING

Chicken à la king is an odd corruption. According to Claridge's Hotel in London, it was invented by its chef to honor J. R. Keene, whose horse had won the Grand Prix in 1881. Others say that Keene's son Foxhall, who called himself the "world's greatest amateur athlete," suggested the dish—diced chicken in a sherry-cream sauce—to the chef at Delmonico's in New York. When the Keenes vanished from the public eye, their name vanished also; chicken à la Keene became chicken à la king.

SALMAGUNDI

Salmagundi is a mixture of minced veal, chicken or turkey, anchovies or pickled herrings, and onions, all chopped together, and served with lemon juice and oil. There are variations. The word entered the language in the 17th century; Brewer speculates that salmagundi may have been invented by a lady of that name in the suite of Marie de' Medici, wife of Henry IV. Others attribute the dish to a shadowy 18th-century chef named Gondi or Gonde. It has even been connected with the nursery-rhyme character Solomon Grundy. Perhaps, says Timothy, there is a side wind from J. F. P. de Gondi (1614–1679), unintentionally made Cardinal by Pope Innocent X, a pope not immune to error. But I see no reason to challenge Webster's speculation that the origin is probably Italian *salmi*, "salt meat," plus *condire*, "to pickle." In 1807 Washington Irving published a humorous periodical entitled *Salmagundi*. A magazine with the same name appeared in the 1960s.

FRENCH
DRESSING

BÉARNAISE

MAYONNAISE

What Americans call french dressing, a combination of oil and vinegar seasoned with condiments, the French call vinaigrette, as in artichoke vinaigrette. To enhance his meat or fish course, the French gourmet might turn to béarnaise, a thick sauce from Béarn, in southwest France; the sauce is made of chopped onion in the United States (but shallots in France), oil or butter, vinegar, egg yolks, and seasoning. He might use mayonnaise: beaten egg yolk, butter or olive oil, lemon juice or vinegar, and seasonings.

During the aforementioned siege of Port Mahon (a corruption of the name of Hannibal's brother Mago) by the Duke of Richelieu in 1756, the duke's chef, finding himself out of condiments, whipped up the first mayonnaise.

TO FRENCH MEAT

FRENCH WINDOW

FRENCH CUFF

To french meat is to cut it into thin strips before cooking, or to trim fat from bone. (Webster lists around 150 terms, by the way, consisting of "French" or "french" followed by other words. Many, such as french window or french cuff, are used commonly with no thought of their origin.)

BÉCHAMEL

Béchamel is a cream sauce thickened with flour, considerably modified from the original creation by the Marquis de Béchamel, dishonest steward of the Sun King, Louis XIV.

SAUCE MORNAY

As a devout Catholic, Brillat-Savarin might hesitate before ordering sauce mornay, since it was the product of a Protestant, but Brillat-Savarin's taste buds would doubtless conquer his scruples. Philippe de Mornay (1549–1623) was chief aide to Henry IV until the king converted to Catholicism; it was during this term of service that he concocted the sauce that bears his name.

LOBSTER NEWBURG

An excellent main course would be lobster newburg— lobster in a rich sauce of sherry, thick cream, and egg yolks. According to Hendrickson, this dish was originally lobster wenburg. It was prepared by the great chef Lorenzo Delmonico at the suggestion of a patron, Charles Wenburg, a 19th-century shipping magnate, and named after him. But one evening Wenburg disgraced himself in the dining room, drinking too much and picking a fight with another diner, so that he had to be ejected. Next day the name of the dish on the menu was no longer wenburg, but newburg.

PORTERHOUSE STEAK

A porterhouse steak might sit well. Introduced about 1814 in the Porterhouse tavern in New York, the porterhouse is a succulent cut taken from the loin next to the sirloin, or, according to Mr. de Rochemont, the sirloin and the tenderloin together—sometimes called a T-bone. A porterhouse in England, not capitalized, was a tavern serving the dark brown beer or ale—very heavily sweetened, for energy—once favored by porters and other laborers.

Out of respect for the 19th-century Paris restaurateur Tortoni, Brillat-Savarin might choose biscuit tortoni for dessert.

BISCUIT TORTONI

Biscuit tortoni is a rich ice cream usually flavored with almonds, often garnished with whipped cream, and served in a paper cup.

NESSELRODE PUDDING

An equally agreeable dessert, whether it be a gelatin containing chestnuts, or a rich ice cream containing chestnuts, candied fruit, and maraschino, is nesselrode pudding. The name is from Count Karl R. Nesselrode (1780–1862), a Russian statesman. The pudding is said to have been concocted by Mony, Nesselrode's cook; but E. Acton's *Modern Cookery* (1845), describing the confection, says, "We give Monsieur Carême's own receipt . . . as it originated with him." Ah, well:

Mony? Carème?
Plus ça change,
Plus c'est la même.

MERINGUE

Or he might prefer a lemon meringue pie; meringue is a delicate mixture, chiefly of beaten egg whites and sugar. It is claimed by both Mehringen, Germany, and Mehrinyqhen, Switzerland.

FRANGIPANI

Then there is frangipani, a pastry supposedly invented by the Marquis Frangipani, a major general under Louis XIV. Since frangipani means "broken bread," this derivation is suspect. The cake is filled with cream, sugar, and almonds. The name is also applied to a sweet, cloying perfume imitating the odor of the *Plumeria rubra* tree or shrub; but I doubt that the perfume was invented by the marquis.

PRALINE

No less delicious is the praline, a confection of nut kernels developed by a chef in the service of Maréchal Duplessis-Praslin (1598–1675).

SUNDAE

If the great authority on cooking did not consider it beneath him, he might even select a sundae—a portion of plain ice cream covered with glop, perhaps crushed fruits, syrups, or nuts. It is natural to assume the name comes from Sunday, that being a special day and the concoction a particularly elaborate ice cream. Ice cream soda first appeared in 1874, and what we now call a sundae was invented at an ice cream parlor kept by E. C. Berners in the 1890s.

SALLY LUNN

A simpler dessert is the sally lunn. Sally Lunn sold her slightly sweetened teacakes, eaten hot with butter, in the streets of Bath in the late 18th century. Dalmer, a well-known baker and musician, bought her recipe, and wrote a song about the teacakes. I wish I had it.

MOCHA

JAVA

HAVANA
STOGY

CONESTOGA
WAGON

As the concluding act in this drama, M. Brillat-Savarin would lean back with a contented sigh and sip his mocha—a word for coffee from Mocha, Arabia. American tramps vernacularized the word, as they did java for another superior coffee grown on the island of that name off Indonesia.

He would puff at his mild cigar, named after Havana; or, if he wished a strong smoke, he might order a stogy, an inexpensive, though not necessarily inferior, cigar with a simple twist at the end. Stogy is a shortened form of conestoga, the heavy covered wagon with broad wheels which was used for transportation during the westward migration. The name of the wagon comes from the Conestoga Valley in Lancaster County, Pennsylvania, where it was manufactured. The valley is named for an extinct band of Iroquois Indians. Many of the wagoners prepared local tobacco for their long trip by rolling it into crude cigars.

The banquet I have described would have warmed the heart of Lucullus (110–56 B.C.), the Roman general who overcame Mithridates VI. Partly due to lack of support at home, Lucius Licinius Lucullus retired into that "elegant leisure, that luxury refined by good taste and tempered by philosophy," for which his name has become proverbial. A lucullan feast is a lavish banquet.

Lucullus and Brillat-Savarin knew toothsome food when they tasted it. There were others, though, who treated eating with more apprehension than appreciation. William Banting (1797–1878), a London undertaker, explained in his pamphlet *Corpulence* (1864) how he reduced his weight from 202 pounds to 156 pounds in a year by abstaining from the likes of beer, port, and farinaceous food. He lived essentially on proteins. To follow such a diet is to bant or bantingize; the diet itself is bantingism.

The American nutritionist Horace Fletcher advocated eating only when hungry, and then chewing one's food thoroughly (thirty chews to a mouthful); to do this is to fletcherize, and the practice is fletcherism.

Sylvester Graham (1794–1851), an American said by some to be a minister and by others a physician—maybe he was both—believed that meat led to hot tempers and sexual excess. Man should therefore eat food the way God grew it, "untouched even by salt and pepper, which would cause insanity." He produced what he considered the ideal food, a cracker made of

GRAHAM CRACKER	whole-wheat flour, so tasty that millions of graham crackers are consumed daily by faddists and non-faddists alike.

PASTEURIZA-TION Whatever your dietary habits, pause for silent tribute to Louis Pasteur (1822–1895), the French chemist and micro-biologist who first identified the minute organisms which cause lactic and alcohol fermentation. Pasteur rescued the silk industry of France by isolating the bacilli of a disease destroying the silkworms. He saved the chicken industry by developing a bacillic inoculation, and discovered a vaccine against hydrophobia. T. H. Huxley expressed the opinion that the money value of Pasteur's discoveries was sufficient to cover the whole cost of the war indemnity paid by France to Germany in 1870. Pasteur is remembered best, however, for discovering a means of killing harmful bacteria in milk by pasteurization, saving the lives of

PASTEURIZE countless children. To pasteurize is "partially to sterilize a fluid at a temperature which destroys certain pathogenic organisms without greatly changing the composition of the fluid."

SIMPSONIZING A dairyman named Simpson was prosecuted in England in the 1860s for simpsonizing—that is, adulterating milk by adding water.

Odds and Ends

TABASCO The source of tabasco sauce is frequently given as Tabasco, Mexico, but the label on my bottle claims it as "the registered trademark for the pepper sauce originated by the McIlhenny family before 1868 and made from special peppers grown only on Avery Island, Louisiana."

PUMPERNICKEL Pumpernickel, a dark, sourish rye bread, once a staple of Westphalians, has various asserted etymologies. One says that Napoleon, during an invasion of eastern Europe, was offered the stuff by local peasants. He tasted it, made a face, and gave the bread to his horse Nicole, saying *Bon pour Nicole*—good enough, that is, for a horse. Hence, by sound association, pum-per-nickel. AH, however, traces pumpernickel to German *pumper*, "to fart" (from being hard to digest) plus *Nickel*, "devil."

EGGS BENEDICT Funk explains the origin of eggs benedict:

In the year 1894 a certain Samuel Benedict, man-about-town and member of New York's cafe society, came into the old

Waldorf-Astoria on 34th Street with a wicked hangover. He knew precisely what he wanted for his breakfast. He ordered bacon, buttered toast, two poached eggs, and a hooker of hollandaise. Oscar, famous maître d'hôtel of the Waldorf, was impressed with the dish, and put ham and a toasted English muffin in place of the bacon and toast, and christened the whole affair *eggs benedict* in honor of the genial rake.

MELBA TOAST

PEACH MELBA

Melba toast stems from Dame Nellie Melba (1861–1931), an operatic soprano who took her stage name from her birthplace, Melbourne, Australia. Melbourne takes its name from Lord Melbourne, perhaps the most gluttonous of England's Prime Ministers. The very thinly sliced, crisp toast was her favorite food, rivaled only by peach melba—a dessert of peaches, vanilla ice cream, and raspberry sauce.

LOBSTER
THERMIDOR

THERMIDOR

Lobster thermidor was named for the drama *Thermidor*, by Victorien Sardou (1831–1908). *Thermidor* opened and closed on the same night, January 24, 1894; but "lobster thermidor," says Craig Claiborne, "is a still-running hit." Thermidor, in the calendar of revolutionary France, was the month of July. Since it was in that month that Robespierre was overthrown in 1794, thermidor has come to be associated with counterrevolution.

CHICKEN
MARENGO

Chicken marengo commemorates Napoleon's victory over the Austrians at Marengo, on June 14, 1800. Napoleon had got so far ahead of his provision wagons that his cook, Dunand, had to scrape up what he could in the neighborhood. The result was "a somewhat scrawny chicken, three eggs, four tomatoes, six crawfish, garlic and oil—and a frying pan." With this, the cook produced a combination which so pleased Napoleon that he ordered Dunand to serve him the same dish after every battle—including, to Dunand's disgust, the crawfish.

MATAPAN STEW

A matapan stew is a meal concocted of leftovers. It recalls the naval battle of Matapan, March 28, 1941. There was no time for formalities, and the cook of His Majesty's Australian ship *Perth* was forced to serve his men a scratch hot meal.

FINNAN HADDIE

The haddie in finnan haddie comes from "haddock"—but the finnan is more debatable. Scotland boasts both a river Findhorn and a village Findon, either of which may have supplied the name. In any event, the haddock is the fish from which Saint Peter took tribute money, leaving as proof two indentations from his fingers beside the fish's gills. The saint-pierre, or john dory, one of the essential fishes used in a true bouillabaisse, also bears the indentations of the saint's fingers.

SANDWICH

An unromantic dish with a diverting background is the sandwich. The title of John Montagu (1718–1792), corrupt 4th Earl of Sandwich, was commemorated when Captain Cook gave it to the Sandwich Islands, which have now resumed their former name, Hawaii. But it was immortalized when it became synonymous with the familiar sandwich—two or more slices of bread, usually buttered and enclosing a thin layer of meat or cheese. The common noun stems from the earl's habit, when spending up to twenty-four hours a day at the gaming boards, of devouring whatever lay between slices of bread (as the Romans had done long before him) without pausing in his play. Frequently quoted is this exchange between Lord Sandwich and John Wilkes, the squinting reformer:

> SANDWICH: I am convinced, Mr. Wilkes, that you will die either of a pox or on the gallows.
> WILKES: That depends, my lord, on whether I embrace your mistress or your principles.

BARMECIDE FEAST

BARMECIDAL

Henry Steele Commager points out that one of the most famous meals of history, perhaps second only to the Last Supper, was a non-meal, the barmecide feast. The Barmecides were a wealthy Persian family which furnished viziers to Harun al-Rashid and earlier caliphs of Baghdad. If the *Arabian Nights* is to be believed, one of them invited the hungry beggar Schabac to dinner, and set before him a series of empty plates. "How do you like the meal?" asks the Barmecide. "Excellently well." "Did you ever see whiter bread?" "Never, honorable sir." Illusory wine is later offered, but Schabac excuses himself by pretending to be drunk already, and knocks the Barmecide down. The host sees he has been outdone, forgives Schabac, and provides him with food to his heart's content. A barmecide feast is an illusion of plenty. Barmecidal is "unreal; illusory."

Bibulous Words

In my adolescence, youths attended YMCA camps, where in the evening they sat around bonfires and sang blasphemous verses ending in the refrain:

> *The things that you're li'ble*
> *To read in the Bible,*
> *They ain't necessarily so.*

SANDWICH

It occurred to me later that these lines were in form the tail end of a limerick, and I prefixed a couplet:

Eve, biting the apple, shrugged, "Oh,
Don't worry — God never will know.
   The things that you're li'ble
   To read in the Bible,
They ain't necessarily so."

"I don't care where the water goes / If it doesn't get into the wine," filched from a Belloc ballad, was part of one of those YMCA songs. It is supposed to have been a remark made by Noah during his cruise on the Ark, when damp and mildew were the order of the day. A limerick version:

Old Noah sang, "Sweet Adeline,
The water's begun to decline.
   Let it rise, let it fall,
   I don't care at all
If it doesn't get into the wine."

I am using Noah's wine-bibbing only as an introduction to the subject of alcoholic beverages. My story really begins not with Noah, but with his descendant Lot.

The Lord, you will remember, saved Lot and his family from the destruction of the wicked city of Sodom. As they left the scene, Lot's wife looked back, against heavenly orders, and was turned into a pillar of salt. This left Lot and his two daughters alone in the world. The result is described in Genesis 19:30-36:

> And Lot went up out of Zoar, and dwelt in the mountain, and his two daughters with him; for he feared to dwell in Zoar; and he dwelt in a cave, he and his two daughters.
> And the firstborn said unto the younger, Our father *is* old, and *there is* not a man in the earth to come in unto us after the manner of all the earth;
> Come, let us make our father drink wine, and we will lie with him, that we may preserve seed of our father.
> And they made their father drink wine that night: and the firstborn went in, and lay with her father; and he perceived not when she lay down, nor when she arose.
> And it came to pass on the morrow, that the firstborn said unto the younger, Behold, I lay yesternight with my father: let us make him drink wine this night also; and go thou in, *and* lie with him, that we may preserve seed of our father.

And they made their father drink wine that night also; and the younger arose, and lay with him; and he perceived not when she lay down, nor when she arose.

Thus were both the daughters of Lot with child by their father.

The incident prompted the following French *jeu*, which I reported in an earlier book:

Il but;
Il devint tendre.
Et puis il fut
Son gendre.

It happens that I chanced some years since upon a rare manuscript copy of the Apocrypha—the only one, I suspect, still extant. It interpolates between chapters 19 and 20 of Genesis the following:

And the Lord visited Lot in a dream, and the Lord said:

Lo! thou hast *known* thy two daughters, the firstborn and the younger; thy daughters were a bad *lot*; they *were* no better than they should be.

And Lot fell on his face, and replied, Nay, Lord; for I was there, *and* they were better; moreover, from the wine I drank they raised seed unto thee, even the sons of Moab and the sons of Benammi; and they are thy seed forever.

And the words of Lot pleased God, and God said to him, Yea, but for the wine that thy daughters did make thee drink, *peradventure* there would be no Moabites nor children of Ammon to praise my name.

And the Lord said, Behold, because the wine has preserved thy seed to praise my name, I will bless thee, and the wine, and the strong waters.

And in Lot's dream, the Lord performed a fandango, *and* the Lord sang:

I bless the wine, the bright wine
That oft has blessèd thee:
The wine that seethes, the still wine,
And all their family.

I bless the doughty brewers,
I bless the bubbling brew;
The stills, and the distillers;
The bottle, cork, and screw.

I bless the hop and rye fields,
The wheat fields, and the corn;
The bibed, and the imbiber;
The toper still unborn.

Then God said, make thee two trumpets of silver, a
greater and a lesser: that thou mayest use the greater for the
calling of men to drink strong drink, and the lesser for the calling of men to drink wine.

And thou *shalt* name all wines and all strong drinks, and
all cocas, and all colas. And the name thou givest them, that
name shall be a covenant between me and thy seed forever.
Then Lot prophesied in his dream, saying:

Old Hochheim, *streamside village,*
God guides thy alpenstock.
The Rhine maids' chorus praises
Thy white wine: "Hoch *to* hock!"

Madeira, *ocean island —*
Fermented, fortified —
Quaff deep, and use as benchmarks
The rise and fall of tide!

From Porto, port *shall issue:*
One sip, and reason spins.
(In stone write this Commandment:
Deploy port widdershins.*)*

Sweet sherry, *brought from* Jerez,
Thy name is Caesar, *since*
A wine so bound with iron
Is fitting for a prince.

The seaport Monemvasia
Is awkward to pronounce.
Its wine shall be called malmsey,
And offered by the ounce.

My eye perceives a future
Where kegs shall grow in girth
Till Scotch *from bonny* Scotland
Intoxicates the earth;

Till bourbon, *of that county*
And of the Bourbon *kings,*
Sends mighty nations reeling
In witless maunderings;

Till rum *(from* Rome *and* romance)
So titillates the tummy
That some go mad from toping,
And others call them rummy.

Montilla, curaçao,
Chartreuse, champagne, cognac,
Iced daiquiri, manhattan,
Bronx, bock, *and* armagnac,

Like gin and it *in England*
(Italian *vermouth),*
Shall comfort babe and dotard
For common lack of tooth.

And Lot named strong drinks for his seed, even the seed
of Moab and the seed of Benammi; and whatsoever Lot called
every drink, that was the name thereof. And he said:

One Matius Calvena
Shall write a cooking book.
Who tipples manzanilla
Does honor to that cook.

In London town, a brewer
Named Lushington *will flush*
His torrents down men's gullets,
Till men for "drunk" say "lush."

Blest be unborn tom collins,
Soft breath of gin and lime.
Oh Tom, I've got to meet you —
My daughters have the time.

My seed shall make a rickey —
One Colonel Rickey *he;*
And Gibson, Tom and Jerry,
And Negus *too shall spree.*

A lord of English sailors
A grogram *coat shall sport.*
He'll serve them rum diluted;
They'll call it grog *for short.*

My seed of seeds, Martini,
Of vodka made, or gin,
With miser hand will dribble
One wee vermouth *drop in.*

And yet one dreadful potion
Must be, my curse despite.
The maker's a Hoochino,
And hooch *is dynamite.*

Now, ere in final skinful
Our remnant wits we lose
Let's lift one shaky goblet
Of booze *to Colonel* Booze.

And Lot made two silver trumpets, and used them even as the Lord commanded.

And Lot dwelt in the mountain for many years, and his two daughters with him; and he dwelt in a cave, he and his two daughters.

And they drank red wine, and followed the commandments of the Lord.

And they prospered exceedingly.

The origins of the above-mentioned beverages:

HOCH   Hoch, a white Rhine wine, is short for obsolete hockamore, from German *Hochheimer (Wein),* wine of Hochheim, West Germany. The name is applied to any white Rhine wine.

MADEIRA   Madeira is a fortified white dessert wine originating in Madeira, main island of the Portuguese archipelago of that name in the Atlantic Ocean about four hundred miles west of Morocco. *A Madeira Party,* written around 1880 by S. Weir Mitchell and reissued in 1977 by Corti Brothers, Sacramento wine merchants, declares each decanter of the reinforced wine must be passed right to left, "with the sun."

PORT   Port, another fortified wine of rich taste and aroma, is native to Portugal, and shipped from Oporto ("the port"), a town on the Douro River. British naval officers meticulously passed this wine "from port to port"—that is, counterclockwise. In 1916, to bring Portugal fully into World War I, Britain made a treaty whose perhaps most important provision binds Britain to admit no wine as port that was not grown in a certain area of the upper Douro Valley and shipped "over the bar of Oporto."

SHERRY   Sherry, a still, naturally light-colored, fortified wine which darkens with age, comes from Jerez, Spain.

MALMSEY   Malmsey, corrupted from the name of the Greek seaport Monemvasia, from which it was originally shipped, is a sweet, fortified white wine, now also produced in Madeira, the Canary Islands, the Azores, and Spain. According to tradition, the Duke of Clarence was drowned in a butt of malmsey by order of his brother, who was to become Richard III.

SCOTCH

Scotch whiskey is of course from Scotland. Though blended, it is made chiefly from barley malt.

BOURBON

Bourbon, a corn whiskey, grew to manhood in Bourbon County, Kentucky. It is also the name of a rose.

RUM
RUMBULLION

RUMMY

As mentioned earlier, rum, short for rumbullion, or rumbooze, goes back to Rome. It once connoted superiority. But by association with the Romanies, or Gypsies, it turned to something questionable; rummy is "queer; odd." No one seems to know which origin is responsible for rummy, the card game in which the object is to obtain sets of three or more cards of the same suit or denomination.

AMONTILLADO

Montilla, in Spain, is the hometown of amontillado, a pale, dry sherry. In Poe's "Cask of Amontillado," Montresor lures his victim, Fortunato, the wine connoisseur, down to the catacombs, pretending a priceless amontillado is stored there. He then proceeds to shackle Fortunato, wall him up with stone and mortar, and leave him to die.

CURAÇAO

Curaçao, a liqueur flavored with the peel of sour orange, was first made on the island of the same name, one of the Netherlands Antilles off the northwestern coast of Venezuela.

CHARTREUSE

The Carthusian monks at La Grande Chartreuse, near Grenoble, France, were the first blenders of the yellow, pale green, or white liqueur called chartreuse.

CHAMPAGNE

Champagne comes from the old province of Champagne, France. Similar wines produced elsewhere may be labeled champagne, if marked with the name of the place of origin.

COGNAC

Cognac is, loosely, any fine brandy. The original is produced around Cognac, on the Charente River, France.

DAIQUIRI

The daiquiri was originally from Daiquiri, Cuba. Sugar with lime or lemon juice is added to the rum.

MANHATTAN

The Dutch used alcohol as a bargaining aid in 1626, when they obtained Manhattan Island from the Canarsie Indians (who did not own it) for twenty-four dollars' worth of bright cloth and beads. There is some question now about who got the better of the bargain. In any event, the sale is honored in the beverage called manhattan, consisting of rye mixed with sweet vermouth.

BRONX COCKTAIL	There is doubt, too, as to whether the bronx cocktail, containing gin, orange juice, and sometimes vermouth or bitters, is named after the New York City borough or the Bronx River.
BRONX CHEER	Nobody doubts, though, that the bronx cheer, or raspberry, made by vibrating the tongue and lips while exhaling, is a product of the borough.
BOCK	Eimbeck, a city in Hanover, was the first home of Ambock, or Eimbecker, now corrupted to bock. It is a strong, dark beer, the first drawn from the vats in springtime.
ARMAGNAC	Armagnac, a superior French brandy, is made near Armagnac in Gers.
MANZANILLA	Caius Matius Calvena, a Roman, wrote a cookbook in the 1st century B.C. Mala Matiana is a Matian apple, made small by the suffix -illa: "manzanilla, a small apple."
LUSHINGTON	A man inordinately thirsty for beer is a lushington, hence lush. The reference may be to the City of Lushington, a club of hard drinkers formed in 1750. Lush in Irish tinkers' slang means
LUSH	"to eat and drink." Lush, meaning "rich; succulent," is unrelated.
TOM COLLINS	The tom collins, presumably named for its inventor, is a tall iced drink made with gin, vodka, rum, or other liquor, and lemon or lime juice, carbonated water, and sugar. The rum type is a rum collins.
RICKEY	Of the rickey, Mencken says, "most authorities agree that the drink was named after a distinguished Washington guzzler of the period [around 1895], but his identity is disputed." He appears to have been a colonel, which at least narrows the field. The rickey is made from any ardent spirits (including applejack), lime juice, and soda water. The addition of sugar turns a rickey into a tom collins.
MARTINI	Jerry Thomas, a new Haven native who became a famous San Francisco bartender of Gold Rush days, once mixed a cooling drink for a stranger "going to Martinez," and named the drink for the town. He published the recipe in 1862. No-one knows for sure whether the Martinez was the forebear of our present martini. The name does not come from the vermouth-making firm of Martini & Rossi, which was founded after the drink was already in existence. The standard English martini, sweeter than ours, is half gin, half Italian vermouth, and is
GIN AND *IT*	ordered as "gin and *it*" (for Italian).

GIBSON   A gibson is a martini with a pearl onion instead of an olive or lemon peel. Hugh Gibson, United States Ambassador to Brazil before World War II, amazed drinking companions with his capacity for liquor. He devised a special drink for himself—ice water and a pearl onion served in a martini glass. Gibson appeared to be drinking straight gin. This, says *Newsday* publisher William Maxwell, is the origin of the gibson—a martini of maximal gin, minimal vermouth, and a pearl onion.

TOM AND JERRY   Tom and jerry is a drink of hot sweetened rum and water spiced with cinnamon, cloves, etc., and beaten up with eggs. As an adjective, tom-and-jerry designates a low tavern, and as a verb, to indulge in drunken roistering. (See page 133 for the origin.)

NEGUS   Colonel Francis Negus, who died in 1732, developed a not too lethal combination of port or sherry, hot water, lemon juice, sugar, and nugmeg for the British soldiery: the negus.

GROG
GROGGY   British admiral Edward Vernon wore a grogram coat in foul weather, and hence was referred to as "Old Grog." In 1740 he issued an order to dilute the navy's rum. One who loves grog not wisely but too well becomes groggy. Because George Washington's brother served under the admiral, the Washington home, now a national shrine, is known as Mount Vernon.

GLADSTONE   If in a London pub you hear a customer order a gladstone, do not think he wants the small hinged portmanteau named after Prime Minister Gladstone. The suitcase is not potable. He is requesting a cheap claret. The name commemorates Gladstone's reduction of duties on cheap wines in 1860.

HOOCH   Hooch is a dreadful liquor distilled by the Hoochinoo, or Hutsnuwu, Indians of Alaska from yeast, flour, and either sugar or molasses.

BOOZE   The word booze is attributed to Colonel Booze, a liquor dispenser of the 19th century. For the true origin, see page 138.

Expressions associated with drinking:

BISHOP BARKER   In Australia the largest glass of beer is a bishop barker. The bishop was an immensely tall Anglican ecclesiastic of Melbourne in the 19th century.

DR. WRIGHT OF NORWICH   If you manage to bring a circulating bottle of spirits to a halt at your elbow, someone may ask whether you have met Dr. Wright of Norwich. The reference is to an 18th-century physician who talked so superbly that no one noticed that the bottle always came to a rest at his side. A related phrase is "to drink with Johnny Freeman," a Royal Navy wardroom play on "free," meaning to get up and leave before your turn to pay for a round.

In Australia a jimmy woodser is one who drinks by himself; I assume there was at one time a misanthropic Jimmy Woods.

A dando, like a johnny freeman, leaves without paying for his drinks. A certain Mr. Dando was the subject of numerous 19th-century popular songs complaining about this habit.

Admiral Lord Nelson was killed at Trafalgar in 1805. Legend says his body was brought back in a cask of rum for the state funeral in London. En route, sailors repeatedly and disrespectfully tapped the cask. Hence the expressions "Nelson's blood" for rum, and "Shall we tap the Admiral?" for "Shall we have a drink?"

In the 15th century an English judge named Littleton wrote *Treatise on Tenures*, the first definitive study of English land law. His work was later commented on weightily by Sir Edward Coke, C.J. A "coke upon littleton" has come to mean a strong drink diluted by a lighter one. Such a combination may also be a "brandy and tent," tent being a hobson-jobson for tinto, a Spanish red wine, or brandy and small beer.

The alexander, a mixture of crème de cacao, sweet cream, and brandy or gin, may be named for Alexander the Great. (My erudite friend Richard Edes Harrison says, "I doubt it."

A British naval surgeon, Sir T. O. Gimlette, diluted gin with lime juice in the belief that the neat drink impaired the efficiency of naval officers. The gimlet is made now with gin or vodka, sweetened with lime juice and occasionally soda water.

From Holland, tasting more of the grain than most gins.

In the 15th century, one Christian Mumme brewed in Brunswick, Germany, the strong beer now known as mum.

A cheap red wine is often called dago red (from San Diego, patron saint of Spain) because such wine fortified Mediterranean workmen. Red biddy (pet form of Bridget) also describes any cheap red wine.

Among alcoholic beverages named for their manufacturers, dubonnet, made by Bonnet, lends itself to an appreciative pun: *C'est du bon, eh?* Frontignac, the fine Languedoc dessert wine, combines in its name Frontignon, a town in the department of Languedoc, and cognac. The name Haut Brion, a laudable wine indeed, is corrupted from O'Brien, an Irish family that culti-

PERNOD
COINTREAU

CINZANO
BACARDI
GUINNESS

BORDEAUX
BURGUNDY
GRAVES
BEAUJOLAIS
BEAUNE
MÉDOC
CHABLIS
SAUTERNE

CHIANTI

CANARY

MALAGA
RIESLING
TOKAY

vated vineyards in France. Pernod, a replacement for prohibited strong absinthe, was a product of the Pernod family. Cointreau, the liqueur, is likewise from a family name. The tonic wine cinzano was first made by a Signor Cinzano, in Turin, Italy. Bacardi, a Cuban rum, is named from the firm that makes it. If you order a guinness, you are drinking stout brewed in Dublin since 1820 by the Guinness family.

Many wines, not to mention stronger drinks, are called for their place of origin or export. Bordeaux wines in France commemorate the port of Bordeaux. Burgundy wines (of many makes and varying bouquets) are from the old province of that name. Graves, a fine light, usually white wine, is a bordeaux from Graves. Others so named are beaujolais (a wine best drunk young), beaune, médoc, chablis, and sauterne (sweet and white).

Chianti is a dry red wine from the Chianti Mountains in Italy.

Canary, from the Canary Islands, is a sweet wine, a yellow bird, and a sprightly French dance. The island was named Canary from the wild dogs (Latin *canes*) found there, making the wine, the bird, and the dance all doggy.

The Spanish province of Malaga exports malaga, a white wine, and malaga raisins as well. The German riesling wine seems to have been grown first in Riesa, Saxony. Tokay wines originated near Tokay, Hungary.

Too much wine puts me to sleep, and I am going to let the subject drop.

Dancing, Strumming, Tootling Words

The very name of Terpsichore, the Muse of dancing and choral singing, is so beautiful it makes my heart thump. She was equally beautiful in person—a young virgin crowned with laurel, holding a lyre or zither in her hand. A terpsichore is a dancer; terpsichore is dancing. Among the memorials to Terpsichore are the entries that follow.

TERPSICHORE

JAZZ

Jazz, first played extemporaneously by Negro bands at the turn of the century, is a highly sophisticated harmonic idiom that builds solo and ensemble improvisations on a strong understructure of basic tunes and chord patterns. Whether the word originated in a proper name will never be proved. One story says it was a nickname for Jasper or Chas, an early practitioner. Philologists prefer a Creole word meaning "speed up." Arabic and Hindustani have similar-sounding words relating to violent sexual desire, a condition which some say is induced by jazz. Jazz is also a slang verb for the consummation of that desire.

JOTA

Harry Randall, editor of *The Selmer Bandwagon*, sent me a list of dance names. One was the jota, which made castanets famous; an unproven story says the dance was declared a criminal offense in the 12th century in Spain, and that its inventor, Aben Jot, was exiled from Valencia for felonious obscenity. (Every new dance is considered obscene by the elderly, and in a few years seems creaky to the young.)

It is impossible to list national folk dances chronologically, since they sprang up spontaneously in the rural areas of many countries. Here are some of them:

POLKA
SCHOTTISCHE
ÉCOSSAISE

POLSKA
POLONAISE

POLONY

The word polka, to us a hopping dance performed by two persons in double time, derives from *pulka*, "half-step," in Bohemia, its place of origin; but Webster believes its ultimate source is *polka*, "Polish woman." A slower variant is called the schottische, for Scottish, by the Germans, and the German polka by the Scots. The écossaise in France is a grave old Scottish dance in triple measure; in double measure, it is quick and lively. Sweden's national dance is the polska, in triple measure and usually a minor key. Not until we come to the polonaise, a stately dance developed from the promenade, are we sure that the word derives from Poland, a name meaning "field dwellers." In the 18th century, polonaise was used, collaterally, for a woman's garment consisting of a waist and drapery in one piece worn over a separate skirt. In the early 19th century it was a man's short overcoat, usually furred. In Scotland it was a one-piece, tight-fitting garment worn by boys, also called a polony.

FLAMENCO
MAZURKA

VARSOVIENNE
TARANTELLA

ALLEMANDE

The flamenco, characterized by forceful, often improvised, rhythms, is named after the Flemings; the mazurka, with the second beat heavily accentuated, for a woman of the Polish province Mazuria or Mazovia; the varsovienne, similar to mazurka but with a strong accent beginning every second measure, for Warsaw; the tarantella, a lively Neapolitan folk dance, for the supposedly poisonous tarantula, against whose bite the dance was allegedly a remedy—the spider taking its name from the city of Taranto. The allemande (from an invading confederation of Germans who called themselves "all-men") was in the

MORRIS

GAVOTTE

16th century a slow dance in 2/2 time, and in the 18th century a lively dance in 4/4 time, both employing the French word for "German." The morris, an English folk dance, arrived from Spain in the time of Edward III (1312–1377). The dancers, wearing costumes prescribed by tradition, represented characters from the Robin Hood stories—an oddity since the steps were developed by the Moors. The gavotte is a 16th-century dance of French peasant origin bearing the name given in Provence to Alpine mountaineers. It featured a raising instead of sliding of the feet.

CIBELL

The cibell, the English form of the gavotte, is named after the goddess Cybele, who, her lover having been slain by her father, roams the world, looking disheveled, to the sound of pipes and drums, these being her inventions.

PAVANE

The pavane is a formal old dance in very slow rhythm, performed in ceremonial costume. It is frequently attributed to the Italian town of Padova (Padua), but probably is really named for the fancied resemblance of the step to that of the Italian *pavone*—the peacock.

BEGUINE

The beguine is a syncopated dance rhythm which repeats the same pattern over and over, without variation. Though native to the Caribbean islands of Martinique and St. Lucia, it derives its name from one of the several Catholic lay orders existing in the Netherlands since the 12th century and known collectively as *béguins*, "beggars," from their founder, Lambert Le Bègue. A Frenchman with a *béguin* on a girl is sweet on her;

SIR ROGER DE COVERLEY

The Sir Roger de Coverley, an ancient and famous English country dance, was named, claimed Addison in the 18th century, after the great-grandfather of Sir Roger de Coverley, Addison's pen name. One assumes that actually the pen name came from the dance.

RIGADOON

Jean Jacques Rousseau asserts that a 17th-century dancing master named Rigaud developed the rigadoon (French *rigaudon*), a lively arrangement, with a jumping step, for one couple. Lowell plays with the word in *The Bigelow Papers*:

"Yes," sez Johnson, "in France
They're beginnin' to dance
Beëlzebub's own rigadoon," sez he.

CONFESSE	The confesse is an English dance of which I know precisely nothing, except that an early English dancing master of that name is supposed to have originated it.
CARIOCA	A native or resident of Rio de Janeiro is called a Cariocan from the local Carioca mountain range; whence the carioca, a dance of African origin related to the samba. In Tupi, the language of the Tupian tribes along the Amazon, carioca means "dweller in a white house" (perhaps because the Carioca peaks are sometimes snow-covered). I have no evidence that aspirants for the American presidency consider mastery of the dance an essential qualification.
CALYPSO	The calypso, a product of the West Indies, is really less a dance than a type of music characterized by improvised lyrics on topical or broadly humorous themes.
MARINERA CHILEÑA	The marinera, a dance with alternating meter, was originally called the chileña, after Chile. But during the war between Chile and Peru (1879–1883), the Peruvians changed the name to *marinera*, "sailor," in honor of their navy (which was annihilated in the first few weeks of combat). The change stuck.

More folk dances from proper nouns:
Bergamasca — Bergamo, Italy
Canaria — Canary Islands
Forlana — Friuli, northern Italy
Granadina — Granada, southern Spain
Habanera — Havana, Cuba
Kazaki — Cossack or nomad
Krakowiak or cracovienne — Krakow, Poland
Kujawiak — Kujawy, Poland
Landler — Landl, Austria
Lauterbach — Lauterbach, Switzerland
Malagueña — Malaga, southern Spain
Murciana — Murcia, southeastern Spain
Siciliana — Sicily
Spagna — Spain
Strathspey — Spey Valley, Scotland
Ungaresca — Hungary
Weggis — Weggis, Switzerland

CASTLE WALK	In the early 20th century Vernon and Irene Castle invented the castle walk, a long-legged walking step in which the woman is backed continually around the room.

CONGA · The conga is a dance of Latin American and perhaps ultimately African origin in which the dancers form a long, winding line. Its name comes from a region in central Africa along the Congo River. I once had a donkey which I called Conga because of a characteristic it had in common with the dance: One, two, three, *kick*.

LAMBETH WALK · The fox trot perhaps receives its name from the short, quick pace of a fox. If the basic one-two-glide step was developed by a Mr. Fox, no one has told me. The step does seem more vulpine than, say, porcine, but that is scarcely an explanation. In any event, the *Times* of London asserted in 1937 that "the tyranny of the fox trot" had been destroyed by the lambeth walk. Lambeth Walk is the name of a street in London, used as the title of a cockney song and dance first performed by Lupino (meaning wolf, not fox) Lane in the London revue *Me and My Gal*. The people of Lambeth were said to greet each other with a thumbs-up gesture and the exclamation "Oi!" In the dance, each chorus ends with the same movement and exclamation: "Next time you're down Lambeth way . . . you'll find them all / Doing the Lambeth Walk. Oi!"

Among other 20th-century dances that have come and, in some cases, gone:

CHARLESTON · The charleston is named for Charleston, South Carolina, where it originated in the 1920s. It is a fast dance in 4/4 time, notable for hands crossing the knees, heel-and-toe progress, and the like.

LINDY HOP · The lindy hop, originating with Harlem blacks, involves a considerable amount of tapping. It celebrates Lindbergh's solo flight across the Atlantic in 1927; the 1920s slang expression "hop" meant both a dance and a short airplane flight.

SUSY-Q · The Susy of the susy-q remains unidentified. The dancer moves sidewise by alternately rotating the heel of one foot and the toe of the other.

KILLER JOE · The killer joe, of which I know only the name, was called after Killer Joe Piro, a dance instructor popular in New York in the 1960s.

FREDDY · The freddy was popularized by Freddy, of Freddy and the Dreamers, one of the first English singing groups to follow the Beatles to the United States. Its primary characteristic is "a kind of spread-eagling, while standing on one foot."

In 1928 Rudolph Laban (1879–1958) introduced a shorthand for dance, enabling a choreographer to score the various complex movements and positions of an entire ballet or musical comedy so that they can be repeated exactly in later performances. The system is known as labanotation.

Instrumental Words

Musical instruments of mythical origin, such as the lyre and the syrinx, have been mentioned earlier. Others derive from a wide variety of sources, sometimes misapplied. As a starter, I give you the French horn; the English horn (not even a horn); the German horn; the English trumpet, lyre, guitar, flute, and banjo; the Russian horn; the French bassoon, flute, lute, flageolet, the trombone; the Irish bagpipe, organ, and harp; the Belgian carillon; the Flemish zither and fiddle. There are types of mandolin in Italy named Florentine, Genoese, Milanese, Neapolitan, Paduan, Roman, Sienese, and Sicilian. A tambourine and accordion are called, respectively, the Basque piano and Polish piano. The name Jew's harp is sometimes considered pejorative, but efforts to rename it have not been successful; Mr. Randall suggests concentrating on one of the hundred-odd substitutes, the twang.

HELLHORN
KENTHORN

Reminiscent of lower regions is the hellhorn, named after its inventor, Ferdinand Hell. The now-defunct kenthorn was similarly named after the dukes of Kent.

SPINET

The spinet was invented about 1500 by the Venetian musical-instrument manufacturer Giovanni Spinetti, and was at first similar to the clavichord. The attribution is not certain; some say the origin is Italian *spina*, a thorn, alluding to the quill points on the spinet as opposed to the tiny hammers on a piano. I prefer to give Signor Spinetti the benefit of the doubt.

STRAD
STRADIVARIUS

WAGNER TUBA

MOOG

The strad, short for stradivarius, a superior violin, was made at Cremona, in northern Italy, by Antonio Stradivari (1644–1737) and his sons Francesco and Omobono. The Wagner tuba has not been lower-cased. A kind of synthesizer—a machine with a simple keyboard, using solid-state circuitry to duplicate the sounds of up to twelve musical instruments simultaneously—is called moog after Robert Moog, its maker.

FENDER BASS
WURLITZER
HAMMOND
STEINWAY
STOMACH
  STEINWAY

One Fender, now living in San Francisco, produced the Fender bass. The Wurlitzer organ is generic as wurlitzer, and the Hammond is becoming so; Steinway stands for not only the piano but the accordion, called the stomach Steinway.

SAXOPHONE

The saxophone is the most familiar instrument to have entered the vernacular from the name of a man. Adolphe Sax, born in Belgium in the early 19th century, grew up accident-prone: he was struck on the head by a brick, swallowed a needle, fell down a flight of stairs, toppled onto a burning stove, and accidentally drank sulfuric acid. None of this prevented him from perfecting, in 1835, the wind instrument named after him, which combined the reed mouthpiece of a clarinet with a bent conical tube of metal, equipped with finger keys. He was also

SAXHORN
SOUSAPHONE

inventor of the less popular saxhorn, a lineal descendant of which is the sousaphone, named after the composer John Philip Sousa.

Edward Putvis, a small, lively British officer who retired to Hawaii in the last century, was nicknamed Little Flea. He became an expert player of a stringed instrument similar to the banjo, played with the fingers in a fashion reminiscent of a flea hopping about. The instrument, brought to the Islands by Portuguese workmen, took Putvis's nickname. The Hawaiian translation of

UKULELE

"little flea" is . . . ukulele.

THEREMIN

The theremin, an electronic console-like instrument often used for high tremolo effects, is played by waving the left hand to control volume, and the right to control pitch. It was invented in the 1920s by Leo Theremin, a Russian-born engineer.

SIXTEEN

TURN ME OUT TENDERLY

Words Men Wear

HOUGH Louise tries to keep my suits pressed, it hurts me to be called dapper. To Milton, dapper meant "quick and alert." To Johnson, it was "little and active, lively without bulk." To me a dapper man is below middle height, with patent-leather hair, a hairline mustache, a corset, a toupee, and perhaps even spats—a M. Poirot without the little gray cells. Besides, dapper is sexist. I have never heard of a dapper woman.

Yet how nice it would be to associate some article of clothing with my person so inseparably that it would carry my name bobbing forever down the stream of time! Prince Albert, Victoria's consort, accomplished that feat with the prince albert coat, and almost accomplished it again with the albert chain, a gold watch chain, now out of fashion, looped across a rounded waist. I have thought of reviving the sensible custom of wearing a cloth around one's neck to protect the front at meals; if the idea caught on, an espy in future generations might be a bib.

PRINCE ALBERT
COAT
ALBERT CHAIN

An early sartorial model was Beau Nash (1674–1762), a gambler who as Master of Ceremonies at Bath made that city the leading English spa. Beau Brummel (1778–1840) was an even more elegant dandy (short for Jack-a-dandy—jack from the nickname for John, dandy probably from the Scottish nickname for Andrew). A beau brummel is a fop.

DANDY

BEAU BRUMMEL

Beau Brummel was for a time on intimate terms with the prince regent, later George IV. There are several versions of the story that he fell out of favor when, strolling at Bath one day, he met George and Lord Westmoreland. "Good morning, Westmoreland," said the Beau. "Who's your fat friend?"

Lord Byron remarked that Beau dressed with "exquisite fidelity," but Byron did not live long enough to learn that the fop lived his later years in a madhouse and died inelegantly in a garret. It is sad that no ring, no tie clasp, no cuff links—not even a moldering pair of spats—carries on the name of Beau Brummel.

By contrast, cheap blue neckerchiefs having large white spots with blue spots at their centers, identified with Jem Belcher, an English pugilist contemporary with Brummel, are still called belchers after more than a hundred years. A Nottingham prizefighter, William Thompson, who went by the ring name of Bendigo (having been born one of triplets; the reference is to Shadrach, Meshack, and Abednego in the Book of Daniel), customarily wore a rough fur cap; such in England are still bendigos in his memory.

BELCHER

BENDIGO

A man could attire himself for the entire day in garments whose names were once proper nouns, though the combination would be eclectic and some of the clothes considerably out of date.

Let us confine ourselves for the moment to male attire. You have just wakened and are considering the wardrobe at your disposal. (If by chance you live in a remote part of Australia, you may be lying under a wagga blanket, consisting of two sacks sewn

WAGGA
BLANKET

together, and named for the Australian town of Wagga Wagga.

JOHN

All right. Out of bed and into the bathroom. Use the john, which is listed in my chapter "Och, Johnny." Then wash.

CASTILE

Perhaps you will use castile soap, a fine, hard, comparatively tasteless variety made from olive oil and caustic soda, and originating in Castile, a province in Spain—unless you prefer

MARSEILLE

marseille, a soap of once similar content (but now often using other fats) from Marseille, France. Next you presumably will shower, shave, and—if this is a hair style you affect—trim your

SIDEBURNS

sideburns. Sideburns are short side whiskers worn with a smooth chin. They were the distinguishing feature of General Ambrose Everett Burnside, at one point commander of the Army of the Potomac in the Civil War, whose side whiskers were widely emulated. The reason for the rhetorical back formation—burnsides to sideburns—is a mystery. St. Clair McKelway once speculated that burnsides degenerated into sideburns as they shrank in size, retreating toward the ear. It is true, at least, that General Burnside—commonly blamed for the Union defeats at Fredericksburg (1862) and Petersburg (1864)—knew something about retreating.

DUNDREARIES

If you let your sideburns spread across your cheeks, they are muttonchop whiskers, or dundrearies, after Lord Dundreary, a character in the play *Our American Cousin* (1858) by Tom Taylor. The lord is remembered for his long side whiskers, his idiotic laughter, and his habit of puzzling his head with "widdles." Abraham Lincoln, at the moment of his assassination, was laughing at Lord Dundreary in a Washington production of *Our American Cousin*. (Marshall Davidson—editor, historian, and authority on American antiques—once sported a particularly handsome set of dundrearies. Through slothfulness, however, he shaved a little less each day, and now he has a full beard.)

MARCEL

Fifty years ago you might have taken time to set your hair in a marcel, a style for both men and women characterized by stiff, regular waves. The fashion, introduced about 1872 by a French hairdresser named Marcel Grateau, lost a bitter fight to permanent waves after World War I, though John Rechy's novel *City of the Night* indicates that it remained a homosexual style. I am told that the grooved irons used for marcels are again available for purchase.

In the 1960s, young men wore long hair as a symbol of disaffection with society. Sometimes they secured it at the back with a ribbon, a rubber band, or a piece of string. Such a ponytail is a cadogan, derived from the 1st Earl of Cadogan, who wore his hair that way in an 18th-century portrait, but not to express disaffection with the system.

I have yet to see a cadogan behind and a vandyke in front. A vandyke is a trim, pointed beard favored in the first half of the 17th century, when Anthony Vandyke was creating his portraits.

AFRO

ISRO
JUDO
POLO
CHINO
ANGLO
ITALO
WASPO
The afro, short for Afro-American but not confined to blacks, is a hairdo created by teasing the hair into a great sphere of tight curls until it looks as if a swarm of bees were nesting there. When worn by Jews, it is called an isro; judo would do as well. You may add polos, chinos, anglos, italos, waspos, and so on as desired.

Once you have arranged your hair to your satisfaction, you start to dress. Your first article of apparel may be a jock strap, a supporter and protector of the genitals, from Jock, a Scottish diminutive of John.

If you are a professional dancer or acrobat, and rehearsal is the order of the day, you may step into a leotard—a short, close-fitting, sleeveless affair, cut low in the neck in front and gussetted between the legs. The inventor was Jules Léotard, a 19th-century French aerialist.

More likely you may wish to don jaegers, men's underdrawers, once the proprietary name of an all-wool clothing material developed by Dr. Gustav Jaeger. Jaegers were manufactured in England about 1890 by the Jaeger's Sanitary Woollen System Co., Ltd. I think we can assume that the rapacious seagull called jaeger is not connected with the doctor's underdrawers; its name probably derives directly from German *Jaeger*, "hunter."

The English are fond of a warm pullover undershirt, the spencer (though you'd better ask for a "pop-top" at the store, or the salesman won't know what you are talking about). This is lineally descended from a short outercoat made fashionable around 1800 by the 2nd Earl Spencer. I'll come to the 18th-century wig bearing the earl's family name in a moment.

Next comes your oxford shirt, named for the college. You are not ready yet for your oxford bags (long-legged, sloppy trousers) or your oxford shoes (low, and lacing over the instep).

Select your cravat tenderly; it is a repository of history. In the 17th century, Croatian soldiers guarded the Turkish frontiers of the Hapsburg territories. A French regiment imitated the linen neckcloth of the Croats, gallicizing the name *hravatsk* to *cravate*, which in English lost its *e*.

ASCOT

Or choose an ascot, a neck scarf named for Ascot Week, held in June at Ascot Heath, Berkshire.

WINDSOR TIE

WINDSOR CHAIR

Though generally reserved for children, a windsor tie might strike your fancy. It is a broad silk necktie, worn in a double bow, and named—why, I do not know—after the royal borough of Windsor in England. (A windsor chair, made entirely of wood, with a curved back, has the same name origin.)

MORRIS CHAIR

For convenience in donning socks and shoes, settle in your morris chair. It is a large easy chair with an adjustable back and removable cushions, first made by Morris and Company in the last half of the 19th century. The Morris of Morris and Company was William Morris (1834–1896), an artist, pamphleteer, and general Renaissance man, who founded his company to reform Victorian taste in wallpaper, furniture, and the like. The chair that bears his name may have existed before he started manufacturing it; but that makes no difference to you. You have more urgent matters to consider.

ARGYLES

NYLONS

KERSEYS

First, your socks. They may be argyles, from the Scottish clan Campbell of Argyll; or nylons, a trade name mentioned elsewhere; or kerseys, made of a coarse ribbed cloth woven in Kersey, Suffolk. Trousers made of kersey were in use as early as the 12th century; they would be a little threadbare by now.

PANTS

PANTALOONS

Once socked in, step into your trousers. These are often called pants, or pantaloons, after Pantaleone, the patron saint of Venice. Pantaleone was transmogrified into a masked character in Italian comedy. He was also the central figure of Molière's *Le Bourgeois Gentilhomme* (1670). He was usually portrayed as a lean old dotard, with spectacles, slippers, and a tight-fitting combination of trousers and stockings.

KNICKER-
BOCKERS

Some golfers, though certainly not many, still wear knickerbockers—short breeches, fitting loosely and gathered at the knee. These were usual costumes of the early Dutch settlers of New York, and are called after Diedrich Knickerbocker, the pretended author of Washington Irving's *History of New York* (1809).

LEVIS

A leg covering as *de rigueur* in some circles as the oxford bags that swept the Western world in the 1920s is levis, originally a kind of denim trousers for rough wear. Young people go to

ASCOT

extraordinary trouble to give new levis an appearance of age and decay. Levi Strauss, an immigrant to the United States in Gold Rush days, crossed the plains to San Francisco as a peddler and prospered there as a clothing merchant. One of his innovations was to add copper rivets to the corners of the pockets of work trousers, so that the trousers would not tear when loaded with samples of ore. Levis still feature these now superfluous rivets.

DUNGAREES

Denims and jeans (page 279), trousers made of rough materials, are now fashionable; more formal leg coverings may raise eyebrows. Dungarees, made of a sturdy cotton cloth once woven in Dhungaree, India, were good enough for California gold miners in 1849; millions of young Americans find them good enough today. Levis, jeans, denims, and dungarees, all equally at home in "21" or on Skid Row, reveal our culture in full flower. Around half a billion yards of cotton drilling for such garments flow from our looms each year.

GALLIGASKINS

But to flaunt galligaskins, a kind of baggy breeches or leggings in vogue among sailors in the 17th and 18th centuries, would be going a little far. The word is a confluence of several etymological streams. One is gascoyne, associated with Gascony; another is *gréguesque*, "in the Greek fashion"; and a third is plain galley-gaskins, "galley breeches," from the galley of a ship. They were also known as slops.

JODHPURS

If it is your day for horseback, your choice of legwear may be jodhpurs, riding breeches that fit closely from the knee to just above the ankle. They were first worn in Jodhpur, Rajputana. Unless you intend to go riding, avoid them.

WELLINGTON

HALF WELLING-
TON

It is time for shoes. If the unexceptionable oxford does not please you, you may have in your closet, left over from your great-great-grandfather, wellingtons, named for the Duke of Wellington. The wellington is more a boot than a shoe. It is loose-topped, the front coming above the knee. A half wellington is shorter, worn under the trousers.

BLUCHER

Or your closet may contain an ancient pair of bluchers, named for the Prussian field marshal Gebhart von Blücher, who by some accounts saved Wellington's boots at Waterloo. The blucher is half boot, half shoe, with "quarters extending forward to the throat of the vamp, their inner edges being loose and lacing across the tongue." Von Blücher's troops presumably marched in bluchers to the aid of Wellington. Surely bluchers deserve a footnote, perhaps even a bootnote, in history.

In the 14th and 15th centuries, says Laver, "men's shoes were markedly pointed, sometimes fantastically so. The 'spikes or points' sometimes reached the length of eighteen inches or more. Such shoes were known as crackowes, or poulaines, the terms being corruptions, respectively, of Cracow and Poland. The names are explained by the fact that King Richard II married Anne of Bohemia and the gentlemen who came in her suite to England wore shoes with extremely pointed toes." You are not likely to wear crackowes, unless you live in a museum.

CRACKOWE POULAINE

Next comes the jacket. You have several choices:

The blazer. These proliferate around boating, cricket, and croquet clubs. Tradition says that the word emerged when the captain of the British H.M.S. *Blazer* ordered his crew to spruce up their appearance by wearing what Brewer describes as "somewhat striking blue and white striped jerseys." Partridge's more pedestrian guess is that the blazer—now generally navy blue, with brass buttons—is so called because it glows.

BLAZER

The cardigan. Much was apparently forgiven the 7th Earl of Cardigan (1797–1868) for having developed or popularized this warm button-down jacket of knit worsted, with or without sleeves. All else in Cardigan's life was distinguished disaster. Within two years after entering the 11th Hussars he had made 700 arrests and held 105 court-martials. As a major-general in the Crimean War, he led (but did not order) the suicidal charge of the Light Brigade which was to be rendered forever famous in Tennyson's poem.

CARDIGAN

The norfolk jacket, with a belt, a pocket on each side, and two box pleats in front and back. In case you are planning to hunt ducks in Norfolk, England.

NORFOLK JACKET

The eton jacket. It is a waist-length affair, with wide lapels and cut square at the hips. Usually worn with wide, stiff collar, it at one time identified pupils of Eton College.

ETON JACKET

Unless you are a priest, you are not likely to pop on a canterbury cap (from Canterbury), worn by the Anglican clergy, or to drape yourself in a cassock, a long, close-fitting garment reaching to the feet. The name of the latter may come not, as often supposed, from Italian *casa*, "house," but from the warlike Cossacks of the Steppes.

CANTERBURY CAP
CASSOCK

You may not let on if you are wearing a wig; wigs are as well disguised as falsies these days. At one time, however, they were as explicit as ruffled shirts. The spencer, worn by a forebear of the Earl Spencer who popularized the short jacket of that name,

SPENCER

LEVIS

BLENHEIM
BLENHEIM
ORANGE
BLENHEIM
SPANIEL

was a fashionable wig. The blenheim was a conservative wig named after its London maker (there is also an apple named, confusingly, the blenheim orange, and there is a blenheim spaniel. Both were first grown successfully at Blenheim Palace, granted to the 1st Duke of Marlborough in gratitude for his victory over the French and Bavarians at Blenheim—German Blindheim, Bavaria, in 1704.) Dalmahoy was a wig style created by one Dalmahoy; the jansen, after the strict-living Jansenist sect, was a plain, short wig; the louis, probably named after one of the kings of France, was extremely formal. So was the adonis, named for the beautiful Greek youth loved by Aphrodite.

DALMAHOY
JANSEN
LOUIS
ADONIS WIG

PALM BEACH

PANAMA

MALACCA

If you are sweating out a hot summer, consider a palm beach suit (a trademark, from Palm Beach, Florida; the fabric is very light), topped off with a panama hat, hand-plaited from leaves of the jipijapa plant of South and Central America, and named after the country of Panama. You might also twirl a malacca. This is an elegant walking cane, rich brown, imported originally from Malacca, in Malaysia.

You are clad now, though outlandishly; you must look a sight. But unless the skies are clear and the day warm, you still need a coat and hat. First the coat:

CHESTERFIELD

On a brisk spring or fall day, you will be well served by a chesterfield, a velvet-collared, single-breasted overcoat reaching to your knees. It is named for a 19th-century Earl of Chesterfield, who gave his name also to an overstuffed sofa. Do not confuse him with the 4th Earl, Philip Dormer Stanhope (1694–1773), a diplomat and statesman known for his elegant manners and his witty posthumous *Letters* (1774), consisting of worldly advice to his bastard son Philip. Or you might prefer a benny, a close-fitting overcoat named after Benjamin, youngest son of Jacob (Genesis 35:18). If a joseph hangs in your closet, shun it; it is a long riding coat with a small cape, outmoded and, in any event, designed for your wife, not you. The joseph owes its name to the coat of many colors made for Jacob's best-loved son (Genesis 37:3). His envious brothers cast Joseph into a pit, whence he was rescued to rise to the right hand of Pharaoh, ruler of the land of Egypt. Joseph later wriggled out of this coat, or some other, to escape the advances of Potiphar's wife; such a joseph would be an anomaly in this permissive age.

BENNY

JOSEPH

RAGLAN

If the weather is bitter, a good choice is your raglan, a loose, heavy overcoat with large sleeves and no shoulder seams. It was a favorite of Lord Raglan, who lost his right arm at Waterloo, and who was criticized, perhaps unjustly, for the sufferings of the British soldiers before Sevastopol in the Crimean War. He does seem, however, to have been a bit woolly-headed; he persistently called his French allies the Russians, and his Russian enemies the French.

PETERSHAM

BALMACAAN

ULSTER

Warm, too, are the petersham coat (made from rough and knotted woolen cloth and named about 1811 after Viscount Petersham, who helped to popularize it); the balmacaan (a loose, full overcoat with raglan sleeves, originally made of rough woolen cloth; it was made at the estate of that name in Inverness, Scotland); and the ulster (a long, loose coat originally worn by both sexes, made of frieze in Belfast, Northern Ireland). In *A Connecticut Yankee at King Arthur's Court*, Mark Twain dresses his baseball team of knights in "chain-mail ulsters."

INVERNESS

If you are a member of the Baker Street Irregulars, try the covering worn by Sherlock Holmes in wild weather—the inverness, or inverness cape, a loose coat with detachable cape. Like the balmacaan, it was first popularized in Inverness, a large county in northwest Scotland.

MACKINTOSH

BURBERRY

TATTERSALL

If it is raining, wear either a mackintosh, a coat impregnated with a waterproofing chemical developed in the first half of the 19th century by Charles Macintosh, a Scottish chemist; or a burberry (originally a trade name), a light overcoat made of waterproof fabric. If none of your coats is warm enough, go out to the stable and steal your horse's tattersall, named after the horse market established by Richard Tattersall in London in 1766. The tattersall pattern is now common in suits and coats as well as horse blankets.

GALOSHES
ALASKAS
ARCTICS

In bad weather, cover your shoes with galoshes—"Gallic boots"; with alaskas, heavy-duty rubberized overshoes named after the chilly state of Alaska; or with arctics, "an overshoe especially for wearing in snow." *Arktos* is Greek for "bear" (because the constellation of the Bear hangs in the north). That the great white polar bear turned out to live in the Arctic was sheer coincidence.

HOMBURG

FEZ

Then dent a little further the crown of your soft felt homburg hat (first worn at the spa of Bad Homburg, Germany), pop it onto your head, and venture out into the storm. If you are a Mohammedan, you may prefer a fez—a hat in the shape of a truncated cone, usually red with a black tassel hanging from the crown, worn mostly in the Mediterranean region. It is named after the city of Fez in north-central Morocco, the religious center of the country.

Unless you prefer some other sort of hat:

GIBUS

In the early 19th century, a Parisian hatter named Gibus invented a collapsible opera hat that could be folded when not in use.

I do not count out the possibility that you are a tea planter in Terai, a swampy lowland belt in India north of the Ganges and at the foot of the Himalayas. In that event, your headwear will probably be a terai, a wide-brimmed, ventilated affair named after the region. Indeed, as a tea planter you are a terai yourself.

TERAI

BUSBY

Certain regiments of the British Army still wear a tall, full-dress fur hat, the bearskin, sometimes called the busby. It was named after the pedagogue Richard Busby (1616–1695), and in the 19th century was a large, bushy wig.

The derby, a hat of stiff felt with a narrow brim and a dome-shaped crown, was first worn at the annual Derby horse race in England, described elsewhere in this book. Indistinguishable from it is a hat introduced around the middle of the 19th century by a Norfolk landowner, William Coke. Finding his tall riding hat frequently swept off by overhanging branches, Mr. Coke asked one Beaulieu, a famous hatter of the day, to design him a hat with a lower crown. The hat caught on, and is called either a coke hat or—hobson-jobsoning from Beaulieu—a bowler. It is also called a billycock, after Coke's first name. To "bowler hat" a British regular officer is to retire him against his wishes.

COKE
BOWLER
BILLYCOCK

STETSON
JOHN B

The best-known hat native to the United States is the stetson, or "ten-gallon hat," particularly popular in the West. It was first called a John B., after John B. Stetson, who originated it in the heyday of the American cowboy.

TAM
TAM-O'-SHANTER

A tam, or tam-o'-shanter, is a Scottish cap, usually of wool, having a round, flattish top much wider than the headband and a pompom in the center. It is called after Tam O'Shanter, who in Burns's poem of that name disturbed a witch revel in the haunted kirk of Alloway. The hags pursued him to the bridge over the River Doon, but there stopped, as they could not cross running water. One, however, plucked the tail from Tam's mare, Maggie.

Now that I have you dressed, I'll leave you to make your way through the day as best you can. Be careful when you cross the street. Spend your money with care; many of my friends are on the high road to needham (Suffolk), which means they are going broke; indeed, I am not doing too well myself.

HIGH ROAD TO NEEDHAM

Oh, as Timothy would say—by the way. If you are going out tonight for a do, you will probably want to change into your tuxedo. At the turn of the century, a barmaid would probably have marked down as a wolf a lone man who wandered into her saloon late, wearing this semi-formal evening dress; and she would have been right, at least etymologically, since tuxedo corrupts the name of the Wolf subtribe of the Delawares, P'tuxit (literally, "he has a round foot"). If the girl responded too quickly to his advances, she might be called the female version of a P'tuxit: "she has a round heel."

TUXEDO

The tuxedo originated in the late 19th century at Tuxedo Park, New York, a favorite resort of the Beautiful People of the day. The Morrises say one of these swells "became irked with the awkward tails on his formal full-dress coat and had his tailor run up the first tailless dinner coat. It was an immediate sensation, and, because of its greater convenience, soon replaced the tail coat on all but the most formal occasions." In this case it was the wolf, not the fox, that lost its tail.

Saratoga Springs, New York, was a popular watering place of the same era. In preparation for going there, families packed their bulky saratoga trunks. Once arrived, they devoured, *inter alia*, saratoga chips, now universalized as potato chips.

SARATOGA TRUNK
SARATOGA CHIPS

When the party is over, you will doubtless do as the cockneys do—go to bedlington.

GO TO BED-LINGTON

Sleep well.

Color

Color has three components: hue, the quality that distinguishes one color from another; brilliance (chroma), the measure of its strength; and saturation, the degree of its freedom from white or gray. These distinctions are generally lost on me. Webster describes both french blue and mazarine as "reddish blue in hue, of high saturation and low brilliance." If identical in hue, saturation, and brilliance, why are they not the same color?

TUXEDO

They seem so to me. Of the two, I prefer the name mazarine, because it has at least a small story attached to it: it was a favorite color of Jules Mazarin (1602–1661), an Italian who became a French cardinal and statesman. He made his affection for it so evident that members of the London city council, since they wore blue gowns, were called mazarines. Beyond this, I should add that my eye detects no flicker of red in the blue of mazarine/french at all.

Only a handful of the hundreds of colors bearing proper names are listed below. I give Webster's technical definition of the first four, and my own untrained reaction to the rest:

Alice blue (because it was much worn at the White House by President Theodore Roosevelt's daughter Alice, now Alice Roosevelt Longworth): greenish-blue in hue, of low saturation and medium brilliance.

Gamboge (from a resin found in Cambodia): reddish yellow in hue, of high saturation and high brilliance.

Indigo (a dyestuff first produced from plants in India, but now generally synthesized, natural indigo being largely confined to Bengal): reddish blue in hue, of low saturation and low brilliance.

Neptuna (named for the sea-god): green in hue, of medium saturation and medium brilliance.

Here is the proper-name background of some other colors, and how they look to me:

Canary, vivid yellow (after the bird; after its original habitat in the Canary Islands; after Latin *canis*, "dog," which may explain why a coward is called a "yellow-bellied cur").

Chartreuse, named for the liqueur produced at the Grande Chartreuse, France, is yellow with a little green in it, except when it is green with a little yellow in it.

Coventry blue, from a blue thread dyed with indigo, means true blue, loyal—because the dye from Coventry holds fast. (See page 158.)

Prussian blue is a dark blue pigment and dye, developed or discovered by H. de Diesbach, a maker of artists' colors in Berlin, in 1704.

Sienna, first extracted from the earth at Sienna, Italy, is brownish yellow when raw and orange-red or reddish brown when burnt. The dictionary and I agree on this one.

Titian, named after the artist, is a sort of red-yellow color.

Turkey (or Adrianople) red, after the place where it was found, is brilliant red with a touch of yellow. It is a durable dye used especially on cotton.

Umber (from a brownish earth found in Umbria, Italy) is just that—brownish. Do not confuse the word with Italian *ombra*, "shade," which gave rise in English to umbrage, first meaning shadow from foliage and later, more usually, offense or resentment.

A few more colors, with their origins following:

Burmese ruby is the color of the red-pink peony. Algerian is a yellow-brown color; mandarin orange is red-yellow; caledonian brown is ruddy when raw, nearly black when burnt; persian orange is red-yellow, and persian red, vermilion; persian blue looks to me like pale violet; wisteria is violet; wisteria blue is blue with red in it.

The origins are generally self-evident: Burma is the country of Southeast Asia, as Algeria is of Mediterranean Africa; a Mandarin was a bureaucrat under the Chinese empire; Caledonia is another name for Scotland; Persia is the Middle Eastern country now called Iran; Wistar was a 19th-century American anatomist, discoverer of the vine whose name misspells his.

Words Women Wear

MAE WEST

The mae west, an inflatable life jacket worn by aircraft personnel in World War II who might have to ditch at sea, memorializes but scarcely idealizes the extraordinary frontage of the film star of the same name. A double-turreted army tank was also called a mae west.

BERTHA

The bertha, a wide, deep lace collar to cover the shoulders of a low-necked dress, is traditionally associated with Queen Bertha, mother of Charlemagne, who affected the style.

DOLLY VARDEN

The dolly varden is a dress with a deep cleavage and bright skirt, in the Watteau style. Dolly Varden is a pretty girl with a roguish face and sparkling eyes who laughs her way through Dickens's *Barnaby Rudge* (1841). A dolly varden is also a large hat with one side bent down, and a species of brilliantly colored trout in western America. It is also a whore.

GERTRUDE

A gertrude, an infant's slip, usually of flannel, is perhaps named after Saint Gertrude the Great, depicted always in a very plain monastic gown. The slip is worn by infants of both sexes.

An English artist, Kate (Catherine) Greenaway (1846–1901), made many drawings of girls in dresses with a long, full

KATE GREENAWAY

skirt, short waist and sleeves, a round neck, and, usually, a sash and ruffled edges. The style became extremely popular. A kate greenaway is either such a dress or the accompanying bonnet, with a frill round the face—"still," says OED, "worn by small bridesmaids sometimes."

BLOOMERS

Mrs. Amelia Bloomer (1818–1894), a militant advocate of women's suffrage, sought to free women from their burden of voluminous clothing, at least during periods of exercise, by dressing them in loose-fitting trousers, gathered tight at the ankle, with a knee-length outer skirt. Though practical, the outfit was scarcely a treat to the eye, and when she began hearing it referred to as bloomers she protested. She was not the inventor, she insisted; she had borrowed the idea from Elizabeth Smith Miller; she did think people should have the courtesy to call the costume millers instead of bloomers. Emancipated women were themselves called bloomers after their wearing apparel.

GAMP

In *Martin Chuzzlewit*, Charles Dickens created a disreputable midwife and nurse named Sairey Gamp, still remembered for her unexemplary drinking habits, her nonexistent confidante, Mrs. Harris, and her bulky umbrella. Gamp remains a common term for an umbrella in England. It is also common, but not flattering, for a midwife.

GEORGETTE

The thin silk crepe of fine texture called georgette recalls Mme. Georgette de la Plante, a celebrated French modiste—a sort of 19th-century Coco Chanel.

FEDORA

The fedora, a soft felt hat with a brim that can be turned up or down and a rather low crown creased lengthwise, takes the name of the Russian princess who wore it in the French play *Fédora* (i.e., Theodora), written by Victorien Sardou and produced in 1882.

TRILBY

Another soft felt hat named for a fictitious woman was worn by the heroine of the George Du Maurier novel *Trilby* (1894). Trilby, an artist's model (and laundress), fell under the hypnotic influence of a repulsive but gifted musician named Svengali, who is discussed elsewhere. With his help she developed a notable singing voice, which she lost when he died. She not only sported a trilby, but her feet were so beautiful that feet became known as trilbies in English slang.

The names of two mistresses of French kings entered the language through their toilettes. The earlier of these was a

POMPADOUR

devout and honorable lady; the latter was one who found it advantageous to love wisely rather than too well.

Louise, Duchesse de La Vallière (1644–1710), was the first, and some say only, true love of the Sun King, Louis XIV. An innocent and modest girl, she was chosen initially as a blind to conceal the king's illicit affair with his sister-in-law, Henrietta. But the pretense soon became passionate reality on both sides; and long after Louis ceased to be faithful, he insisted on keeping his dear duchess close at hand. Not until she had arrived at the ripe old age of thirty-two did he accede to repeated pleas that she be permitted to enter the Carmelite convent in which she was to breathe her last "in gentle piety" thirty-four years later.

LAVALIERE

The only recorded frailty of Louise, setting aside her infatuation for a loose-living king, was for precious jewels, particularly those suspended at the throat from a chain. She wore these beautiful pendants daily, and the ladies of the court and country soon began calling any such ornaments lavalieres in her honor. Today the name is also applied to a microphone that is hung around the neck.

Jeanne Antoinette Poisson, Marquise (later Duchesse) de Pompadour, born eleven years after Louise died, was a more down-to-earth type, educated specifically and avowedly to be a king's mistress. One of her lures in this touchy game was her hair style, the straight-up, high-over-the-forehead effect now familiar as the pompadour. Whether or not this attraction was decisive, she managed to entice and entrap Louis XV. She then moved with skill and determination to grasp in her soft hands complete control over the major political decisions in France. She kept her influence over the king even after his ardor cooled, and is said to bear responsibility for the alliance with Austria which brought on the disastrous Seven Years' War.

POMPADOUR

A style of dress cut low and square in the back; certain silks and ribbons with small, thready designs in delicate colors; and a small South American bird of brilliant reddish-purple color—all these, with the hairdo, are called pompadour after the irresistible marquise.

ALPINE

If you have ever seen Mont Blanc or the Matterhorn, you remember the soft felt hats of the Swiss guides, often green or red, and usually decorated with a feather through the band. These hats are alpines. In the circular way words have, alp goes back in Gaelic not just to that familiar mountain range in Switzerland, but to any high mountain. In Teutonic folklore it means a nightmare, and is akin to both elf and oaf.

BIKINI

The bikini is a swimsuit for women—preferably, from a male viewpoint, for well-shaped women—consisting of two strips of cloth separated by a span of sunburned skin. A number of atomic test blasts were set off on Bikini, a Pacific atoll, after World War II; men seeing the two-piece swimsuits found them equally explosive. The word is probably connected also with Malay *bikine*, meaning "to make."

CAMBRIC

CHAMBRAY

Cambrai, a textile-manufacturing city of northern France, produced the finely woven white linen or cotton fabric we call cambric. The thin whiteness of a drink for children, made of hot water, milk, sugar, and usually a small amount of tea, was so reminiscent of the fabric in appearance that it adopted the name, and is called cambric tea. Chambray, a fine, lightweight gingham woven with white threads across a colored warp, celebrates the same city.

DAMASK

DAMASCENE

"A sword, a silk, a linen, a rose," said Brown; "all these have at some time, and even at the same time, been damask." They emanate from Damascus, Syria. Because linen is blanched and bleached, says Brown, damask suggests whiteness, as in Bacon's line: "Roses, damask and red are fast flowers of their smell, so that you may walk in a whole row of them and find nothing of their sweetness." The sword, mentioned earlier, is of fine damascus steel; the silk is a reversible figured fabric, bearing on one side a satin pattern on a background of plain weave, and on the other a pattern in plain weave on a satin background. The rose, notable for its pinkness and fragrance, gave us attar of roses. To damascene a metal is to decorate it with a special watermark. When a king or a queen regnant of England dies, the Great Seal is damasked—that is, defaced with the blow of a hammer by the Lord Chancellor, leaving a pattern of cracks reminiscent of damask.

SILK

Silk is from Greek *Serikos*, "of the Serics or Oriental people" (perhaps Chinese), from whom the thread was first obtained.

CANOPY A canopy is a cloth covering fastened or held horizontally above a person or object for protection or ornamentation. It was developed in the Egyptian city of Canopus, reason enough for its name; but the word also incorporates Greek *kōnōps*, "mosquito," mosquito netting being a very prevalent kind of canopy thereabouts. Perhaps the city was named after the mosquito.

BALDACHIN Baldachin, baldaquin, or baldac(c)hino, a rich, medieval fabric of silk and gold, is used for church vestments and decorations. A canopy of baldachin, used in ecclesiastical ceremonies, bears the name, as does a structure in canopy form placed over an altar. The baldachin in St. Peter's is about ninety-five feet high. Baldachin came from Baghdad, which in Medieval Latin changed to Baldac and in Italian to Baldacco.

MANTUA Mantua is a loose gown, as well as the fabric from which the garment is made. This robe may have been developed as a protection from marsh-caused chills of Mantua, Italy. Mantua was doubtlessly influenced by Italian *manto*, French *manteau*, English mantle. Webster separates the fabric, which it considers a corruption of mantle, from the dress, which it attributes to the city.

MARTINGALE The martingale is, first, a loose half-belt or strap placed at the back of a coat or jacket; second, part of a harness designed to prevent a horse from throwing back its head; third, a strut strengthening a ship's bowsprit and jib boom against the force of the headstays; finally, a form of gambling in which one doubles the stakes after each loss. The word may spring from Spanish *almartage*, "checkrein," but is more traditionally associated with the Provençal village of Martigues, perhaps because of the first of the foregoing definitions: the natives of Martigues were long ridiculed by other Provençals because they fastened their trousers in the back.

Sometimes a regional name for an article of clothing refuses to stick. The Morrises report that Scottish weavers once named four new shirt fabrics after great universities: Oxford, Cambridge, Harvard, and Yale. The last three shirtings have long OXFORD vanished. Oxford, though, has not only hung on to its shirt but added shoes and trousers.

Samson destroyed a temple (along with himself and a clutch of reveling Philistines) by pulling the pillars down about his blinded head. The temple was located in Gaza, in Canaan. Long afterward, Gaza began to export a thin, transparent fabric with a

GAUZE	loose, open weave, used for curtains, clothing, and surgical dressing. It was too fragile to be named samsonite; so, from its place of origin, it became gauze.
TULLE	Tulle, France, originated the fine, silk, open-mesh fabric called tulle, used for veils and light dresses.
MELTON	Melton Mowbray, of Leicestershire, England, produced a heavy woolen cloth used for making overcoats and hunting jackets. An article of such material is a melton.
MADRAS	Madras, associated with the southeastern India city of the same name, is a fine cotton fabric, usually corded or striped, sometimes figured or plaid, used for dresses and shirts.
SHANTUNG	Shantung silk, a kind of pongee, comes from the province of Shantung, China.
HESSIAN HESSIAN BOOT	Hessian is a coarse, strong cloth of jute or hemp, originally made in the grand duchy of Hesse, Germany. During the American Revolution, Yankees equated hessian with mercenary, because the British employed thirty thousand Hessian troops in the war. The money obtained by the House of Hesse for the hiring out of its troops was turned over for investment to the famous banking family of Rothschild, and is said to have contributed considerably to their enrichment. Hessian boots—high, and tasseled at top front—became fashionable in England early in the 19th century.
JERSEY	The jersey, a soft, plain-knit fabric, was first woven from the wool of sheep on Jersey, the largest island of the English Channel—a name conjecturally cognate with Caesar: "Caesar's Island." Jersey fishermen used the wool for sweaters. The opera singer Lillie Langtry, "the Jersey lily," popularized jerseys around 1900, making her an early sweater girl.
MACKINAW	Less glamorous but no less useful than Lillie Langtry's sweater is the mackinaw, a heavy, double-faced wool coat named for Mackinac, Michigan, a distribution point in the 19th century for supplies needed by trappers and Indians. In the Ojibway language, mackinaw means "great turtle." It is applied to the coat, the namaycush trout, and certain boats and blankets.
ANTIMACASSAR	In Victorian times, Makassar, a city in Indonesia, produced an oil highly popular as a men's hair dressing. Unfortunately, the dressing left stains behind. In self-defense, housewives sewed or pinned tidies called antimacassars to the backs of chairs and sofas. Antimacassars are not as pervasive as they used to be,

either because men's hair is less oily than it once was, or because women don't care as much.

NINON

A sheer fabric of silk, rayon, or nylon, made in a variety of tight, smooth weaves or open, lacy patterns, is ninon, a French nickname for Anne. The derivation is probably from Anne Lenclos, known as Ninon de Lenclos (1620–1705), a French *salonière*. She was famous for her beauty and wit, with some of the most distinguished men of the day among her lovers. "Old age," said Ninon, "is the hell of women."

MERCERIZING

Mercerizing is a process in which a cotton fiber or fabric is treated with a caustic alkali to make the material stronger, more receptive to dyes, and lustrously silky in appearance. The technique was developed in the 19th century by John Mercer, an English calico-maker.

GOBELIN

Gobelin tapestries are noted for their rich pictorial designs. They were first produced in the Paris dye works founded by the Gobelin family in the 15th century.

DOILY

The doily, sometimes used also as a table napkin, was created by one Doily or Doyley, who kept a shop in the Strand, London, in the late 17th century.

DENIM

JEAN

A coarse cotton drilling, first used for overalls and carpeting, is called denim because it was originally imported "de Nîmes," a manufacturing city in central France prominent before the French Revolution. Jean, a similar material of which jeans are made, was woven in Genoa (called Gênes in Old French); it invaded these shores as sails on the ships of Columbus.

POPLIN

Poplin is a corded fabric, usually silk or worsted, attributed by some to the Belgian town of Poperinge, but more often, as by Partridge, to *papalino*, from *Papa* or Pope, "because made at papal Avignon." Avignon, in southeastern France, was a seat of the papacy from 1309 to 1377, during the so-called Babylonian Captivity, for the latter part of which there were popes in both Avignon and Rome. Merchants during this period advertised the fabric as "Pope's linen," which may have been abbreviated to poplin.

"Haven't seen hide nor hair of him," we boys used to say when asked about a missing classmate, suspected of playing hooky. The old expression is redolent of an interrelationship between man and beast taken for granted in the backwoods village of my youth. It is meaningless, I suppose, now that few of us personally butcher the steer that furnishes our steak or shear the sheep that produces our wool.

Primitive man used the hide before the hair. Until he caught on to weaving, which took him a good many thousand lifetimes, he had to hunt down his clothing—first slaying his victim, then flaying it. The stench of a well-dressed cave man must have been abominable, and that day blessed when the first stinking hide, dropped into a bath made with oak or hemlock bark, came out as fragrant leather.

Leather serves not only for shoes and boots but for such varied items as handbags, book covers, saddles, jackets, skirts, belts, and punching bags.

MOROCCO

Its quality varies widely, according to the condition of the skin and the skill of the tanning. One highly esteemed leather is morocco, made of goatskin tanned with sumac. It is named for its country of origin in North Africa. Book collectors reserve morocco bindings for their most precious volumes.

NAPA LEATHER

Napa leather is a soft variety first developed in Napa, California.

SUEDE

In Sweden a clever fellow got the idea of rubbing the flesh side of leather on an emery wheel to make the fuzzy surface now so popular in shoes, coats, handbags, and gloves. The French named this variety of leather *Suède*, "Swedish."

Skins as writing material were priced out of the market when the Egyptians found a cheap way of pressing the pith of a common sedge, papyrus, into a writing surface. Papyrus became an Egyptian monopoly, a fact of life discovered to his cost in the 2nd century B.C. by Eumenes II, of the Asia Minor kingdom of Pergamum. Eumenes planned to build a grand new library, and needed papyrus for the books. But the Egyptians, wanting no rival for their world-famous library at Alexandria, refused to supply the papyrus. Eumenes was forced to have his books copied in the old-fashioned way, on skins. By good fortune, his scholars discovered a trick that made both sides of the skin suitable for writing. This cut production costs in half, and Eumenes proceeded to develop a book collection quite as extensive as that of the Egyptians.

PERGAMENE

These specially treated writing skins were called pergamene for the kingdom and its capital city. If life were fair, that name would be more familiar than it is today; but, as remarked by

Presidents Kennedy and Carter, among others, life is *not* fair. The Romans absorbed Pergamum in 133 B.C., leaving Parthia the dominant kingdom in Asia Minor. More and more, favor-currying folk referred to the skins not as *pergamene* but as *particaminum*, "Parthian leather"—in good English, parchment. The word now describes any excellent waterproof, grease-resistant paper.

PARCHMENT

Mountainous Turkestan, including parts of China, Afghanistan, and the Soviet Union, is dotted with lakes named Karakul, and with herds of sheep called karakul after the lakes. The fur of karakul lambs, usually black, has the same name, differently spelled: caracul.

CARACUL

Astrakhan, in the Russian part of Turkestan, is home of the astrakhan sheep, a relative of the karakul, but with a fur even more highly prized, the hair being longer and with a looser curl. Its name is applied also to its fur, and to a fabric with a similar curled pile.

ASTRAKHAN

CASHMERE

In the same way, cashmere is the name not only of the coveted downy wool at the roots of the hair of the Kasmir goats of India, but of a shawl made of this hair, a wool fabric of twill weave, and knitted garments made of the wool.

Just as leather is animal skin with a tan, furs are only leather without a shave. Both date from man's beginnings. It was not until the invention of weaving that hair came to rank with flesh and hide in the hierarchy of animal usefulness.

Sheep's wool is the best hair of all. It is warm, it is durable, and it can be woven into scores of distinctive, eye-catching fabrics. A number of these have lower-cased the names of their places of origin. Among them are berlin, a light fabric used in making gloves (a carriage has the same name); shalloon, a twill weave, used chiefly for lining, first manufactured at Châlons-sur-Marne, France; and worsted, a cloth of firm-textured, compactly twisted yarn made from long-staple fibers, produced originally at Worthstede, now Worstead, in Norfolk, England.

BERLIN
SHALLOON

WORSTED

TWEED

The Scottish form of twill, "tweel," was read by mistake as "tweed" for the River Tweed.

ARGYLE

The pattern of vari-colored, diamond-shaped areas on a solid-color background which was once familiar in argyle socks was first worn as the tartan of the earls and dukes of Argyll, heads of the great Campbell clan in western Scotland.

AFGHAN   An afghan may be either a kind of worsted blanket or wrap originating in Afghanistan; a Turkoman carpet of large size and long pile, predominantly wine-red; or the yellowish-red color Chippendale.

TARTAN   The word tartan (attributed by Webster and AH to *tiretaine*, Old French for linsey-woolsey), meaning any pattern of stripes of varying widths and colors crossed at right angles against a solid background, each the exclusive plaid of a particular Scottish clan, may go back to Tartary and the Tartars. The manifold variations, however, date only to the new weaving methods introduced with the industrial revolution. In the Bible, as in Assyrian history, the tartan was the commander-in-chief, second only to the king.

PAISLEY SHAWLS   At the turn of the 19th century, the great ladies of France and England shared a passion for soft woolen shawls from Kasmir having colorful, swirled pattterns. Since the two countries were at war, each intent on cutting off the other's trade routes, cashmere shawls were progressively harder to come by. So both nations began manufacturing their own. The British shawls were made at Paisley, Scotland. At first considered inferior substitutes for true cashmere, paisley shawls took on a vogue of their own when Queen Victoria, by establishing her residence at Balmoral, brought all things Scottish back into fashion.

The list of fabrics and related objects below shows but a small portion of those whose names derive from proper nouns.

ABERCROMBIE   Abercrombie, a Scottish tartan from Abercrombie, is characterized by a blue-and-black ground and an overcheck of green and white.

ACCA   Acca, a rich fabric of silk decorated with gold threads, was originally made at Acre, Israel.

ADELAIDE   Adelaide is fabric made of wool shipped from Adelaide, South Australia, a city named for the Queen of William IV.

AGRA   Agra, India, is the home of agra carpets, made of knotted wool or cotton and mingling blue, green, and brown colors.

ALBERT   Albert, a filling-face cotton fabric, is made into albert cloth, albert cord, albert crepe, and albert diagonal. Other uses of the word are mentioned elsewhere.

ALENÇON   Alençon is a needlepoint lace from Alençon, France.

| AMANA | Amana is a textile first made at Amana, Iowa, in the community-owned plant of the Amana religious sect. Ownership of the concern was later turned over to a joint stock company. The Amana society takes its name from the Song of Solomon 4:8: "Come with me from Lebanon, my spouse, with me from Lebanon; look from the top of Amana, from the top of Shenir and Hermon, from the lions' dens, from the mountains of the leopards." |

AMIENS   Amiens, a closely woven, twilled fabric in solid colors, stripes, or novelty patterns, was originally made in Amiens, France.

AMY ROBSART   An English fabric with a floral pattern traced in gold or silver thread on a white ground is an amy robsart, after Lady Amy Dudley, whose husband was believed to be the best beloved of Elizabeth I. On September 8, 1560, Lady Amy was found dead by her servants under mysterious circumstances.

ANDREWS   Andrews, a variety of sea-island cotton having an extra long staple, is named after some Andrews, but whether man or place I do not know.

ANGLESEY   Anglesey wool is taken from a large, soft-wool breed of sheep raised in Anglesey, Wales.

ARRAS   Arras, in northeastern France, became notable in the 15th century for the distinguished and energetic style of its tapestry weaving; an arras is a rich tapestry fabric with inwoven figures or scenes, or a wall hanging or screen formed by such a tapestry.

BALBRIGGAN   Balbriggan is fine unbleached fabric or hosiery made at Balbriggan, Ireland.

CALICO   Calico, a cheap cotton cloth, was first imported from Calicut, India, now known as Kozhikode, and not to be confused with Calcutta.

CHEVIOT   Cheviot is wool from a hardy breed of sheep raised on the Cheviot Hills in Scotland, or a napped, usually twilled fabric of such wool. It is also a moderately heavy cotton fabric used for shirts and waists, and a lightweight paper, decorated to simulate the weave of a cheviot fabric, for covering and ornamenting boxes.

CRETONNE   A heavy unglazed cotton, linen, or rayon fabric, colorfully printed and used for draperies and slipcovers, is cretonne, after Creton, Normandy, where it was first made.

DUFFEL	Duffel is a blanket fabric made of low-grade woolen cloth with a nap on both sides, and by extension clothing or other personal gear carried by a camper. A large cloth bag of canvas or duck for carrying personal belongings is a duffel bag. The name is from Duffel, a town near Antwerp, Belgium.
DUFFEL BAG	
HOLLAND	Holland, originally manufactured in that country, is a fabric of linen or cotton, often glazed, and used for children's clothing, window shades, and upholstery.
JACQUARD	In 1752, J. M. Jacquard, a French inventor, developed a device which, when applied to a loom, caused the warp threads to be lifted producing figured fabrics. Jacquard is a fabric woven by the jacquard method.
LAWN	Lawn is a fine, sheer, plain-woven linen or cotton fabric, thinner than cambric, used for dresses and handkerchiefs. It is also a sieve made of lawn. The source of the word is probably Laon, a linen-manufacturing town of France.
MARSEILLE	Marseille, a heavy cotton fabric with a raised pattern of stripes or figures, was originally made in Marseille, France, and was first called marseille quilting. It is also a kind of soap.
MILLINER	A milliner is one who makes or sells hats, bonnets, laces, ribbons, and suchlike articles of women's apparel. The word was originally Milaner, an inhabitant of Milan, Italy, or someone who imported women's finery from Milan.
MONTENEGRIN	Montenegrin, a close-fitting outer garment for women, ornamented with braiding and embroidery, uses wool from the thick-fleeced Montenegrin sheep. Montenegro is the Western European name for Crna Gora, the Black Mountain, home of Nero Wolfe and now a constituent republic of Yugoslavia.
MUSLIN	Muslin, a cotton cloth ranging from very thin, fine, and soft to heavy and coarse, was first made in Mosul, Mesopotamia, now Iraq.
NANKEEN	Nankeen is a brownish-yellow cotton cloth from Nanking, China.
NAVAJO	The navajo blanket is a woolen blanket, of bright colors, made by women of the Navajo Indian tribe of the southwestern United States.
QUINTIN	Quintin, a kind of fine lawn, is named from the town in Brittany where it was made.

SARCENET	Sarcenet, a fine, soft silk cloth, is from Anglo-French *sarzinett*, "Saracen cloth," which appears to have come to the attention of western Europe when the Christians were battling the Saracens in the Crusades.
SATIN	Satin is a silk fabric having a thick, close texture and a glossy surface. The name is traced, though not with assurance, to Zaytun, Arabic form of Chinese Tseutung, now Tsinkiang (or Chuanchow). This was the city known to Marco Polo as Zaitun. A great seaport in the Middle Ages, it appears to be the place from which satin was first exported.
SENDAL	A light, thin cloth from India, used in the Middle Ages for fine garments, church vestments, and banners, is called sendal from Sanskrit *Sindhu*, "the country of the Indus" (the river).
SISAL	Sisal, a fleshy plant indigenous to Mexico, is widely cultivated for its large leaves, which yield a stiff fiber used for cordage and ropes, but with a limited use also in the manufacture of coarse fabrics. The plant is named after a former seaport of Yucatan; *sisal* in Mayan means "cold waters."
SLEAZY	The adjective sleazy, applied to a cloth, means flimsy. Webster attributes it to English dialectal "sleeze," meaning to part asunder; Partridge ventures that the word may trace to obsolete Sleasy for Silesia. But he adds that the linen made there was not noticeably sleazy.
TABBY	A tabby may be a gossiping woman, from Tabitha, or a striped or brindled cat; but it is also taffeta, originally manufactured at Al'attabiya, a Baghdad suburb named after one Prince 'Attab. The striping of the cat is similar to that of the cloth. To my best knowledge, the gossip has no stripe.

Words on Wheels

A generation or more ago, a lady who was dressed for the day might call for her carriage and pair and drive out to visit friends. As uncommon, improper nouns, our motor cars are no threat to those buggies of the last century. No name of an automobile has achieved the generic, with the cantankerous exception of the tin lizzie. Oh—and the jeep. Jeep started as an acronym for a G.P., or "general purpose," vehicle in World War II, but is now vernacular. The Volkswagen, beloved as that beetle is, has not lost its capital letter. Chevrolet, Plymouth, Cadillac, Dodge, and the like have not even come close.

SEDAN

Most car styles—touring car, coupé, and so on—have always been common usage. The sedan was first a portable enclosed chair for one person, having poles in front and rear and carried by two men. It is not a product of the French city of that name; its source is Spanish *sillón*, "easy chair." Longfellow's "wonderful one-hoss shay"

> *That was built in such a logical way*
> *It ran a hundred years to a day*

corrupts French *chaise*, "chair."

LIMOUSINE

Limousine, though, was once a proper name. In Limousin, a former province of central France, it was first a hood or cloak; went on to become an enclosed, horse-drawn carriage, and persists as a large motor-driven sedan, used especially for airport bus service.

COACH

So too with the coach, a product of Kocs, a village in Hungary. Once a large, closed carriage with four wheels, the coach has adapted its name to a motorbus, a railroad passenger car, a low-priced class of passenger accommodation, a person who trains athletes, and a private tutor employed to prepare a student for an examination. The last two meanings are associated with the extreme difficulty of handling a coach-and-four. English novels of the 19th century abound in coach accidents.

Some carriages named for their place of origin:

SURREY

The surrey, a two-seated pleasure vehicle from Surrey, England. The surrey with the fringe on top praised in the musical *Oklahoma* is of a later, American vintage.

ROCKAWAY

The rockaway, with four wheels, two seats, and a standing top. It was put together in the latter part of the 19th century at Rockaway, New Jersey.

LANDAU

The landau originated in Landau, Germany. It has four wheels and is covered. The top is divided into two sections, so that the back can be let down or thrown back, while the front can be removed or left stationary.

CONCORD

The concord, from Concord, New Hampshire, had side-spring suspension.

FIACRE

The fiacre, a small hackney coach, is so called from the Hotel de St. Fiacre, Paris, where the first station for these coaches was established about 1650 by one M. Sauvage.

Carriages were named for people, too:

SHILLIBEER

The shillibeer is an omnibus, or a hearse with seats for mourners, developed by George Shillibeer (1797–1866), an English coach proprietor.

VICTORIA

The victoria, after Queen Victoria, is a low, four-wheeled pleasure vehicle with a collapsible top. It was designed for two passengers, with a raised seat in front for the driver.

STANHOPE

The stanhope, a light open carriage with one seat and either two or four wheels, was built for the English clergyman Fitzroy Stanhope (1786–1864).

HANSOM

The hansom is a light, two-wheeled covered carriage with the driver's seat elevated behind, the reins being passed over the top. It was patented in 1834 by architect John A. Hansom, and was called by Benjamin Disraeli the gondola of London.

CLARENCE

The clarence, a four-wheeled closed carriage with seats for four passengers, was named after the popular Duke of Clarence (1765–1837). He lost much of his popularity after assuming the throne as William IV. Britannica describes him as "a genial, frank, warm-hearted man, but a blundering, though well-intentioned, prince."

BROUGHAM

The first Lord Brougham (1778–1868) made Cannes, France, a popular resort by building a house there in 1838. He used to ride about the streets in the "odd little kind of garden chair"that bears his name—a four-wheeled closed carriage seating two or more persons and drawn by a single horse or pair. He was, by the way, a remarkable man. While still a student at the University of Edinburgh, he wrote two papers on light which were published by the Royal Society. He founded the *Edinburgh Review* in 1802, and filled it with his own articles on subjects ranging from science and politics to literature and the fine arts. A whig, he bitterly fought the slave trade, and as Lord Chancellor in the 1830s pushed through a bill emancipating all blacks in the British colonies. Though he never became Prime Minister, as he had hoped, he lived actively and happily into his ninetieth year.

BLACK MARIA

Perhaps out of place here is the black maria, a police van used for the conveyance of prisoners in the 19th century. The

287   TURN ME OUT TENDERLY

name is supposed to commemorate Maria Lee, a Boston black who kept a lodging house. "She was of such great size," says Brewer, "that when the police required help they sent for black Maria, who soon collared the refractory men and led them to the lock-up."

TILBURY

If none of the foregoing conveyances pleases you, try the tilbury, a two-wheeled carriage with or without a top, called after a London coach-maker. Surely one of these carriages should be a satisfactory replacement for your automobile. Remember, the energy crisis can only grow worse.

SEVENTEEN

WHATSOEVER ADAM CALLED EVERY LIVING CREATURE, THAT WAS THE NAME THEREOF

BEASTLY WORDS

N HIS delightful *Naming-Day in Eden*, Noah Jonathan Jacobs speculates on how Adam named the bat:

> Did its blindness move him to call it *murcielago* (Sp.), its baldness *chauve-souris* (Fr.), its shyness *pipistrelloe* (It.), its leathery skin *Laderlapp* (Swed.) . . . its preference for the night *nukteris* (Gr.), its resemblance to the mouse *Fledermaus* (Ger.) . . . the sound of its flapping wings *watwat* (Arab.), its winglike hands *chiroptera* (Gr. *chir*, hand, plus *pteron*, wing)?

Perhaps so, but not unless Adam was reincarnated frequently. Genesis notwithstanding, many creatures of earth, air, and sea were discovered and named long after Adam was laid to rest.

LAPU-LAPU

I give you as an example a fish swimming off the Philippines called the lapu-lapu. The name honors dishonorable Lapu-Lapu, treacherous king of Cebu. In 1521 Lapu-Lapu contracted a close friendship with the navigator Magellan, sent him on an expedition to conquer in the king's name the neighboring island of Mactan, and arranged to have his landing party slaughtered. The poor fish in this case was the explorer, not the king; I think the lapu-lapu should be renamed the magellan.

TEDDY BEAR

The teddy bear is a toy; but it represents an animal, and the story behind its name can stand one more telling. President Theodore Roosevelt, known affectionately as Teddy (this was in the days when Americans were occasionally affectionate toward their presidents), was an inveterate hunter of big game. Once, in 1902, it is said he refused to shoot a captured baby bear, considering such an act unsporting. The stuffed plush toy that appeared soon thereafter may have been called a teddy bear on account of that act of compassion, but more likely as a playful allusion to Roosevelt's penchant for hunting.

It would be possible to stock a sizable exhibit with fauna bearing names from mythology. Some potential specimens are listed here:

CECROPIA MOTH

The cecropia moth, a large North American variety with red, white, and black markings on the wings, was named for Cecrops, legendary founder of Athens, who had snakes in the place of legs.

ARACHNID

An arachnid, which may be either a spider or a scorpion, is an arthropod, its body being divided into two principal regions. Unlike a true insect, it has no antennae. The allusion is to Arachne, a Lydian girl vain of her weaving skill. She challenged the goddess Athena to a contest, lost, and was turned into a spider.

NEREID

The nereid, a clamworm with a long, flat, segmented body, having a pair of paddles on each segment, is named for the nereids, attendants on Neptune and daughters of the sea deity Nereus. These were first represented as beautiful nymphs, but later as beings with green hair and a lower body like that of a fish. Even so, they would not have been flattered by the association of their name with a clamworm.

In Greek mythology, Phoebe was a daughter of Uranus and Gaea. Her name, from a Greek word meaning "to shine," was sometimes applied also to Diana, goddess of the moon. She

PHOEBE

persists as a common noun in the phoebe—also called the pewee or pewit—a flycatcher that makes a *fee-bee* sound. The bird has a slight crest, and is grayish brown above and yellowish white below. A western serranoid fish is likewise a phoebe, and Phoebe is the ninth satellite of Saturn.

RHESUS MONKEY

The rhesus monkey of India, used extensively in biological experimentation, is named for Rhesus, mythological king of Thrace and ally of the Trojans, to whose aid Rhesus marched with a large army. An oracle had declared that Troy would be safe should the horses of Rhesus drink from the River Xanthus and feed upon the grass of the Trojan plains. The Greeks, however, slew the king and galloped off on the horses before the terms of the oracle could be met. They made a monkey of him.

LEMUR

The lemur is a pop-eyed, monkey-like animal of Madagascar, so named because it is nocturnal, like the Lemures. In ancient Rome, the Lemures were the maleficent spirits of the dead, who prowled about the house until appeased by a ritual of feeding.

RHEA

I have noted elsewhere the story of Rhea, mother of Zeus. She is the eponym of the rhea, a South American ostrich.

CYCLOPS

A fetal monster with a single eye, or any animal having two eyes fused, is a cyclops, alluding to the one-eyed Cyclopes mentioned earlier, whom Gaea bore to Uranus. Largest and strongest of the Cyclopes was Polyphemus, who captured Odysseus and his men and immured them for food in the cave where he kept his sheep. After four of the men had been eaten, Odysseus managed to intoxicate Polyphemus and then to deprive him of sight by plunging a pointed stake into his eye. Next morning, despite his agony, Polyphemus as usual rolled away the stone which blocked the cave entrance, so that the sheep might go out to graze. Odysseus and his men escaped by fastening themselves to the underbellies of the sheep, of which the blinded monster checked only the backs.

ARGUS-EYED

Argus was a giant with a hundred eyes—whence argus-eyed, "sharp-sighted." He was instructed by Hera, queen of heaven and consort of Zeus, to keep all hundred eyes fixed on Io, one of her husband's lights of love. Io had been transformed into a white heifer—either by Hera to conceal her from Zeus, or by Zeus to conceal her from Hera. To put an end to the chaperonage, Hermes, cunning son of Zeus, contrived to sing all hundred of Argus's eyes to sleep, and then, it is said, killed the giant with a stone. Hera next sent a gadfly to torment the heifer, who fled until, arriving on the banks of the Nile, she resumed her original form, and bore Zeus a human daughter. In her flight, Io had to swim the Bosporus (meaning "ox-ford" in Greek), the strait separating Greece from Turkey. This is as good a reason as any for shouting "Come, boss. Come, bossy" when calling home the cows. A bosporus, by the way, is a strait between two seas, or between a lake and a sea.

BOSSY
BOSPORUS

As a memorial to Argus, Hera set his eyes in the tail of her favorite bird, the peacock. His name is now applied to the closely related argus pheasant.

ARGUS
PHEASANT

Triton, god of the sea, blew a pointed, spirally twisted shell as a trumpet. The god had the head and trunk of a man, the tail of a fish, and innumerable progeny in his image. All that remains of these now is a gastropodous mollusk, the triton, which sports a shell of the sort the god used to blow. Wordsworth cited Triton as a symbol of the natural life from which man has become disaffected:

TRITON

> . . . *Great God! I'd rather be*
> *A Pagan, suckled in a creed outworn;*
> *So might I, standing on this pleasant lea,*
> *Have glimpses that would make me less forlorn;*
> *Have sight of Proteus rising from the sea;*
> *Or hear old Triton blow his wreathèd horn.*

The *Roman de Renart*, a medieval beast epic satirizing contemporary life, appeared in Latin as early as the 12th century, and in French and German soon afterward. The ape in the story was named Martin, and apes are frequently referred to as such. The same name is applied to a small European swallow — perhaps, says Weekley, "in allusion to the southward flight of this swallow about *Martinmas*," a feast held November 11. The son of Martin the ape was called Monekin in Old French, and Moneke in Low German. This altered to our monkey (perhaps with a little help from monk, in allusion to that holy man's brown-capped head). The fox, Renart, is the chief character of the epic; the name was once spelled Regin, and evolved to Reynard, vernacular in English for a vulpine.

MARTIN

MONKEY

REYNARD

CHARLEY

For a hundred years, by the way, the English called a fox a Charley, from Charles James Fox (1749–1806), a brilliant and casuistic politician who was three times Foreign Secretary. In his own affairs, however, Fox was not so shrewd; he was regularly fleeced at gambling. Since the moneylenders to whom he resorted were Jews, he called the room in which he did business with them his "Jerusalem chamber." When his elder brother had a son, damaging Fox's prospects for inheriting from his father, and thus the prospects of his creditors for getting their money, Fox said the boy was a second Messiah, who had appeared for the destruction of the Jews. "He had his jest," went a saying of the time, "and they had his estate."

BRUIN
COWARD
CHANTICLEER

Bruin, another character in the *Roman de Renart*, is still Bruin the bear. Couart, the hare, meaning in Old French "with tail between the legs," turned to Coward, while Chanticler, the crowing cock, is our familiar chanticleer:

> *The beasts forgathered for a vote*
> *On which to most revere.*
> *"The sun itself obeys my call,"*
> *Said cocky Chanticleer.*
>
> *But Reynard sneered, "Yon rooster*
> *Survives but at my whim.*
> *When he is in my belly,*
> *What beast will honor him?"*

The verse goes on (or will, if I ever get around to finishing it) to tell how each of the other beasts extols his own superiority, with the exception of Coward, whose long ears have picked up the approaching footsteps of Man. Coward slips into his hideyhole, and as one by one his friends are slaughtered above his head he lies placidly, reflecting

> *He who lives to run away*
> *Will live to run another day.*

BALUCHITHERE

Far older than even the earliest myths is the baluchithere, an extinct rhinoceros-like mammal of the Oligocene and Miocene epochs, twenty-five to fifty million years ago. It was twenty-eight feet long and stood thirteen to eighteen feet at the shoulder. It could pull down tree branches twenty-two feet in the air. The name comes from Baluchistan, Pakistan, where fossil remains of the great beast were first found in 1911.

MOSASAUR

Even more ancient is the mosasaur, a lizard with some characteristics of a fish. Its fossil remains first appeared in 1780 near the Meuse River—Mosa in Latin.

PHEASANT

The name of the pheasant, a large, long-tailed, brilliantly colored fowl, is shortened from Phasian bird. The fowl were common around the Phasis, a river of the ancient province of Colchis, ease of the Black Sea.

TURKEY

GUINEA COCK

TURKEY BUZZARD

The turkey, American by origin, bears its present name because it happened to reach England by way of Turkey. The guinea cock, imported from Guinea, Africa, through Turkey, was once called the turkey cock, and the American fowl was for a time confused with it. The turkey buzzard is an American vulture bearing a slight resemblance to a turkey. The name is applied also to a number of plants (the turkey beard, turkey berry, turkey blossom, turkey corn, turkey fig, turkey foot, turkey grape, turkey gum); to a louse which feeds on the turkey; to a sponge, a candy, and a dance; and to other objects too numerous to list here.

GUINEA PIG

The guinea pig, a nearly hairless cavy about seven inches long, is so commonly used in biological experiments that guinea pig has come to stand for any subject of an experiment. It originates not in Guinea, but in Guiana and Brazil; its name seems to have come from the Guineamen, or slave traders, who carried it from South America to England.

CAPTAIN COOK

A wild pig in New Zealand is known as a captain cook, pigs having been introduced there by Captain Cook during his explorations. Australians call New Zealand the Pig Islands.

TARANTULA

TARANTISM

Taranto, an Italian seaport, gave its name to the tarantula, in Europe a large wolf spider. Its bite was once associated with tarantism, a nervous affliction characterized by melancholy, stupor, and, contradictorily, an uncontrollable desire to dance. Some say the tarantella, a lively dance, was developed to cure the bite of the tarantula; others, that the bite was fairly harmless but gave an excuse for dancing at a time when to dance was considered sinful. Probably the dance as well as the spider were simply named for the seaport. Large hairy spiders of Texas and the American tropics are called tarantulas, as is a type of whip scorpion.

SPANIEL

The spaniel, a short-legged dog with long hair and drooping ears, was developed in Spain. The three main classes are the field, or springer, spaniel, used for hunting small game; the water spaniel, larger and with curly hair; and the small English toy spaniel, kept as a pet. As an adjective, spaniel means "cringing; fawning": "Looking at her with spaniel eyes," said Sinclair Lewis. To spaniel is to sport about or, more rarely, to fawn.

SHELTY	A shelty is a sheepdog or a pony, both rough-coated and hardy, from the Shetland Islands.
JENNET	The jennet, a small Spanish horse, derives its name from the Berber tribe Zanatah. The word originally meant a mounted soldier. There is also a jennet ass. The jenny, or female, ass, however, is named for some Jenny.
JENNY ASS	
BOCACCIO	The Italian poet and diplomat Giovanni Boccaccio (1313–1375) had something of a reputation as a big mouth. The bocaccio, a rockfish of American waters, has a big mouth too; indeed the word for "big mouth" in Spanish is *bocacha*.
LITTLENECK	The littleneck clam is so called not from the size of its neck, but from its location in Littleneck Bay, Long Island. It is the young of a quahog, small enough to eat raw. By extension it is any clam suitable for this purpose.
FLAMINGO	A large wading bird of tropical regions is the flamingo. It has reddish or pinkish plumage, long legs, a long, flexible neck, and a bill turned down at the tip. The name derives from the Flemings of Flanders, apparently because they were noted for their gay attire. It may also incorporate a play on a Portuguese word meaning "flame." A deep pink color is called flamingo.
CARIBE	A voraciously carnivorous freshwater fish of the American tropics, the caribe, is named for the cannibal Caribe Indians of northern South America and the Lesser Antilles.
CAYUSE	The cayuse, an Indian pony, was first associated with the Cayuse tribe of Oregon.
GUPPY	A guppy is one of a species of tiny tropical fish presented to the British Museum in 1868 by R. J. Lechmere Guppy, president of the Scientific Association of Trinidad.
GARVIE	In Scotland, a garvie is a sprat, or herring. It probably takes its name from Inchgarvie, an island in the Firth of Forth. The sardine, a small fish of the pilchard family suitable for preserving in oil or tomato sauce for food, is called in the same fashion after the Greek coast of Sardinia.
SARDINE	
GIBBON	The lowest and most arboreal of the anthropoid apes, the gibbon, takes its name from a familiar form of Gilbert. Weekley remarks that "the tombs of the Gybbon family at Rolvenden, Kent, dating from c. 1700, are surmounted by an ape's head, the family crest." Perhaps they could trace their descent all the way back to a gibbon.

COLORADO
BEETLE

The colorado beetle is a native of Colorado, and hard on potatoes.

LONK

And a lonk, of course, is a sheep from Lancashire.

Other domestic animals whose names trace back to proper nouns follow.

Dogs

BEDLINGTON

The bedlington, a swift, game, rough-coated terrier, after Bedlington, on the River Blyth in Northumberland.

BOSTON
TERRIER

The boston terrier, a cross between a bulldog and a bull terrier, after Boston, Massachusetts.

CHOW

The chow, a profusely coated, lion-headed dog with a short tail curled close to the back, originating in China and connected both with chow, a pidgin word for "food," and Chow, Australian slang for "Chinese," in reference to the Chou dynasty (the name may also relate to food).

COLLIE

The collie, a large sheepdog of Scottish beginnings, after Colin, a common Scottish name.

DALMATIAN

The dalmatian, a short-haired, spotted coach dog, after Dalmatia, a region in Yugoslavia.

GREAT DANE

The great dane, a big, strong, short-haired dog, after Denmark.

HUSKY

The husky, an Eskimo dog of unstandardized breed, probably after Eskimo.

LABRADOR

The labrador, a black, smaller variation of the newfoundland, after Labrador, a peninsula of northeastern Canada, which in turn is named after the Lavrador of Terceira, the pilot who guided John Cabot's ship to this Canadian coast in 1498.

NEWFOUNDLAND

The newfoundland after Newfoundland, a province off the coast of Canada, where it developed from a cross between the native dogs and large dogs brought from England.

PEKE   The peke, or pekingese, a dog originally the property and
                the prerogative of the imperial family of China; after Peking, in
                imperial days the northern capital.

POM   The pom, or pomeranian, a small, long-haired dog with a
                foxlike head, from Pomerania, in northern Prussia.

SAINT BERNARD   The Saint Bernard, a gigantic life-saving dog, after the
                hospice of Saint Bernard in the Swiss Alps, where for nearly a
                thousand years it has been rescuing travelers in the snowdrifts of
                the Alpine passes.

DOBERMAN   The doberman, or doberman pinscher (*Pinscher* meaning
                "terrier" in German), a large, smooth-coated terrier developed
                about 1890; after its first breeder, Ludwig Dobermann.

SALUKI   The saluki, or gazelle hound, after Saluq, an ancient city of
                southern Arabia.

SEALYHAM   The sealyham, a short-legged, strong-jawed terrier first
                bred to hunt badgers, otters, and foxes; after Sealyham, the
                country estate of Captain John Tucker-Edwardes, where it was
                developed about 1860.

SCOTCH   The scotch (or scottish) terrier, probably the oldest indige-
    TERRIER   nous North British dog, short-legged, large-headed, and deep-
                chested; after Scotland.

SKYE   The skye, a terrier of a very old breed, after Skye, the largest
                isle of the Inner Hebrides.

Cats

ANGORA   The angora (also a goat or rabbit), after Angora, a city in
                Asia Minor.

MANX   The manx, which has, as Partridge puts it, "a ridiculously
                rudimentary tail but is not the least ashamed of it"; after the Isle
                of Man.

SIAMESE   The siamese, a short-haired cat, having blue eyes and a pale
                fawn or gray coat with darker face and extremities; after Siam,
                though there is apparently no evidence that it originated there.

BANTAM   The bantam, a dwarf domestic fowl of combative disposi-
                 tion, or, by extension, a small combative person, after Bantam, in
                 Java.

COCHIN   The cochin china, or cochin, a large domestic fowl with
                 densely feathered legs, after Cochin China.

LEGHORN   The leghorn, a small, hardy fowl with yellow legs and white
                 earlobes, after Leghorn, now Livorno, a port in northwest Italy.

ORPINGTON   The orpington, a deep-breasted fowl with a single comb and
                 short legs, after Orpington, Kent, England.

RHODE ISLAND   The rhode island red, a heavy bird useful for both eggs and
    RED   meat, from Rhode Island.

Several Horses and Two Asses

CLYDESDALE   The clydesdale, a heavy draft horse, from its place of origin,
                 Clydesdale, Scotland.

DONKEY   The donkey, after Dunky, diminutive of Duncan.

GALLOWAY   The galloway, a small and hardy horse (also a hardy,
                 medium-sized breed of hornless cattle), from Galloway, in
                 southwestern Scotland.

MOKE   Moke—a pet term for any donkey in Australia—derives
                 from either Michael or Molly, according to the sex of the animal.

MORGAN   The morgan, an American saddle and trotting horse, after
                 Justin Morgan (1747–1798), owner of the stallion from which
                 the breed is descended.

PERCHERON   The percheron, in this country a draft horse (Webster, AH);
                 abroad often a light, stocky, fast-trotting cart horse (Partridge);
                 after Perche, a region in northern France.

                 Other horses named for their place of origin, but more
                 usually capitalized than not, are the Arabian, the Belgian, the
                 American standardbred, the shire (from any of the English
                 counties ending in -shire), and the Suffolk.

EIGHTEEN

PRESTO! YOU'RE A FLOWER

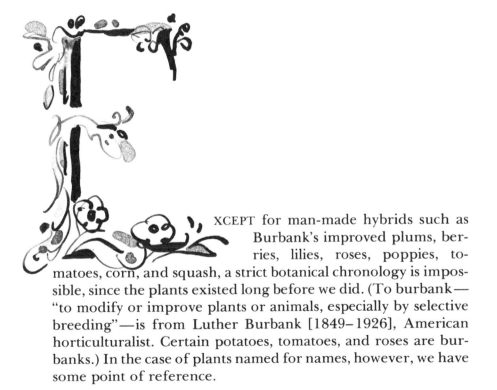

VEGETABLE WORDS

BURBANK

XCEPT for man-made hybrids such as Burbank's improved plums, berries, lilies, roses, poppies, tomatoes, corn, and squash, a strict botanical chronology is impossible, since the plants existed long before we did. (To burbank — "to modify or improve plants or animals, especially by selective breeding" — is from Luther Burbank [1849–1926], American horticulturalist. Certain potatoes, tomatoes, and roses are burbanks.) In the case of plants named for names, however, we have some point of reference.

The Greek gods were in their heyday in 1200 B.C. It is as good a date as any to use for the origins of the plants attributed to deities.

MYRRH

Take the myrrh tree. Myrrha was mother by her own father of the beautiful boy Adonis. For the crime of incest she was changed into the myrrh, which secretes a gum resin used in perfume—a fact presumably irrelevant to the incest. As to

ADONIS

Adonis, now lowercased for any preeminently beautiful young man, a boar ripped him to pieces. From his blood there sprang the genus of red or yellow buttercup that bears his name.

Hyacinthus was a beautiful boy beloved by Apollo and equally by Zephyrus, the west wind. He was competing one day with Apollo at discus throwing, when the god made a particularly long cast. As Hyacinthus ran for the quoit, it rebounded and struck him a mortal blow in the face. Perhaps Zephyrus, enraged that Hyacinthus preferred Apollo's attentions to his, had deliberately blown the flying disk against the youth's head.

HYACINTH

Apollo turned him into a delicate flower, the hyacinth, with breathtaking spikes of white, pink, yellow, or purple flowers. On the petals Grecian fancy saw traced *ai, ai*, the notes of grief. (Funk believes the original flower was not our hyacinth at all, but "some sort of small iris").

Though Apollo was the god of light, the sun itself was personified by Helios, who drove his golden chariot daily across the sky. Helios was wildly loved by Clytië, daughter of the king of Babylon. Discovering that her sister Leucothoë had replaced her in the god's affections, Clytië persuaded her father to have

LEUCOTHOË

Leucothoë buried alive. Helios, arriving too late to save his beloved's life, changed her into the sweet-smelling shrub that bears her name. Clytië herself then faded away out of remorse and despair. For nine days and nights she slept naked on the ground, going without food or water, and quenching her thirst only with the dew and her own tears. Her body at last took root in the soil; her head became a flower bright as the violet. Each day she turns it ceaselessly toward the god she continues to worship.

HELIOTROPE

Thus the heliotrope. An ancient gemstone bears the same name.

On any page of Greek mythology some nymph is running, some god pursuing. Keats muses in "Ode on a Grecian Urn": "What men or gods are these? What maidens loth? What mad pursuit? What struggle to escape?" Among those for whom such pursuits beat jogging was Pan. With Pan hot on her heels, the Arcadian nymph Syrinx took refuge in the River Ladon, and prayed to be changed into a reed. The prayer was granted, and of the reed Pan made his famous pipes. The reed mouth organ is called a syrinx, as is the vocal organ of birds. The mock orange and a species of lilac are syringas. Also named for the altered nymph is the syringe, a small hand pump used among other things for injecting a fluid into the body.

SYRINX
SYRINGA
SYRINGE

Cupid, a mischievous lad, one day shot his golden arrow of love into the heart of Apollo, and his leaden one of aversion into Daphne, daughter of the river-god Peneus. Apollo pursued and Daphne ran. At length, exhausted, Daphne fell to her knees, stretched forth her hands, and cried out to her father for protection. In a flash, she was transformed into bark and leaves. Even as the exultant Apollo sought to embrace her soft, pliant form, he found he was holding rough bark; she was no longer the nymph Daphne, but a daphne, or laurel tree. He rained kisses on the unfeeling wood, and the laurel was ever after held sacred to him.

DAPHNE

Arethusa, daughter of Oceanus and attendant of Diana, returning one day from hunting, entered the clear waters of the River Alpheus to refresh herself. She heard a splash; the god of the river rose towering before her, eyes afire with lust. Following the custom, the nymph fled and the god pursued her. At last, her strength failing, she prayed to Diana for relief. Immediately she was dissolved into a fountain. Alpheus countered by resuming his aqueous form, and as an underground river succeeded in mingling his waters with hers. It was only later that Diana, if indeed Diana deserves the credit, changed the ravished fountain into the flower arethusa. By that time it was already too late.

ARETHUSA

The nymph Echo, condemned (for deceiving Juno) to lose all power of speech except to repeat the sounds she heard, loved beautiful Narcissus, who ignored her. She wasted away till nothing remained but her voice, which echoes still. Nemesis punished Narcissus by making him fall in love with his own reflection. He died of longing, and was turned into the narcissus, a cluster of trumpet-shaped white or yellow flowers. Narcissism is morbid self-admiration.

ECHO

NARCISSUS
NARCISSISM

When Cepheus and Cassiope were king and queen of Ethiopia, Cassiope foolishly boasted herself fairer than Juno and the nereids. This so enraged Neptune that he inundated the coasts and sent a sea monster to ravage the land. Informed by

ANDROMEDA Jupiter that the calamity could be removed only by delivering their daughter Andromeda to the monster, the royal couple obediently secured her to a rock. She was awaiting her doom there when Perseus, returning through the air from the conquest of the Gorgons, saw, saved, and married her. On her death she became a low shrub of the moorwort family, with drooping, pinkish flowers. In the skies she is the constellation Andromeda, the Chained Lady.

IRIS
IRIDESCENT An iris may be either the rainbow, the diaphragm suspended in the eye, or a translucent, orchid-like, sweet-smelling flower of many colors. Iris, goddess of the rainbow, was the swift-footed messenger of Zeus and Hera. Iridescent is one of her words.

CALYPSO Calypso, a nymph, daughter of Oceanus, so loved Odysseus that she detained him prisoner on her Mediterranean island for seven years. She survives as an orchid of the North Temperate Zone, having a pinkish flower with a slipper-shaped lip. She is also a type of West Indian music.

PEACH
PEACHY Greek armies returning home through Persia in the time of Alexander the Great brought with them the Persian melon, which became *persicum malum* in Latin, *pêche* in French, and peach in English. Peachy, "splendid; fine," takes its flavor from the fruit. To peach, "tattletell," does not; the forebear of the word is Middle English *pechen*, "impeach." "An apple is an excellent thing—until you have tried a peach," says Geeoge Du Maurier in *Trilby*.

CEREAL

FLORA Ceres, the Roman goddess of agriculture, gave us cereal, meaning an edible grain, or food prepared from such a grain. Flora, the goddess of flowers and vegetation, gave us flora for plants or plant life in general. Anthon says Flora's festival, celebrated at the end of April and the beginning of May, "degenerated in the course of time and became so offensive to purity as not to bear the presence of virtuous characters." Having made her flower beds, Flora was constrained to lie in them.

MAY
MAY BUSH
MAY BLOOM
MAY TREE
MAY APPLE
MAY BLOSSOM May is named for Maia, goddess-helpmeet of Vulcan. A number of plants that bloom in or around that month are referred to as mays, among them the hawthorn (called also may bush, may bloom, and may tree) and the spirea. The may apple, or American mandrake, has a single, nodding white flower and oval yellow, edible fruit, but poisonous roots, leaves, and seeds. The lily of the valley is a may blossom, and a kind of melon is

MAY COCK
MAYWEED

called a may cock. The mayweed, however, derives not from May but from "maythe," an obsolete word for various composite plants.

CHERRY
CERISE

The Roman general Lucullus, leading an army into the kingdom of Pontus, on the southern shore of the Black Sea, found near Cerasus groves of trees with fruit containing a small, hard stone. The fruit was so delicious that he brought back specimens for home planting, sowing the way for our present-day cherry—and the cherry-color cerise.

APPLE

The word apple descends from Abella, in the province of Campania, Italy, but the fruit may have originated in the region immediately south of the Caucasus. Apples were introduced by the Romans to much of Europe, including Britain.

MARIGOLD

Marigolds, bearing showy yellow or orange flowers, are supposedly named for the Virgin Mary. In 19th-century slang, a marigold was a gold sovereign.

CANTERBURY
BELL

When pilgrims traveled to Canterbury in medieval England, small bells jingled from the harnesses of their horses. Because of a fancied resemblance, a plant widely cultivated for its showy bell-shaped, violet-blue flowers is called the canterbury bell.

SAMPHIRE

The samphire is one of several fleshy European plants that grow along the seacoast; we sometimes pickle it. Samphire hobson-jobsons *l'herbe de Saint Pierre*, "herb of Saint Peter." Apparently the plants like steep dunes; Edgar, in *King Lear*, stands on a hill and says:

> *How fearful*
> *And dizzy 'tis to cast one's eyes so low!*
> *The crows and choughs that wing the midway air*
> *Show scarce so gross as beetles. Half way down*
> *Hangs one that gathers samphire, dreadful trade!*
> *Methinks he seems no bigger than his head.*

SPRUCE

Though inhabitants of the North Temperate Zone have always lived around spruce trees, it was not until the end of the 16th century that these were first cultivated. Plantings were taken to settlements in America early in the 17th century. Widely cultivated for lumber, ornament, pulpwood, and turpentine, the tree takes its name from an early spelling of Prussia. It was considered particularly handsome, which is why a neat, dapper person is spruce; when you spruce up, you wish to look your best.

SPRUCE UP

The expression is perhaps reinforced by spruce (Prussian) leather and by the Prussian reputation for military smartness.

BANYAN

It was in the 16th century also that European explorers and traders found in East India the banyan (Anglo-Indian, mysteriously, for "undershirt"), a tree whose branches send out numerous aerial roots that reach down to the soil and form props or additional trunks. A single tree may cover an area large enough to shelter thousands of men. It is named for the Banians, a caste of Hindi merchants and traders who abstain from meat; and specifically for a famed tree, near Bandar Abbas, Iran, beneath which the Banians once built a pagoda. By association, sailors in the Royal Navy came to call the two days a week on

BANYAN DAYS
BANYAN
  HOSPITAL

which no meat was served banyan days. "Banyan hospital" became slang for an animal hospital, in reference to the Hindu dislike for taking the life of an animal.

CAYENNE
  PEPPER
CAYENNE
DRY GUIL-
  LOTINE

A century later the French settled French Guiana, naming the capital city after a river and island called Cayenne. A condiment made from pungent seeds growing in the area is known as cayenne pepper. If the peppers are fed to canaries while the feathers are growing, the plumage comes out red, and the birds are called cayennes. In the Napoleonic Wars, Cayenne was known as the "dry guillotine" because political prisoners were sent there to die. Out of sight, out of mind. The same name is applied to a variation of whist.

SWEET WILLIAM

STINKY BILLY

A certain plant having flat, dense clusters of varicolored flowers is known as the sweet william, after William, Duke of Cumberland (1721–1765), who whipped the Scots in the decisive Battle of Culloden (1746). The Scots call the man Butcher Cumberland and the flower stinky billy.

GARDENIA

LUCIA

Alexander Garden (1730–1791), a botanist of Charleston, South Carolina, either imported or crossbred a kind of tropical tree or shrub with showy white or yellow flowers, called after him the gardenia. His success is said to have enraged Dr. Lewis Mottet, another botanist of the locality. Dr. Mottet announced that he too had developed a new flower. "And I, too, have named it," he said. "I've named it the lucia, after Lucy, my cook." But the lucia was never heard of again.

BOUGAIN-
  VILLEA

The colorful life of Louis Antoine de Bougainville (1729–1811) included the discovery and importation of the vine named after him, the bougainvillea, which has brilliant red or purple floral leaves. Bougainville dabbled in activities ranging from calculus and the law to diplomatic and military service. Not the least of his achievements was managing to escape the 1792 Reign of Terror in Paris. In the 1760s, after failing to get backing for a proposed expedition to the North Pole, he made a three-year voyage of discovery around the world, bringing home the bougainvillea and leaving his name to grace two straits and the largest of the Solomon Islands.

SEQUOIA

The giant redwood tree of California has living specimens dating back to the time of Christ. Its name, sequoia, comes from a Cherokee Indian, Sequoyah, son of a white trader named Nathaniel Gist and an Indian woman related to King Oconostota. Sequoyah, born about 1770, and lamed in a hunting accident, set out to discover the secret of writing for his people. He finally completed a table of characters representing all eighty-six sounds in the Cherokee spoken language. His alphabet was adopted by the Cherokee council in 1821. The tree was named in his honor in 1847.

DOUGLAS FIR

Early explorations of the West also revealed a tall evergreen of great size, the most important timber tree of the American West. It was named the Douglas fir for its discoverer, David Douglas (1798–1834), a Scottish botanist who from 1823 to 1825 collected plant specimens in America for the Royal Horticultural Society. His life was short; he was killed by a wild bull in the Hawaiian Islands at the age of thirty-six.

CURRANT

Currants, imported from Corinth, Greece, were first called raisins of Corinth.

MOREL
SCALLION

Morel, the name of an edible mushroom, means "dark brown," and is associated with Moor. The scallion ("actually," says Holt, "a sort of diseased onion") was named for the now destroyed Palestinian seaport of Ascalon. The word was used by gossip columnist Walter Winchell as the opposite of orchid; one sent a scallion to convey disesteem.

Apples

Since any number of products have any number of varieties, this work would have to be enlarged monstrously to encompass even a fraction of them. There follow a few arbitrary samples from collections in various categories; and apple, since it begins with *A*, is as good a place as any to start.

In 1900 at least a thousand varieties of apples were sold in the markets of the United States, and no doubt many have been added since. Some have names that are clearly proper, others that are clearly generic. Many fall in between. The decision as to whether to capitalize or lowercase the name of an apple depends on how established it is and how universally it is recognized. I vernacularize the jonathan, named "as a compliment" after Jonathan Hasbrouck, a gentleman of Ulster City, New York; and the baldwin, which F. A. Waugh called "exactly the apple for the ordinary man—it is an ordinary apple"; and the gravenstein, supposed to have originated at Gravenstein in Holstein, and once esteemed the best apple in Germany and the Low Countries; and the aromatic macintosh, discovered by John McIntosh in 1796. But the Virginia Greening, the Kansas Keeper, the Pennsylvania Longstem, the Missouri Pippin, the York Imperial? Or the Adirondack, or the Greenville, or the Olympia? I cannot bring myself to it. Among apples named after people, besides the baldwin and the macintosh, none seems vernacular to me: the Abe Lincoln, the President Napoleon (*sic*), the Blenheim, the Milligen (for a Mrs. Milligen of Washington City, Pennsylvania), the Starkey (for Moses Starkey), the Ingram (for Martin Ingram, who farmed near Springfield, Missouri), the Shannon (from a chance seeding on the farm of William Shannon, Coshocton County, Ohio), the Sleight (for Edgar Sleight, of Dutchess County, New York)—all remain proper names.

And all are drawn from *All About Apples*, by Alice A. Martin (Houghton Mifflin, Boston, 1976), whom I have to thank for reminding me that an apple a day keeps the doctor away.

Other Plants

AGARIC

A fungus of the family *Agaricacae*, including the common cultivated mushroom, or meadow mushroom, is called agaric, after Agaría, a city in Sarmatia.

ANGOSTURA
BARK

Angostura bark is the bitter, aromatic bark of either of two Brazilian trees, formerly used as a tonic. Angostura is the former name of Ciudad Bolívar in Venezuela, whence this bark was

ANGOSTURA BITTERS
exported. Angostura bitters, a tonic of which the bark is a principal ingredient, is seldom lowercased.

BEGONIA
A genus of succulent herbs, native to the tropics, was named begonia by Charles Plumier, the 17th-century French botanist, after Michel Bégon, governor of Santo Domingo.

BIGNONIA

TOURNEFORTIA
The bignonia, more popularly known as the trumpet flower or cross vine, was named by the French botanist Jean Pitton de Tournefort (1656–1708) to honor Abbé Jean Paul Bignon, court librarian to Louis XIV. Tournefortia, a large genus of tropical trees and shrubs, is named after the botanist.

BOURBON LILY
The common white bourbon lily takes its name from the Bourbon dynasty of France.

BOYSENBERRY
The boysenberry—a prickly bramble hybridized from various berries—and the large, wine-red, edible berry borne by this plant were developed by Rudolph Boysen, 20th-century American horticulturalist.

POINSETTIA
The poinsettia is a genus of chiefly tropical American herbs and woody plants with inconspicuous yellow flowers and bright-colored, usually scarlet leaves. Joel R. Poinsett (1799–1851), of South Carolina, came across this flower while Minister to Mexico, and brought it to the United States.

SHADDOCK
The shaddock is a pear-shaped citrus fruit (*Citrus maxima*), resembling the grapefruit but differing from it in having coarse dry flesh, usually of poor quality. It is the largest known citrus fruit. In the East Indies the shaddock is known as a pompelmous. It is named for Captain Shaddock, who brought the seed from the East Indies to Barbados in 1696.

SHALLOT
The shallot is closely related to the onion, cultivated for its edible, mildly flavored bulb. The word corrupts French *échalote*, from Old French *escalogne*, from Ascalon, a city mentioned a page or two back.

TANGERINE
The tangerine is a yellowish-red orange with easily detached rind. The word traces to Tangier, Morocco, from which such oranges were first imported.

WISTARIA
The wistaria, any of several climbing woody vines having compound leaves and drooping clusters of purplish or white flowers, is named for Casper Wistar (1761–1818), American anatomist. "Wisteria," born of ignorance, is a common spelling.

ZINNIA	The zinnia is any of various plants of the genus *Zinnia*, native to tropical America. *Z. elegans* particularly is widely cultivated for its showy, variously colored flowers. The plant is named for Johann Gottfried Zinn (1727–1759), German botanist and physician who was professor of medicine at Göttingen.
CAMELLIA JAPONICA	The camellia, an ornamental greenhouse shrub with glossy evergreen leaves and red or white double flowers resembling a rose, was first brought from Japan by Georg Joseph Kamel (1661–1706), a Moravian and a Jesuit missionary. It is also called japonica.
CANDYTUFT	Any of various plants having clusters of white, red, or purplish flowers is a candytuft. Candy is a variant of Candia, largest city of Crete.
CANTALOUPE	Cantaloupe is a variety of melon having fruit with a ribbed, rough rind and aromatic orange flesh. It was first grown at Cantalupo, a papal villa near Rome.
CAOUTCHOUC	Caoutchouc is natural rubber, named after the Quechua, a tribe of South American Indians once constituting the ruling class of the Inca Empire.
CASABA	A variety of winter melon having a yellow rind and sweet, whitish flesh is the casaba, from Kasaba, former name of Turgutlu, Turkey, where these melons grew.
DAHLIA	The dahlia is a small genus of Mexican and Central American tuberous-rooted herbs of the thistle family, having rays of many shapes of red. It is named in honor of Anders Dahl, an 18th-century Swedish botanist.
DAMSON	The damson, a plum tree native to Eurasia, bearing an oval, bluish-black, juicy fruit, is from Damascus, capital of Syria, where the tree thrived.
FREESIA	There is a dispute about the origin of freesia for any of several plants native to southern Africa having one-sided clusters of fragrant, variously colored flowers. Webster says the plant was named for Elia Magnus Fries, a 19th-century Swedish botanist; AH says it was named for Friederich H. T. Freese (d. 1876), a German physician.
FUCHSIA	The fuchsia is any of various chiefly tropical shrubs widely cultivated for their showy, drooping, purplish, reddish, or white flowers. The name honors Leonhard Fuchs (1501–1566), a German botanist.

GENTIAN   The gentian is any of numerous plants of the genus *Gentiana*, characteristically having showy blue flowers. The supposed discoverer of the medicinal properties of the plant was Gentius, king of Illyria (2nd century B.C.). Gentian is used as a tonic and a stomachic.

GREENGAGE   Sir William Gage, of Hengrave, Suffolk, imported greenish-yellow plums of high quality from France about 1725, and they were given his name.

JENNETING   A variety of early apple is named jenneting (from Jeannet, Jean, John, Latin *Joannes*), from being ripe about St. John's Day, June 24.

JIMSONWEED   Jimsonweed is a coarse, poisonous plant having large trumpet-shaped white or purplish flowers. It was first the Jamestown weed, after Jamestown, Virginia.

JOE-PYE WEED   Either of two tall perennial American herbs bearing clusters of purplish flowers is a joe-pye weed. Joe Pye is said to have been the name of an Indian who cured typhus fever in New England by means of this plant.

LIMA BEAN   The lima bean is any of several varieties of a tropical American plant having flat pods containing large, light-green, edible seeds. It is sometimes called butter bean. The name is from Lima, capital of Peru, a country in which the bean is widely grown.

LOBELIA   The lobelia, any of numerous plants having terminal clusters of variously colored flowers, is named for Matthias de Lobel (1538–1616), a Flemish botanist.

LOGANBERRY   The loganberry, a red-fruited, upright-growing dewberry-raspberry combination, is of sentimental interest to me because J. H. Logan (1841–1928), the jurist and horticulturist who developed it in 1881, used to keep his neighbor—my grandfather, D. S. Richardson—apprised of the progress of his botanical experiments.

MAGNOLIA   The magnolia, a tree or shrub bearing conspicuous and often fragrant white, pink, or purple flowers, is named after the French botanist Pierre Magnol (1683–1715). There are about thirty-five widely distributed species.

NOISETTE   The noisette is a hybrid between the China rose and the moss rose. One John Champney presented a specimen to Phillip Noisette, a contemporary of Alexander Garden in Charlotte,

South Carolina. Mr. Noisette popularized the flower and gave it his name (somewhat confusingly, since *noisette* is French for "hazelnut").

JIM HILL
MUSTARD

A type of yellow-flowered mustard plant, common along railroad sidings, is named "jim hill mustard" after Jim Hill, a great railroad entrepreneur of the last century.

NINETEEN

MITHRIDATES, HE DIED OLD
POISONOUS WORDS

IT APPEARS that I am somehow offending society, or ecology, or nature, because I eat eggs, which contain a suspect element called cholesterol (or perhaps chlorophyll). I have even been known to sprinkle sugar on a halved grapefruit. There is a legend in my family that we once devoured a swordfish that had been mounted over our fireplace; we served it because we had nothing else around for Thanksgiving dinner. If some forward-looking scientist had kept a cutting from that swordfish, it would no doubt have proved to be three-quarters mercury, or some other carcinogenic substance.

Nature is not to be trusted. I did not put the cholesterol in my morning egg; the hen did. Nature was playing tricks on us for a million years before we caught on, and we can never beat her at her own game. The best we can get from her is a mixed bag.

Venus, Roman goddess of love, personified some of nature's most delightful drives. But her drives were as mixed as yours and mine. The root of her name is *wen* or *ven*, "to desire"; whence Latin *venari*, "to desire (and therefore) pursue"; that is, to hunt. This attribute of the lovely creature is the inspiration of Racine's line *C'est Vénus toute entière à sa proie attachée*—"the hunter is inseparable from the hunted." Thus the curious identity between the venery involving the dear with whom one is holding hands or rubbing noses, and the venery of trailing the deer that will soon be venison. Russian *voina*, "war," is an etymological cousin of Venus. Directly attributable to her is venerate—to regard with reverential respect. Venereal, "pertaining to sexual love," is her word, made monstrous in venereal disease. There should be a different name for that. And for venom. Venom began life as a love potion, a draft to appease Venus; but it was corrupted early. Love gone rancid is a poisonous brew indeed.

The Veneti, "the beloved ones," were a hunting tribe after whom the city of Venice was named. Hunter, lover—the curious conjunction repeats itself. From the city, from the tribe, from the goddess developed the venice glass, a goblet supposed to burst if a poison—venom—was poured into it.

A form of venom popular in 18th-century Italy among young wives wanting to get rid of their husbands was *aqua tofana*, a liquid containing arsenic. Brewer says it was invented about 1690 by a Greek woman named Tofana. She called it the manna of Saint Nicholas of Bari, after an oil of miraculous efficacy supposed to flow from the tomb of the saint; but posterity decided her own name was more appropriate.

An antidote to poisons was theriaca, from the Latin for an antidote to snake bites. In Venice this was called Venice treacle, and consisted of about seventy drugs pulverized and mixed into a base of honey.

How does nature justify poison hemlock, nux vomica, poison ivy, water hemlock, locoweed, pokeweed, black nightshade, jimsonweed, may apple, the castor oil plant, poison sumac, opium poppy, sheep laurel, monkshood, death camas, belladonna, foxglove, henbane, mescal, hemp, upas? Don't talk

VENERY

VENISON

VENERATE
VENEREAL
VENEREAL
    DISEASE
VENOM

VENICE GLASS

AQUA TOFANA

VENICE
    TREACLE

to *me* about abusing nature. I'll call off the dogs if nature will.

There is no dearth of harmful natural products whose names were once proper nouns. We have turned some of them to our own use, but nature deserves no credit for that.

COLCHICINE

Colchicine, for instance, is a poisonous alkaloid, used medically to treat gout. It is processed from the dried seeds of various bulbous plants, such as the autumn crocus, of the genus *Colchicum*, named after Colchis. Why Colchis? Because that was the Black Sea home of Medea, the witch who enabled Jason to acquire the Golden Fleece.

HASHISH

MARY JANE

The early cannabis, or hashish (perhaps stemming from the Old Man Hasan referred to below), was apparently far more potent than its watered-down descendant, called grass, marijuana, pot, or mary jane. Mary jane literally translates marijuana (Spanish Maria and Juana), but nobody can say who the two girls were, if indeed they were. Unquestionably, the plant was harmless until we started harvesting it. But man is not made to leave plants growing in the meadows. Marco Polo reported that in the 11th century a Moslem religious leader, Hasan ibn-al-Sabbah, used hashish to refine the practice of assassination. He would enlist youths from twelve to twenty, "such as had a taste for soldiering," and ply them with the drug. When sleep overcame them, he removed them to a remarkable garden:

> When, therefore, they awoke and found themselves in a place so charming, they deemed that it was Paradise in very truth. And the ladies and damsels dallied with them to their heart's content . . . So when the Old Man [Hasan] would have any prince slain, he would say to such a youth: Go thou and slay So-and-So; and when thou returnest my Angels shall bear thee into Paradise. And shouldst thou die, natheless even so will I send my Angels to carry thee back into Paradise.

ASSASSIN

Etymologists generally agree that assassin stems from Hasan. They are less certain about hashish.

DITTANY

Nature's cruelty is unintentional. So is her kindness. Dittany is one of those kindly accidents. The name of the plant descends from Dikte, a mountain in Crete, where it was credited with many medicinal virtues—"especially," says Brewer, "in enabling arrows to be drawn from wounds and curing such wounds." Perhaps nature will develop a new kind of dittany, one aimed, say, at drawing the barb from an atomic explosion. But I doubt it.

CALAMINE

I look kindly on calamine (a mineral dissolved in mineral oils and used as a skin lotion) less for its usefulness to the skin than for the story of its name. First located near Thebes, the city founded by Cadmus, it was called in Greek *Kadmeía,* "Cadmian" (earth). (Artists are familiar with a light tomato red called cadmian red.) Cadmus was a legendary Phoenician prince who killed a dragon and sowed its teeth, from which sprang up a crop of armed men. When Cadmus saw them rising he flung stones at them; and they, thinking the attack came from among themselves, fell upon and slew one another. Only five survived. With Cadmus, these five were the first inhabitants of Thebes. A jolly little bedtime tale.

Coleridge apotheosized the city of Cologne, Germany, as follows:

In Köln, a town of monks and bones,
And pavements fanged with murderous stones,
And rags, and hags, and hideous wenches,
I counted two-and-seventy stenches,
All well defined and separate stinks!

Ye nymphs that reign o'er sewers and sinks,
The river Rhine, it is well known
Doth wash your city of Cologne;
But tell me, nymphs, what power divine
Shall henceforth wash the river Rhine?

COLOGNE

I suggested once that the answer to Mr. Coleridge's question might be *eau de cologne. Eau de cologne* is a perfumed liquid composed of alcohol and aromatic oils, named for the city. Cologne in turn was originally named Colonia Agrippina, "Colony of Agrippina" (A.D. 16–59), after the Roman empress who was born there. Agrippina would have added a breath of fresh air to any city. In forty-three brief years she poisoned, says tradition, at least one of her husbands, committed incest with her brother, the emperor Caligula, and married her uncle, the emperor Claudius. A man does not run into many women as enterprising as that, and it is a pleasure to say a good word for the fragrance associated with her.

BACITRACIN

DUFFY FACTOR

Bacitracin is an antibiotic obtained from a bacillus and used externally as a salve. The substance was first isolated in 1945 in the body of an American child named Margaret Tracy. The name is an acronym: baci(llus) + Tracy + in. The duffy factor in blood is also named for a patient.

The Food and Drug Administration could have usefully employed Mithridates VI (132?–63 B.C.), king of Pontus. Mith-

MITHRIDATE
MITHRIDATISM

ridates attained immunity against poison by taking gradually increasing doses of it. An antidote against poison is therefore known as a mithridate, and mithridatism is the immunity so produced. Housman reports:

Easy, smiling, seasoned sound,
Sate the king when healths went round.
They put arsenic in his meat
And stared aghast to watch him eat;
They poured strychnine in his cup
And shook to see him drink it up;
They shook, they stared as white's their shirt.
Them it was their poison hurt.
—I tell the tale that I heard told.
Mithridates, he died old.

Mithridates was defeated and captured by Pompey in 67 B.C. He tried to commit suicide by poison, but failed because of his self-created immunity, and had to have himself run through by the sword of a slave.

ORVIETAN

A counter-poison is sometimes called an orvietan. The source is the town of Orvieto, Italy, where a notorious charlatan would pretend to take poison, swallow a brew of mustard and water, and proclaim himself cured.

SALMONELLA

SALMONELLOSIS

Salmonella, the bacteria that causes a disagreeable and sometimes deadly form of food poisoning called salmonellosis, has nothing to do with fish; the name honors Daniel Edward Salmon (1850–1914), a veterinarian and one-time investigator for the U.S. Department of Agriculture who isolated the guilty germ. Salmonellosis is caused by infected and insufficiently cooked beef, pork, poultry, and eggs, or food, drink, or equipment contaminated by the excreta of infected animals.

It is bad enough that nature does not protect us from our mistakes; she does not even bother to protect us from *her* mistakes. Why does she not keep such poisons as atropine, the belladonna extract, out of our way? Don't tell me we need atropine to dilate our pupils. We see too much already.

NICOTINE

God may have let the serpent into the Garden of Eden, but nature let in tobacco. In 1560, Jean Nicot, French ambassador to Portugal, was presented with some tobacco seeds which Portuguese sailors had brought from America. In his honor the active principle of the plant was called nicotine. It is a poisonous alkaloid, better suited for insecticides than for smoking. In 1560 he sent a sample to Catherine de' Medici, queen of France, and tobacco quickly became a universal addiction:

"A woman is only a woman," said Kipling, "but a good cigar is a Smoke." Oscar Wilde said, "A cigarette is the perfect type of a perfect pleasure. It is exquisite, and it leaves one unsatisfied." Robert Burton said, "Tobacco, divine, rare, super-excellent tobacco, which goes far beyond all the panaceas, potable gold and philosopher's stones—a sovereign remedy to all diseases." And Walter Savage Landor said, "For thy sake, tobacco, I / Would do anything but die."

As it turned out, for tobacco's sake a good many million people did die, and are still dying. I wonder whether even Mithridates could have immunized himself against it.

CATHARTIC

Catharine or Catherine, the given name, comes from the Greek word for "pure." So does cathartic, a purgative. Whether you trace cathartic to Catharine or back to the original Greek depends, I suppose, on how, if a woman, you feel about yourself, or how, if a man, you feel about women.

SARDONIC

The repulsive word sardonic attained its meaning of "disdainfully or sneeringly derisive" through folk etymology. Sardinia, second largest island in the Mediterranean, is the home of the bitter Sardinian herb, which "renders men insane, so that the sick person seems to laugh." This laugh was called in French *rire sardonique*, and in English, sardonic. (Timothy tells me that sardonic appears to be cognate with the Welsh word *chwerddhu*, having much the same meaning.)

Sardonic is the kind of expression that lies behind nature's lovely smile when she tells me all the delectable things she is going to do for me if I just treat her right. I am not going to treat her right. When she turns her back, I am going to bop her.

TWENTY

PORCELAIN COMES FROM PIG
EARTHEN AND MINERAL WORDS

CHINA

S WE have seen, words frequently travel tortuous paths and end a long way from home. Porcelain, for instance, a fine earthenware made from clay—translucent, and superior in whiteness, hardness, and sonority—is named for its resemblance to the lovely porcelain shell or cowrie—named in turn from the shell's having the shape of a pig's back (Latin *porcellus*, "little pig"). An interesting transformation. Unfortunately, porcelain is not an improper, uncommon noun. China, however—identical with porcelain in all essentials—is indeed improper and uncommon, since it is a common noun named after its place of origin. Other earthen products descended etymologically from proper names:

DELFT

Delft is a style of glazed earthenware, usually blue and white, or any pottery made in this style. It originated in Delft, a city of the Netherlands, five miles southeast of The Hague.

FAIENCE

Faience, a decorative earthenware as opposed to tableware, is named after Faenza, Italy, but was originally applied to coarse ware made in France from the 16th to the 18th century.

MAJOLICA

Majolica is a Renaissance Italian pottery, glazed and richly colored and ornamented, or a modern imitation of it. It was first made at Majolica, the old name of the Mediterranean island Majorca, and was brought from there to Italy.

PARIAN

Parian, a fine white porcelain used for making statuettes, vases, and the like, comes from Páros, one of the islands of the Cyclades in the Greek archipelago.

JAPAN

Enamels, lacquers, and glazes are vitreous substances used to produce a durable, glossy finish. One of the best-known black enamels is japan. To japan is to lacquer; a japan is any object decorated and varnished in the Japanese manner.

CHALCEDONY

SARD

Chalcedony is a variety of translucent pale-blue or pale-gray quartz. If variegated it is an agate, onyx, carnelian, etc. The name comes from Chalcedon, a town in Asia Minor opposite Byzantium. A deep orange-red variety is the sard ("Sardian stone"), after Sardis, the capital of Lydia.

JET

Jet is a velvet-black mineral, discovered in Gagas, a town and river in Lycaea. In French, Gagas evolved to *jaiet*, *jais*, and *jet*, in which last form it entered the English language. As an adjective, jet is "lustrous black."

TOPAZ

A topaz is a semiprecious stone, characteristically yellow, but sometimes white, greenish, or bluish. Chrysolites not unlike topaz were first discovered at Topazos, the Greek name of an island in the Red Sea.

TURQUOISE

The turquoise, a blue to blue-green mineral highly esteemed as a gemstone in its polished blue form, was first called *la pierre turquoise* ("the Turkish stone") by the French, either because it was first found in Asia Minor or because it reached Europe through Turkey. The first two words sloughed away.

COPPER   Copper is a ductile, malleable, reddish-brown metallic element, an excellent conductor of heat and electricity. The name is applied also to a minor coin made of copper or a copper alloy. The derivation is from Kypros, the anciently Greek island we call Cyprus, whence the best copper was once taken.

MAGNET   A magnet is a piece of iron ore having the natural property of attracting iron. The stone first came to attention in Magnesia,

MAGNESIA   a district in Thessaly. Magnesia, a mild cathartic, was made from magnesium salts, available on the same island.

TASMANITE   A light-colored, shaly coal is known as tasmanite, after the mineral tasmanite of which it is largely composed. Tasmanite yields a large quantity of oil on dry distillation. It was found in Tasmania, an island state of Australia discovered in 1642 by the Dutch navigator Abel Tasman and named by him Van Diemen's Land after the governor general of the East Indies. The name was changed to Tasmania in 1853.

Mineral terms drawn from proper names run into the thousands. Here is a sampling—a small fraction of just the words beginning with *A*.

Absarokite, from the Absaroka Range, Wyoming
Acadialite, from Acadia, poetic for Nova Scotia
Adamellite, from Mount Adamello, Italy
Adularia, from the Adula Mountains in Switzerland
Aegirite, from Aegir, Teutonic god of the sea
Afwillite, from *Alpheus Fuller Williams*, its discoverer
Agpaite, from Appa, southern Greenland, "place of the auks"
Aikinite, from Arthur Aikin, British mineralogist
Ailsyte, from Ailsa Craig, Scotland
Akerite, from Aker, Norway
Alabandite, from Alabanda, Asia Minor
Alalyte, from Ala, Tyrol
Alamosite, from Alamos, Mexico
Albertite, from Albert, New Brunswick
Alboranite, from Alboran Island, Spain
Aleutite, from the Aleutian Islands, Alaska
Alexandrite, from Alexander I of Russia
Algovite, from the Algäu Alps
Alisonite, from R. E. Alison, of Chile

TWENTY-ONE

TRADE ME A MARK
&
PROPRIETARY WORDS

HE epitaph Daniel Henniger wrote recently for the alleged death of public interest in celebrities was as iridescent as a soap bubble. The bubble burst in his last sentence: "The big blimp Celebrity is looking for its Lakehurst." The reference is clear enough: the celebrity racket is shambling toward some still unimagined event that will destroy it. Slashed across your memory, if you are old enough to remember 1937, is the sudden anguished cry of Herb Morrison, a radio announcer who had been routinely reporting the mooring of the lighter-than-air craft *Hindenburg* at Lakehurst, New Jersey: "It's burst into flames! Oh, my God . . . it's burning, bursting into flames . . . Oh, the humanity and all the passengers!" Viewers of the newsreels that were shown at every motion picture theatre in the 1930s saw the eight-hundred-foot dirigible puff into nothingness; cinders that a moment before had been human beings rained down from the sky.

But Mr. Henninger erred in calling the *Hindenburg* a blimp.

BLIMP

A blimp is a small, nonrigid airship; the name, says Partridge, was probably coined in 1915 by one Horace Short, and may stem from bloody plus limp or, though this is doubtful, (type) B plus limp. Or both. Blimps were used by the British in World War I to patrol cities threatened by German airpower. (David Low's cartoon personification of outdated upper-class British attitudes was portly Colonel Blimp, full of hot air, lacking backbone, and deficient in motive power.)

ZEPPELIN

The *Hindenburg* was a different breed. It was a zeppelin, not limp but rigid, with a long, cigar-shaped body supported by internal gas cells. The zeppelin's creator and eponym was Count Ferdinand von Zeppelin (1838–1917), a German army officer who visited the United States during the Civil War to view the balloon operations of the Union forces. Impressed by the military potential of aircraft, he spent the next thirty years trying to design a practical dirigible. He began operating commercial zeppelin transportation in Germany as early as 1910.

During World War I the Germans produced zeppelins, six hundred feet long and powered by four motors, at a rate of one every two weeks. The pottering ways and great bulk of the vessels made them easy targets, however, while the hydrogen they needed for buoyancy rendered them highly inflammable. They added little to German military might. Yet after the war, more than 32,000 passengers flew in German zeppelins without incident, until the Lakehurst catastrophe put a tragic end to the era of lighter-than-air transport.

Names like B-limp and Zeppelin are often registered as trademarks. This does not prevent them from evolving into common nouns. For instance:

MASON JAR

In 1857 a New Yorker named John Mason patented a widemouthed glass jar with either a glass or metal screw top, used for home preserves put up for consumption between vegetable seasons. As a proprietary product, it had to be capitalized: Mason jar. But it has been vernacularized to mason jar for going on a hundred years.

DIESEL

Rudolf Diesel, born in Paris of German parents in 1858, developed a way to utilize compressed air that resulted in a more efficient internal combustion engine. (Unfortunately, Herr Diesel did not develop a storehouse of compressed air for his own body. One night in 1913, crossing the English Channel, he fell from the mail steamer and was drowned.) The diesel engine is now commonly lowercased.

DAGUERREOTYPE Louis Jacques Mandé Daguerre (1789–1851) trademarked a pioneer photographic process in which mercury vapor developed an impression made on a light-sensitive, silver-coated metallic plate. The daguerreotype first came into general use in 1839; if you have photographs of mid-19th-century ancestors, they were produced by this or some closely related means. (One was the tintype; in my childhood, the expression "Not on your tintype!" meant "Absolutely not!")

LISTERINE Sir Joseph Lister (1827–1912), son of the man who invented the compound microscope (and, in an idle moment, the photographer's tripod), founded antiseptic surgery. Lister demonstrated that scrupulous cleanliness in surgical procedures minimized post-operative infection. He objected vainly to the use of his name in the trademark Listerine, a product so popular that the name became generic for any antiseptic mouthwash.

LUCIFER Lucifer, as I mentioned earlier, was the rebel archangel who became first Satan and then, 150 years ago, a trade name for a friction match. The word soon entered the vulgate. By World War I a popular song assured British Tommies they never need yield to hopelessness

. . . while you've got a lucifer *to light your fag.*

Today, lucifers are a dim memory, and fags are no longer cigarettes but homosexuals. Or at least they were until homosexuals kidnaped the word gay, robbing us of one of the lightest and loveliest words in the language.

FERRIS WHEEL For the Chicago Exposition (1893), a tinkerer from Galesburg, Illinois, built a great wheel. It revolved on a stationary axle, stood 268 feet high, and carried 36 cars, each capable of seating 60 persons—a potential of more than 2,000 passengers. The tinkerer was G. W. Gale Ferris, and some version of his *chef d'oeuvre* now dominates every amusement park and carnival. None, however, matches that first ferris wheel in grandeur. Because the first wheel stood at the Midway Plaisance in Chicago, any central avenue for the exhibition of curiosities or
MIDWAY amusements is called a midway.

KLIEG LIGHT

The brothers John H. and Anton T. Kliegel created a powerful carbon-arc lamp in the early years of the 20th century. A klieg light, being especially intense, is indispensable in the making of motion pictures.

MACADAM

John Loudon McAdam (1756–1836), a Scottish engineer, made a fortune in his uncle's counting house in America. When he returned to Scotland, he was appalled at the poor conditions of the local roads. He spent the rest of his life developing better ways of road surfacing. Hence macadam, a roadbed paved with layers of compacted small stones, usually bound with tar or asphalt. A bituminous binder for roads, or roads made with such a binder, is called tarmac: tar plus Mc(adam). Tarmac was once generic for airfield, as in: "However many planes Russia may have on the tarmac . . ."

PULLMAN

George M. Pullman (1831–1897) improved on earlier versions of a railroad passenger car for the elite—one with comparatively comfortable furnishings, even beds. When railroads were the arteries of America, better-heeled types traveled by pullman; hoi polloi traveled in coaches, dozing the night through as best they could on hard, springless seats.

SELTZER

The Nieder Selters spa in the Wiesbaden area of Germany was once a magnet for visitors, apparently because its water fizzed. Seltzer water was bottled and widely sold. Vichy, France, similarly produced Vichy water. A current favorite, Perrier water, is produced by a French company of that name.

HEROIN

A kind of morphine was trademarked as Heroin, apparently on the assumption that the drug would make its user feel like a conqucring hero.

VERONAL

The name Veronal was applied to a hypnotic barbital, by two German chemists from Verona; the allusion is to the Italian city where Juliet drank her fatal sleeping potion in Shakespeare's *Romeo and Juliet*.

KLEENEX

Kleenex, a specific brand of soft cleansing tissue, refers conversationally to any such tissue.

CELLULOID

Celluloid, the first synthetic plastic, drops its capital letter when used as a slang term for motion pictures.

CELLOPHANE

Cellophane, a moistureproof wrapping made of thin, flexible, transparent cellulose (the word contains cellulose and French *diaphane*, "transparent; diaphanous"), was once a trademark, but is now generic in the United States by court decision. Cellulose ($C_6H_{10}O_5$) is the main constituent of all plant tissue and fibers.

It is hard to be sure which trade names maintain their copyright; I sometimes wonder whether the company lawyers themselves know. Aspirin, a white crystalline derivative of salicylic acid used for the relief of pain and fever, was introduced into medicine by Herman Dreser in 1893. It was trademarked once, but is now generic.

ASPIRIN

COKE

Coke, abbreviating Coca-Cola, is trademarked, but if you accept your host's offer of a coke you may find yourself drinking Royal Crown, Pepsi-Cola, Dr. Pepper, or some dietetic oddity like Tab. The Coca-Cola Company does not like this, but it is the price one pays for success.

ORPHEUM

Orpheum, once the trade name for a chain of motion picture and vaudeville theaters, is now generic for any motion picture house. The name refers to Orpheus, the mythological Greek musician whose lyre could tame beasts and make stones and trees move.

MARCONIGRAM

Guglielmo Marconi (1874–1937), an Italian electrical engineer, produced the first workable wireless transmitter and receiver in 1896. Nobody knows or cares today that marconigram was once a registered trademark.

NYLON

Nylon originated as an acronym: from either N.Y. (New York) + *Lon*don, or *ni*trogen + -lon. In any event it began as a trademarked name for a cloth or yarn (often shaped into leg or body stockings) made from a family of high-strength, resilient, synthetic materials.

BAKELITE

Bakelite was a trademark wrung from the last name of Leo Hendrick Baekeland, who developed the synthetic resin used to harden rubber and celluloid. Born in the United States in 1863, he formed the Bakelite Company in 1910.

FRIGIDAIRE
HOOVER
FRIDGE

Trademark owners seem to have split personalities. On the one hand, they will advertise a name unceasingly in order to convince consumers that there is only one true frigidaire or hoover. (In England, fridge and hoover are used generically for refrigerator and vacuum cleaner.) But should a proprietary name truly become a common noun, the customer tends to apply it to other brands. Having spent millions of dollars to make his product generic, the advertiser then goes to court to prevent the

VICTROLA

name from being used generically. Ordinarily, time cures the difficulty. Victrola once edged out Edison as a word for record player; the public, in its wisdom, ultimately lumped both as simply . . . record players. Gramophone, a trade name, won the day in Great Britain.

XEROX

To Xerox is to copy a printed page by a quick photographic process. Though still legally a trade name, Xerox as both noun and verb has become—like mimeograph and photostat before it—an everyday word in office work.

MIMEOGRAPH
PHOTOSTAT

ESCALATOR

Escalator, for a stairway or incline arranged in an endless belt, so that the steps or treads ascend or descend continuously, is a name trademarked by the Otis Elevator Company. Any similar product, however patented and trademarked, would be thought of by most of us as an escalator—just as many of us refer to a sanitary napkin as a kotex, or a camera as a kodak. If our lack of sophistication permits us, we even refer to a simple camera as a brownie, from the Brownie Kodak developed for duffers by George Eastman, founder of Kodak: "No, I don't have one of them fancy cameras. I do fine with a brownie." I do not know how Eastman chose the name; perhaps he was thinking of the Brownies, a division of the Girl Scouts comprising girls from the ages of seven through ten.

KOTEX

KODAK
BROWNIE

KLAXON

Klaxon, a trade name, merged once with the vernacular, but now seems to be withdrawing. The klaxon was a loud horn used especially on automobiles; its name was taken from a Greek word meaning to make a sharp, piercing sound, or to roar.

If you ever travel by rail, you occasionally may see men leaning on their shovels, picks, or some other tool, waiting for your train to pass so that they can resume their work on the roadbed. These workers are gandy dancers, from the rhythmic movements associated with handling tools produced by the now-defunct Gandy Manufacturing Company of Chicago. The gandy dancers have a song of their own:

GANDY
DANCERS

Oh, a gandy dancer is a railroad man,
An' his work is never done.
With his pick an' his shovel an' his willin' hand
He makes the railroad run.

BABY

You may think a baby is someone or something young and new, and you are right. But in South Africa, a baby is a machine to separate diamonds from the soil; to baby is to employ this machine. The word is derived from Babe, surname of the American who invented it.

BESSEMER

BESSEMERIZE

Bessemer, a process for de-carbonizing melted pig iron into steel by means of a blast of air, was invented by Sir Henry Bessemer (1813–1898). To bessemerize is to treat with a blast of air, as in the Bessemer process.

SINGER

BONNAZ

Sewing machines were once called singers after Isaac Singer (1811–1875), who first popularized them, though the actual inventor was Elias Howe (1819–1867). Howe was no salesman, and spent years in poverty; he was so poor for a time that he had to borrow a suit from a friend in order to attend his wife's funeral. Howe's rights were established after much litigation in 1854, and I hope he prospered after that. In any event, his ghost has the satisfaction of knowing that he, not Singer, gets the entry in Britannica. (An embroidery called the bonnaz is named for another tinkerer with the sewing machine; he developed the stitch that will not pull out.)

TWENTY-TWO

ARE YOU A MAN OR
ARE YOU A MEASUREMENT?
SCIENTIFIC WORDS

CURIE

ROM the 19th century on, particularly among physi-
cists, it has been common to honor outstanding
scientists by incorporating their names into the
scientific lingo. Thus the curie, a unit of mass of radium emana-
tion, was named after Marie Curie (1867–1934), the Polish-born
chemist who twice received the Nobel Prize for her work on
radium.

Bear with me, as I labor to explain the meanings of terms I
do not understand. (In the 1950s, *Fortune* asked me to describe in
layman's language the scientific implications of the Phase

Theory, an equation worked out by a Yale mathematics professor named Josiah Willard Gibbs (1839–1903). The equation established the basis for modern physical chemistry. Without it, we might have no metallurgical industry today, nor nitrate fertilizers drawn from the air. We might have had to call off World War I in the third inning for lack of gunpowder. I interviewed some of the most distinguished and articulate of the nation's physical scientists, hoping they could get the Phase Theory through my head. It was impossible. My article never appeared.)

FARADAY

The faraday is as good a scientific term to start with as any. It is named for Michael Faraday (1791–1867), an English physicist who made the first rough experiments on the diffusion of gases and produced several new kinds of optical glass. Here is my definition of a faraday:

> A faraday is a unit or quantity of electricity, being about 9.6494×10^4 coulombs. A coulomb, named after French physicist Charles A. de Coulomb (1736–1806), is a measure of the amount of an electric current that passes a given point in a conductor at a given time. It is the quantity of electricity conveyed in one second by the current produced by the electric force of one volt acting in a circuit having a résistance of one ohm; the quantity transferred by a current of one ampere in one second; or the quantity on the positive plate of a condenser of one-farad capacity (the farad, after Faraday, being the capacity of a condenser which, charged with one coulomb, gives a difference of potential of one volt) when the electromotive force is one volt. The coulomb is equal to
> $$\frac{3 \times 10^9 \times 10^{10}}{4.80} \text{ electrons.}$$

FARAD

COULOMB

That is to say, the coulomb is the quantity of charge transferred in one second by one ampere, named for A. N. Ampère (1775–1836), a French physicist who was instrumental in developing the science of electromagnetism. An ampere is the intensity of an electric current produced by one volt acting through the resistance of one ohm.

AMPERE

HENRY

The inductance of a circuit in which an electric force of one volt is induced at the rate of one ampere per second is a henry, after Joseph Henry (1797–1878), American physicist.

VOLT

The volt is all that remains of Alessandro Volta (1745–1827), the Italian physicist who invented the battery, and is a unit equal to the difference of electrical potential between two points on a wire carrying a conducting current of one ampere.

Before proceeding, I must clear up the ohm, a unit of electrical resistance in which a current of one ampere is produced by a potential difference of one volt, with which you are

now familiar. The ohm has as its reciprocal the mho, both memorializing Georg Simon Ohm (1787–1854), German physicist, who was first to state that when an electric current is flowing through a conductor, the intensity of the current equals the electromotive force driving it, divided by the resistance of the conductor; that is, current equals volts divided by ohms.

Bear in mind that my description of the volt applies only when the power dissipated between the points is one watt, a volt-ampere, or approximately 1/746 of an English horsepower. The name is from James Watt (1736–1819), the Scottish engineer who invented the modern condensing steam engine. In his last days he also invented a machine for making reduced copies of sculpture, which he presented to his friends as the work "of a young artist just entering his eighty-third year." I hope you and I will feel as young at that age. Wattage has been extended to other than electrical energy; my friends tell me, for instance, that

I am "a person of low wattage." Watt had little to do with development of the modern science of electricity; his name was applied to the electrical unit to honor his general contributions to applied science.

A watt equals one joule per second. The joule, named for James P. Joule (1818–1889), the English physicist, is a unit of energy equal to the work done in one second when a current of one ampere is passed through the resistance of one ohm; or, if you prefer, when the point of application of one newton is displaced one meter in the direction of the force. Webster puts the matter differently; he says a joule is a unit of work or energy which is equal to 10^7 ergs, and is approximately equal to .738 foot-pound, or 0.24 small calorie. Webster also says that the physicist's own pronunciation of his name was pretty certainly jōōl, and may have originally ben jōl, but that joul (jowl) is frequent for the unit throughout the English-speaking world. This takes care of the joule, but not of the newton that slipped in a moment ago.

A newton is the unit of force required to accelerate a mass of one kilogram one meter per second per second. That second per second is not a slip of the typewriter. It is equal to 100,000 dynes. I do not have to explain a dyne, which is not an improper, uncommon noun. A newton, as you know, is named after Sir

Isaac Newton (1642–1727), English mathematician, scientist, and philosopher, whose works include the theories of universal gravitation, terrestrial mechanics, and color, and the invention of differential calculus.

That is all you need to know about the faraday. If you do not understand it by now, you are plain stupid.

A few other words in electromagnetism that were once proper names:

BEL

A bel is a unit used in the comparison of two levels of power in an electrical communication circuit. Non-technically, it is an expression of sound intensity; Kenneth Amis once wrote of "relaying a girls' choir at a volume of a couple of bels." The source of the word is A. G. Bell (1847–1922), inventor of the

DECIBEL

telephone. A decibel, much bandied about these days particularly in reference to the noise level of aircraft, is one-tenth of a bel.

DEGAUSS

You can neutralize the magnetic field of a ship or a television receiver or other things of the sort by degaussing it, if you know how. I suspect that if my television set were degaussed it would no longer produce an image; but that is only a guess. Whatever the practical effect of degaussing may be, the word was named after Karl F. Gauss (1777–1855), German mathematician, astronomer, and physicist. A gauss is a unit of magnetic

GAUSS

flux density, equivalent to one maxwell per square centimeter.

MAXWELL

A maxwell is a unit equal to the flux perpendicularly intersecting an area of one square centimeter in a region where the magnetic induction is one gauss. James Clerk Maxwell (1831–1879) made great contributions to the theory of magnetism.

MAXWELL'S
DEMON

Maxwell's demon is a hypothetical being of intelligence and molecular proportions imagined by Maxwell to illustrate limitations of the second law of thermodynamics. This says that when energy or heat is exchanged between two bodies at different temperatures, the hotter loses and the colder gains energy.

HERTZ

A hertz, named after the German physicist Heinrich Rudolph Hertz (1857–1894), a pioneer in electromagnetic phenomena, is a unit of frequency equal to one cycle per second.

GALVANISM

Galvanism, the branch of physical science treating of the properties and effects of electrical currents, is the work of Luigi Galvani (1737–1798), professor of physiology at Bologna, Italy. He devised a theory of the production of electricity in animals,

GALVANIZE and was one of those who (about 1780) brought about the discovery of current electricity. To galvanize is to subject to the action of electrical currents; hence, to stimulate or excite as if by an electric shock.

FERMIUM

EINSTEINIUM

Many scientific attributes outside the field of electromagnetism are also named for men. The metallic element fermium, for instance, is for Enrico Fermi (1901–1954), the nuclear physicist; and einsteinium, a synthetic element first produced in a thermonuclear explosion, for Albert Einstein (1879–1955), who formulated the theories of special and general relativity.

MORSE

To morse is to signal by the Morse alphabet. Samuel F. B. Morse (1791–1872), a well-known American artist, promoted, but did not invent, the telegraph (patented 1840). He did, however, invent the Morse code, a system of communication in which letters of the alphabet and numbers are represented by short and long patterns, which may be conveyed as sounds, flashes of light, written dots and dashes, or wigwags of a flag.

TWENTY-THREE

PATIENT GRISELDA

UPPERCASED WORDS WITH
LOWERCASED MEANINGS

When Charon ferries me across the Styx,
And Cerberus acknowledges I'm dead,
Pray, Boswell, carve some legend at my head!

Say that I sharpened Machiavelli's tricks;
Out-Croesused Croesus and his golden bricks;
Loved on when Casanova wearièd;
Pushed back Canute's rude ocean in its bed;
Was funnier than Chaplin in the flicks.

Dear Boswell, will you carve in stone how I
Awhile to Joan was Darby, and awhile
To Damon, Pythias? Will you descry
Jack Ripper's rictus underneath my smile?

More likely, Boswell, you will not recall
A blessed thing worth writing down at all.

So I once wrote. All these names are Patient Griseldas—a term which in this book refers to expressions still associated with their eponym, and so still capitalized, yet generic in meaning.

PATIENT
GRISELDA

The expression "Patient Griselda" is a random example of the concept. In Boccaccio's *Decameron* (1353), Griselda's husband takes away her two children and tells her they are murdered. He divorces her and sends her home, saying he is about to wed another. "The trials to which the flinty-hearted marquis subjects his innocent wife," comments Benét, "are almost as unbelievable as the fortitude with which she is credited to have borne them." Perhaps it is just as well that, as Chaucer says in his "Envoy" to the Clerk's Tale:

Grisilde is dead, and eke her pacience,
And both at once buried in Italie.

Griselda has become, like Job, a prototype of one who undergoes seemingly endless afflictions with fortitude and faith. For those of you who believe in ultimate justice, it should be stated that she eventually was reestablished in her place as honored and beloved wife. What a dog's life her husband must have led thereafter!

Here are some Patient Griseldas meaning never:

When all the world grows honest;
When the Yellow River's clear;
When Calais meets with Dover,
Do you suppose, my dear,

I shall forget I've lost you? . . .
Not until St. Tib's Eve,
Not for a year of Sundays
Shall I forbear to grieve —

Till noon strikes Narrowdale; till
Latter Lammas dawns;
Till Queen Dick reigns; till Fridays
Arrive in pairs like swans;

Till the Greek calends, and the
Conversion of the Jews.
I'll mourn you till the coming
Of the Cocqcigrues.

Obviously, the world will never grow honest, the Yellow River will never clear, and Calais will never meet with Dover. There is no Saint Tib, no year of Sundays. Narrowdale is the local name for the narrowest part of Dovedale, Derbyshire, where dwelt a few cottagers who never saw the sun all winter; in the spring the sun's beams pierced the dale for a few minutes in the afternoon, but never at noon. There is a Lammas Day in Scotland and England (August 1), but no latter Lammas. Richard Cromwell, who succeeded his father as Protector of England, was referred to as Queen Dick; he managed to maintain power for less than a year. Queen Dick has become a contradiction in terms. Fridays never arrive in pairs. The calends were the first day of the Roman month; the Greeks had no calends. It is not expected that the Jews as a people will ever become Christians. The Cocqcigrues, fabulous animals of French legend, have become labels for any idle story; cf. Kingsley in *The Water Babies*: " 'That is one of the seven things,' said the fairy Bedonebyasyoudid, 'I am forbidden to tell till the coming of the Cocqcigrues.' " All these words are Patient Griseldas.

Volumes would be required to list all the prototypical names in our language. The random sampling that follows may lead you to add Patient Griseldas of your own.

AESOPIAN
LANGUAGE

A statement in which one word is to be taken for another is considered aesopian language, after the slave Aesop, who put morals into the actions of animals. In the early days of their quarrel with China, the Russians would excoriate Albania instead. The English cartoonist Vicky portrayed Mao Tse-tung carrying a placard that read "600 million Albanians can't be wrong."

ALADDIN'S LAMP

An Aladdin's lamp, from the story of Aladdin in the *Arabian Nights*, is a magical talisman that overcomes all obstacles.

BENEDICT
ARNOLD

Benedict Arnold was an admired American general in the Revolution who went over to the British, and became a symbol for treachery.

In the late 18th century one Giuseppe Balsamo, claiming to be a certain Count Cagliostro, cut a wide swath through the

CAGLIOSTRO

highest circles of Europe, selling love philtres and the elixir of youth along the way. Women were said to find him irresistible. He died in prison in 1795. A Cagliostro is an impostor.

CINCINNATUS

The supreme type of patriot, a man who rises to a great occasion and then returns to his previous simple life, is a Cincinnatus. Cincinnatus left his farm to save Rome in battle, then returned to his plow.

COLUMBUS'S EGG

Columbus's egg stands for "simple when you know how." To prove an egg could stand on its end, Columbus simply tapped the lower part to establish a base.

DARBY AND JOAN

Darby and Joan are the type of loving, old-fashioned, virtuous couple, no longer in fashion, but made famous in a ballad written by Henry Woodfall in 1835:

> *Always the same, Darby, my own,*
> *Always the same to your old wife Joan.*

Among the French, an expression of somewhat similar import for inseparables is *St. Roch et son chien*, referring to the legend that his hound daily brought Saint Roch bread as he lay dying of plague.

DRESDEN SHEPHERDESS

A Dresden shepherdess—a fragile, delicate young woman—is named for the ceramics portraying such.

I DO NOT LOVE THEE, DR. FELL

A Dr. Fell is someone disliked for no tangible reason. John Fell (1625–1686), a noted Oxford scholar (who gave his name to the Fell typeface), ordered an undergraduate named Tom Brown to translate a passage from Martial on pain of being "sent down"—that is, dropped from school. Brown's loose rendition:

> *I do not love thee, Dr. Fell;*
> *The reason why I cannot tell;*
> *But this I know, and know full well—*
> *I do not love thee, Dr. Fell.*

EL DORADO

An El Dorado is any place of fabulous wealth or opportunity. At the time of the discovery of the Americas, the Indians of what is now Bogota, Colombia, in an annual ceremony covered their king with gold dust, making him *el dorado*, "the gold-covered one." The word was later applied to the country over which he reigned.

FLORENCE NIGHTINGALE

A Florence Nightingale is a ministering angel, especially a nurse. Florence Nightingale went to the Crimea in 1854 to tend the wounded in the Crimean War. Known as "the Lady with a

Lamp" after a Longfellow poem, she vastly improved the practice of nursing.

GIBSON GIRL   A Gibson girl was a type of wholesome-looking American girl portrayed by the illustrator Charles Dana Gibson as representative of the fashions and manners of the 1890s.

GOLCONDA   Golconda is a source of great riches, as a mine. The allusion is to a now-ruined city of India, where great wealth was obtained in the 16th and 17th centuries.

HOBSON'S
CHOICE   Hobson's choice means take it or leave it. Thomas Hobson (1544–1631), a Cambridge livery-stable keeper, let out his horses only in strict rotation. Milton's epitaph to him included the lines:

Ease was his chief disease; and to judge right,
He died for heaviness that his cart went light;
His leisure told him that his time was come,
And lack of load made his life burdensome.

HONEST INJUN   Honest Injun means "on my word of honor." Indians, suspecting their word was sometimes taken lightly, were supposed to have used this expression to convince whites of their veracity.

INDIAN GIVER   One who gives a present and later asks for it back, as early American Indians were said to have done if they got nothing in return, is known as an Indian giver.

INDIAN SIGN   An Indian sign is a hex, initially ascribed to Indians.

JENKINS'S EAR   The trivial cause of a great quarrel is a Jenkins's ear. Brewer recalls that Captain Robert Jenkins, of the brig *Rebecca*, claimed he had been attacked by a Spanish coast guard vessel off Havana in 1731 and that the Spanish had severed his ear. This he carried about in a bottle, so inflaming the populace that in 1738 Walpole was forced to yield to the general clamor for war against the Spaniards. It was widely suspected at the time that the ear may have been cut off in a pillory.

Jim Crow began as a black song-and-dance routine featuring one Jim Crow; to dance Jim Crow was to jump or dance according to the requirements of the song.

First on de heel tap, den on de toe,
Ebery time I wheel about I jump Jim Crow.
Wheel about and turn about and do jis so,
And ebery time I wheel about I jump Jim Crow.

JIM CROW	Today Jim Crow symbolizes social and economic discrimination against blacks.
JIMMY VALENTINE	A Jimmy Valentine is a romantic burglar. The character was featured in a story by O. Henry (1862–1910). In 1909 Paul Armstrong adapted the story into a successful play, *Alias Jimmy Valentine*.
JEEVES	A Jeeves is a manservant much smarter than his master. From the P. G. Wodehouse novels revolving around Bertie and the gentleman's gentleman who repeatedly saves him from his addlepatedness.
LAND OF COCKAIGNE	The Land of Cockaigne is an imaginary country of idleness and luxury. In Old French it means "land of cake."
LAST OF THE MOHICANS	The Last of the Mohicans is the last of anything, after the noble Indian in James Fenimore Cooper's novel of that title.
LET GEORGE DO IT	Georges Cardinal d'Amboise (1460–1510), a prodigy who excelled in all his activities, became a bishop at fourteen, and rose to be minister of state to Louis XII. "Let George do it," Louis would say when a particularly difficult problem arose. We are still letting George do it today.
LONG MEG OF WESTMINSTER	Long Meg of Westminster is anything huge. Long Meg was a giantess of the 16th century.
MARY CELESTE	Mary Celeste is any unsolved mystery of the sea. The brigantine *Mary Celeste* was found abandoned with sails set between the Azores and Portugal in 1872. No trace of the crew was ever discovered.
MAY-DECEMBER MARRIAGE	A May-December marriage is a marriage between an elderly and a youthful person, commonly an old man and a young girl. Jimmy Walker, a charming if venal mayor of New York City in the 1920s, wrote a song with the refrain:

Will you love me in December
As you used to do in May?

MICKEY MOUSE	Mickey Mouse, a familiar character in the animated cartoons of Walt Disney, works as hard for a piece of cheese as Alexander worked to become ruler of the world. Mickey Mouse means "much effort and many complications for a little result": "I had to go through a lot of Mickey Mouse to get that."
MONA LISA SMILE	Mona Lisa was the subject of a portrait by Leonardo da Vinci (1452–1519). Her expression is enigmatic; a Mona Lisa smile covers thoughts and emotions at which one can only speculate.

337   PATIENT GRISELDA

MONA LISA SMILE

NAPIER'S BONES   Napier's bones are counters for multiplication and division, invented or discovered by John Napier (1550–1617), Scottish mathematician.

NERO WOLFE
MAIGRET
PETER WIMSEY   Many fictional detectives are referred to generically: Nero
SHERLOCK   Wolfe, Maigret, Peter Wimsey, Sherlock Holmes, Hawkshaw,
    HOLMES   Nick Carter to name a few. Add your own favorites.
HAWKSHAW
NICK CARTER

NEVER NEVER   Never Never Land is the land that will never be. In J. M.
    LAND   Barrie's *Peter Pan* (1904), the Lost Boys and the Red Indians lived there. In the Australian outback, it refers to the Northern Territory.

NORMAN BLOOD   Norman blood connotes snobbery. When William of Normandy conquered England, his associates established themselves as the aristocrats of the country. Partridge compares "Norman blood" in England with American descent from the Pilgrims of the *Mayflower*.

PAGLIACCI   A Pagliacci is one who makes others laugh though his heart is breaking. Pagliacci is the clown in Leoncavallo's dramatic opera of that name (1892).

PARKINSON'S   Parkinson's law is the satiric promulgation by C. Northgate
    LAW   Parkinson (1957) that the amount of work done is in inverse proportion to the number of people employed, that the time
MURPHY'S   required is whatever time is available, etc. Murphy's law declares,
    LAW   in the same vein, that anything that can go wrong will.

PHILADELPHIA   A Philadelphia lawyer is a casuistic debater; earlier a bril-
    LAWYER   liant advocate, from the days when Philadelphia was the metropolis of the Colonies.

            When Prince Potemkin of Russia was showing Catherine II through certain regions of her realm, he is said to have had stage
POTEMKIN   sets of pleasant cottages and pastoral scenes built along the road
    VILLAGE   to hide the poverty behind. A Potemkin village is a false front.

            To put your fingers to your nose, parodying Queen Anne's
QUEEN ANNE'S   coquettish manner of concealing part of her face with her fan, is
    FAN   to create a Queen Anne's fan.

RASPUTIN   A Rasputin is an evil person of tremendous power and seeming invulnerability. Such was Gregory Efimovitch (1871–1916), nicknamed Rasputin, meaning "debauchee." His doctrine was "Sin in order that you may obtain forgiveness."

A favorite at the Russian court in its last years, he survived poisoning by potassium cyanide and finally was assassinated by shooting.

RIP VAN WINKLE
A Rip Van Winkle, someone out of touch with the times, recalls the Washington Irving character who slept twenty years.

ROBIN HOOD
A Robin Hood is one who takes from the rich and gives to the poor. The legendary outlaw is said to have flourished in Nottinghamshire in the 12th, 13th, or 14th century.

ROCK OF GIBRALTAR
The phrase Rock of Gibraltar for an impregnable stronghold derives from the strongly fortified rock and town on the southern coast of Spain, held by Britain since 1704.

RUBICON
To cross the Rubicon is to make a fateful decision from which there is no turning back. When Julius Caesar in 49 B.C. crossed the Rubicon, a small stream between Italy and its province of Cisalpine Gaul, he automatically declared war upon the Roman senate.

RURITANIA
Ruritania is any small nation where politics, romance, and melodramatic intrigue are the order of the day. The name is that of the imaginary kingdom which is the setting of Anthony Hope's novel *The Prisoner of Zenda* (1894).

SARGASSO
Sargasso, a state of being becalmed, alludes to the Sargasso Sea, which is frequently without wind, and where great masses of floating vegetation impede the passage of vessels.

STAKHANOVITE
A Stakhanovite is an exemplary worker. In the 1930s one Alexei Stakhanov, a coal miner in the Donets region of the Soviet Union, substantially increased his output by improving his work methods. Stalin hailed him as a hero and urged other workers to follow his example.

TALLEYRAND
In diplomacy, a Talleyrand is one who stretches the rules of negotiation to the limit, but does not exceed them. Such was the French statesman Charles Maurice de Talleyrand (1754–1838), who represented his country at the Congress of Vienna (1815).

TIN PAN ALLEY
Tin Pan Alley is any area frequented by composers, agents, and publishers of sheet music. Denmark Street in London, and an area around 14th Street in New York—later 48th to 52nd Street—are called Tin Pan Alley.

TOM THUMB
A Tom Thumb is any tiny male. In the fairy tale, Tom was the size of a man's thumb. In Barnum's exhibits, he was an American dwarf, Charles Sherwood Stratton (1838–1883).

TREE OF
PORPHYRY

The Tree of Porphyry is a complex hierarchy of logical choice, named after its originator, a Greek philosopher of the 3rd century A.D.

WAGNERIAN

Wagnerian is apocalyptic, overwhelming, as a Wagnerian opera—or, often, the bust of a Wagnerian diva.

WALL STREET

Wall Street symbolizes the money market and financial interests in general. Wall Street, at the southern end of the borough of Manhattan, is the chief financial center of the United States, if not the world. It was originally a rather flimsy barricade established by the Dutch of New Amsterdam against the English, who eventually took over New Amsterdam and renamed it New York.

TWENTY-FOUR

O THOU IMPROPER,
THOU UNCOMMON
HODGE-PUDDING
LEFT-OVER WORDS

ODGE-PUDDING is an obsolete word meaning a pudding of many ingredients; by extension, any sort of confused mixture. I wish it were an improper, uncommon noun derived from a man named Hodge, plus pudding. It would have made a good title for this book.

But the hodge in hodge-pudding is the same as the hodge in hodgepodge, or hotchpotch, which comes from French *hochepot* and Dutch *hutspot*, meaning "stirred pot; ragout." No proper name there. I can revive the word only to describe this last chapter, which is indeed an alphabetized hodge-pudding of improper, uncommon nouns that did not fit anywhere else. Some of them are not very interesting, and if you are growing restless, this is a good place to stop reading.

An expression that may seem generic to you may still be specialized and uppercased to me. Architectural terms that are generic to architects, and engineering terms that are generic to engineers, may be proper names to musicians and taxi drivers.

BIEDERMEIER

In the 19th century, for instance, Ludwig Eichrodt (1827–1892) created an imaginary author named Gottlieb Biedermeier, author of philistine poetry—that is, poetry indifferent or antagonistic to artistic and cultural values; boorish; barbarous. Biedermeier's name was applied to a German style of furniture somewhat resembling the French Empire style, but simpler and heavier. Curved lines in chair and sofa backs, and straight lines with little decoration in cabinets, are characteristic of the style. In an architect's mind, Biedermeier is a lowercased word representing bourgeois elegance; in mine, it is capitalized.

BOLTON

A bolton is one who flatters by false humility. Bolton, a courtier of Henry VIII, refused to play cards with his master "unless you give me the advantage of an ace."

BUNGALOW

A bungalow is a house of one story or a story and a half, preserving the low, sweeping lines and the front verandahs of bungalows in India. The name is from a Hindi word signifying "pertaining to Bengal." Says Brown: "The English have been great importers of housing words and the citizen of today inhabits his bungalow (Hindi) or villa (Roman-Italian) with its veranda (also Indian but used, too, in Spain). If it be storeyed, there may be a balcony (Italian). His windows may be French, his blinds Italian. If his bungalow garden is at all ambitious there will be a pergola (Italian)."

BURTON

A burton is a light tackle having double or single blocks, used to hoist or tighten rigging. These were first called Breton tackles, from Brittany; the word shifted shape over the years.

CANTERBURY

Some Archbishop of Canterbury, I know not who, built the first stand or rack surmounted with upright openwork partitions, used for holding papers or music. A canterbury is generally a magazine rack.

CATLINITE	George Catlin (1796–1872), American artist, devoted his life to studying the Indians. He executed the series of Indian portraits now in the National Museum, Washington, D.C. He was the first white man to see the quarries in Minnesota from which Indians obtained the soft stone they carved into pipes; and this pipestone is called catlinite in his honor.
CHARLEY NOBLE	A charley noble, the galley funnel of a merchant ship, bears the name of a merchant service captain who kept his copper galley funnel brightly polished. Don't ask me who.
CHEYNE-STOKES BREATHING	A Scottish physician named William W. Cheyne and an Irish physician named William Stokes observed simultaneously in the 19th century that before death, breathing frequently builds to a gasping climax, ceases for five to fifty seconds, and resumes— until it ceases forever. A. E. Housman first read about the Cheyne-Stokes phenomenon in Arnold Bennett's novel *Clayhanger*, and recognized it in himself when he lay dying.
DERBYSHIRE NECK	In many parts of England, goiter is referred to as derbyshire neck, because the water of Derbyshire was once deficient in iodine, with the result that goiters were of frequent occurrence there.
DUTCH CAP	A close-fitting cap, with two flaps that turn up over the ears, is referred to as a Dutch cap. So is a familiar contraceptive.
FALLOPIAN TUBE	The oviduct in female mammals (one of the tubes that conduct the egg from the ovary to the uterus) is called the fallopian tube, after its discoverer, Gabrielle Fallopius (1523–1562), a physician of Modena, Italy. He also devised a primitive condom of linen.
GEYSER	An intermittently eruptive hot spring is called a geyser. In England, a faucet bears the same name. The word is from the Geyser, a hot spring in Iceland, which in turn capitalizes Icelandic *geysa*, "to rush furiously."
GHAN	In Australia, a transcontinental train or highway is a ghan, once a camel service crewed by Afghans, imported from Afghanistan. In 1965, the last surviving ghan was in an old people's home in Alice Springs, Australia, still worrying about ongoing arguments over ritual among the Muslims of Bosnia, Yugoslavia, where he had never been.

Herbert Hoover, who presided over the collapse of the world economy in 1929, became one of our most unpopular

Presents. Yet it is hard to think of another President whose name entered the vulgate in so many guises. Hoover was food controller during World War I, when families were encouraged to grow their own vegetable gardens, which became known as hoover gardens. A gardening apron was called a hoover apron. Hoovervilles were settlements of the unemployed made from packing boxes, tin sheets, and the like; and hoover villas were the constituent structures.

HOOVER
GARDEN
HOOVER APRON
HOOVERVILLE
HOOVER VILLA

MANILA

A durable brown or buff paper used often for envelopes is called manila, because it was made originally from Manila hemp.

Thank You, Timothy

The book was being typeset. My mind was meandering down other paths. The telephone rang.

"By the way," said Timothy. "John Doe, Richard Roe, John Styles, Richard Miles, John-a-Styles, John-a-Niles? All fictitious names for parties to an act or proceeding. A jobation, from Job, for a long, tedious reproof?"

"Timothy," I said, "you don't understand. I have to *pay* for author's alterations."

"Precisely. You have Dalmatian. But did you know that the expression 'running dogs of capitalism,' much used by Marxists, is from the Dalmatian dogs that used to run under the coaches of the great? *Omm . . . mmm . . . mmm.* Yes Yes Yes. Dogs. Happy hot dogs, for the young lawyers trained by Justice Felix Frankfurter? From *felix*, Latin for 'happy,' and hot dogs for—"

"I understand," I said.

"Thermidor—the reaction after a period of radicalism? The French Revolution went into reverse when Robespierre was overthrown in the month Thermidor. Piker for a cheapskate—someone from Pike County?"

"Webster," I said, "cites picky as the origin. Bartlett prefers picayune."

"Pike County," said Timothy firmly.

"Of course. Pike County. Thank you, Timothy."

"God Bless," said Timothy.

INDEX

Argyle, 261, 281
Aristotelianism, 114
Arkansas toothpick, 174
Armageddon, 82
Armagnac, 247
Arnold, Benedict, 334
Arras, 283
Arriet, 208
Artemisia, 23
Artesian well, 106
Ascot, 261
Aspirin, 324
Assassin, 313
Astrakhan, 281
Athanasian wench, 222
Atheneum, 115
Atkins, Tommy, 197
Atlas, 118
Atropine, 14
Attic, 50
Attic, bats in the, 51
Attic faith, 50
Attic figs, 177
Attic salt, 50
Attic story, 51
Attic style, 50
Augean stables, 34
Augustinism, 91
Aunt sally, 208
Aurora, 18
Austerlitz look, 55
Azteca, 45

Baal, 68
Babbitt, 141
Babble, 67
Babel, 67
Baby, 325
Bacardi, 250
Bacchanal, 25
Bacchants, 25
Bacitracin, 314
Backward up Holburn Hill, to
    ride, 169
Badminton, 215
Baedeker, 134
Baedeker raids, 189
Bain-marie, 68
Bakelite, 324
Balaam, 70
Balaam's ass, 70
Balaclava helmet, 55
Balboa, 45
Balbriggan, 283
Baldachin, 277
Baldwin, 230
Baldwin apple, 306
Balkanize, 185
Ballyhoo, 194
Balmacaan, 267
Baloney, 232
Baluchithere, 293
Bant, 236
Bantam, 298

Bantiginize, 236
Bantigism, 236
Banyan, 304
Banyan days, 304
Banyan hospital, 304
Barani roll, 219
Barb, 49
Barbarian, 49
Barbarous, 49
Barlow knife, 171
Barmecidal, 239
Barmecide feast, 239
Barmy, 89
Barnum, 110
Barnumism, 110
Barnumize, 110
Baroque, 101
Bartlett pear, 230
Bastille, 170
Bath, Turkish, 99
Bats in the attic, 51
Battology, 47
Bayard, 144
Bayonet, 179
Béarnaise, 233
Beatrice, 124
Beau brummel, 258
Beaujolais, 250
Beaune, 250
Béchamel, 234
Bedlam, 91
Bedlington, 296
Bedlington, go to, 269
Bedouin, 98
Beecher's Bible, 188
Beef bourguignon, 232
Beef stroganoff, 233
Beelzebub, 68
Beg, 99
Beggar, 99
Begonia, 307
Beguine, 252
Bejesus, 88
Bel, 330
Belcher, 258
Belga, 45
Bellerophontic letter, 32
Ben day, 143
Bendigo, 258
Benedick, 128
Benedict Arnold, 334
Bengal lancer, 174
Benny, 266
Berkeleianism, 119
Berkelium, 119
Berlin, 281
Berserk, 167
Bertha, 272
Bess, brown, 203
Bessemer, 326
Bessemerize, 326
Beth o'bedlam, 91
Bethel, 67
Bethlehemites, 78

Burberry, 267
Burgundy, 250
Burke, 165
Burmese, 272
Burton, 343
Burton, gone for a, 187
Busby, 268
By Jove, 86
Byronic, 133

Cabal, 153
Cadogan, 260
Caesar, 95
Caesarean, 95
Cagliostro, 335
Cain, 66
Cain, raise, 66
Cain-colored, 66
Calamine, 313
Calcutta, black hole of, 174
Caledonian brown, 272
Caliban's rage, 145
Calico, 283
Californication, 61
Calliope, 21
Calypso, 253, 302
Cambric, 276
Camellia, 308
Camembert, 231
Canaan, 68
Canary, 250
Canary yellow, 271
Candytuft, 308
Canfield, 219
Cannibal, 168
Canopy, 277
Cant, 153
Cantaloupe, 308
Canterbury, 343
Canterbury bell, 304
Canterbury cap, 264
Caoutchouc, 308
Captain cook, 294
Capua, 177
Caracul, 281
Carbine, 179
Cardigan, 264
Caribe, 295
Carioca, 253
Carronade, 180
Carter, Nick, 339
Carthaginian peace, 177
Caryatid, 47
Casaba, 308
Casanova, 130
Cashmere, 281
Cassandra, 40
Cassock, 264
Castile soap, 259
Castle walk, 253
Catamite, 222

Catch a tartar, to, 168
Catch-22, 188
Cathartic, 316
Catherine wheel, 90
Catlinite, 344
Caudle lecture, 135
Cayenne, 172, 305
Cayenne pepper, 305
Cayuse, 295
Cecropia moth, 290
Celadon, 128
Celeste, Mary, 337
Cellophane, 323
Celluloid, 323
Centaur, 31
Cerberus, 29
Cereal, 302
Ceremony, 24
Cerise, 303
Cesarewich, 54
Chablis, 250
Chaeroneia, 177
Chalcedony, 318
Chambray, 276
Champagne, 246
Champaign, 105
Chanticleer, 293
Chapel, 93
Chaplain, 93
Charlatan, 100
Charleston, 254
Charley, 169, 292
Charley, good-time, 202
Charley horse, 204
Charley noble, 344
Charlotte russe, 203
Chartreuse, 246, 271
Charybdis, Scylla and, 41
Chassepot, 184
Chateaubriand, 233
Chaucerian, 125
Chautauqua, 118
Chauvinism, 161
Checkmate, 217
Cheddar, 231
Cherry, 303
Cheshire, 231
Chesterfield, 266
Cheval-de-frise, 178
Chevaux-de-frise, 178
Cheviot, 283
Cheyne-Stokes breathing, 344
Chianti, 250
Chicago piano, 187
Chicago quadrangle, 58
Chicken à la king, 233
Chicken marengo, 238
Chileña, 253
Chimera, 32
Chimeric, 32
China, 317
Chino, 260
Chivvy, 100
Chow, 296

Homeric laughter, 122
Honest Injun, 336
Hooch, 248
Hood, Robin, 340
Hoodlum, 166
Hooker, 222
Hooligan, 166
Hoover, 324
Hoover apron, 345
Hoover garden, 345
Hoover villa, 345
Hooverville, 345
Horatian, 123
Horatio Alger, 140
Hottentot, 174
Hudibrastic, 204
Hulled, to be, 189
Humbug, 182
Humpty-dumpty, 206
Hun, 167
Hunnish, 167
Hunting pink, 213
Husky, 296
Hyacinth, 300
Hyde, Jekyll and, 140
Hydra-headed, 34
Hygiene, 29
Hymen, 25
Hymeneal, 27
Hyperbole, 49
Hypnosis, 30
Hypnotism, 30

Iamb, 28
Iambic, 28
Icarian, 37
Ignite, 33
Immelman turn, 185
Incubate, 225
Incubus, 225
Indian giver, 336
Indian sign, 336
Indiana volunteer, 183
Indigo, 271
Innocent, 204
Inverness, 267
Irenic, 21
Iridescent, 302
Iris, 302
Irish kiss, 197
Irish up, get the, 196
Isabel, 179
Isro, 260
Italo, 260
Ivan, 197

Jack, kitchen, 201
Jack johnson, 187
Jack ketch, 170
Jack rabbit, 201
Jack sausage, 54
Jack the Ripper, 165

Jack up, 201
Jackanapes, 100
Jackass, 201
Jackboot, 202
Jackdaw, 201
Jackknife, 201
Jackpot, 202
Jack-in-the-box, 202
Jack-in-the-pulpit, 201
Jack-of-all-trades, 201
Jack-o'-lantern, 202
Jacks, 201
Jacobin, 107
Jacquard, 284
Jacquerie, 184
Jaeger, 260
Jake, 208
Jakes, 42
Janiceps, 19
Janitor, 19
Jansen, 266
Jansenist, 92
Janus-faced, 19
Jap, 186
Japan, 318
Japhetic, 16
Japonica, 308
Jarvey, 195
Java, 236
Jazz, 250
Jean, 279
Jedburgh justice, 160
Jeeves, 337
Jehu, 68
Jekyll and Hyde, 140
Jemimah, 207
Jenkin's ear, 336
Jennet, 295
Jenneting, 309
Jenny, spinning, 207
Jenny ass, 295
Jenny howlet, 207
Jenny scaffold, 207
Jenny winch, 207
Jenny Wren, 207
Jeremiad, 71
Jeroboam, 73
Jerry, 73, 197
Jerry, Tom and, 133, 248
Jerry-built, 73
Jerrycan, 73
Jersey, 278
Jesse, 110
Jesuitic, 76
Jesus freak, 74
Jet, 318
Jew, 198
Jew down, 198
Jewfish, 198
Jewish lightning, 198
Jezebel, 68
Jilt, 207
Jim Crow, 337